DEARLY BELOVED

Letters To the Children of My Spirit

By

Catherine de Hueck Doherty

Volume One

Madonna House Apostolate
Combermere, Ontario
Canada

Cover: Catherine at the shrine on her island where these letters were written.

Nihil Obstat: Rev. Robert D. Pelton

Imprimatur:
J.R. Windle
Bishop of Pembroke
Aug. 15, 1988

The Nihil Obstat and Imprimatur are a declaration that a book or pamphlet is considered to be free from doctrinal or moral error. It is not implied that those who have granted the Nihil Obstat and Imprimatur agree with the contents, opinions or statements expressed.

Canadian Cataloguing in Publication Data
  Doherty, Catherine de Hueck, 1896-1985
    Dearly beloved

ISBN 0-921440-10-3

  1. Christian life — Catholic authors.   2. Doherty,
Catherine de Hueck, 1896-1985.   I. Title.

BX4705.D64A3   1988   248.4′82   C89-090000-0

ISBN 0-921440-10-3

Published by:
MADONNA HOUSE PUBLICATIONS
COMBERMERE, ONTARIO
CANADA
K0J 1L0

DEDICATION

To all the Children of my Spirit,
those who are with me now and those
who are as yet unborn.

INTRODUCTION

Catherine de Hueck Doherty could be described in various ways: a pioneer for interracial justice in North America; a great lover of the poor; a woman of immense faith, capable of inspiring faith in others; a passionate lover of Christ; a powerful preacher of the Gospel without compromise. All these descriptions would be true. But just as various ingredients are mixed in a bowl, and a bread is poured out which is more wonderful than each ingredient by itself, so all the various dimensions of Catherine's life resulted in a grace that was the harmonious blending of all others. She became, in the Russian sense of "staretza," a spiritual mother: she daily fed her children, in all their needs, with the bread of Gospel wisdom.

This is the particular importance and significance of these volumes entitled *Dearly Beloved*. For the last forty years of her life Catherine was called by God to form a community of love in which the Gospel would be incarnated in every dimension of that life. As problems, situations, needs, joys, feast days, questions would arise, Catherine sat down and penned these letters to (as she called us once in one of these letters) "the children of my spirit."

The family of Madonna House, therefore, considers these letters as perhaps *the* most important part of Catherine's legacy to the Church and our civilization. In them we have, from the depths of her maternal spirit, the daily, concrete, nitty-gritty application of the Gospel to the whole of life. In the West of the last five or six hundred years, we simply have no experience any longer of what that means. Catherine taught us again.

"If you love Me," said the Lord to Peter, "feed My lambs. Feed My sheep." In these letters (published for the first time) Catherine responded to this longing of the Saviour that His children be fed with the daily bread of the Gospel. We hope and pray that these volumes of *Dearly Beloved* will help restore the Gospel vision to the whole of our civilization.

The Editors

Madonna House, Combermere

Feast of the Assumption, August 15, 1988

CONTENTS

OUR WONDROUS VOCATION

February 21, 1956

Dearly Beloved,

I have been praying much about our family and every member in it. With every step toward a clarification of our wondrous vocation, I felt the burden of my unworthiness grow and grow. Yet there was a joy in that realization, for the more I realize both my unworthiness and weakness, the more I know the Lord beholds my poverty and sends his mercy to fill it with himself.

Most assuredly, the Lord of Hosts, and his gracious Mother, will make up what is wanting so much in me. Therefore, quite humbly and simply, yet firmly, with the assurance that comes from faith, humility and obedience, I proceed to do my best about directing our little flock, knowing that where I fail, Jesus and Mary will make good my failures.

I began by saying that I pray much these days, as the vision of the whole opens widely before me, and I see the immense possibility of the vocation that God has called us to.

As I begin to realize that the words the Holy Father addressed to me in 1951 are really filled with prophetic, holy, and deep significance, my heart rejoices. If you remember, he said to me: "Madam, persevere, for on groups like yours depends the fate of the Church."

Busy about the little things of the Lord that form the warp and woof of our days, all of us sometimes lose sight of the overall picture. I can't, because it is my duty to look at the Apostolate as a whole, and at each of its parts. Each must be taken care of lovingly, gently, without ceasing. So when I pray, that is the way I pray: first for each, next for the whole; first for the heavily burdened, next for those less so; first for those just coming in, next for those who have been here a long time; then again for the indivisible whole that is Madonna House.

I thought I would share with you my way of praying, for I want you to know that though my heart desires with a great desire to be with each of you all the time, though my heart greatly desires to share the burden of day-to-day existence, working and praying in the Apostolate with each one of you personally, I can not do so. More and more I must open my hands and let go of things and people that are more precious to me in the natural order than life itself. Such is the way of the Lord — He does not allow us to attach ourselves even to the Apostolate but only to himself. That is why I meet you now all the time in his heart, because that is the only place where I can do so.

Many thoughts pass through my head, heart and soul as I pray, thoughts of time, poverty, and especially of hospitality, the gracious fruits of *caritas*, engraved on our cross.*

First let us consider. We are preparing ourselves to take vows, one of which is poverty. This is the particular virtue which is supposed to detach our hearts from everything and everybody, and attach it to Christ alone. He desires many things. One is the proper use of the one commodity, the one piece of gold left to us — *time*. What are we going to do with it? How are we going to use it? Waste it? Will we waste sixty seconds? Sixty minutes? An hour or two? Will we fritter time away in useless motion, in useless conversation, in taking a long route instead of a shorter one? Or are we going to use every second for God?

What do we have? Twenty-four hours between Masses. Our tomorrows are his. We have but twenty-four hours. And if you want to come down to fine points, frankly we don't even have that; we have just a moment at a time.

A woman in this area left her husband and child to go to the movies and to take a little drive to see a sick relative. The husband was going to make a lunch for them when she came back from the movies. Thus they had planned. Less than one hour later, less than sixty minutes later, she was here on a stretcher with a concussion and a broken foot — the victim of an automobile accident.

Perhaps the example is trite, often repeated. But it is still worth repeating, for it brings us back to the only wealth we have to offer God — *time*.

But there is more to time than just wasting it or using it. Time is a cord with which to flagellate our sluggish spirits. Be quiet. Listen. Remember what you have read and meditated upon in the Gospel so many times. You can hear heavy cords, knotted with

---

*Pax, caritas, peace and love in Latin, is inscribed in the Madonna House cross.

big knots, whistling through the air and hitting the back of the Sinless One tied to a post.

Can you see the strong, well-developed shape of the Roman soldiers? With bulging muscles and sheer brute force, they ruthlessly, methodically lift those cords and keep hitting the sinless flesh that suffers for your sins and mine. Can you see them?

We have no Roman soldiers in Madonna House. But we have cords made out of strands of time, a minute here, a minute there, a second here, a second there, a half-hour here, a half-hour there. We could weave them all together and make them strong and heavy and allow them, wielded by our own hands, to flagellate our laziness, our sluggishness, our love of comfort, the thousand things that we have to drive out of ourselves.

Five minutes late for dinner. Seven minutes late for Mass. Needless wear and tear. Useless walking back and forth to our various houses and premises. If we tried hard enough, we could do our job in fifteen minutes; but we take half an hour.

Be quiet. Listen. The Roman soldiers were strong. The cords whistled through the air, and the flesh of the Sinless One was torn and hung in ribbons with each blow. What about those wasted minutes, seconds and hours? What about them now?

The vow of poverty deals with time, our only wealth, but it also deals with the spirit of generosity and with the spirit of detachment.

Now I would like to discuss hospitality, the gracious fruit of charity. Can you visualize charity without hospitality? Remember the saying of St. Benedict: "Let every guest be received as Christ." I seldom find fault with the hospitality of anyone in the Apostolate, but at times there is a slackening, a sort of indifference about the whole affair.

Let it be clearly understood that whether it is our day off or our time to rest, if anyone comes to our door, we forget our sleep, we forget our day off, we forget everything, to serve Christ in them. It would be rather foolish for us to pray before the Blessed Sacrament by the hour on our day off, if we haven't understood that the greatest prayer is meeting Christ directly in our neighbor. Remember the words of the Lord: "It is not those who say 'Lord, Lord' who will enter the Kingdom of Heaven, but those who do the will of my Father." The will of his Father is expressed again to St. Catherine of Siena when he said, "How can you love me whom you do not see if you cannot love your neighbor whom you do see?'' Let no one in the Apostolate forget this, lest God vomit from his mouth our prayers before the Blessed Sacrament.

Now I would like to write about doubts not doubts of faith, but doubts about the vocation.

There are doubts and doubts. There is a doubt that is normal. It is a wondering, a wishing, an asking for light, a making sure. This is a good wondering; that is a good doubt. You can recognize those doubts if tranquillity and order remain in the hearts of those who have them. They are not upset by those doubts, but even strengthened by them. It is quite possible that God permits those doubts for that very reason — in order to strengthen the will. Those doubts are seldom accompanied by tizzies, tiredness, crying spells, and what have you. They are easily dealt with by the people in charge.

The other kind of doubts are violent, upsetting. They are to be thrown out, for they are either from ill health or from the devil. In the first case proper medical or psychiatric help should be given; in the second there should be recourse to the director of the house if possible, but most certainly to one's spiritual director.

Yet be sure of one thing, doubts will be with us till we die. They are like sit-up exercises for our will. Eventually, we will be able to deal with them quite simply by paying no attention to them. But that will not happen today or tomorrow. As we grow in the spirit of caritas, so we will grow in the second part of the motto of our vocation: *pax*.

Yes, I pray for you constantly. These are a few of the thoughts that pass through my soul as I pray about Madonna House. Please, dearly beloved, pray for me too. I need it so much more than you do.

May this Lent be a time of great blessings for you. May it be fruitful through Our Lord and Our Lady. May it make you strong and pure and joyous before the Lord.

Affectionately in Jesus and Mary,
with a motherly blessing,

A FEARSOME SURRENDER

March 23, 1956

Dearly Beloved,

On this tremendous feast of Easter, I want to wish you all the joys of the Risen Christ! Isn't it marvelous that God so loved man that he gave his only Son to be born, to die for us, and then to rise and enter into glory so that we might follow him! Alleluia! Happy, holy, fecund, Easter to you, for I know it will be our constant strength, inspiration, and joy throughout this coming year.

I have been thinking about the meaning of the words vocation, dedication, and charity in our Apostolate. While arranging the files recently, I came across that of the ex-members. It was a source of both joy and sorrow.

In some souls, I clearly saw the hand of God leading them to other vocations, which evidently had become clarified through their months or years in Madonna House. When I looked at these names, I rejoiced and thanked God that we were able to help them find the niche that God wanted them to fill.

But before other names I paused, and a great weight, a strange pain filled my heart. These were the names of those who didn't leave to pursue a different, clearly-defined vocation, but who went forth because of one sentence spoken eons ago by a creature of the Lord so filled with light that he was called Lucifer, "angel of light."

That sentence is only made up of four little words heavier than the universe. Four little words were placed before God and created an abyss of darkness into which the angel of light plummeted for eternity. Four little words became mother and father to all the sins of the world. Four little words: *"I will not serve."*

These words are radically opposed to light and to joy, love, to everything that is of God. When they were spoken, hell was born. Evil entered creation. Lucifer, the angel of light, became Satan, the king of darkness.

I felt cold when I read the names of those who had left

because of those words. The fruit of those words is a one-letter word in English — "I."

These people had pitted their "I" against the will of God. They thought they were doing right. Oh, rest assured that they had every seemingly valid reason for thinking so. Yet they missed the whole point.

From the depths of my memory, their voices echoed clearly. They even found priests who agreed with them because, consciously or unconsciously, they so marshalled the facts that discernment was impossible for someone who had not lived with them day by day, as I had; who had not shared their joys and pains, their problems and tizzies, their silences and their thoughts.

Satan is the greatest logician of all!

I am not ashamed to tell you that in the wee hours of the night, when I took out the file again to read and pray over these names, I cried. Am I presumptuous in saying that while I wept, I thought of Christ weeping over Jerusalem?

It came to me that many vocations are lost because of a lack of dedication. To be dedicated, says the dictionary, is to be surrendered, given over, totally consecrated to a person or a cause. It came to me that to be totally surrendered to God is *fearsome*. It is fearsome because our little minds cannot see very far; our vision is narrow. And what usually blocks our vision with regard to the Apostolate is an immense cross: the cross of monotony.

We come to the Apostolate full of joy, which is mostly emotional, with high resolutions and glowing hopes. Then we meet the drabness and greyness of our days. We chafe under the monotony, day in, day out, day in, day out. Another day of getting up sleepy and weary from our thoughts of rebellion or boredom. Another day of going to chapel to pray the Mass which at times seem to mean nothing. Another day of cooking, filing, typing, sewing, washing, scrubbing. Even if variety is present, our chores become boring after a while.

The words "vocation" and "dedication" shrink into insignificance. An endless vista of terrible days opens before us with cruciform arms. We shiver. Even asleep, we turn restlessly and moan. From some unknown depths, a voice says, "Just look at your drab little apostolate and its childish, foolish little rules. This isn't for you. Maybe for someone else. Why don't you go and talk it over with Father X., present the situation, and free yourself from the binding, useless cords of dedication.''

As I lay sleepless in the dark of the night, I could almost see those thoughts taking shape in the minds of young people who have as yet not even come. It seemed to me that my room had become very cold, as if Christ had departed from it. He is fire and warmth; Satan, his opposite is as cold as despair.

Suddenly my room was filled with a whisper: ''I will not serve.''

Like a crescendo, the sad words beat against the walls of my room, and I was afraid. I took refuge in that shiny, shimmering, warm, glorious word *love, caritas*, which is the essence of our Apostolate. Love is a Person, God. I relaxed. The words *vocation* and *dedication* came back to me. I know now that they had to do with love and that both of them could only be examined *in the light of a loving heart*.

And so, dearly beloved in Christ, on the feast of Love, the Resurrected One, the Conqueror of death, I pray with all my heart that you might realize that vocation is simply *to love*. All the rest will be added unto us. Dedication will come running if we love. Where is there a loving heart that does not wish to bound in every possible way to the Beloved?

Let us pray that God may enlarge our narrow hearts, and pour into them the fruits of his love, so that we in turn might love unto folly. Nothing else will do.

Without love there is no dedication. There will only be unfaithfulness to the vocation that God has given so clearly, but which some refuse to follow to its glorious end.

Yes, let us spend the coming year asking God to teach us to love more and more, until we finally become one with Love, one with God.

> With my motherly blessing and all
> my love, in Mary's Immaculate Heart,

INTO A KINGDOM OF LIGHT

April 1956

Dearly Beloved,

Since the beginning of Lent we have been studying the Liturgy of the Church. It is time we began to nourish our souls on the ''meat of the saints,'' for when all is said and done, our greatest school of love is the Liturgy. Our days are spent between two Masses. That is all the time we have. Our tomorrows are God's, our yesterdays are his, and our today is rooted in the morning Mass. Each day we pray that the fruit of these Masses will be heaven, where our living with Christ, begun in faith, will be completed in his marvelous light.

Before you go on with this letter, get your Bible and read the Epistle for Easter Saturday, 1 Peter 2: 1-10. Linger long and lovingly on it. The humble commentary that I want to make is the fruit of a lifetime of meditation, for I have loved that Epistle even before I began Friendship House.*

What Peter has to say in this Epistle applies so well and so clearly to all of us. ''Dearly beloved, leave off all malice, all guile, dissimilations and envies and all detractions.''

Think of it. This is an exact description of a lay apostle, born anew in the resurrected Christ. ''Daily we die in Christ to be reborn in Christ,'' says St. Paul. We leave off all malice, guile, dissimulation, envy, detraction. In utter simplicity of heart and humility of soul, we go forth to seek all that the will of God, which is our sanctification, desires for us in this twenty-four hour period.

Filled with the charity of Christ, we go forth unafraid into the kingdom of envy, malice, detraction, guile and dissimulation. This is our challenge day after day. In the same Epistle we read, ''Christ, who called us out of darkness into his marvelous light. . . .'' It is into this marvelous light of his love, his kingship, that he has called us.

*Lay Apostolate begun by Catherine Doherty in Toronto, and later in Harlem and Chicago. Often referred to as F. H. Madonna House, Combermere was founded as the Canadian branch in 1947, and later separated from Friendship House.

Why should we be afraid? Why should we answer malice with malice, envy with envy? Here, at the very beginning of the Epistle, is his blueprint for our humble Apostolate. You might say, "Surely you do not think we are envious or malicious?" But truly, beloved in Christ, how weak we are, how watchful we must be, and how often we should meditate on this Epistle.

Let us take one example. You may be someplace where another apostolate might be more successful than yours; it may have newer better or more radical ways. How easily envy enters one's heart, and how readily we say, "Oh, they are wonderful; if only. . . ." Examine your hearts. I have often examined mine in the light of that Epistle and asked God and St. Peter to clear my heart of all that flotsam and jetsam described in its opening sentence.

Let's go on. Here is a sentence that I have made mine for many years: "But to them that believe not, the stone which the builders rejected . . . is a stone of stumbling and a rock of scandal." How many times have I tried to penetrate the inner meaning of that sentence! Think of all the persecution, misunderstanding, problems, and difficulties that come to us from those who do not believe and to who Christ is indeed a "stone of stumbling and a rock of scandal." Just think of the long, drawn out months and years of misunderstanding that some of you have suffered from your parents. Recall the endless pointed questions that are addressed to us day in and day out. Even men of God sometimes seem to see Christ as a "stone of stumbling and a rock of scandal." But we do not set ourselves up as judges. "Without guile, without malice, without envy; in peace, encompassed by the marvelous light of Christ, we keep doing the will of God between our two Masses.

How beautifully St. Peter speaks about that: "But you are a chosen generation, a kingly priesthood, a purchased people; that you may declare his virtues who hath called you out of darkness into his marvelous light." Here we have it, our true constitution, given to us from heaven! The "vision of the whole," that I always talk about so stammeringly, is in this Easter reading! The answer is clear, simple enough that even little children can understand it.

Christ is risen! Death is conquered! We are baptized and have become part of his Body, apostles all. We are sent to declare his virtues, and the glad tidings that men shall die no more, that Christ will come again and will reign over his Kingdom, that we shall be made whole, body and soul in the Parousia, the coming of the Lord!

It is for *this* that you have left home, family and friends. For *this* you have taken your vows. For *this* you are engaged in the social apostolate of the Church in the far corners of the world. As in the Gospel of today, you are running eagerly, like John and Peter, to the tomb of the risen Christ.

This is it. And I write you this letter with an overflowing heart, filled with joy and gratitude to God and to our Holy Father for the new Liturgy and for the clear vision that it brings to us. I repeat to you the words of Christ on another occasion, when he was speaking to his apostles: "Fear not little flock." You are part of that stone that is the Rock. Men shall stumble over you, but you are the beautiful Temple of Christ, the new Jerusalem. Alleluia! Alleluia! Alleluia!

Lovingly yours in the Risen Christ,

[signature]

THE PRIMACY OF CHARITY

May 16, 1956

Dearly Beloved,

I have been praying for you more than usual, though that seems impossible, for I pray for you without ceasing, as the Lord said we should. In my thoughts, throughout the day, I lift you up to Our Lady. As I pass through the chapel, as I glance at her pictures, I quietly say, "Take care of them; spare them not; make them saints, make them saints." On this last sentence my mind rests. I desire with a great desire that you be sanctified, individually and collectively, and for this I would sacrifice all other things. For me there is only one word that is synonymous with sanctity, and that is *caritas*, love, and its fruit, *peace*.

All evaluations that I make of any house always consist in this: How deep, how constant, is the charity of the house? How great is its internal peace? And then I go to the individual, for the same yardstick is applicable. *Nothing* matters, except charity and peace.

Where charity is, peace abides. There God abides. Above all, I desire that the members of our apostolic family love one another deeply. If they don't love each other with the love of Christ and his peace, how can they love the poor?

The center fire, and model of that love, is the director of the house. Through thick and thin, through blind pain and sorrow, through sickness and health, through weariness that truly is a crucifixion in recreation and in work, in prayer and in sleep, the heart of a director watches and loves, watches for the well-being of the staff and the tranquillity of order. This love is like a vine of Christ, and its fruit is the Apostolate. The vine is laden with grapes, because the vine is truly grafted onto Christ.

The members have their own role to play in that *caritas* and in that *pax* which is the essence of our vocation. You are all in the process of growth. You are the little shoots of the vine that tomorrow will be heavy with fruit too. Without the members the director is sterile; together, you are filled with the fecundity of God.

Humility, love, trust and openness are the characteristics of a member of Madonna House. Each one knows that he or she is part of a team, and that the team is only as strong as its weakest part.

We are a family. We are all one, children of Our Lady of Combermere, living in a house that belongs to her. We are one in soul, mind and heart; one in aims and goals. We are all walking the same way — the little, steep path of our Apostolate that is a part of the narrow, royal road of Christ. It is this oneness that we have to safeguard above all else. It is the spirit of the family whose true Mother is Our Lady, Queen of the Universe, in whose glorious month this letter is being written to you.

Anything that breaks this unity is a tragedy beyond compare. The spirit alone matters, the "being before God" that must express this unity, make real and palpable that charity, clothe everything with peace. Then the works will be added to this unity

12

and they will glow like precious stones in a crown. But if there is no crown, where shall we put the stones? They will have to remain hidden, and their light will not shine on the top of a mountain, but will be buried under a bushel.

With deep longing and a great desire, I want you to discuss this unity, this charity. Pray about it. Live it. Make it real, so that the modern pagans might truly behold us and say, "See how these Christians love one another!" Then indeed we shall renew the face of the earth and extend Christ's Kingdom.

Caritas, pax to you, my beloved,

In Mary's Immaculate Heart,

IN THE CELL OF PEACE

July 9, 1956

Dearly Beloved,

I have been thinking in the quiet of the night, as I often do, about how much I love you and how much, in the natural order of things, I miss each one of you. Yet my heart rejoices because each day I realize more and more, through the grace of God, the great depth, height, and breadth of the bond of charity that unites us all. You have become dearer to me than my own blood family, and distance does not seem to make much difference.

This is the immense lesson in detachment that the Church teaches us. It is so simple a lesson that in the hurly-burly of everyday life, under the thousand pressures of the Apostolate, we are apt to miss it and allow loneliness to take hold and walk with us once again. Loneliness for a place, Madonna House Combermere. Loneliness for a person with whom we desire to be.

The secret of detachment is that if we detach ourselves from created things, including people, and attach our hearts to God, we suddenly rediscover all that we have left behind, and we have a foretaste of Paradise. In his immense love and mercy, he gives us back, in his Sacred Heart, the very people we loved most and from whom the separation was so painful. We have given up all things for Christ's sake, and now he returns them to us.

When I come to this point in my meditation, suddenly you are all with me — warm, alive, closer than you could ever be if you were here physically. It is then that I feel palpably the bond of charity that unites us.

The more I think about Our Apostolate, the more I dwell on the word *peace*. In the Gospel, Christ says, "By their fruits you shall know them." One of the basic fruits of the Apostolate, a fruit of our life together, should be peace, a deep, inner peace in every individual.

What is there to be unpeaceful about? Difficulties will abound. Trials will dwell with us constantly. Little pressures and big pressures will encompass us with their eternal demands. Temptations will beseige us from within. Loneliness will knock at the door of our hearts. The devil will roar all around us, not only like a lion but like underground thunder. Mental, physical and spiritual weariness will chant their endless lullaby. The flesh will seek escape into sleep.

These things will happen, but if our soul remains in its cell of peace, dwelling at the feet of the Prince of Peace, all this will be as if it were not, for peace is the fruit of charity, and nothing can penetrate that cell unless we let it.

I was praying to Teresa of Avila, and I recalled her words: "Let nothing disturb you. Let nothing affright you. All things are passing. God alone remains."

Let us try then to dwell at the feet of the Prince of Peace. Let us work in the noonday darkness, in the many dark nights of the spiritual life, holding high the torch of peace. If we do that, then faith will become strong, the vision of our priorities will be clear, and peace and love will grow.

Lovingly yours in the Prince of
Peace,
And in Our Lady, Queen of Peace,

14

GRATITUDE FOR YESTERDAY — COURAGE FOR TOMORROW

August 15, 1956

Dearly Beloved,

During this holy and blessed month of the Assumption, forgive me if I reminisce a little on the past. Truly miraculous are the ways of God! How incredible to think that a little group of six lay people, who banded together in the Lord's name twenty-five years ago, should become an Apostolate of laymen, laywomen and priests! It took many years for this to happen, but herein lies a lesson which we should all keep before our eyes. It is the lesson of a faith that knows no obstacles — a faith that always remembers that for God, the impossible takes just a tiny bit longer. It is the lesson of trust in Divine Providence that remembers these words of God and clings to them through all contingencies — "Ask and you shall receive."

It is the lesson of abandonment to God's holy will in child-likeness and simplicity. It is an abandonment that stands straight and tall content to rest along banks filled with sunshine, or in dark valleys, or anywhere that God's will leads it.

Nor let us forget patience, that humble virtue without which our little Apostolate could never survive. Patience with one another, patience with oneself, patience with superiors, patience with those we serve, patience with those who hate and persecute us. Patience, always patience.

The flower of all this is the motto on our cross: "Pax-Caritas." It is a peace that surpassess all understanding — and a charity that understands and forgives all things.

It is good to reflect on the past, and to receive courage from it. Each one of us has such a past. You remember the difficulties, the darknesses, the sorrows that were yours. Unite them with those who went before you until you come to the pioneers, who perhaps suffered most of all, and whom we should remember always in our prayers.

Yes, it is good to pause and look back, and to see the mercy and grace of God leading us through so many dangerous paths and quicksands to the place where we are today. Let this backward glance give us courage for today and readiness for tomorrow. Let this month be one of gratitude and joy before the face of the Lord and his gracious Mother. Let us pray for perseverance and steadfastness and the growth of our wondrous vocation.

May Our Lady cover you with the blue mantle of her love and keep you safe.

Affectionately yours in her,

OUR FAMILY SPIRIT

September 17, 1956

Dearly Beloved,

One of the greatest difficulties of those leaving Madonna House, Combermere for the missions is caused by their tremendous love for their motherhouse, the cradle that received and shaped their vocation. But there is a subtle distinction that has to be considered. For the problem is not as obvious.

A family spirit is never limited to a house, a geographical place, nor to specific people. Naturally, there will be a soft spot in one's heart for the mother and father of one's soul — for myself or another director general or for one's spiritual director. But love is not dependent on the physical presence of that person. If there is to be a real family spirit in Madonna House, then the director of every house will be seen as the image of Our Lord or Our Lady. Our loyalty, love, and respect is automatically given to that director, because the eyes of faith will see in him or her the gracious figure of Christ or his Mother.

Here I would like to quote from the constitution of St. Ignatius of Loyola, found in a book called *Perfect Obedience* by M. Espinosa Polit, S. J.:

> Obedience vastly conduces to rapid spiritual advancement. Therefore, all should give themselves to perfect obedience, acknowledging the superior, whoever he be, in place of Christ . . . and yield to him not only outward but inward reverence and love. And they must accustom themselves not to behold who he is whom they obey, but rather *who he is for whose sake they obey* — that is, Christ our Lord.

St. Ignatius states very concisely the principle on which all obedience is based:

> They regard not the individual whom they obey, but in him Christ our Lord for whose love they obey. For the superior is not to be obeyed because he is prudent or virtuous or excels in any other divine gift, whatsoever it be, but for this only: that he is in the place of God, and has authority from him who says: "He that heareth you heareth me, and he that despiseth you despiseth me."

Obedience is due not only to the superior, but also to subordinates who receive their authority from him; for instance, department heads in Madonna House. St. Ignatius writes:

> When anyone goes to the kitchen to help the cook, he must obey him with much humility in all things pertaining to his office, showing him always complete obedience; for if he does not, it is not likely that he will show obedience to any superior, since true obedience is not concerned about the person to whom a thing is done, but for whom; if he does this for our Creator and Lord alone, the same Lord of all is obeyed. Wherefore, one should not look to see whether it is the cook of the house, or its superior, whether he who commands is one or the other, for neither to them nor for them is this obedience shown, but only to God and for God, our Creator and Lord.

The following is another point for your meditation, a very deep one — for if ever there was a superior lacking in everything, it most assuredly is myself. It is consoling to read the following from Dom Columba Marmion, a great Benedictine. He discusses the hiddenness of Christ in the Eucharist, and continues:

> In the same way Christ conceals himself from us in our superiors. In spite of his imperfections, the Abbot (or any superior) for us is the representative of Christ. Christ hides beneath the sacramental species. Just because the superior is placed above all others, the daily intercourse which we have with him betrays his deficiencies; wherefore we feel tempted to exclaim: "This man is not Christ; his poor judgment is not infallible; he can make mistakes, in fact does; he cannot comprehend my plans; he allows himself to be guided by this or that preference." But faith answers, the Abbot is believed to act in the place of Christ; whether Christ gives us Solomon to take his place, or a man without talent to the eyes of faith it is Christ that the man represents. And then when I have faith, I will say *Credo*, I believe; I obey this person, whoever he may be, because in him I obey Christ and I remain thus united to Christ. . . . .

To see Christ in the director or superior, there is no need to believe, through some misconceived idea of loyalty, that the superior cannot make a mistake, or that he is not subject to the weaknesses of human nature. Returning to the book on St. Ignatius, we read:

> St. Ignatius on the contrary expressly says that these deficiencies may and do actually exist in the superiors that rule us. He has no reluctance in admitting the case of a superior's lack of prudence and even scanty virtue, and he warns us *at once* that similar imperfections do not weaken in the least the strength of the principle which ought to sustain the edifice of our obedience. Let us give ear to his words: ". . . neither, on the other hand, if he be of less understanding or prudence, is he therefore to be the less obeyed in that wherein he is superior, since he bears the Person whose wisdom cannot be deceived, and who will supply whatsoever shall be wanted in his substitute, whether it be virtue or other qualities. Wherefore, Christ our Lord, when he had said in express and open terms, 'The Scribes and Pharisees sit upon the chair of Moses,' presently added: 'All things, therefore, whatsoever they shall

say to you, observe and do, but according to their works do ye not.' ''

I could go on quoting from this wonderful book, but I think I have written enough to show you that the family spirit depends on yourselves and your attitude to your director and to each other. Like love, this spirit is intangible. Every group of Madonna House staff workers constitutes a family. Every staff worker who might be assigned to work alone somewhere, in the future, to teach in a university or to nurse in a hospital, still knows that he or she is a member of that family, whose love embraces him forever. The essence of the spirit of the Secular Institute* is that it can easily dispense with the outward signs of a corporate existence so familiar to religious life.

Nor need a family spirit express itself in being together physically at regular times. Naturally, the staff members and director will be happy when they can enjoy each other's company alone. But the Apostolate will make demands upon that intimate little body of apostles. Christ will say, ''Do you wish to be together and enjoy each other while I stand outside and wait, in the person of a stranger, to join the small circle of your inner family, when charity demands that you extra help me in someone else's?''

Do you see what I mean, dearly beloved? The family spirit is not a tangible thing that has to be brought to life at appointed times, for example, the common recreation of the religious. In the lay apostolate, we who eat Christ every morning must be eaten ourselves by others, and must surrender everything, including those outward signs of our inward unity. We must always remember that this unity is strengthened through this immense sacrifice on our part. So let the nostalgia for Combermere depart from your hearts and be replaced by a strong, warm love, and by gratitude for what Madonna House has done for you.

Another point that I want to discuss is this matter of canonizing the techniques of Madonna House. Just because the horarium of Madonna House is thus and so, just because we do things here this way or that, does not mean that we should carry these techniques into the mission field. The only thing that we never change but deepen and sanctify, is the *spirit of the Apostolate*.

*At one time Madonna House was seeking Secular Institute status, but it is no longer doing so.

Charity can make short work of methods, customs, and even traditions, for these are always subject to the needs of our brethren, the Apostolate, and the milieu in which we find ourselves. We must be flexible like rapiers, malleable like wax. We change these techniques at a moment's notice, to be of better service to God and humanity. Unless we do this, we will be hidebound, dead wood, and of no use to the Lord.

We have been discussing these matters quite a bit lately at Madonna House, and I am sharing with you the thoughts that have crystallized in my own heart from these discussions.

Lovingly in Mary,

FACING THE REALITY OF CHRIST'S PAIN

December 7, 1956

Dearly Beloved,

Slowly, the immense vision of the Secular Institutes* given by the Holy Spirit to Pope Pius XII is unfolding before me. The heart of this vision depends on our interior life and on our spiritual and emotional maturity. We have to get out of ourselves. We have to concentrate on the things of the spirit. We will only be as strong as the life of our spirit. This life cannot grow in emotional immaturity. The time has come for all of us to *face the reality of Christ's pain*.

The pain is immense. Think of Christ in the world today. Meditate on him. Steep yourself in his pain.

*At one time Madonna House was considering becoming a Secular Institute.

Of course, he is in the poor, the forgotten, the neglected, the hungry, the cold and homeless. He is in the thin children with old eyes, he is in the restless, unmoored youth. He is in the alcoholic, the psychotic, the neurotic. You know his pain in these people; you are familiar with his presence there.

But do you see the pain of Christ in the priests and in the bishops who are concerned about their parishes and dioceses, who spend themselves beyond all human prudence in an effort to assuage the pain of Christ in those entrusted to their care?

I have seen bishops and priests cry slow, heavy tears. It seemed to me that I saw Christ cry in them. My heart stood still, I would have died for them right then and their if my death could have stopped those heavy tears. I saw Christ in these priests, Christ's need of us to extend their efforts. I realized the need for unselfishness, for maturity, and for an end to this eternal concern with our puny, demanding little selves.

The weapon of knowledge has been given to all of you that you might mature emotionally. Months and sometimes years have been spent showing you the way to that maturity. These methods are now in your hands. Lay them at the feet of Christ. Ask him for the grace to forget yourself completely, to become the linen cloth that will wipe his bloody face, the hands that will take him off the cross, so that he will not be recrucified.

Look with the eyes of your soul and see how he needs you. There is no time to spend on that self that should die so completely to make room for him.

Our time is now. Now! Now! Now! Not tomorrow, *now!* For the pain of Christ is real. It has to be shared, assuaged, and stopped. Now!

Have you seen his pain in the hungry heart of mankind? Have you seen his pain in the "poor rich?" Have you seen his pain in the intellectual life of the universities and schools, the teachers and professors who, day in and day out, teach empty words that are but a skeleton of truth without the flesh of him who is Truth?

Have you seen the pain of Christ in the municipal, state, provincial, national and international governments? Do you feel the horror of the United Nations, so divided because Christ does not sit on their councils?

Stop! Look! Listen! Behold the pain of Christ — a white-hot iron that should set your heart afire so that you might share his pain and become a flame that lights and warms the world.

At this point, you may well ask, how do I propose that you do this, you who are working in that part of the vineyard he has allotted you and who are already assuaging his pain in hundreds of people? My answer comes to you simple and direct: *Love more*. To love more, *pray more*. Pray not only the prayers of the Mass, the Office, the rosary, which are the foundation of all prayer; but pray the prayer of the presence of God. Walk in that presence. Ask those who direct your soul to teach you. Love. Love God. Love every minute, with every step that you take. Love him sleeping or waking, eating or working. Love. For only each individual loving God as he should be loved will bring peace to the world. This is Caritas.

Let each of your souls become the cradle, the manager of the newborn Christ. Let us become the cities and villages of his public life, the earth he walked upon, until finally we become a Golgotha, where he will be the cross and we the crucified. Then, someday, we shall also know his Ascension, and we too will ascend. But not alone. We shall take with us all those whom the fire of our love, our surrender, and our dedication, have brought to Christ. This is my wish for you this holy season of Christmas.

In the unity of prayers and
love in Mary,

Catherine

CRUCIFIED CONTEMPLATIVES

January 26, 1957

Dearly Beloved,

We all know that the spirit of Madonna House is the cross. But have we thought about how difficult it is to lie stretched upon that cross?

To allow oneself to be stretched out upon the cross requires fidelity, perseverance and vision. It is this vision that gives one the courage to climb the hill to Golgotha. You may walk upright with even, forceful steps, or bent over and burdened. You may have to drag yourself inch by painful inch, exhausted and wounded, on bruised hands and knees, up the Hill of the Skull towards that desired goal, the cross.

Without that clear vision and singleness of purpose, without complete dedication and surrender, you might not reach the cross. You might be tempted to pause on some gray-green meadow or some warm hill. You might give in to fatigue, to your emotions, to the dark night of the spirit.

To reach Christ's cross, you must know where you are going and why. You do not need knowledge, but the knowledge that comes from Love itself.

You need prayer, constant, unflagging prayer. You need the prayer of silence, contemplation, and repose in the heart of Christ.

We cannot love unless we are willing to be crucified. To be crucified with Christ, we must become one with him. How much must happen in order that a human being become so empty that he might be filled with the immensity of Christ!

This cannot happen unless we die to everything in us that belongs to the old man. We must die to all that is a result of original sin, to desires that lead away from life and truth, to instinct that, unless tamed and sublimated, will carry us into the bottomless pit of hell.

All this must die in order that our *true* self, the self redeemed by the immense gift of God in Jesus Christ, may live. Just think, dearly beloved, we are called to be one with Love himself!

To die this way, in order to be reborn, requires a courage that men call foolhardy, a gallantry men call stupidity. It demands that we become fools for Christ's sake, for the foolishness of the saints is wisdom before God.

It requires utter indifference to human respect. Short of giving scandal to the little ones, we cannot care about what people think of us, but only about what God thinks of us.

When we have walked this way of fidelity, perserverance, prayer and courage, we will be ready to be stretched out on the cross of Christ. One with Love, we will know the meaning of *Caritas*, engraved on our silver cross. We will know the meaning of *Pax*, the second word on our crosses, for his peace will be ours, and no one will be able to take it from us. We shall have stepped out of the prison of self into the freedom of the children of God. We shall be in the hallways of heaven.

I have mentioned the need for contemplation. While, on a human level our Apostolate is one of the most active imaginable, I think it has also been destined by God to be deeply contemplative.

Unless we become contemplatives, how will we ever be able to face a lifetime of doubts, temptations and fears? Unless we enter the great silence of God and his peace, how will we be able to face the daily pain that grinds us like sand. Resting on his breast, listening only to the sound of his heartbeats, we will hear, in proportion to our inner stillness, the depth of his love for us. From this love will come the joy that will lighten problems, pain and darkness.

We are a new breed of contemplatives. Our monasteries are the busy streets of new pagan cities, the noisy thoroughfares of immense metropolises that sing the hymns of the world, the flesh and the devil. Our convents are rural roads, deserted because they are no longer travelled by men who know and love God.

We are a new breed of contemplatives, whose prayer is accompanied by clanging sirens, honking horns, blaring radios and tramping feet.

We are a new breed of contemplatives, and our bells are the poor, knocking ceaselessly at our blue doors.*

We are a new breed of contemplatives, and we must learn to rest on the heart of God, listening to the perfect harmony of his heartbeats while we go about his business in the midst of the most discordant music the world has ever known.

This is what I wanted to share with you, my dearly beloved.

Lovingly in the immense charity of Christ and the gentle love of Our Lady,

*The doors of Madonna House are painted blue in honour of Our Lady.

ARE WE READY FOR THE PASSION?

February 24, 1957

Dearly Beloved,

With Lent approaching, my mind turns to the passion of Christ, and the realization that this same passion continues daily in his Mystical Body, the Church.

This means in us. In you, in me, and in every human being. The question arises in my heart: how are we, who have been called to this special vocation, who are children of his Sacred Heart and of the Immaculate Heart of his Mother, how are we to bear his pain in our own minds, bodies, and souls? More precisely, how are we to *share* it? And sharing it, how are we to assuage it in others?

To share Christ's passion is to bear its marks, deep and searing. Are we ready? Are we ready to die to self, to so forget ourselves that we feel an exultant joy in being wounded as he has been wounded, hurt as he has been hurt, counted as nothing as he has been counted nothing? Are we ready to be unjustly accused as he was, flagellated, if not with the cat-o'-nine tails, then with the whips of evil, uncharitable, thoughtless tongues?

Are we ready to be persecuted by the thoughtlessness of those closest to us, by personalities that rub salt into the wounds of our minds and hearts, even as the dust of Via Crucis bit into his? Are we ready to be persecuted by the misunderstandings of those we look up to, by the crown of thorns that responsibility weaves around our head, by the loneliness into which this responsibility leads us?

Are we ready to spend our nights with him in Gethsemane, sweating not blood, but tears? Are we ready to go with him into the desert and be tempted for forty days? Can we leave father, mother, brother, sister, husband, wife or children, as he wanted us to do when he called us into his special service? Can we leave our families behind, not only physically, but inwardly, repeating, "I have no brothers, I have no mother." Can we really mean and live what we say? Finally, are we ready to be stripped naked of self, not caring that we are exposed to the gaze of multitudes who do not understand us; who, at best, ridicule us; and in the end, crucify us.

This is what it means to share Christ's passion. Have you ever thought of it that way, dearly beloved? If you haven't, I beg of you to do so. Only then will we begin to enter into that passion, deeply desiring to bear it's burdens, to identify ourselves utterly and completely with him. Then we will be willing to pick up the cross of our austere, glorious vocation, to be pierced with the sharp nails of days and nights spent for others without a thought for our own comfort, consolation, needs, desires, or dreams. We will be crucified with the nails of a routine so familiar as to be excruciating at times, by a monotony and weariness that seem to seep into the very marrow of our bones.

Let us ask ourselves these questions this Lent, and let us ask them in the presence of God. If we grow in a positive response, it will be a good Lent. Unless we really steep ourselves in Christ's passion and identify ourselves with it lovingly, joyously, whole-heartedly, we cannot go forth into the world and seek out the suffering Christ in our brother. We will not understand his pain. Without understanding, there is no love, and without love, there is no healing.

I have been thinking of these things since Septuagesima Sunday, contemplating them before his Face in the Blessed Sacrament, meditating on them in the few spare moments of a busy life, in the quiet hours of the night when sleep will not come. Sometimes it seems to me that I am drowning in the sea of Christ's sorrow and that of Mary. The sight of his pain in our brethren is forever present before my eyes. At times it feels as if I have been bled dry by the wounds this sight inflicts upon my soul, heart and mind. At times I think I will not be able to get up in the morning, for the pain of Christ has bowed me down and made me weak. By his grace alone, I do get up. If I ask you to share his pain, I too must do so.

Have you ever thought what it must have been like for Mary Magdalene and St. John the Beloved to stand at the foot of the Cross? Sometime, when all is quiet and the night has hushed a long day, go into the chapel and meditate. You are Mary Magdalene. You love Jesus passionately. You are always with him. You know the Pharisees, the Sadducees, the rich people of Jerusalem, the ordinary country folk. Close to Jesus, you sense the storm gathering around him. You watch the hate rise, you see the suffering of Mary his Mother, and you are helpless to prevent what you see coming. All you can do is to love more, suffer more, pray more, keeping ever closer to him who seems intent on entering that storm of hate.

Try being John the Beloved. You see what Mary Magdalene saw, but with a man's eyes, and a heart that loved so much that it remained steadfast to the end. Imagine yourself at the Last Supper. Your head rests on his breast, and in your ears beats the heartbeats of God? Ecstasy? If St. Paul was taken up to the third heaven, as he writes in one of his Epistles, what heaven did St. John reach when he listened to the heartbeats of God who is Heaven!

St. John and St. Mary Magdalene saw their Love whipped, spat upon, and made to carry the Cross, a gibbet of shame. They saw him crucified like a common criminal between heaven and earth. Compare your faith and love with theirs. Do we love like they did? Do we believe like they did? Do we share his passion like they did?

I have purposely not mentioned Mary. We who have barely learned to walk in the way of Christ's passion should, perhaps, first take St. John the Beloved and St. Mary Magdalene for our patrons, this Lent of 1957. Let us ask them, who were so close to Mary, to lead us slowly to her. Next year or the year after, we might, on our knees, approach the suffering of Mary, and ask her to take us into that final novitiate that will reveal the secrets of God's pain, which are the secrets of his love.

A holy Lent to each one of you. May its fruit be great, for the pain of Christ cries out around you.

Lovingly yours,

YARDSTICK OF SANCTITY

April 1, 1957

Dearly Beloved;

Christ is risen! Alleluia! Verily he has risen! Alleluia! May the ineffable joy of this Feast be yours forever!

I know that we will all be united this week during the holy Easter Vigil. We will also be one in spirit on Holy Thursday when many of us will renew our promises to love and serve Our Lord in the House of Our Lady. Of course, this does not mean that we are not united throughout the year. We are; but for those who love God there are special moments when this unity can almost be seen and touched. Let us rejoice in these days and thank God for them.

I've been thinking about some of the difficulties experienced by people in the houses, and I have prayed much over them asking God to give me light. It seemed to me that perhaps it was good that there were so many difficulties, for it meant that the Lord was sharing his Passion with all of us.

When you are sent to the missions after your initial training period at Madonna House, the Lord puts you through his own novitiate, the only goal of which is to make you saints. Don't worry too much about the work. We become saints through the work, but let us not try to analyze it too much. Instead, let us *love* much beginning with those in the house.

I am always afraid when any member of Madonna House starts to be too concerned and prays too much about matters outside the house. We get caught up with ideas, techniques, and the problems of those we serve, and we forget that everything must begin *in the family*. If there is no unity and charity among ourselves, any attempt at clarification will fail; all techniques will be sterile, and the seeds of any discussion will fall into stony ground.

In our Apostolate, there is only one yardstick of sanctity: How much do we love God? How much do we love one another, and then how much do we love those who we serve? We cannot love the poor if we do not love one another.

As this beautiful Feast of Easter approaches, I stand before God's face and behold my utter poverty. I know I am emptier than a husk. I have only one prayer for myself and for all of us — that we may grow in love of him and love of one another. Then we too shall rise with him.

Christ is risen! Alleluia! Verily he has risen!

In Christ,

[signature]

CHRIST IN THE MISSIONS

July 11, 1957

Dearly Beloved,

I have been remiss in sending you my monthly letters! I miss you all so much. I miss the little get-togethers we had discussing the things that mattered. So I thought I would sit down and talk with you as I used to do.

So many have gone to another house only recently and every thing is strange and maybe a little frightening. Probably it was all very exciting at first; but now, perhaps, some of you feel discouraged or bewildered saying to yourselves, "Is this what it is really like? There's nothing glamourous about it! Why did I think it would be exciting? Look at this hard work, the lack of privacy, and the sea of needy people constantly pressing upon us!"

This is the time to review what we have discussed during your training. Remember how wonderful it all sounded then as I painted word pictures of a God waiting to be loved, of the lonely Christ at the crossroads of the world, of the pain of Christ in others! How silent you were! You went into the chapel to talk it over with the Lord, and you assured him, I know, that you loved him and were ready to die for him.

Now you are experiencing the dust of Arizona or the inconveniences of the Yukon. Seeing the face of Christ in others is not at all as easy as you imagined it to be. That face seems distant and blurred. Heat, dust, cold and the constancy of serving people with different manners and standards of cleanliness — how far all this seems from those word pictures! How frightening!

You are on your own now. There are no set schedules. You make mistakes and they stand out glaringly. There is no longer the security of someone saying, "Now do this; now do that."

There is no one except God. He speaks to you in the duty of every moment in which chores have to be done, though you are weary. Too, you are still tired from the residue of the emotional problems which we have all had to face in ourselves. Now is the time to ask Our Lord *to open our eyes* so that you might see the pain of Christ in your fellow men.

You might find it in a group of boys who ask you to go swimming with them. Why should you? The only reason is that the boys are Christ and have invited you. What work of grace might take place at that swimming hole! Even if nothing happens, friendship has developed between you and the boys — between you and the boy Christ. The law of charity has been fulfilled and that in itself is an immense grace. That is our Apostolate.

Ask our Lord to open your eyes to millions of little services that are right there to be performed with love. They don't need to be scheduled. Our children need to be constantly told what to do. Lovers of God see the obvious.

I remind you also, dearly beloved children of my spirit, that each house is only as strong as the love, openness, obedience and joy that reign among its members. If these qualities are not present, then no matter how great the activity, the members of that house will not grow in wisdom and grace before the Lord.

The work must always be the fruit of a spiritual growth, for unless the foundation of love is present, the works will be shallow. Let all the members constantly examine their consciences upon this, for our houses must be built with the help of the Lord not by our hands but by our souls.

The directors have been chosen by God to be the cornerstones. Think of the weight they carry! Let, them, therefore, live in the heart of Christ. Let them think with the mind of Christ;

see with the eyes of Christ; hear with the ears of Christ, and love with the heart of Christ. Then the weight will be light as a feather, for it will be carried with him and in him; and in him all things are easy.

Affectionately yours in Mary,

THE CHALLENGE OF BEING APOSTLES

July 30, 1957

Dearly Beloved,

August is the month of Our Lady's Assumption. This is one of our patronal Feasts and one of the days the new members of Madonna House receive the silver cross.*

As I look back over the years, gratitude and joy fill my heart. God has certainly been merciful to me, a sinner, in giving me this wonderful vocation and a little glimpse of his vision for the whole Apostolate. I thank Him for my ever-growing spiritual family; for all the joy, pain, suffering, and gladness of these years — for every second, minute and hour.

As I sit in my office I am keenly aware of my responsibilities. As the evening of life approaches, I ask myself: ''What account will I render to the Lord for these years?'' I ask: ''Have I been a good steward? Have I used well and faithfully the talents he has given me?'' As I examine my conscience, I know that I could have

---

*One of the days the members of Madonna House make Promises of poverty, chastity and obedience.

done many things better, but I know also that I have tried to do them the best of my ability.

I pause. A strange hesitancy enters my soul. It is almost a fear, I ask myself: "Have I truly done all that is possible for my spiritual children, the members of Madonna House? Have I done all that is possible, and then, in faith undertaken the impossible?"

This is the point where darkness envelops me. I make a deeper examination of conscience. Why do I feel uneasy about this part of my life? The answer comes: because it is the most important part, and because when I appear before God, the first question he will ask me will be about each of you. I am disturbed because I wonder if I am responsible for the shortcomings I see in you. I ask you, the children God has given me, to think about my words in the depth of your souls before God; for it is you who must answer this question.

"By their fruits you shall know them," says the Lord. I look at the fruits. On the whole they are good. The houses prosper. They grow in size. Their apostolic works expand. But are all the members of the Apostolate growing in wisdom and grace before the Lord as they should be?

I cannot say that everyone is. There are some among you who are still very self-centered. They look at the whole world through the narrow, confining window of self. This also affects your relations with your brothers and sisters in Christ which should be filled with *caritas*, thoughtfulness and joy. Some are far from being this way.

You still react to your brothers and sisters in an immature fashion. You seem unable to adapt to different personalities though you may have spent years together. Even if you had not, just because you are brothers and sisters in this glorious family of Madonna House, just the sight of our cross — *pax-caritas*, should be enough to remind you that peace, love and service must begin in your own spiritual family.

No wonder I hesitate during my examination of conscience. No wonder in the dark of the night I toss sleeplessly on my bed. No wonder I arise and go to our silent chapel and weep and pray before the Blessed Sacrament. Why do I weep? I weep for myself partly, for somewhere in the course of your training, I have failed God and you.

I weep also for you who drag your feet before the greatest challenge ever given to human beings — the wondrous challenge of being apostles in the marketplace where you could be feeding multitudes with your burning charity! But how can charity take fire in a soul all wrapped up in itself in the deep, green wood of a mind that refuses to be a channel of light?

I have written of the vision of our Apostolate which grows. I have written about the pain of Christ. I might as well have remained silent! My words fall on deaf ears, cold hearts, and souls stifled in the thick blanket of selfishness.

I don't want to hear any more about emotional problems. You have been given every means to rid yourselves of them. Are you clinging to them as an excuse from plunging into the depths of God's heart? Or because you shrink, not only from the shadow of the cross, but from the cross itself? You know well that you must embrace it if you are to rise with Christ at Easter and fulfill your vocation to love.

Don't talk to me about emotional problems but look deeply into your souls, and stop worrying about associations, transfers and other psychological mechanisms. Start living in *caritas*. Arise and begin that journey inward and upward which you have been taught to make.

Don't you understand that each moment that you waste on yourself, on your little two-by-four emotional reactions, is precious time wasted? It is God's time. If you weren't so self-centered and so wrapped up in emotions, you would be one hundred per cent engaged in the work of God. Then you would bring him ten souls where now you barely bring him one?

You say you are all "cooped up in one place." What does it matter? Millions of human beings are cooped up without any recreation, with nowhere to go, no bed, and nothing to eat. Stop and think of our own Canada, of the U.S.A., of India with its teeming millions — of China. How those people would like to change places with you! What kind of apostles are we, if we are worried about our spiritual family living so closely together? The fruits of that life should be gaiety, laughter and joyful recreation.

The hardships of the Apostolate today are nothing to what they will be later in missionary countries. There, unable to understand the language living in a hut, perhaps, getting used to strange new food and new ways we shall *really* be cooped up together.''

How do you think a long face affects your particular house?

Do you think saints are sad? We are extremely sensitive to one another. You, who are trained in the ways of the spiritual life, should know that each change of countenance or attitude, whether you do a task happily and efficiently or slowly and moodily has direct consequences on others. The guilt of having made your spiritual family unhappy should weigh heavily upon you.

I expect you to be modern martyrs, heroes of love and selflessness. This is what I practically killed myself to tell you in season and out. Have you forgotten? I repeated until I was hoarse that all I could give you was a cross; that I couldn't even promise you three square meals a day; that your housing might be a hut or an old palace, a dilapidated convent, or a broken-down army shack. This is what you will often have to be satisfied with in the missions.

The only way to achieve peace within yourself is to grow in *caritas*. The only way to grow in caritas is to become utterly poor, not only in material goods but in the surrender of your will. There can be no "ifs," "ands," or "buts," but only a joyful obedience. A whole house can be held back by one individual! God help me if I am that individual! God help me if I have failed to indoctrinate him or her! For that failure would be partly mine!

I could carry the burden of an apostolate much larger than this one, but I cry out in agony before the sight of one of my spiritual children failing the Lord or our spiritual family. I, who seldom weep, feel the weight of unshed tears in my weary soul. I think of the endless talks I have had with each of you. I think of the many hours spent teaching you, healing you, loving you, and I ask myself: "Were they enough?"

The darkness deepens around me, and the weight of the cross grows heavier. This cannot go on, dearly beloved. If the fault is mine, please let me know. I shall prostrate myself at your feet and humbly ask your pardon. And I shall atone with all the power of my soul. If the fault is yours, I beg you simply to desist. Otherwise a chink is opened to the devil, and no one in his right mind wishes the prince of darkness to have so much as a foothold in any one of our houses!

Many of you may be surprised at this letter; some hurt; others bewildered. All of you will ask yourselves: "Is it I?" Those who recognize themselves will understand. But, in any case, it is good for everyone to realize that, at some time or other, he or she may have been guilty of the same thing.

Let us put an end to this immaturity — this fear of growing in wisdom and grace and sanctity. Let us arise and fly to God.

Lovingly yours in Mary,

DEVOTION TO THE SACRED HEART

August 29, 1957

Dearly Beloved,

I have been thinking lately about the Sacred Heart. I have never been able to develop the kind of devotion to It which many Catholics have. That devotion, though warm and human, seems to me a little sentimental.

Each person worships according to his own background and culture, and in my own devotion to the Heart of Christ is inextricably woven into the Mass. Only God, passionately in love with man, would give himself to us in this incredible proof of his love which is renewed eternally on our altars. His heart was wounded with a lance. All hearts that love are wounded with the lance of love. At every Mass love shouts out and begs us to *love him back*.

So to me, devotion to the Sacred Heart is far from sentimental. Christ's Heart is the symbol of his love, part of the sacred humanity and his infinite Godhead. He compels me to look at my heart and ask myself whether or not I love him as I should.

This shakes my whole being and forces me to look deeply into my own heart and ask myself, whether or not I love him as I should. I see my utter poverty. I realize that if I enter the heart of God and accept his love, then I shall know how to love him back as he desires.

The Sacred Heart calls us in the Apostolate to give him our hearts, which means to give him ourselves. We must hold nothing back. He asks that we offer ourselves as a holocaust, that we become ashes in the fire of that heart.

What does that mean? It means that if we truly loved God as he wants to be loved, we would begin to assume full responsibility for our actions. We would not be afraid of the approval nor the disapproval of anyone in authority. We would assume responsibility because that is our vocation; because that is what God desires of us, and because in calling us he has given us all the grace that is necessary. Having accepted responsibility, we would accept both praise and censure peacefully, acknowledging the first as proper to God, and the second as proper to us sinners.

If we truly loved God as he wants to be loved, we would work for him with great foresight, planning every step of each job so as to perform it perfectly. We would do our work efficiently, since love cannot bear to bring pain to the Beloved by wasting time. He thirsts for souls. The work of our hands, of our minds and bodies are the coins that will enable us to purchase souls.

What an incredible mystery this is! Our humble efforts at washing dishes, dealing with the disturbed, arising in the night to open the door to the homeless, enduring other's noise or raucous music — all can be used by God to bring him souls for which he thirsts.

It is an awesome, joyous mystery that warms our hearts. In its presence, how can we not be concentrated in our work, be it large or small, never counting the cost? We offer up our boredom, our tiredness, our irritability and lo, they vanish for love has taken their place.

To me this is true devotion to the Sacred Heart of Christ, a devotion that consists of simply loving him back, and offering that love in atonement for our sins and the sins of our neighbor. It means loving him so much in the nitty-gritty routine of our daily routine that we make up for the coldness of others hearts. We should love him as though we had millions of hearts, and then ask him to enlarge them so that tomorrow they will become millions of hearts!

We prove our love by taking responsibility and by listening attentively to orders and performing our duties efficiently. If we put into practice all that we have been taught, we will gladly do all that we have been given. We will do it with our whole being never thinking of ourselves nor of how it affects us. Then indeed, we will assuage his thirst for love. Our devotion will flame like a fire and renew the face of the earth.

Let us begin.

With love,

[signature]

THE INFINITE LONELINESS OF CHRIST

December 20, 1957

Dearly Beloved,

The joyous season of Christ's birth is upon us. I want to wish you, my spiritual family, all the incredible blessings of this time, and to share with you the thoughts which have been in my mind this Advent.

During this time of preparation, the picture of Christ's loneliness has come before my eyes with ever-increasing poignancy. In a few days we will see him in our minds, born once again in the endless modern Bethlehems of our towns and villages. Those who listen may even hear the angels singing the glory of his birth. But where will be the shepherds coming to kneel in adoration?

Millions of people this year will not raise their voices to God making the cold of winter seem warm. Their love will decorate no stable. Today, millions of people do not know Christ, or knowing him do not care about him — or more tragic of all — even hate him. How intense must be the loneliness of Christ in Bethlehem this year!

His loneliness continued throughout his life with the flight into Egypt. There the Holy Family became the first refugees of the Christian era. Was there anyone to help or console them? Today, how many thousands of Christs live in the refugee camps of the world? How many exiled ones have taken the same flight into Egypt and found it a desert because we do not love enough — we who live the comfortable and normal life! How lonely is Christ the Refugee in our day!

My spirit falters as I try to imagine the loneliness of Nazareth where the Creator was subject to his creatures — even such loving ones as Joseph and Mary. Imagine the ineffable, incomprehensible, all-encompassing God imprisoning himself in human flesh! Imagine him whose word built the whole universe, whose thought created the forests, painstakingly planing a board in his carpentry shop! How lonely the sound of wood shavings falling to the floor! That was long ago, but how about that now?

Today, I feel the loneliness of all the lonely people in the world. What is more lonely than the sound of laughter in the street, heard from some little room in a shabby boarding house? Or a kiss outside the window, overheard by a woman who doubts the fidelity of her husband? So many sounds can be heard everywhere by the lonely Christ in hearts, minds and souls all over the world. I shiver to think of it. Don't you?

Think of the loneliness of Christ's public life when perhaps only the breeze caught his holy words and gathering them close to its heart carried them across the face of the earth. How many millions of people hear Christ's words today and do nothing about them, letting them die before they reach the heart? How many ears hear without hearing? How lonely must be the Christ of our day as he continues his public ministry and sees the dwindling crowds and the shrinking priestly vocations!

There is the loneliness of Gethsemane, with its terrible agony of mind and soul that so affected Christ that he sweat blood. How many thousands are in Gethsemane now! Think of the alcoholics, psychotics, neurotics — each spelling out painfully in their lonely lives each letter of the word Gethsemane!

Finally, there is the loneliness of Golgotha, of the Crucified One on the Cross. From how many thousands of Golgotha does Christ look down upon the world today! There are the crucified ones of the concentration camps behind the Iron or Bamboo Curtains. There are the poor, the sick, the lonely, the crucified in our very midst. Often their sufferings are forgotten as we hustle and bustle about our Christmas shopping.

The crowning loneliness of Christ was that of the cold tomb, a heavy stone rolled before its emptiness. Such is the loneliness of those in prisons. How many are there because they suffered the loneliness I tried so poorly to describe!

I could go further and further into the depths of Christ's infinite loneliness in his Mystical Body today. But what would be the reason for entering these depths unless they brought us to the heights of Christmas and its joy and its love? We must remember that the essence of our Apostolate is to smash the loneliness of Christ; to share it and assuage it.

In a few days, we shall kneel at the crib. Let us be filled with the desire to comfort him. Let us pray to the Christmas Infant, before whom we kneel so happily, to give us the grace to implement this desire in the reality of our daily lives.

Lovingly yours in the lonely Christ,

A TIME OF STOCKTAKING

January 14th, 1958

Dearly Beloved,

To all of us the Lord has given another year of grace: 1958. Knowing our weakness and our unpreparedness to meet him, he is graciously giving us his gift of time to grow in wisdom and grace.

Let us not waste any of it, not a little second, not a minute, not an hour. Just stop for a moment and think that you are dying, even as the year 1957, has just died. They say that before death one's whole life passes before one's eyes. I wouldn't know for sure, but I imagine that to be true.

I was several times near death. I do not remember thinking very clearly about my whole life, but I still remember realizing very vividly that all I wanted back again was the time I wasted. In those moments, time was the most precious thing I seemed to have wasted.

Dimly too, I remember that a strange, enormous and dark fear suddenly possessed me. Somehow, through pain and agony, I was given an understanding, clear and sharp, that I would have to account before God for everyone of those wasted seconds, minutes and hours. If we just meditated seriously about dying and wasted time, I think we could approximate the reality of a deathbed very quickly. It would not be a morbid meditation at all, but a very wholesome one. Youth would do well to meditate on death; they have so much time to give to God or to waste.

The first month of the New Year is usually a time of stocktaking. Reviewing the past, we find it laden with God's graces for which I hope we thank him constantly. We should also examine ourselves on what we have left undone or done badly, so as to eschew the same mistakes in this new year.

Consider our emotional lives. Most of you have been with Madonna House for a while. Even the newest members of the various houses have been with the Apostolate for at least a year. Yet so many of you still wallow in your moods. You forget the beautiful prayer of St. Francis which has been the very basis of your Madonna House training:

> O Divine Master, grant that I may not so much seek to be consoled as to console, to be understood as to understand; to be loved as to love; for it is in giving that we receive, in pardoning that we are pardoned; and in dying that we are born to eternal life.

This one little paragraph contains a whole gospel of spiritual life. It is the perfect answer to every neurosis in the world.

What does an emotionally immature person want above all else? *To be consoled.* And next? *To be understood, and to be loved.* But if we are constantly treated this way, then we become intensely selfish in that warm house which these three false illusions create. Then we are loathe to venture out of that house of illusions and to become mature and holy.

You might ask, "Why is being consoled, loved and understood an illusion?" The answer is very simple. It is the wrong type of love. When someone really loves you, he tries to direct your life into the way of giving rather than receiving.

Imagine a world where everyone gives and nobody desires to receive, except from God. Paradoxically, everyone would be loved, understood and consoled. The world would indeed be the *kingdom of heaven and earth*!

Let us apply this idea to everyday living. Suppose all of you were mature. Suppose you yourselves were like St. Francis of Assisi. How delicate your spiritual pitch would be! Your whole being would be a single burning flame of love, consolation, and understanding. Your spiritual ears would be acutely attuned to other peoples' needs.

What would your speech be like then? Would you ask silly, curious questions about those whom you serve? Would you thoughtlessly discuss drunkenness, oblivious to the fact that on the other side of a Dutch door some victims of alcohol are having a meal? Would you thoughtlessly relate pitiful accidents which might seem funny to you, who as yet are not too experienced with human failings and the tragedies they can bring? Would you chatter on about the problems of the disturbed who come to us seeking compassion? Idle talk and curiosity about things that do not really concern us are born of emotional immaturity. They take us far from the direction of sanctity.

Or take another situation. Will you be shocked when some tired priest, who himself is under terrific strain, might in a moment of weakness share with you matters that normally he would never have discussed with anyone? Will the human weakness, the Simon in the Peter, as it were, send you reeling in a round of doubts, temptations, and emotional crises? Why? All you have to do is look at your face in the mirror and remember that this either has happened, or will or can happen to you. You have to realize that the immensity of an office does not preclude the weakness of humanity. Otherwise Christ would not have made Peter the cornerstone of his Church.

An all-embracing charity, even in a small, humble lay apostle, can burn so fiercely so as to be of help even to one's betters without oneself being adversely affected. True, such cases are rare, but they might happen. And there are a thousand variations on the theme. None of them should harm you, for you understand that your vocation is *to understand, to console and to love* the sinner and the saint; the latter has his moments of weakness or he could not become a saint.

What did you expect to find at the mission houses? It is the reality of life which you have to meet sooner or later. We cannot simulate this life at Madonna House. We have no missions here to the Indians. Here we do not feed six thousand meals to Brothers Christopher in three weeks, nor do we deal with hundreds of children all day and half of the night. No. We give you the principles of approach and conduct but we cannot simulate the reality. You have to apply the principles given here.

And please do not begin your mission work by concentrating on yourself or how it affects you and what it does for you. No. Concentrate on what you can do for others how you affect others, and you will be all right. The graces of your vocation are there. Pick them up and make it snappy.

A holy, little motto that I received at Christmas hangs over my desk. It comes to mind right now and I will give it to you for an occasional meditation. It reads:

Let my silence bring forth *the Word*
My rest, his *action*
My death, *his life*

If you look it over, you will have the answer to my letter here. Let my silence bring forth the Word. My silence regarding questions which should not be asked at certain times and places; my silence about questions which should not be asked at all, for they are idle curiosity.

My rest, his action. That means my inner rest, the state in which I do the things that the Apostolate requires. If my mind, soul and heart are full of turmoil and self-centeredness, then he cannot act in me. His face will not be seen in my actions, for the curtain of these things will blot out his face or hide it.

My death, his life, means my death to self. I needn't enlarge upon that, for you have heard that many times from my lips.

Another little point which I wanted to discuss has been bothering me quite a bit. I have, of course, no desires to stop you from eating that which the mercy and kindness of God sends you. But I would like you not to become choosy because you now have so much from which to choose. Don't choose only that which you prefer.

We are coming close to Lent, and it is a wholesome thought to think of mortification. Remember we don't seek any mortification without the permission of our spiritual directors. It is necessary here to explain the state of your health if the priest does not know it, and it isn't obvious.

With these provisos, I would like to remind you of the words of our song which so well illustrate the spirit of Madonna House in this matter:

"Eat what is put on your plate."

If there is a choice of drinks on the table — cocoa, milk, tea, coffee — make a habit of not choosing what you like best, but often taking what you do not like.

In the various houses where thee are so many less people than in Madonna House, it is easy to slip into careless ways of eating as far as that type of mortification is concerned. I, being the watchman in the tower of our Apostolate, must remind you of this even though I presume that this rarely happens.

So let us review what I have written, as I want to really impress upon you these "big, little things." Watch your conversation for charity grows or dies there. Keep a rein over what may be idle curiosity. You will be told all that you need to know. If you are unsure about asking a question, check with your spiritual director to make sure you know what idle curiosity is. You will learn that way.

Remember that your Apostolate is to everyone in the marketplace — the rich and the poor, the saint and the sinner, the hobo and the priest (in a small, human measure, of course) the nun and the prostitute, the young and the old, the babies and the children, the men and the women — all who live in the marketplace. Thank God that you may be of assistance sometimes just by listening.

Don't be naive. It is not a virtue. To be childlike is wonderful at any age; of such is the kingdom of heaven but being childish after twenty-one is silly and spells emotional immaturity.

Observe and listen. Silence is gold and speech is silver. Remember there is in every house one person who will give you the right answer according to our spirit that is the director of your house. Be open to him or to her. Trust them. You do not place this trust in them because you personally like or dislike them, but because God has placed them over you.

Think this letter over. God love you! May keep you!

Lovingly in Mary,

DYING TO SELF

May 26, 1958

Dearly Beloved,

I recently found myself comparing the development of a member of our Apostolate to the evolution of the airplane. When people first arrive, they fly joyfully with the Wright Brothers at about five or ten miles an hour.

As time progresses and they grow in knowledge and cooperate with the grace of God working in them, they become like Lindbergh's "Spirit of St. Louis." They may take many hours, but they are capable of venturing out across the seas of life, the spiritual Atlantic.

Time passes — that is not what is important — but their dying to self and their growth in holiness. They become a DC-7, a four-motor plane which travels at six hundred miles an hour. Soon they become jets. Now a real miracle takes place in the souls of some members. It could happen to someone who has been here only a year, or to someone who has been here five years. They crash the supersonic barrier and enter into the stratosphere of God's most Sacred Heart!

Now they have arrived! The Holy Spirit fills them with his gifts, and you sense a difference. You can almost touch their total dedication. The only thing that seems to matter to them is loving God, which is reflected in the love they have for their neighbor.

Thoughts of self have fallen away like worn garments. Their one concern is to spread the kingdom of God. They have no more desire for days off than a man or woman in love wants days off from the beloved. Not only do they mind being eaten up by work and people; they welcome it. They have nothing to show for it, except to those who really have eyes to see.

In what airplane are you flying? With the Wright Brothers? Lindbergh? The DC-7? The jet? Or are you in that supersonic plane that can crash the very barriers of self? Why not make an examination of conscience and ask yourself, ''Where am I? Why don't I move upward? Even if you are in the supersonic category, don't rest on your laurels. Tomorrow there is the moon to reach! If you can reach the moon, then you can reach the very essence of the Holy Trinity. You can begin to enjoy a foretaste of the Beatific Vision, if you die completely to self.

Let us face the facts of life in Madonna House. You don't need any special privileges. All you need is to realize that you are an apostle of God. Sometimes you will be tired, sometimes you will feel emotionally drained. We are all human, but we go on in spite of this.

You can have no mental agony that will ever equal that of Christ in Gethsemane or that of his Blessed Mother under the Cross. No one will ever be as tired as Christ was on that Cross. So what are you getting excited about? You feel lousy? Fine. Keep going. You are an apostle — a man or woman in love with God and totally dedicated to him in the world.

Stop taking your psychiatric pulse. Stop worrying about your aches and pains, your little tensions and fatigue. Keep going! You've been told you are on your way to the cross, so drag your feet at a hundred miles an hour to get there. Physically you are well taken care of. All your legitimate needs are being met. You are loved and cared for so what's the problem? Christ is waiting.

Let's look at those personality clashes. X gets on the nerves of Y. Okay, let him. Keep smiling. Be extra-charitable to him. Don't withdraw. Be like the Little Flower with the nun who rattled her rosary. This is only a tiny splinter of the cross on which you are supposed to be crucified. What are you worried about? Keep going.

You have problems? The type of work you are assigned is

worrying you? All kinds of nagging little fears fill your mind? Christ must have been filled with fears too, when he saw them preparing to flagellate him, when he was mocked, etc. Unite yourself with him in his Passion, and *keep on going*.

Do you know what the basis is for happiness and peace in a give house, besides the love of God and death to self? It rests on complete trust in your superiors. Their primary concern duty and obligation is *you*. In order for them to direct you well, they must have your complete openness. Otherwise, you suffer. If love, trust and obedience are your motto, all will be well with you spiritually, mentally and emotionally.

In conclusion, I remind you once more that your prayer life should not be worked into your schedule. It *is* your schedule, prayer is the foundation of your life, and all the rest ebbs and flows around it. That is most important to your well-being and that of the houses.

Love to all in Mary,

DEALING WITH TEMPTATIONS

June 14th, 1958

Dearly Beloved,

More and more I am realizing my terrific responsibility before God, as regards the spirit of our Institute.

I have come to the realization that I must take hold of my office as Director General and come closer to you in order to help you as much as is humanly possible. Often the only way I can do this is by letter. Many of you feel that a given letter is addressed to you personally, but usually when I write I am responding in a general way to the information which comes through your letters.

At first, it may be hard for you to understand my request that each member write to me at least twice a month. It is difficult for a young person to be put under such an obedience, but I ask you to do so because it is only through your letters, flowing in at regular intervals, that I get the full picture of any given house. Quite unconsciously, your letters reflect its atmosphere. Believe me when I say that no one can direct in a void. Knowledge must be the basis of all direction.

Because you are young and inexperienced, you say to yourself, ''What am I going to write to her about? I have nothing to talk about, except the little things of every day.'' The funny part is that by and by you will learn not only to write me about the unusual happenings in the house such as a picnic, an interesting movie or extraordinary visitors, but about the deeper things of your heart and soul.

It is very important that you tell me *how you feel about things*. None of us are saints yet; we are saints-in-the-making. Someone might be irritated about cooking, another might have a personality clash with one of the members, someone else might find the director difficult. All of you are bound to have temptations against your vocation, for that is an old weapon of the devil. You will have moments of fear, disappointment, frustration, joy and sorrow. You will have difficulties, large and small, in prayer, in the common life, and in the work assigned to you. There will be feelings of helplessness, ignorance, joy and wonder. You will find the men difficult, the children obnoxious, the native people impossible. The studies required may, at times, seem very demanding. Sometimes you will feel shut off from what goes on in the house; at other times, you will feel that too much responsibility has been placed on your young shoulders. You will wonder at the differences between Madonna House and your new mission house. The vagaries of the human person are endless and I want to hear about them.

You have not yet understood that whatever you are going through, I have gone through myself. Even though I say it very humbly, there isn't a person in the Apostolate who understands your problems as well as I do. Help is at the end of a postage stamp, but you have not yet learned to avail yourself of it. That is what I much teach you before I die.

Your combined letters will help the common good, for when you write of your particular difficulties, joys, sorrows, and temptations, you are voicing those of every member, present and future. As we help you solve your problems and share your joys, we will eliminate many difficulties in the future and enhance many of the joys. I hope you get at least a glimpse of the tremendous importance of your letters.

I want to talk to you about several other things now. One of them is temptation. The devil is not too clever. He uses temptations, obsolete even for our modern times, presuming that human nature never changes and he is partially right. I can make a list of his temptations and I bet I won't be far from wrong. I have gathered from the many who have passed through Madonna House and myself many of his techniques. Let me try and list a few:

1. Fears.
2. Temptations about vocation, no matter how long you have been in the Apostolate.
3. Discouragement.
4. Personality clashes.
5. The monotony of a given job (he will hammer on that)
6. Confusion. Examples:
   "Why does she want me to write letters?"
   "What is this big idea of family life and going on outings together?"
   "Such forced recreation! We should have some privacy."
   "I want to work more. Why do they give me time off when others don't have it?"
7. "Bees! Never a free evening! (What do they think I am a machine?")
8. "Why do they make me do this and that?"

I could go on indefinitely. Add a dash of day-dreaming (at which the old boy is post-master), salt it with self-pity (he produces it out of nowhere), add a dash of paprika (which is withdrawing from the family) with a feeling that no one understands me — not even God, and throw in a few herbs of "What's the matter? I need psychiatric help and they don't give it to me these days." Serve it all on a platter of disobedience and the desire to be left alone. You have put together the devil's masterpiece, and you have the old boy's stock-in-trade.

Only untutored eyes miss the point. I bet if you reread this carefully, no one in the Apostolate could say it hadn't happened to him or her in one fashion or another.

Here are some of these weapons:

1. Be open with your local director and the director general. They know more about both the devil and God than you do, and they can help you by their experience.
2. Be open with your spiritual director by letter or *viva voce*.
3. Sprinkle holy water on yourself, and especially on your bed and place of work.
4. Use common sense, together with a sense of humour and the ability to laugh at yourself.
5. With regard to personality clashes, ask yourself:
   "If so-and-so is such a pill to me, maybe I'm more of a pill to her."

Now I want to talk to you about charity. Charity whose other name is love is very much misunderstood even among us. Charity is a very powerful reality. One cannot dissect it as you would a dead body in an autopsy. That will kill it. Yet there are some parts which belong to Charity without which it is not charity, but an illusion.

1. Constant watchfulness over the needs and pleasures of others.
2. The desire "not to be loved but to love, not to be understood but to understand.
3. Watchfulness over one's own little mannerisms and habits that may annoy others.
4. Care that moodiness, irritations and fears, menstrual tensions in women, not darken the souls of others.
5. Applications of good manners to daily living. For instance, talk about what interests you, but not to the exclusion of what interests others. Don't monopolize the conversation. Observe little courtesies at mealtimes and create harmony. Surrender graciously to the wishes of others when decisions are made based on preference (whether to go to a movie or on a picnic, etc.)
6. Charity is simple too. Accept work "bees" in the same spirit as you accept free time. Believe me, directors don't schedule either just because their left toe itches. The tension and pres-

sure might be so great in some jobs, that people must have time off if the common good is not to suffer.

7. Charity is trustful of superiors and of one another. Charity never judges another person's motives. Charity is not puffed up. No one knows it all. Length of time in the Apostolate does not mean that one has the vision of the whole and can teach it to others.

8. Charity is not gooey or sentimental. In an Apostolate like ours, the days of hugging and kissing (this applies to the female sex) are past. Such childish constant display of affection is of the high school stage, or below it. It doesn't befit a member of our Apostolate. Once in a while there is a place for a display of affection, but the Pope demands of us a mature approach to life, a capacity for good judgment and the ability to take responsibility. Let us be watchful in these areas.

9. Charity takes cognizance of little things. Don't linger in the bathroom when you know others are waiting to get in. Charity serves and denies itself constantly, and makes the road smooth for others while shouldering the hardships as much as possible oneself.

Do you begin to see what I mean?

Charity can be as pitiless as a surgeon's knife, for it knows when to say no. Theology provides us with a good rule of thumb, that the personal good is always subjected to the common good. If you remembered that and understood it, many of your problems would be eliminated.

Let us analyze the problem of giving sandwiches to men outside of the ordinary time. At first glance, it seems so simple to give a sandwich, already prepared, to a hungry man; but bitter experience has shown that if this is done on Sunday, it passes along the grapevine and one hundred and fifty men appear for sandwiches. This is bad for the common good of our house and it is not good for the men either. On Sunday they have other places to go. After this they found other places for food and that was good.

In another house out of mistaken notion of charity, children were allowed in at all hours, disrupting the house and tiring the staff making them irritable without anything very positive being achieved. All this coming and going was haphazard. When this was eliminated, much more order was established in our house and in the children's homes. Toys were given to the families so that the children could play at home in the evenings. This is where they should be if we wish to restore home life.

In another place, Indians were often bailed out of jail and allowed to sleep on the school premises and generally babied, until the government authority himself pointed out how bad this was for the common good of the people. The government desired the Indian to be independent and not a burden to the country, and this was not helping to produce that — another mistaken idea of charity. Other examples could be multiplied, but I know you will read between the lines too.

I am working very hard on revamping the whole training system of Madonna House and better integration between here and the other houses. If I am to do that well, I need your letters.

Love in Mary,

RECREATION AND TOGETHERNESS

June 19, 1958

Dearly Beloved,

This time I want to discuss *recreation*. Some voices have come to me from various houses asking for clarification. Most of you have already had the explanation of the word "recreation". It means *re-creation* to make new. That is the real meaning of the word. In ordinary language, it means a change of occupation. It doesn't mean *doing nothing*, which is very boring.

It definitely does not mean going to bed and sleeping. If

someone stayed up all night, or if there was a late collective "bee," or if the Apostolate demands emergency work that tires someone like nurses, then rest is indicated. A nurse who has been up all night must be given twenty-four hours' rest to recuperate. She will not be given twenty-four hours recreation. Even our language does not lend itself to such an interpretation.

To recreate then, does not mean to do nothing — to rest; it means to be engaged in an activity of re-creation. I want to be explicit. You might be swimming and having a lot of fun. Re-creating your spirit in that way is an activity. Then afterwards, lying in the sun, you might take a snooze for fifteen minutes for half an hour or so; or you might be reading a book quietly to yourself, recreating your mind with new horizons and more creative understanding. That is okay too.

However, the best re-creation is *togetherness*. "A family who prays together stays together." A family who re-created together stays together lovingly on the natural level. Doing things together makes us know and love each other more. Joy binds us, and laughter cements our relations. Knowledge gathered and shared with one another creates a deeper union. Creating things together, devising a skit and planning well-known games help to make us one in spirit and in truth.

Thus recreation can also become teamwork and team play. These are a must for democracy and for good social intercourse. Good team play is a weapon of the Apostolate. If your recreation includes, as it has and will, members of minority groups, or the poor, or any people you work with, a new spirit will develop.

People who play together can never hate each other. On this, incidentally, the British Empire was built. British fair play and teamwork fostered the virtues of justice, charity, and in ordinary language, fair play and sportsmanship. All of these natural virtues are really the reflection of the Ten Commandments applied to recreation.

Now let me take you back a bit. Some of you will remember when finally, after much deliberation and seeking advice from priests, I inaugurated the rule that recreation would be in common at Madonna House on all free nights. All would stay at Madonna House until 10:15. I was very aware of the wail which went up in the various dorms, and the pouting of some. I was also aware that at the moment I was the most unpopular individual at Madonna House for having brought this rule into existence. All felt that something precious had been taken away from them; even though that precious thing was prolonging their neuroses and killing the family spirit. Preserving the family spirit of Madonna House is my joy and duty. It is this spirit which distinguishes us and makes us a marvel for all visitors.

That family spirit is also the mother of the joy, simplicity and ease with which we receive everyone. But at the same time, when recreation in common was inaugurated, the members, who are now directors and seniors, did not understand. They felt that common life was biting a little too deeply.

During the last visitation, I perceived the danger of individual, so-called separate re-creation which was no re-creation at all. It was only a separating of oneself from others and re-creating privately, utterly unconscious that this way of doing things would eventually lead to the break-up of the family spirit of any given house.

This can be linked to the liturgy. Many older Catholics feel almost insulted when a priest begins to discuss the corporate worship of the liturgy. Such Catholics say that they are lost without their individual devotions, that there is something wrong with a worship which does not allow them to talk personally to God.

They cannot fall asleep as they feel like doing, or what is worse, daydream in a pietistic sort of way. They go on to say that following the missal is an austere discipline which does not allow them to say their individual, beloved prayers (usually sentimental or self-centered.) "Missa Recitata," they will tell you, kills them. "Do we have to pray in common all the time? What is the Pope coming to with all those newfangled ideas!"

The same applies to recreation. I leave it to your imagination to make the parallels more explicit.

To return to our Madonna House history. They pouted and wailed and they looked unhappy and they thought they were martyrs; but they obeyed, alleluia! And slowly, painfully, they reaped the reward. Madonna House family spirit came into being which couldn't have happened through work alone. One has to pray, work and recreate together to make the family spirit come alive.

You ask: "What is better-organized recreation or spontaneous recreation?" I would say that both have a place in a family. But organized recreation must have a definite place and I suggest that once a month on Sunday be devoted to it; and the rest of the month be left for spontaneous recreation with just a tinge of organization. That is, even unorganized recreation has to be somewhat planned.

Perhaps you will visit a museum and decide what to do afterwards. You might discuss art or the pictures you have seen or perhaps make plans to have someone discuss art or some other subject with you. You might plan picnics or reading nights together. You might just have free recreation of whatever develops in a given house.

In the winter, one might plan such things as poetry reading together, skit presentations, story reading and discussions. You might engage in handicrafts such as making Christmas cards, or perhaps share some good records you may have borrowed. Slowly recreation will become what it is meant to be — fun, builder of unity, a refresher of the mind, spirit and body — all of which will help to mold the family into a whole which knows and loves each other better.

Be simple about those things. Try to recreate this way and that way, and eventually you'll find the best way to recreate in your house. Let the intellectuals have their say, the sport fans their say. It is give and take. That is what teamwork is and that is what love is.

And never think that anything is really forced. Sometimes, in the way I had to do it, it appeared forced — an order in council — and it might appear that way to you with more family recreation in the mission houses. But that is only a temporary impression.

You are the children of a society that divorced fun, moneymaking and business from God — everything but Sunday. This is called secularism, and it is a great heresy. Because you have not been given the knowledge of what a real family should be like, and what *home* really means — a little *church* — you have to be taught for a while by order-in-council. Then you will get used to doing things together, and by doing them learn how much you grow in knowledge and love of one another. Then, in a perfectly natural order you will see how much fun it is.

I hope this has clarified the matter of recreation for you. Remember that the key word is *togetherness*. Don't go on a picnic and separate yourselves, each in a corner, for the whole day, coming together only for a hasty picnic meal. Do things together. If you read a book, share what you have read with the others. If you have a snooze in a shady corner after swimming, join the others after the snooze. *Togetherness is the foundation of recreation.*

May the Lord of all creation be with you and inspire you to recreate in tune with him and his Blessed Mother.

Affectionately in Mary,

LOYALTY AND CHASTITY

June 27, 1958

Dearly Beloved,

As I told you before, you will be hearing quite a bit from me from now on. These letters will be coming at odd times and whenever I think I have something to say to all of you.

Before I start the theme of this letter, I want to thank you one and all for the mail that you are sending. Your personal letters to me are simply a delight. First, as you are beginning to realize, I think, that I love you very deeply in the Lord. I love each of you separately and uniquely and all of you together.

Those letters of yours are such a tremendous help to me in getting the feel of each of your houses, and sharing in a small way its life. This is a dream of mine coming true through these letters! Moreover, without realizing it probably, you are helping the whole Apostolate in a most stupendous way by being open, direct and loving in those letters. I have before me many letters from the houses all interesting and informative. Though they are personal, together they often show some common problem. These give me wonderful help for clarification and much food for thought. They also lead me to examine our training and my approach to this common state of affairs, and the instructions that I can give to the directors are the same, never revealing the source (for I consider all of your letters confidential, even if not so marked). But what is most important is that it allows me, I hope, to help you personally and to clarify your questions be they personal or common. All this brings peace, increases charity, and makes for light.

So now to the theme of this letter.

All of you remember your lectures during the training course; at least I hope you do. There was a series of lectures, rather short, called "Dedication, Loyalty and Stability." However, I understand full well that it is one thing to hear a lecture on these important virtues, and another to try and live them in the crucible of Madonna House or any mission.

So from time to time it is needful, I think, to refresh one's memory, and remember how we were taught to evaluate them in the light of our daily experiences, and to see how we measure up in these important and vital, I repeat, apostolic virtues. They are part of the immutable foundation of our Institute. If we fail in them, the whole structure will crumble!

Let us consider *loyalty*. As I told you long ago and far away, loyalty, the dictionary tells us, is a state or quality of being loyal, of allegiance to a government, in friendship to a person, to a *cause*. The Catholic Church defines it as a child of love or *caritas*, and the sister of trust and of hope.

Let us see how all these definitions apply to everyday life. You understand, of course, loyalty to government. The spy trials of Canada and America have made us all aware how tragic it is when a human being becomes a traitor to his country, by revealing its most vital secrets to the enemy. Even in the immense charity of Christ, in the natural and supernatural order, we feel a strange revulsion to people like that. We would find that we needed an immense charity to shake their hands! Being apostles of Christ, we would do that, for we are commanded to love our enemies; but we would do it reluctantly. It would be an act of the will.

In everyday life, we don't think much of a person who is *disloyal* to a friend. Here things are a little clearer. WE wouldn't think much of a person who would divulge what we told him in confidence. We wouldn't think much of a person who, once we had left his premises, started gossiping about us, saying: "She is a good person, but . . ." and then tear our reputations to shreds.

Yet, if he or she met us again, that person would be nice to our face, seek our tust and our confidence, and then repeat the offence *ad infinitum.*

Nor would we have respect, speaking always on a natural basis, for a person who, though not betraying the confidence in a manner of speaking, would have to tell us all about another person whom we both know, explaining in gory details how much he suffered at the hand of that person? Even if what he was saying were true, there would be left in the mouth of the hearer a bitter taste that he could not define. For the question would arise: ''Why does he or she have to tell me all that? If this person is all that I'm hearing he or she is, I would respect the person who is speaking much more if he kept those faults, foibles and imperfections to himself.''

All of this would happen to us on a perfectly natural basis. The world, you understand, gripes. The army folks may gripe. Why? Because a huge number of people from all parts of a country, with various backgrounds, are brought together compulsively and put under such a rigid discipline, which most have never experienced, that griping, as every army psychologist knows, is a good outlet for the emotional storms created within an individual under such circumstances. Yet in time of war, a strange feeling of uneasiness comes to those who listen to those gripes. Deep down, each one of us wishes that a soldier wouldn't gripe. There is a little bit of a shadow of disloyalty in it, even in an army.

What would you think of a Jesuit who took another Jesuit aside and started to tell that person all he thought about another Jesuit priest? Suppose you were the second Jesuit. Would you be sympathetic to such a state of affairs? Would you consider griping about a priest to another priest appropriate under such circumstances? I wonder.

Some of you have had, alas, the experience of a neurotically disturbed priest expressing in no uncertain terms his gripes about his bishop or his superior. I have had such experiences also. Let us be truthful, though. In the charity of Christ, we have to listen, for it might be helpful to this priest in a psychiatric sense. But we all shrink from it, and there is a strange void, and a great fear comes upon us, as if something sacred had been desecrated.

For quite properly we feel (with the exception of myself in the role of a psychiatric nurse, and even then I found it difficult) that if the priest had any grievances, the proper and right thing to do would be to discuss them with his superiors. Instinctively we know that is what we would expect him to do. They very injudiciously select us lay folks, and because we are weak boughs and reeds, we find it hard to support these problems which are hung onto us; we shake and shiver, for they seem heavy and crushing.

We understand, in a dim sort of way, that those people, be they priests or any of the others I have depicted above, lack loyalty, trust, hope, and common sense. For when all is said and done, what has been achieved? True, the emotions were released by this binge or blow-up. But was that the proper place to do this? A healthy and helpful blow-up should have taken place in the office of a spiritual director, in the confessional, in the office of a superior or a bishop, in a doctor's office — as the case might be. For even in psychological sickness, there is a proper place and time for blowing up.

The same applies to the one who gossips — the girl or the man who impulsively reveals the weak points of someone else, who is a friend or acquaintance. And the same applies to the Jesuit priest I mentioned. No one is better for having spoken or listened in that way. Both parties feel uneasy, unhappy, and the griper feels guilty and this adds to his emotional and spiritual burden. The listener inwardly squirms and wishes he never had to listen, and feels somehow tainted for having shared in this disloyal action.

There is the classical example that to this day brings horror, fear and trembling to our souls: *Judas, who betrayed with a kiss.* How did his disloyalty start? The Gospel shows us. He was not open with Christ, his Superior, his Bishop, his Director, his Friend, his Master. He griped to the other apostles about the acts and deeds of the Lord, constantly judging his motives. To judge another person is a terrible thing. The scripture says: "Judge not and you shall not be judged." What do we know of the intentions behind the actions of our fellow men? And who are we anyhow to pass judgment on them?

Truly it is a terrible wound to charity to judge, to gripe behind someone's back; to share with others unfounded judgments about someone else. We do not gain anything. Our confident and listener is left with a thought that we are not a pleasant person to be with. In his heart is an uneasiness; perhaps the person who made him his confident and listener today, might tomorrow make someone else his confidant, and this time *he* will be the topic of conversation. There is sadness in us under those conditions and we begin to mistrust such people.

This letter might appear to you long and dry, but alas, these situations can be found in Madonna House Apostolate. If we allow them to continue, they will grow like a cancer on the body of our Apostolate; and, though we might be an immense establishment, physically speaking, the decay of death will be in our collective soul.

Let us take a few imaginary situations. A member of our Apostolate has difficulty in getting along with another member. The difficulty is real. No one denies it. One of the classical means of sanctification is to endure the rubbing of personality against personality. That is why *common* life, as understood by canon law, and, in fact, family life in every home, lived properly according to God's design, is called the *greatest school of sanctity*. It is considered the fastest means of growing in charity and self-discipline, as well as in dying to self. This is where each one of us feels the Cross. It bites deeply, and dimly we begin to understand the pain of Christ.

But let us continue. So we have difficulty getting along with someone. Tell me: Why do we feel compelled to discuss people's private affairs with another person? What exactly do we get out of that discussion? It is not going to help us to love him better, for the means to grow in love are not found in idle conversation, but in *silence and prayer*. There is no one in our Institute who is unaware of this. Yet, can we pick up a stone and cast it at someone else? Have we not been guilty at one time or another of the same sin. For sin it is. What matters if it be venial or mortal! *Any type of sin is an added pain to Christ*.

Such discussions may have helped us emotionally, but the same effect would have been achieved if we had discussed this situation in the privacy of the confessional or with our superiors. We could then get help and clarification from sources that are the *true channels of grace*.

If you want to tear Madonna House into shreds, I'll give you a recipe that is guaranteed to do so in the shortest time possible. All you have to do is to get another member or a little group of them as the case may be, and begin to gripe, to judge, and to misjudge your superiors. It won't take a year before you will see the fruit of your griping: a house in shambles, charity lying in the dust of the road, torn apart, bleeding and dying. The foundation will be shaken. You will endure a sight too horrible to behold — the works of God destroyed by a small part of the human body — the tongue — which was used for selfish purposes. And all that you will reap from it is a greater sense of guilt and unhappiness. And if you have emotional problems, they will be a hundred times worse.

Getting along with various people in one house is the hardest thing that anyone of us can do, even though we love them very much. Nevertheless, if we have even the slightest understanding of what we do to Christ in our brethren, we would not indulge in any kind of griping. Griping is destructive, critical, and uncharitable.

Now you will ask yourself, after hearing this long, somewhat dry letter of mine, "Why does she write like this?" The answer will come to you very directly, as all my answers do. I have noticed a tendency creeping in, in a small way, thanks be to God, (for we are a most united family). Somewhere, somehow, the idea has come about that blowing up and griping are good for the emotions. Then too, some of us still suffer from a neurosis known as compulsive talking.

Whatever the reason, let us get one thing clear. It is true that both griping and blowing can be good for emotional problems; but since we are an apostolate of charity, the proper place to do this is the office of our director, or under the seal of the confessional — preferably both. Then our souls will be at peace, and the Apostolate will not be wounded.

Believe me, dearly beloved, from vast experience I can tell you that if you do your griping and your blowing up in the wrong places, you will reap only one harvest: an increase of your emotional problems through guilt complexes, and the disruption of the Apostolate.

Now I want to go on to another point. I do so with great love. Believe it or not, I do it with infinite gentleness and delicacy, as a surgeon who uses a scalpel not to hurt but to heal.

We must realize that we are an *Apostolate on probation*. Secular Institutes* are very new to the North American continent. The heirarchy, the clergy, religious orders, many Catholics, and many non-Catholics are watching this experiment with an eagle eye. "Boys and girls living together in chastity in a lay state!"

*At this time Madonna House was seeking Secular Institute Status.

says the hierarchy, "Well! Well! Since the Pope says it is possible, we will allow it. But believe you me, we will be watchful. It has to prove that it can work."

"Boys and girls living together in chastity in the lay state, even though approved by the Holy Father — I don't believe it is naturally possible," say some priests and religious. "But since we have one in our midst, we shall watch it closely!" So they do.

"Boys and girls living in chastity together? Baloney!" say many of the older Catholics. "There must be some hanky-panky. Let us go down there and see for ourselves. We aren't as easily fooled as the bishops and priests, for they are unworldly people but we are men and women. We know. A glance, a word, a gesture will be enough for us. Boy, are we going to have fun debunking that situation! Wait until we check it out! We will open the eyes of the bishops and priests. We certainly will." And so it goes.

And, you little lambs of God, innocent enough most of the time — in fact all of the time I would say — barely suspect all of this. At Madonna House, you are protected (even though you don't know it) by the priests living here. Their presence silences many tongues which otherwise would speak. You proceed to be gay and simple and you joke and fool around without any concern, not realizing that you are playing with dynamite.

Let me give you a few examples that I heard personally:

a) "I saw a boy slap a girl on her fanny." To that person that was a vulgar gesture of affection — a breach of good manners (and I agree that it is. No man ever slaps a lady on her fanny unless he is her husband, and they are in the privacy of their own bedroom). This gesture could be taken as unchaste relations. Then the gossiping, disloyal tongues begin their evil work.

b) From a priest: "Baroness, how do you explain the conduct of a young man under vows of chastity, publically discussing holding hands at the dinner table? It took me an hour to explain that nobody in Madonna House holds hands anywhere. It was just a joke made from an innocent heart unwise in the ways of the world. It didn't show too much sense nor tact.

c) From a lay person: "I heard a boy call to a girl, "Hi gorgeous, you really send me!" That took three hours to explain. The results were unsatisfactory.

Words, gestures, jokes, glances, all form part of this pattern. Each member of the Apostolate must realize that Madonna House and all its foundations are so public that extreme care must be exercised constantly. We are guinea pigs, and make no mistake about it. In a manner of speaking, on people like us depend the implementation and realization of an immense dream of the Pope given to him by God "the vast army of Secular Institutes."

We, the bold ones, the imaginative ones, have been led by Our Lady to form a most extraordinary and rare kind of religious family composed of *priests, laymen and laywomen*. There are very few of them. Our bishop said that our chastity was a great blessing and asset to our type of Apostolate. He hoped it would continue to be a blessing and an asset in the years to come.

So do you want to destroy all this by a thousand little things that you don't even notice? I hope you don't.

I hope this letter has helped to clarify some points. I repeat: there is only a little griping and blowing up going on in the wrong places, and as yet little harm has been done. But much harm will be done if it isn't stopped.

One piece of advice I give to you: When you feel like griping about someone else, stop. Say a Hail Mary and think. How much material for griping does this person have about you? If you are honest with yourself, that should silence you pronto!

Lovingly yours in Mary,

PRUDENCE AND TRUST — HANDMAIDENS OF POVERTY

July 2, 1958

Dearly Beloved,

Here I am again. Through these letters I enter your common room, and I sit down with great joy in a most comfortable chair and visit with you. I cannot think of anything that brings me more joy, though I know that for you these letters are sometimes a chore. I hope that the net result of my writing them and your listening to them will bring much needed clarification.

Also, under obedience, I must write many outlines (which will eventually become books) at least for our Apostolate. It is the last assignment given to me by my spiritual director. Thus I will finish leaving behind me the information that the priests say will be invaluable for the coming generations of our Institute. I take their word on sheer faith and joyfully obey this directive, recording what the priests so beautifully call "God's voice in the soul of the Foundress."

During the last visitation, I saw clearly that there must be an even closer relationship between my office and all of you. Otherwise there will be confusion in our missions.

Today I just want to mention something about our material possessions. You have been often reminded that ingenuity is part of the Apostolate, and that when we lack certain goods, be it office supplies, tools for the workshop, a new furnace, any furniture, or furnishings of a house — even food — we may do one of two things: invent something to take its place, or make do with what we have. For instance, we could temporarily substitute a blanket for curtains on a window.

This is all true. But perhaps you have been too busy with all the things that you have to learn, and with all the new ideas that you have to absorb that you fail to notice that poverty always goes hand in hand with *utter trust in God*. Often I have plunged into the purchase of some of the above mentioned vital needs of the Apostolate with utter disregard of an overdrawn bank account.

Some of you who have been bookkeepers in Madonna House went through seventeen hells at the sight of such seemingly reckless actions. I need not remind you how many times you have been in my room, worried stiff about such strange procedures. You were almost weeping and very tense. You had a battle on your hands between spiritual truths on the one hand, and "reality" on the other.

"How is it possible," you used to argue, "to go and buy a thousand dollar furnace, a new car, or even rakes and hoes for the garden, when we are overdrawn $2000 or more, and the bills unpaid will amount to $3000 or more?" "What about the virtue of prudence?" you used to say. "What about sheer common sense?"

"What about just debts that we owe?" Your inner battles would really rage, and you would be almost angry at me when I would simply say: "Be at peace, child, for I see the matter demands serious consideration and I'll attend to it at once. *I will go and pray to the Infant.*" And I will go to Our Lady of Combermere or to the Holy Spirit or to some saint, as the Spirit might move me; but most of the time I would go to the Little Infant of Prague — an old helper of mine.

This seemed utterly inadequate to you, and you were bewildered, as many of you may yet be. But now that you are in the missions, a small group of you know and share the terrible burden that the directors carry so courageously. Those of you who have need of some goods such as I mentioned just now, might be going through a private, little hell of your own, trying to solve the seemingly unsolvable.

Yet the answer is so simple. It lies in that utter trust in God's Providence which I spoke to you about. Two things are necessary. First, ask the Holy Spirit to enlighten your intellect so that you might consider the need of a given object in prayer before God, and decide (with his help of course) if he desires you to exercise the virtue of prudence or the virtue of trust. The virtue of poverty is always taken for granted. However, prudence and trust are her handmaidens. But you must be very clear about prudence, too. At no time would I even mention the prudence of the natural order. Such prudence is hesitant and fearful. No, I speak of the *virtue* of prudence, the prudence of God. That virtue is young, strong, wise with God's wisdom, and knows when to trust in his providence completely.

This prudence will not be afraid to plunge into God's providence. Having prayed as though all depended upon God, it then acts as though all depends upon the person.

So first you think things over and see if you can beg or borrow what you need. Whether it be a large or small item, and you have time to beg, and have the faith to wait.

But let us suppose our furnace is on the blink, and there is no time for waiting. Prudence and wisdom will indicate that you trust in divine providence. The furnace will be paid for in due time and all will be well.

So what is the rule-of-thumb? First, the urgency of the need and its effect upon the common good. Living in cold rooms is going to make everyone ill and will hinder the works of the Apostolate. So evidently a new furnace is a must. That is the sort of thing that I mean. Once that decision is made, you go and buy the furnace on credit because there is no time for begging. The money will come later.

There are other approaches. If a given need is not an emergency, and there is the possibility of substituting something else or repairing an old item, you should do that.

Also as a regular practice all the members of a house should list all their needs monthly, be it a rake, a hammer, or pots and pans. Those needs should be made known to the director. Then at meetings, the directors should discuss with everyone whether these needs are realistic.

If they are real, they can either beg or buy the necessary item. Then the director does not hestitate. In utter simplicity and childlikeness, and after much prayer, she buys the item then begs the money for it.

In this way holy poverty is not injured. Faith and trust in God's Providence grow by leaps and bounds; order and peace in the house and in souls flourish.

The Apostolate cannot be less efficient than the children of the world. Remember the saying of Our Lord: "The children of this generation are wiser than the children of light. Be wise as serpents and as simple as doves." It would be tragic if the Apostolate went about its work in an inefficient, lackadaisical manner. To be efficient, one has to have the proper tools.

When the bank account gets very low, then the local director must pray and do something about it, such as talking to some influential friends or writing a few letters to some old benefactors and collecting some money. Our Lord and Our Lady will help them. In fact, I would say that in all circumstances there should be peace of heart, untroubled conscience, complete trust in Divine Providence and utter abandonment to God's Will. Yet, there should be good business sense, a dynamic imagination, and the ability to implement begging for Christ in the reality of practical, daily living.

One more word and I'm finished on the theme of material possessions and begging. It is this: there is no rule forbidding a member, with the permission of the director, to beg from the volunteers and friends in a given house.

God love you and Mary keep you! I'll be back some time with another theme.

Lovingly yours in Mary,

A SYMPHONY OF CHARITY

July 16, 1958

Dearly Beloved,

Here I am again with a new letter for you.

A strange problem presents itself these days. With growth we have become better known. More and more people visit with us. More and more people are interested in our Apostolate. Some are desirous to help; some perhaps, interested in joining us. Bishops, nuns, brothers, priests, seminarians and members of the government, social works, librarians, university professors, the poor and the rich, the learned and the unlearned all come to observe, learn, admire and criticize. We must remember one thing — to all of them we represent an interesting, marvelous development of a new religious family in the Church. There is no use denying that we are a bit like guinea pigs in a lab, like a butterfly on a pin. That is all right too, except for one frightening thought — on us may depend, in many cases, their relation to Christ himself.

There is no denying that to many people, we represent the Catholic church; and many seek Christ through us as it were. They wish to touch Christ in us — perhaps to strengthen their faith, to find hope or courage, to find their vocation, or just to know and love him better. A sobering thought — one that we cannot avoid, and which we must face.

Christ was truly a gentleman and we are his brothers and sisters. Mary was indeed a perfect lady and we are her children. So we must be very careful that nothing that we do or say disfigures the face of Christ in us for any of these people. For externals are the first things people observe. This brings me to the topic of manners and dress.

Manners are like little brooks running into one another forming a river that in turn flows into a lake or sea. They have an accumulative effect. To my desk, from here and there, come letters mentioning that a priest, a nun, a layman or laywoman has been in one of our foundations. They give me their impressions of Madonna House.

Or quite often in conversation with visitors, little remarks of criticism and astonishment creep in. Many of them deal with posture, table manners, chapel behavior and such. These people are kind and humble and seem reluctant to mention such things, and yet they do so because they love us. We mean so much to them and seem to bring them closer to Christ, except for these little things which are really very important.

So, as usual, I turned to the priests of the Apostolate for counsel. They too, had heard such statements from others but out of kindness to us, did not repeat them to me. But when I mentioned them, then they opened up and said that something had to be done.

We all agreed that often there was no guilt involved. Many did not receive their early childhood the basic training in manners and etiquette. This would not prevent them from becoming great saints, except for this — it is our Apostolate of little things that are important. We view manners, tidiness in dress, etc., as part of charity that everyone must practice to become a saint.

I remembered what my parents taught me about the amenities of life. They explained that having good manners was not snobbishness — a sort of nose-in-the-air attitude — the dowager looking through her specs on a long, silver chain. Manners was not a "better than thou" attitude. Rather, it was a matter of politeness; of making life easier for the other; this politeness was the fruit of charity.

Father used to explain that eating with a knife, or licking a knife with jam on it, annoyed the onlookers. They would be afraid you would cut yourself. A hammer is used to hit nails, an axe to cut wood, and a table knife is used to cut things on your plate.

People who burp or produce other noises in public make life unappetizing for those around them. The same with coughing or sneezing without covering one's mouth. These are all faults against charity and justice. Christians must be ladies and gentlemen, not because they are born into the upper classes, but because they belong to Christ and Mary.

So here is a list of good manners for all:

1. Come to the table and the chapel with clean hands and face. You must be tidy in dress and appearance thus honoring God in the chapel and Christ in others at meals.
2. Be punctual for the breaking of bread at both tables. Remember that in order to break bread with God, one must prepare oneself with prayers throughout the day. All official prayers are such a preparation. So be on time for all of them unless the duty of charity prevents you. But especially *be on time for Mass and meals.*
3. Sit down quietly and wait to be served. Concentrate on the needs of your brethren before your own. As one of the songs says: "Pass the butter without being asked." Please stop that boarding-house reach at the dinner table. Give your fellow men a chance to serve you. Ask for what you need.
4. Do not put your elbows on the table bending over the soup, lapping it noisely as though you were a child or an animal. Sit up straight and bring your spoon to your mouth quietly. Don't put half or a whole hamburger into your mouth at once. Don't put your spoon or knife into the honey, jam or pickles: the server should see to it that there is enough cutlery on the table. It is truly unappetizing for everyone, especially the visitors, to eat from dishes into which everyone has dipped his spoon. The same applies to the sugar bowl.
5. Do not pick your nose, scratch your head, clean your nails, or read your mail at the table. The cleaning part is reserved for the privacy of the bathroom or your bedroom. Reading a letter or newspaper or a book to oneself at meal time is impolite to the others. In Canada and America, it is not considered polite to use a toothpick at the table, though this is done quite normally in Europe, and toothpicks are on the table. At all restaurants on this continent when one pays the bill, one can get a toothpick — a clear reminder that everyone expects you to do your teeth cleaning after you have left.

6. Don't slouch in the chapel. Sit, kneel and stand straight. Don't put your legs under yourself when you sit in the chapel. We worship God with our bodies. I suggest that you all read *Sacred Signs* by Guardini. That book shows clearly how we worship God with our bodily posture. Men should not put their hands in their pockets while in chapel. At all times observe decorum, remembering that you are in the presence of God, the great King.

5. Let me add an addition to the above paragraph. The church and the chapel of God are also the home of our Father, where we might be quiet and "at home." So for spiritual reading there, you can relax, lean back, or you can sit on the floor. In the evening, or during private prayer when you make a visit, your posture can be relaxed and comfy, but not ostentatious. Don't sprawl over a bench as if asleep; but you could prostrate before the tabernacle, if you're alone or just the family is present.

6. This brings me to another point: namely, the diversity of social manners. Remember the saying: "When in Rome, do as the Romans do." That is good manners too. Let us not impose our manners on foreign countries; let us accept their manners instead, no matter how strange they may seem to us. That, too, is part of charity.

7. Out of respect for the representatives of Christ, by order of the priests of Madonna House, the men rise when I walk in. It would not be a bad idea to adopt this practice in the foundations. No matter how young the director might be, he or she is the representative of Christ even as the priests.

8. The men are the protectors of the women, and chivalry should not be dead in the little Christian society that is our Apostolate. Whenever the occasion arises let the men stand aside and let the women go first. If the latter are carrying heavy things, and a man passes, he should help to carry it. I know that in Madonna House this is not often done. Our women almost have to be carpenters. Due to necessity, they often must carry heavy burdens. But still, the man should open a door for a woman, and generally behave as a man in the presence of real womanhood. In this, they help to restore their own masculinity.

Women, on the other hand, must remember the nature of womanhood and must accept these things graciously not saying: "I don't need all these trimmings of etiquette."

The nature of women is to be feminine and men instinctively react to that, and it helps them to come closer to God. For God demands that each living thing act according to its nature. A tree grows upward. A fish swims in the water. A woman is feminine. She never boasts about being "like a man." All she will get for such boasting is that men will feel let-down. They will not know how to react to her. In the depths of their being, they will feel unhappy and disturbed as though something beautiful has been desecrated.

A man must be virile, strong and yet gentle. A woman must be feminine, strong, and gentle too, according to her nature. Then life flows on peacefully, and both complement each other — a beautiful sight to behold.

There are many little things I could go on mentioning, such as breaking your bread or cutting it — instead of tearing it with your teeth; being watchful about stirring the sugar in your cup and not leaving it at the bottom for someone to wash down the drain. This pertains to holy poverty and justice but charity is involved too. Watchfulness over jokes and conversation in general have already been discussed.

So I think I'll close this staff letter, reminding, you that all these ideas are given to you because I love you so deeply and want you indeed to be perfect before the face of the Lord. To me, you are such wonderful people that I have to see a few little easily-corrected notes spoiling a lovely symphony.

God bless you! Mary keep you!

Lovingly yours in Mary,

[signature]

P.S. Oh, yes, I forgot: when you offer a cigarette to anyone, especially your brothers and sisters in the Apostolate, pass the whole pack for them to select one. Trust them to take no more than one: Don't take a cigarette out and pass it across the table. Thanks.

THE VARIOUS FACES OF COURAGE

July 26, 1958

Dearly Beloved,

Here I am again for a little visit. It may seem that I come often, and yet I get lonely for a chat with you. Time goes by pretty fast at Madonna House, but for me at times slow, because I do desire to go home to the Lord. But it seems to go fast when I think of all that I want to share with you whom my heart loves so much.

I have been thinking and praying about *fire* — especially the fire in the Yukon — and I have been wondering what was really in the heart of everyone at Maryhouse. Was there much fear, fright, and worry? There should have been. Courage does not consist in the absence of those emotions, but in overcoming them for the sake of a greater good.

The soldier on the battlefield is afraid, but he loves his country, and so he goes ahead courageously. The missionary who knows that his hour has come, and that the martyrdom he read about as a youth and dreamt about in his young adulthood, is now close at hand, is humanly afraid, of course. However, fear has another quality in a man who has spent many years in the wilderness and in the country of souls. He has been stripped of his childish emotions. He is still afraid of pain; where is the man born of woman who isn't? Mostly, however, he thinks about his soul, and prays to God to give him the flaming, fiery courage of the martyrs who went before him. He prays that in his last hour, he might show the face of the Lord to those who might have never caught a glimpse of it. His is a courage tempered by daily living, and by drinking at the source of Love Itself for many years.

Thousands of Christians are now being subject to psychiatric tortures in jails, concentration and labor camps too horrible for us to even read about. They are also examples to us of great courage. The eye-witnessing accounts that come to us from Nazi Germany, and are still coming from countries behind the Iron Curtain and Bamboo Curtains, show the great courage of these people who have quite a history of martyrdom.

The fire in the Yukon is the test that God has given us there. The directorate there, of course, understand that; and I know they are showing steadfast peace and courage without any childish fears. I hope that the same can be said about every member. And that every member of the house stood ready to be the last to be evacuated. The last should be the bishop and the priests, for captains and their assistants are always the last to leave a sinking or a burning ship.

I have no knowledge about any reactions contrary to my above words. From the letters sent to me, the spirit of the members of that house is just what it should be. And I rejoice in this, and in fact I am proud of it. This whole episode of the fire in the Yukon became for me a matter of deep meditation and examination of conscience which I make when anything unusual happens. Always before my eyes is the eternal question: How well have I done my job of making saints out of the spiritual children the Lord has begotten through me?

In our times, this preparation for sanctity will possibly include martyrdom, and all kinds of trials by flood, fire and earthquakes. In possibly a few days or weeks, or even in a few hours, our Apostolate could be under attack from missiles sent from Russia exploding everywhere. No place on this continent of North America will be safe.

The mission lands present a million dangers. There are sicknesses we as yet know little about. We are not accustomed mentally or physically speaking to their climates. There is the suspicion and enmity of native peoples to whom our white skin is like a red jacket to a bull. They might come and quietly kill us in the night as they did Charles de Foucauld. They might do this to avenge a member of their race who was killed by a white person. They might desire our meager possessions which seem like wealth to them; or they might just because they feel like killing a white person.

Many of the countries which our teams will be going are subjected to floods, earthquakes or fires. Communism is alive and active in many of these countries and is ready to eliminate anything which stands in its way. War also often flares up amongst various tribes and peoples.

This is the life which you will be leading in a few years. Have I prepared you for it? Have you yourself given any thought to it? I wonder. Yet this is the acceptable time to meditate upon it prepare oneself.

Perhaps we should begin in small ways to train ourselves to grow in courage, to shed fear, to grow in faith and love of God — a faith and love that humbly simply prays:

> Lord, I am ready to live and die for you, and I accept whatever form of death that your will has selected for me. But I am weak, and my soul is housed in a house of clay. Be thou my strength, and give me but one gift — the gift of perfect love of you that casts out all fears. So that if my death that you will for me, is my last witnessing to you, may I have the courage and the love to witness joyfully, gladly, with a song in my soul, and with full possession of myself. Then those who brought about my death will see your blood-covered Face and understand that, in a small way we too have laid down our lives for our very killers who still are our friends and our brothers. By dying thus, O beloved Christ, we shall bring you into their midst, and you yourself will complete what your holy will has begun by our death. Amen.

This is a little prayer that I composed as I wrote this letter to you. I didn't have that prayer on my lips when, as a young woman, I was put against a fence by the Communists to be shot. The only reason I didn't die was that the soldier was too drunk to aim right, so instead of hitting my forehead, he hit my upraised hand.

No, I did not have that prayer, I confess humbly and truthfully. But I also have to say that at that moment I knew God was present, and I do not remember being afraid.

I have faced death many times, how and when, you will know in detail when death finally comes to claim me. Right now I don't feel much like speaking about it. Suffice to say that I learned slowly, as I hope you will, the various faces of courage, which I repeat, is not the absence of fear but the conquest of fear for a greater motive.

I have said that we should begin in a small way to prepare ourselves for the day when fear and pain will really come to dwell with us. So let us be done with such small things as griping about the weather. Our brethren in Winslow are often broiling 100 degree weather. The same applies to cold, food or insects. It does not behoove spiritual athletes-in-training to be worried or upset about such incidentals.

And should disaster strike, as it almost did in Whitehorse, utter peace should remain in our hearts. The only concern should be: Am I in the state of grace? And having taken care of that, we should not think of ourselves, but be ready to see every woman and child, all the crippled and the aged evacuated before ourselves. We must be determined that under such conditions, our Apostolate is witnessing to Christ. We must shout to people his love not through words but through deeds of courage and of faith.

Do you think I am an alarmist? Do you think that I exaggerate Oh, no! At times, it seems that I might name those who may die a martyr's death. My heart rejoices as the rosary of names passes through the fingers of my mind. However, my dreams do not matter. What matters is that we are going into foreign missions soon. What matters is the international situation that may any day explode right here in Canada and U.S.A. in the most literal and physical sense of the word "explode."

So let us thank God for the blessings and comforts we now enjoy, and our temporary safety from war and martyrdom. But let us also make our souls, hearts, minds, and bodies ready, at a moment's notice, to face all of these dangers — ready to face even death when it comes for the love of God.

Lovingly yours in Mary,

PARTICULAR FRIENDSHIPS

July 30, 1958

Dearly Beloved,

Often a question that seems solved at twenty years of age, raises its head again and requires further discussion. More experience in life demands greater clarification.

So today, I would like to consider the problem of love, particular friendships, *love of God and neighbour, detachment from people and things,* and *holy indifference.* Why do I consider these particular themes at this time? Because quite a few discussions have arisen in Madonna House regarding, what seems to many, contradictory virtues. So let us begin with love.

The commandments tell us that we must love God first, with our whole hearts, our whole minds, our whole souls, our whole selves. Then we must love our neighbor *as ourselves.*

God shows us in what manner he wants to be loved, in what one might both term the natural order and in the vocations that he has given us. There are four vocations the priesthood, the religious life, the married life, and the consecrated, single life.

Through these vocations God shows us the way in which he wants to be loved. All these vocations demand passionate love for God since they all lead to sanctity and the Beatific Vision, if properly embraced and lived. For the priest, this passionate, total way of loving is public. Through the Sacrament of Ordination, he is officially and publically set apart for loving. He does this through his ministry, the dispensation of the sacraments, a life of chastity, obedience, and often poverty under a vow. His vocation to love is public, evident, official, consecrated. In both the natural and supernatural order he has no other calling but God.

The same applies to the religious vocation, with the exception that diocesan priests often remain in the midst of men, whereas religious priests are removed from the world. Many of them though, such as the teaching, nursing and active orders in general, serve the world part of the time. Nevertheless, they too are completely set apart for loving and serving God.

The married vocation is also a vocation to love God, but through a man or woman and children. This loving must be done in the marketplace, in the midst of people. Besides going to God through one another and their children, married people must also be apostles to others — apostles of like to like, of families to other families. If the husband is a doctor, to other doctors etc.

The single vocation demands the same consecration as the priest, religious, or married person, but it is not so evident. The vocation of the single person is also God, spiritually in the hidden life of Nazareth and publicly as one of the crowd.

All these vocations if lived deeply, demand the totality of the person. A priest, for instance, cannot have any particular friendships with another priest, or with a lay person. And that brings us to the explanation of what a particular friendship is, and how it differs from a normal friendship.

A particular friendship is a friendship that concentrates on one person, to the exclusion of all others, and often to the exclusion of God. Let us say I have a particular friendship with a member of our Apostolate. I am so engrossed with him or her that I am looking for every spare moment to spend with that one person. At dinner, I want to sit next to him; all my remarks are addressed to him; I listen enraptured to all that he has to say; in fact I am wrapped up in that person. I seem to need him. There is almost a physical need for me to be in his presence. I live and breathe, as it were, happily and normally, only when I am in his orbit. I am happy if I can work with him. I desire to help him, serve him, make him comfortable; I haven't the same depth of feeling towards anyone else. I am kind to others, I love them but I do not feel the same way about them.

I ask you frankly, friends, what would you say if I had such a friendship with one person in the Apostolate? The resentment of the others would be the first thing to develop. That state of affairs would be obvious in no time flat. Secondly, those who were not in the orbit of my particular friendship, would feel rejected and neglected. They would feel angry and there would develop a feeling of injustice and perhaps jealousy. Certainly a house where such friendship existed would feel the impact of this disordered affection.

If the object of my particular friendship were a woman, all of this would happen and would be bad enough. If it were a member of the opposite sex, it would also become a scandal, and rightly so. It would be dangerous for the salvation of my soul, not only because I might fall in love, but because I would disturb the chastity of others while being in danger of losing mine. Because of a promise of chastity, things that are not sinful for people without such a promise become sinful for those who have it.

But a particular friendship strikes even more deeply into the heart of the matter for people whose vocation is *God* alone. For, by a particular friendship, we are distracted from our love for him and direct our love towards one of his creatures in an excessive and wrong manner. Thus we do not fulfill the vocation that he has given us, and do not walk the way he has chosen for us to love him.

What would you say if a married woman had a particular friendship with a single man? Oh, they weren't in love with each other. They had mutual interests. Both were artists. Both liked playing golf, going hiking, or listening to music. They were very compatible. They had much in common. Sex was not yet involved. If particular friendship exists between members of the opposite sex, it will come to falling in love eventually, for it is axiomatic that there can be no platonic love between men and women. Platonic means love without sex.

What do you think the world, the husband, family, friends would say about such an innocent, unsinful friendship? I leave it to your imagination. Do you think God would look favourably upon it since by giving this woman the vocation to love him through her husband and children, he sees her diverting part of that love to a stranger?

What would you say if that same woman had a particular friendship with another woman, where sex was not involved at all, but this woman became almost a standard fixture in the household and shared many of the family meals? The wife and mother concentrated on what that friend said, excluding the conversation and interest of the husband and children? What would you say if in most of the family outings this female friend was included, if she were the third party more often than not? It doesn't take too much imagination to see that the household would be disrupted in a very short time.

Particular friendships in a convent, monastery, family, and in the lives of single people dedicated to God always bring havoc and chaos in their wake. For, fundamentally speaking, any particular friendship of that type detracts from the love of God which is the ultimate goal of every vocation; in other words, that way of loving deviates into the paths of the devil. Our feet are taken off the narrow path to God and placed onto the smooth paths of Satan.

I hope you begin to see why we cannot countenance such particular friendships, any more than can a monastery, rectory, convent or family.

Now we come to another point. Since all vocations lead to total, passionate love of God, according to the designs of his will, then *detachment* and holy indifference must follow for they are the handmaidens of such a love. Let me explain this a little more fully.

As an example, I will take a husband and wife. Here is an apparent contradiction. God gives you the vocation to love a man or woman, marry and bear children. At the same time, he calls you to be detached. Contradiction? Only seemingly.

If a woman is so in love with her husband that he is her whole world, and then if God should take him away by death, this woman may even leave the Church, and even begin to hate God. She loved God while she had her idol, but it was not true love. God realized that this woman was untrue to him by making such an idol out of her husband. Because of this terrible sin, God, loving her soul so much, took away her husband to save her soul. You begin to see that holy detachment must ultimately be part of loving God.

Holy detachment should be an attitude in a woman's heart that goes something like this: "Dear Lord, I know you have given me the vocation to love you through this man. But I also know that I must be detached from him if I am to serve you in this vocation as you wish me to. So I am ready and willing, with your help and grace, to give you back this man through death, if this be your holy will, because I love you and your will above everything else."

The same holds for a mother and a child. When a child is sick and at death's door, a mother who understands her vocation may pray for a miracle of recovery, but not without adding: "Not my will, but yours."

The same is true for a priest. He might become very attached to his congregation, his parish, Madonna House. But he must at all times, control that attachment, be inwardly detached and ready to change at the will of his bishop or his superior. A nun might be greatly attached to her work with the sick, but she must be inwardly detached, at all times, to go and teach in a nursing school if her superior desires it.

For if there is no such detachment in our hearts, souls and minds, we are detracting from our ability to love God with our whole being. A part of us is attached to a creature and by creatures we mean persons, places, books, anything created that is not God.

The quality of our detachment comes next, and here is where holy indifference enters in. Our aim is to be like the Host, Who is the Lord Himself. Think of the helplessness, the holy indifference of the Lord in the consecrated Wafer. He goes where the priest carries Him. He lies where the priest puts Him. Here you have loved unto absolute annihilation of self — the perfection of holy detachment. The Lord does not care where He is taken nor what is done to Him. Such is the holy indifference of the Lord Almighty.

Do you understand now to what extent holy indifference and holy detachment are part and parcel of that immense *caritas* that the first commandment enjoins?

If you have that holy indifference, there will be that detachment from everything but the will of God, and the love of creatures will fall into its proper place. It will not become inordinate and selective, but you will love all things in harmony with God's will.

If you love in this way, God will give you the grace to love those who might be repulsive to you — alcoholics, prostitutes — those who grate on your nerves and annoy you. Now you will love with an almost divine love. You have become Christlike — Godlike. The image of God the Son is almost completed in you, and the Father is well pleased with you.

The Scripture says that God loves all his creatures; his rain falls on the just and the unjust; his sun shines on the good and on the bad. Wouldn't it be strange if God had a particular friendship with a nation, a group of people, or a person, in the way I have described particular friendships? What would happen to the rest of the human race if he concentrated on some to the exclusion of others? It would be just too bad for the world, wouldn't it?

There is just one more point that I want to bring out about loving your neighbor. Don't forget you are called to love him *as yourself*, no more, no less. Your first duty is to save *your* immortal souls. That is what all this love is about. We love God and our neighbor as ourselves because that is the only way we can save *our* souls.

If we are not detached from creatures, and we are not filled with holy indifference, we will not love our neighbor in a manner that will save our souls; our love of our neighbor and service to him will be disordered.

For instance, by having an inordinate, particular friendship with one person, we could actually be endangering our souls, and hence not properly loving either ourselves or our neighbor.

In the great tranquility of God's order, therefore, *love*, whose other name is *caritas*, walks along the path of holy detachment, holy indifference, and a rightly ordered love. This love avoids any emotional attachments, and loves with a will directed by reason and illuminated by faith.

I hope I have made clear to you this matter of holy indifference, holy detachment, and love and explained why particular friendships, which are usually based on emotional attractions, are a sin against divine love. If you have any questions on this subject, don't hesitate to write me.

Lovingly yours in Mary,

CALL TO CHRISTIAN MATURITY

August 12, 1958

Dearly Beloved,

Here I am again for a little visit with you. I have another theme: namely, priests.

Let me review a little what happens in the life of someone to whom God has given the vocation to Madonna House. Here is a very nice individual who loves God, practices his or her religion very well, and by all standards is a good Catholic. However, with rare exceptions, young people coming to Madonna House have a certain amount of emotional disturbance.

During their life in the world, these young people have not had close contacts with priests. Of course, every Catholic has had some contact with priests either in grade school, high school, in catechism classes, or confession. Some have had very intimate contact with priests, for instance as chaplains of specialized movements. These holy priests have never been able, in most cases, to give the individual much time. Some have had some individual attention but not enough to meet his needs. However, these people were still more fortunate than others.

Other young people may have had intimate contact with

priests because a brother or an uncle was a priest. They were drawn into the intimate, social side of priests. They know one side of them — the human side — better, perhaps, than many other young Catholics; perhaps better than the lay members of specialized apostolates. But even in the case of such close family ties, and even belonging to the intimate circle of a given priest and his friends, this did not necessarily satisfy their own emotional needs. As a rule, priests do not deal spiritually with the members of their own family any more than doctors do. They will send their relatives to other priests for that kind of help, for there is always a little bit of reticence between brothers and sisters, nieces and uncles, etc.

The mother might be prominent in works of charity, and then the children will grow up in a clerical atmosphere, but this will not necessarily bring them close to the priests and bishops whom they meet. Again they will rarely seek spiritual advisors for themselves among these priests. Instinctively, they feel it is too much of a family affair.

The next contact many young people have with priests is in Catholic high schools or colleges run by priests and brothers. But that again does not seem to have brought them much help. Again and again we find that graduates of such schools are still looking for priestly help. Why this should be is, in part, a mystery to me, but it is a fairly well known fact that I have observed for twenty-eight years of the Apostolate. Perhaps this occurs because the priests have a very busy schedule. There are exceptions, of course, but they are rare.

Very wide contacts open to all Catholics are, of course, the confessional and visits to the rectory. In both cases, the time element seems to interfere with a complete and satisfactory relationship between youth and priest. Saturday and pre-holy day confessions are conditioned by a long waiting line. Any discussion is limited. Private interviews in the rectory, at times more satisfactory than in the confessional, are often avoided because of the shyness of the young people.

They find it difficult to explain their problems briefly and often the busy priest gets called away from time to time. This is unsettling for both as they try to get at the heart of a problem and find a satisfactory solution.

Finally, the best contacts that people might have with a priest are in spiritual direction. This would be very satisfactory if

Catholics of the North American Continent understood spiritual direction, and priests were trained in mystical theology. This at present, is not the case in our seminaries. We have a strange phenomenon that, not withstanding repeated injunctions and encyclicals by various popes, priests are not familiar with spiritual direction. If they know about it, they are usually not prepared to give it. Catholic people though not needing direction desperately, do not understand how much they need a spiritual guide on the way to heaven. The few who do have a guide are fortunate.

So many young people arrive at Madonna House ignorant of the need for spiritual direction, or how to go about obtaining it, while inwardly needing such help. Also emotionally disturbed youth come to Madonna House filled with what we call slight neuroses. They live in the prison of their own emotions which mar their whole lives. Moreover, they usually come (especially in North America) from disturbed homes. Often the proper upbringing and love-giving which could have made normal men and women of them were absent.

What happens to them? They enter a loving place and see Christian charity lived out. They see that charity is not an abstraction, but a Person — God Himself. They find him here, without words, present in the hearts of everyone who deals with them. They find his Mother too. They find the people responsible versed in the psychological problems of humanity. Moreover, these people are also filled with the love of God.

And on top of everything else, there are priests filled with God's love, and with psychiatric understanding. Both are blended with their knowledge of ascetical and mystical theology. All of this guidance is suddenly available to a tired, emotionally disturbed young person who truly seeks to love God.

For the first time in their lives, these unmoored, emotionally damaged young people come to port a port that is the House of Our Lady and her Divine Son. Here Catholicism and charity are not only present, but surround them completely.

Suddenly they acquire a full-grown family — a father, mother, brothers and sisters — thus satisfying the emotional hunger that has been so overwhelming and unfulfilled by their own families. They find too, that those priests whom they have been seeking so shyly and with so little success are right here, ready and willing to listen to them by the hour.

They experience too, that physically and materially in most

cases they are taken care of, as they never would have been by their families or by themselves. Dental care is given to them and their diet is watched. Their life becomes regular. They have plenty of time to sleep. They begin to use their muscles and to work outdoors. If they are sick, they are sent to a doctor, and tender, loving care is given to them by the nurses of the Apostolate. They have sufficient food, clothing and shelter. They are given challenging, academic courses which stimulate their minds. So we have a group of people who for the first time in their lives, are in ideal surroundings with all their needs satisfied, or at least on the way to satisfaction.

Of all these needs, the one that the priest will fill is the most cherished and the most important. At first, like hungry little babies, they literally latch onto a priest and talk to him almost every day. Slowly as time goes by, they talk perhaps only once a week. Also, they know they can talk things out to their hearts content with others also when there is a need to. This creates a sense of security that transcends all human security.

This is one of the reasons why there is such a shock of separation when a member of Madonna House is sent to a foundation. Homesickness, especially for the priests of Madonna House, has almost become a malady with everyone. They have been separated from a newly-found family that was well nigh ideal; separated from all the care and attention which meant so much in their lives. This loss has played a great role in their adjustment to the foundations.

They finally had to realize that they were adults, they had been given more than most other people in the sense that God had favored them very much. Now they had to pass on the graces they had received. To many this realization did not come easy. Many still had difficulties and many will have some difficulties for some time. I understand. It is not easy to grow up but we must grow up. Growing up includes the realization that the foundation has no Madonna House priest. It was hard enough not to be able to see priests before one came to Madonna House; but to have *found* the ideal situation, place and priest, to be listened to, guided, loved, and understood by these and then to lose them! That *demands maturity*. Not everyone has that maturity yet. But you are all coming to it slowly as you must.

There is a mystery of faith involved here which God permits. We find it in all the lives of the saints. We can be misunderstood, ridiculed by people outside the Faith until the cows come home, and not one hair of our emotional heads will be lost. But to be misunderstood, ridiculed and hurt by Catholics especially by priests, devastates us. That is the mystery. It places us with Christ in Palestine and allows us to suffer what he must have suffered from the fact that the Jewish Priests, versed in the Scriptures, rejected and crucified him.

When we are in that darkness removed from the understanding of Madonna House and its priests; when our souls are torn with homesickness; when Catholics do not understand us; when other priests, if they do not ridicule us, at least lift their eyebrows; when we can't find a priest who understands our Apostolate; then indeed, the little chalice that God gives the young apostle of Madonna House lost in the wilds of a foundation, is truly filled to the brim.

It is not a big chalice. It is small like the shining cross of the new member who goes to the foundations. God will give him the grace to drink from the chalice and be crucified on this cross. In a little while, the cross will grow and so will the chalice, and the bitter draught that the chalice contains. But that is for tomorrow for which special graces will be forthcoming.

Dearly Beloved, you have to face the fact that until God sends us enough priestly vocations to have a priest in each foundation, you will have to share Christ's chalice, and bear the very great loneliness of not having a priest who understands you and the Apostolate.

Incidentally, your foundress knows this road which you are treading, for she trod it first, and she is still here to tell the tale!

In the foundations you are lucky to have other members to talk to. Thank God for this mercy and don't forget it. You may also have priests who, even though they don't completely understand Madonna House, are by your side, and try to support you. That too, is a blessing beyond compare.

So count your blessings and start growing up whether you are still here at Madonna House or at one of the foundations.

Lovingly yours in Mary,

Catherine

LOVE   SERVES

September 17, 1958

Dearly Beloved,

Now that I am separated from Madonna House Proper and its local directorship, and living on my "Isle of Patmos" at St. Kate's, I have a clear realization (that grows daily with prayer and meditation) of the immense scope and responsibilities of my office. It can be summed up in one sentence: TO GOVERN IS TO LOVE. . . . AND TO LOVE IS TO SERVE. I spend every moment of my life trying to do just that.

But LOVE is never static — it grows — and in growing it desires to serve and sacrifice itself even more. It seeks to be ever more pleasing to the Beloved and to serve him better; and I know that to prove this love, to render this service, I must bring him souls and serve him in others.

You, the children of my spirit and his, are the first. *Through this clarification of love, you have become my primary concern these days.* Being who I am, I keep examining my conscience as to how I might have failed in teaching you, in forming your souls and minds in the Apostolate. In examining my conscience, I came across questions for which I have no answers. So I am presenting them to you for your consideration and meditation, hoping that you will enlighten me *by your answers.*

It always seems to me that we do one thing fairly well in Madonna House, and that is teaching you the dignity of labor. Since Christ was a carpenter, we put great emphasis on manual labor done well. We also try to teach you respect for the wood, the machines, the earth — whatever materials we might be using.

But evidently, either the teaching has not been well absorbed, or it has been of an inferior quality. Throughout the Apostolate we have a strange phenomenon constantly occurring. You, the members of the Apostolate, do not see the work which has to be done. You have to have it pointed out to you again and again. Can you tell me why?

It would seem to me that our deep love for the Apostolate

should make us all alert to what needs to be done in a working day to keep the House of Our Lord and Our Lady shipshape. There should be a deep concentration upon, and a constant growth in accepting responsibilities, instead of the directors' having to forever repeat the same directives: "Put things where they belong." Can't you see the thousand little things that have to be done without always needing to be told?

For some reason you do not see these things (though this is not true of everyone). Yet by this time, no one should be guilty of this. There are enough problems in the foundations without constantly having to point out the obvious to people whose vocation is to love and to serve.

I admit this bothers me very much. Does it bother you? Do you make it a point to examine your consciences nightly about these things? If you don't, you should. Let me hear your answers to these questions.

Then there is a situation (incomprehensible to me and to most of the directorate). It concerns higher education. There seems to be a total lack of humility in this regard. A "heretical" theme keeps occurring. So deeply ingrained is this attitude in American and Canadian youth, that we of the directorate are at a loss as how to deal with it. It is rampant everywhere. Even after years of training it persists in the Apostolate.

The essence of this "heresy," which very hesitantly I would say is a sin of pride, goes like this: "If a man or woman has any kind of degree or is a white-collared worker, it is degrading for him or her to be asked to do any kind of menial work."

Just to read that sentence makes one shiver! Our Lord chose to be a carpenter for fifteen or twenty years of his life. He from Whom all knowledge flows, from whom all intelligence has its being, must have had a reason to make that choice!

Again the same Lord and God washed the feet of his disciples. On that occasion, he gave us a sentence that should knock that "heresy" out of us with one blow. "I have come to serve!" Remember he said this when he washed the feet of his apostles. In his day, this was a most menial task, assigned to slaves and servants who were considered chattel and despised.

Aren't the words of God sufficient for us? If we need more proof, we have the example of every saint in the ages of faith. Kings and queens pushed wheelbarrows to build the Cathedral of Chartres. Nobles, kings and queens, popes and prelates, priests and lords, served pilgrims, paupers, the sick and lepers rendering the most menial services to all.

Trappists and Trappistines, Carmelites of both sexes — all the great religious orders have manual labor as part of their constitutions. Every founder clearly understood the dignity of manual labor. God the Father worked when He created. Adam was told to care for Paradise. Christ and St. Joseph were carpenters and Mary was a housewife. I could go on and on and write a book about it. This "heresy" persists among us and breaks the bonds of charity, creating confusion and chaos. These are the fruits of the Prince of Darkness.

We observe also that those amongst us who have no degrees often keep trying to prove that they, too, could be scholars if they had an opportunity. At times, in an effort to impress others, they spout utter nonsense gleaned from what they have heard or read.

Why, for example, is there so much talk about various spiritualities? Some talk of the Jesuit, others the Carmelites, others of Dominican spirituality. Unspellable words are used which the speaker perhaps remembers from a book. All of this seems to be a lack of humility. Is it insecurity, a search for neurotic approval, or what is it?

I don't think I have failed through the years to give you a personal example of love for manual labor. Personally, I have done it with great joy and gladness; from gardening to cooking; from scrubbing floors to sewing and mending; from nursing in very menial ways to being a servant of the poor with great joy.

Why does this "heresy" persist among us? Why do people try so hard to impress others? Why do we worship degrees and white-collared jobs? They are idols which lead to perdition bringing with them the very breath of hell.

Another point for our discussion is stewardship of time. I wonder if we understand what time is. Do we realize that it is part of eternity — a tiny, fleeting part from which we came and to which we are going. It is disasterous for our souls to waste even a moment of time. The Lord of Hosts, having performed his miraculous multiplication of loaves and fishes, ordered his apostles to "gather the fragments lest they be lost." He will demand an account of every fragment of our time. He abhors waste. Do you?

Time is often wasted in this manner: You are given a job to do, and deep down you are aware that you have neither the knowledge nor the ability to do it. Why waste time trying? Why not simply go and tell the person in charge humbly and directly: "I don't know how to do this job. Is there anyone who does? Perhaps he could show me." This would be an honorable truthful, and humble question and the proper way to deal with the situation.

Instead what happens? Men and women often go into huddles, but no one knows any more than the one asking. No one has the courage to say, "I don't know." Everybody putsy-wutsys. Minutes, days or even weeks are wasted. Is this a Christian way of doing things? Is this an apostolic way to react? To me, it is frightening because it wastes time — that little part of eternity that God has given us to save our souls. Does it frighten you? I would be glad to hear your answers.

Doesn't every one of you, as a member of Madonna House, feel that you are approved, trusted and taken into a loving family? The fears of childhood have been alleviated. Your neuroses have been dealt with and love surrounds you. You don't have to prove anything. You are loved just as you are. We are all here to help one another. The priests and directorate exist to help you to teach the ultimate in love and security — the Beatific Vision.

Why can't we realize that the time for impressing others is past? The only one we can trust to "impress" by our simplicity, humility, joy, spiritual childhood, thoughtfulness and kindness, is *God Himself.* Why can't we just discuss things simply, acknowledging the pools of ignorance in each of us? Why do we try to impress each other by quoting from half-digested books or half-remembered lectures? Can you answer that?

God love you. Mary keep you. My prayers and love are always with you. I am always at your service. Do answer my questions. It would help me so much in directing the Apostolate better.

Lovingly in Christ and Mary,

THE FOG OF ENDLESS "WHYS"

October 1, 1958

Dearly Beloved,

There are two themes which I would like to discuss with you. One, especially, has been haunting me. So I will discuss it first.

I understand perfectly that modern youth has been grievously wounded by history, whether or not they realize it. Two world wars and a depression have affected both parents and children. They are also influenced by the atomic age which causes fear of destruction.

These young people come to Madonna House because God has chosen them, out of millions, to become lay apostles. I am prepared to face the fact that many of them will be emotionally disturbed and will need help. I have also known, for a long time, what every American and Canadian magazine, paper, and book are now discussing: namely, that the youth of America and Canada have also been sinned against by their elders who shortchanged them educationally. Students graduate from schools and colleges often without being able to correctly use their native tongue, the first sign of an educated person. Their geography is hazy, their historical knowledge more so. They also lack cultural knowledge. They are not too familiar with the great literature of the world nor with the arts. As time goes by in Madonna House, this becomes clearer, but one can see a desire for knowledge growing in these young people.

Recently the events in Formosa, Lebanon, in the Near and Far East, showed quite definitely an appalling lack of knowledge amongst the members of our Apostolate. Most people did not know where those nations are. They know little about their historical background and why the world was so concerned about this trouble in the East. This too, I understand well, and I try my best to enlighten them and to enlarge their intellectual background by any means that ingenious loving can invent.

I do not need to repeat how Madonna House tries to give you the vision of the whole, spiritually speaking. We have holy priests giving you various courses, retreats and days of recollection. There is personal, spiritual formation by experienced spiritual directors. Everything that can be done is done.

I understand why, in the majority of cases, people come to us with only part of the vision of the whole. Again, it is not their fault. Homes and schools, even the Church with its way of teaching religion — all, in a manner of speaking, have failed them. There is a revival now, and the Church is asking itself a lot of questions. The Pope is leading us out of the twilight into the brilliant sun of that vision of the whole which Madonna House attempts to give to you. Here again, I understand.

I understand the struggles which all of you have to face. I understand and sympathize, for we are all human, and all sinners. I know this will take time, but what baffles me is when people who have been in Madonna House for some time, and who have been recipients of all of this knowledge, this constant attention, and loving care, continue to act as little children. They continue to act as if none of this had happened; often continue to wallow in the mire of self; continue to be self-centered often using the excuse of emotional difficulties to hide spiritual problems.

We have had a lot of discussion about hostility that has a transfer onto authority figures. Understood in this way, it becomes unnecessary then, to examine one's conscience about the sin of pride; then one does not have to face the fact that obedience is not too pleasant, and that we are spiritually adverse to it. Yes, it is possible to hide behind these emotional explanations. Yet, it puzzles me why one does that, because sooner or later, all those false pretenses and reasonings will have to fall off like an old cloak. For when all is said and done, God is not mocked. I am amazed that members of Madonna House still think that they are working for human beings, instead of grasping the one simple idea: we are all working for God.

I had a letter from Thomas Merton recently, and I was telling him how unworthy I was to be a superior. He replied: "The great paradox of superiorship is that no one can be a superior unless he is fully worthy, and yet no one is fully worthy. There is only one solution: *that Christ Himself, in us, must be the Superior, for he alone is worthy.*" And so, does one really have a *transfer of hostility* to Christ? I wouldn't know. Would you?

We are working for God. Examine your conscience, dearly beloved. Are you satisfied with the type of work that you produce for God? Is it the kind that you would do in your own home, if you had one?

This question was asked of me by one of the local directors. She mentioned a little story about a young, married couple who had just enough money to purchase a rather dilapidated house. They bought it and moved into it. The husband was an intellectual, white-collar worker, who had never held a hammer in his hand. Somehow, through sheer necessity, he repaired, rebuilt, and remodeled the house, and they were both so proud of their achievement. Their friends were amazed, knowing his former manual inability. Smilingly, they both answered: "Love can do everything. Love does such things."

Does it? Do you see what has to be done without having to have it called to your attention again and again? Are your attitudes to work eager and willing, yet humble and truthful? Do you candidly acknowledge that you do not know how to do a job, but that you are desirous of being taught? Do you understand that this is a job for God — a job for Love Who is a Person, Who is Christ? Does your love do such things? Do *you* feel that *love can do everything*? Or do you "sanctify" your superiors by crucifying them over and over again on the cross of constant repetition and constant schedule-making? If you were truly in love with God, you would not need this repetition because you would be recollected.

Why is it that God has to put up with childish attitudes from adult men and women capable of begetting and rearing children, and founding new homes. Why do you retard your emotional, spiritual, and intellectual growth by these attitudes?

Perhaps I should be brutally frank, for I am so tired of getting letters from weary local directors whose theme song is: "How long, O Lord, how long do I have to keep this up — this monotonous repetition of the obvious? How long must I show people over and over again tasks which should be familiar to them but are still unnoticed or done badly? How long, O Lord, how long?"

They say it lovingly; they say it jokingly; they say it tearfully; they say it smilingly; they say it patiently, seeking from me new lights and advice. But what have I to give them? The same attitude prevails in Madonna House!

Those of us responsible, through meetings and consultation with experts, are trying to pierce the fog of these endless "whys."

Baffled and weary, we search our consciences — I especially. These "whys," like an endless litany, become as monotonous as the sound of a tom-tom beating endlessly and relentlessly against our brains. I begin to think of them as thorns weaving themselves into a sharp, piercing, crown that someone rudely places on my tired head until the pain is excruciating. Then what can I do but prostrate myself before the Face of the Almighty and ask for the gifts of *caritas*, patience, understanding and light?

The litany is always the same: a pattern of emotional problems flaring up and dying down; a pattern of not seeing the obvious that has to be done; a pattern of needing crutches for healthy feet — in the shape of schedules that try to cover every possible contingency. We see healthy human beings who cannot take a step without crutches. We hear much discussion of big ideas, but a strange reluctance to face, day by day, the little things that really matter, and without which the big things are sounding brass and tinkling cymbals.

Above all, these questions reveal to me *a waste of God's time*. Jobs which could be done in an hour even by a person unfamiliar with the job, take hours instead. There is a putsy-wutsy about everything. People go into huddles, attempt to look wise, discuss what is the matter with the stove, or a machine, as if they know, instead of humbly saying: "I don't know what the matter is, I am sorry to say." They waste precious time fiddle-faddling with things which they do not understand.

There is an emotional need to assert oneself and a lack of humility to state that one does not know. How long will this state of affairs continue? Not everyone is guilty, of course, but it is a pattern for the majority in our Apostolate. I could go on endlessly. Why should I? You get the picture. Help me and help your local directors by having sessions about it. Discuss it and get to the bottom of it. Do anything that you can to end this state of affairs. For while this fiddle-faddling goes on, the pain of Christ mounts, and waste of time brings deeper agony to his Sacred Heart. We have so little time to save our immortal souls so that we might enjoy him for all eternity. We have so little time to assuage his thirst. How dare we waste it?

We make God wait while we putsy-wutsy with our jobs, refusing to grow up, refusing to implement our vocation one hundred per cent. How long, O Lord, how long do you have to wait for us?

I beg you on my bended knee to give me an answer. For I am asking myself: "How long can I endure this sight that constantly lingers before my eyes?" So much for the first theme that fills my heart.

The second then, seemingly on a smaller scale, is the question of our cross which we wear, and on which is inscribed: *Pax-Caritas*. It is the symbol of our vocation and the seal of God upon our hearts and persons.

There has been much discussion about whether we should wear the cross inside when we are not on the premises of the Apostolate — when we are on vacation, or when we might be employed somewhere. The approaches to that are very simple, but very profound.

First and foremost, examine your souls deeply before the Face of God regarding the reason why any one of you should ask that question. Are you ashamed of your cross? Are you uncomfortable, humanly speaking, in a worldly way, to display the sign of your salvation and vocation?

Have you doubts about that vocation? Do you want to be free for a little while on your own, making believe that you have no obligations?

Or perhaps your intelligence and your love for God have told you that in a particular case, to better win souls for Christ, you can put your cross inside and let Christ shine through your *caritas*, and your desire to serve.

In the case of men going downtown on ordinary business, you may or may not display the cross, depending on the situation, the job, the reason for being downtown. In picking up donations, for example, the cross displayed outwardly, might be of help to the benefactors. In some areas, there might be a valid reason for not displaying it. The best thing to do is to take advice from the local director who knows the situation.

But will you give me one solid reason why a girl on vacation should wear her cross inside? For a young woman going on her vacation, the cross is a protection from unwanted male attention. It often offers her an opportunity to explain to someone who might ask, not only what it stands for, but to speak about the God who was crucified on it. I can see no reason for a girl on vacation to put her cross inside. And to those who say that wearing the cross outside, identifies us as religious, I say that many women today wear crosses for ornamentation or for other purposes.

For men going on vacation, I can see many reasons for not wearing it. Because of the mores of Canada and America, it is often thought sissified for men to wear adornments. They may wear the cross outside or not. The important thing is to be guided by the proper motivation. I would trust the men of the Apostolate to make their own decisions, having consulted their superiors and their spiritual directors. But I feel that it should be a rare occasion when a woman of the Apostolate has to hide her cross. I would deeply question her motivation, except in very unusual cases.

God love you! Pray for me.

In Christ's infinite charity and Mary's love,
Yours lovingly,

CHECKING OUR MOTIVATIONS

October 7, 1958

Dearly Beloved,

It seems that you and I come together more often these days. Perhaps it is because we have so much to talk over. I get lonely also, for the "sight of you" and "the sound of your voices" (symbolically speaking). Often too, I see that you need to have more clarification about the Apostolate or spiritual life. Several of your letters bring forth points that I feel have to be answered. I love to talk to you, my spiritual children, and here I am again to discuss several matters together.

This time I am trying, not only to clarify or lay down definite rules, but also I want to go more deeply into some recurring questions: the cross, hairdos, liquor, clothes, blessing oneself before and after meals in public places on trips, and similar issues which may occur as days go by.

So let us plunge into the depths from which these questions arise. If we ponder them for a moment, we do not find God's Fatherhood as their origin. It is not from his depths that they arise. They appear to be neutral questions, but if we look into their depths we see that they all stem from human respect.

Don't throw your hands up in horror right away, but ask yourself if I am right or not. The question of wearing the cross inside or out is definitely influenced by the opinion of others, the need for explanations which one is reluctant to make, the fear of appearing as a holy Joe or holy Jane, of being somewhat embarrassed to belong to Christ or of appearing to be a sissy. Granted, I clarified the matter in my last letters. I begged you very seriously to examine your inner intention for wearing the cross. I am trusting you to find out for yourselves, with the grace of God and the help of Mary, when you are moved by human respect, when you refuse to stand with Christ and proclaim that you are his, when, in order to promote his kingdom, you temporarily wear the cross inside, so that at some future day, it may be revealed in all its glory. You do this latter sadly, telling him so, remembering that he too, once did not reveal himself immediately to his two disciples on the road to Emmaus. So much for the cross.

Now for the hairdo. If we look into the murky depths of our motives, we shall see the human respect float up along with vanity. Then they vanish. Some unseen hand has made them vanish, a frightening dangerous hand, belonging to one who loves the darkness. Perhaps, even these depths will vanish and a strange light will appear. From that light will issue a voice full of unction and intelligent, logical words. Like parrots, we repeat these words which come from the depths of a false light, without stopping to analyze the quality of this voice, its false lucidity and deadly intelligence.

If anyone in the Apostolate, after having thoroughly examined her conscience before the Blessed Sacrament, can honestly say that the reason why you care for your hair is not human respect nor that vanity of any kind bothers her conscience, then let her do whatever she wants to do with her hair. I am not going to judge anybody. I mustn't or I myself would be judged.

Now as regards to liquor. I come from an European Country where wine and beer are part of the meal. I could quote the Bible, holy doctors and saints, and make a very good case for the normal use of liquor. Our Lord used it, himself, and made wine into his Blood.

Were I to write a moral treatise, I would mention all of these things, but there is another side to the picture. There is alcoholism — a disease sweeping the world. Even France which used to drink moderately, is now plagued by a drunkenness that destroys minds, souls and bodies. Drunkenness that breaks up homes, makes of man an animal, fills insane asylums, attacks youth and all ages. Alcohol has become a tool of the devil, for he always uses that which can be abused.

In many cities of the world, many nuns and monks (e.g. Trappists and Trappistines) arise in the night interrupting their sleep, to pray for those whom alcohol has enslaved, for those who have made the flesh and food their god. They atone for good things gone wrong, like sex, wine, drugs which were meant to cure and food that was meant to sustain.

There are few bodily mortifications that we of the Apostolate seek or have imposed upon us. Would it be asking too much from us to refrain sometimes from drinking for the same reasons that these chosen souls chastise their bodies? Is it too much to ask that in countries whose mores proceed from heretical ideas, in regard to the use of some of the good things of the Lord, is it too much, to ask, I repeat, that we abstain from liquor, except at the times and places permitted, so that truth might prevail and sin be atoned for? Is it too much to ask that our lay apostles, if they choose, would have the courage to say to their relatives and friends: "I do not drink wine, cocktails nor highballs because I want to atone for the sins of drunkenness and other kinds of abuses."

Again we go back into the depths and examine our motivation: human respect, the desire to be one of the crowd, the fear of being different, the fear of being placed squarely on the side of Christ, and jeered at and mocked? Is it the desire to compromise, somehow, and to clothe the compromise in intelligent and logical words that are always half-truths and whose father is the devil?

It is not so much the questions that bother us as the depths from which they always come. We are looking for holy indifference, common sense, proper intentions, the cement that serves as the foundation of the house of sanctity.

Again, I would like to state my clarification in the following way:

1) No one in the directorate of Madonna House is opposed to alcoholic beverages in any way.
2) Should our Apostolate have foundations in countries where wine and beer are part of daily meals, we would, without hesitation, allow the taking of alcoholic beverages.
3) The general ruling, at present, stands as follows: throughout the Apostolate, we drink wine on specified, liturgical feasts in the houses of the Apostolate.
4) That once in awhile, at the discretion of the local director, alcoholic beverages might be used to celebrate a special occasion.
5) That on vacation, after thoroughly examining one's conscience alcohol may be used. But this has to be done with good judgement. For there are places where young people go on vacation, where to take a drink would be to let our Apostolate down. There are places where drinking would be of no consequence, such as with members of the family.

Such therefore, is the clarification of liquor. I beg you to examine your motives, in wanting to have a drink. If you are simply drinking out of human respect and not for the reasons given above, don't drink. If you are prudent, and your motives are recreation and conviviality, then take one. It is always a matter of examining your intention.

Thank you for listening to me. I hope I have made myself clear.

Lovingly yours in Mary,

TEARING THE SEAMLESS ROBE OF PETER

October 22, 1958

Dearly Beloved,

Today, I want to discuss with you what is known, in the Church, as the *mysterium romanum*, or the mystery of Rome. It may be illustrated by a story which Bishop Sheil once told. He knew a very intellectual man who was interested in coming into the Church. However, this man had one tremendous stumbling block the history of which he knew well. His stumbling block was the human frailty of the hierarchy — even the popes.

On the surface, he had a point; and Bishop Sheil answered him this way: "Dear friend, don't you see why the Vatican Library made its historical files so available? It was not afraid of the truth, sad as some of it is. Such frailty has been additional proof of the divinity of the Church. Bishops, priests, and popes by their human sinfulness and weakness have hurt the Church for two thousand years, but it still stands!"

Recently, we were discussing the behind-the-scenes politics in Rome, especially during the election of a pope. I myself, during my visits to Rome, have been given descriptions of various factions there that are constantly in disagreement. These resemble lobbies in Washington or Ottawa, and are sometimes just as dirty, humanly speaking.

Let us go back to the beginnings of the Church. Christ chose his apostles. They weren't such hot potatoes, and I doubt if any of us would want those characters as our intimate friends. We certainly would not choose them for our associates in such a tremendous undertaking. There was Peter who denied him. What do we think of friends who leave us in the lurch at the moment when we need them most?

Judas sold him down the river, and betrayed him with — of all things — a kiss! The dirty bum! That makes two pretty shady characters. Where, please, were the eight when he was crucified? They disappeared so fast no one knew where they were hidden. That leaves us with only one who was okay.

Yet note: After his resurrection, Jesus never mentions a word to Peter about his infidelity, but builds his Church on him. That brings us to two thoughts: we definitely do not think, see or act with the mind of God. We judge too quickly and with too little to go on. I suppose it's because we cannot read human hearts as God can, or because we ourselves are pretty weak creatures.

Several inevitable conclusions follow from the above: God did not build his Church on angels, but on human, sinful, weak, frightened men who loved him, and, slowly co-operating with his grace, became what they should have been. Therefore we who are still directed by weak men must understand that we need to look beyond the person to the office he holds. That office is Christ.

Again I quote to you from a letter that I received from Thomas Merton. As you remember, I had written to him about my inadequacy as a Director General. It is important enough to mention it again:

> The great paradox of superiorship (re popes, priests, religious superiors, etc.) is that no one can be a superior unless he is fully worthy, and yet no one is fully worthy. There is only one solution: that Christ Himself, in us, must be the superior, for he alone is fully worthy. And we must be content to struggle to keep out of his way.

That brings us to a conclusion: because Christ is in the Church, he is in every office, from the pope down to the local director of a Secular Institute. Otherwise, there would be no Church.

That is what Bishop Shiel meant: that no matter how much the men and women in office try to wreck their part of the Church's fabric by their humanness, hence sinfulness and unpleasant personality traits, it does not happen. Christ in their office does not allow the Church to be wrecked because of the weakness of the persons who represent him.

That brings me to the theme of this letter which I want to make very clear to you. I know from deep experience, that many young people have never given thought to these things. They expect every religious superior (from the pope on down) to be a saint.

I well remember the first time this happened to me. A member who had been in Friendship House for about eight months, came to me and with the bluntness and courage of youth said: "B, I'm quitting. You know that I came here because I heard you lecture and I thought of you as a saint, and so I came to learn at the feet of a saint. In the last eight months I have discovered that you have clay feet, and at times I think that you are all clay — a phony!''

So I smiled, even though it hurt, and explained to her that she had a very childish and sentimental idea of those in authority. I explained that every priest is commissioned, by his ordination, to preach the truths of Christ, even though he has a hell of a time living them himself. ''That is the paradox not only of the priests,'' I said, ''but even of ordinary lay folks like me.'' I explained that God had given me some knowledge about the faith, the Negro, and the apostolate. At the request of Church authorities, it was my duty to go and proclaim those truths. That I didn't live them to the hilt was evident to everyone, especially to me.

Then I quoted to her from the Constitution of Saint Ignatius Loyola. You can find it in a book used in all the novitiates of the Jesuits. It is called *Perfect Obedience*, originally written by Fr. Rodriguez, S.J., a contemporary of Ignatius Loyola, their first novice master, I quote:

> Obedience vastly conduces to rapid spiritual advancement. Therefore, all should give themselves to perfect obedience, acknowledging that the superior is in the place of Christ, and give to that superior not only outward, but inward reverence and love. They must accustom themselves not to behold whom it is they obey, but rather who he is for whose sake they obey, that is, Christ, the Lord, for whose love they obey. For the superior is not to be obeyed because he is prudent or virtuous or excels in any other divine gift, whatsoever it be, but for this only, that he is in the place of God and has authority from him who says, ''He that heareth you heareth me, and he that despiseth you, despiseth me!''

Now, dear friends in Christ, this brings to a focus the theme of my letter. I tried to present a story to emphasize that theme. Let us now apply it to the Apostolate. Starting with me and proceeding to every local director, and on to the head of every department, or even to someone in charge of a temporary, little job, what do we have?

Let us paint a dark picture. Let us say that, in each case, the superior, foreman, or local director has the worst personality conceivable, and that every person has enormous difficulties dealing with him or her. Let us say that all his or her mannerisms irritate you. If you are a man, you dislike being ordered by a woman; if a woman, you dislike being ordered by men. I'll let you fill in the rest of the picture.

So we feel we have a louse for a superior! Let us now return to those luminous words of St. Ignatius. We are dealing with the *mysterium romanum*, and — what is more to the point — dealing with the passion of Christ and the behavior of the apostles. There are only two possible conclusions: either the Catholic Church *is* divinely founded, and Christ is in all the superiors who rule his Church, or there *is* no Catholic Church, and the whole thing isn't worth belonging to. Take your choice.

But let us take a little more from St. Ignatius that is very pertinent for us:

> When anyone goes to the kitchen to help the cook, he must obey him with much humility in all things pertaining to his office, showing him always complete obedience. For if he does not, it is not likely that he will show obedience to any superior, since true obedience is not concerned with the person to whom a thing is done, but *for whom*. But if he does this, obey the cook in all humility, for our Creator and Lord alone, the same Lord of all is obeyed. Wherefore, one should not look to see if it is the cook of the house or its superior, whether he that commands is one or the other; for neither to him or for him is this obedience shown, but only to God and for God, our Creator and Lord.''

How about using these luminous words of a saint for your meditation?

Here is another point, this time from Dom Columbia Marmion:

> In the same way Christ conceals himself from us in our superiors. In spite of his imperfections, the abbot (or any superior anywhere) for us is the representative of Christ. Christ hides behind the weaknesses and imperfections of the man, just as he conceals himself beneath the Sacramental Species. Just because the superior is placed above all others, the daily intercourse which we have with him betrays his deficiencies. Wherefore we feel tempted to exclaim: ''This man is not Christ. His poor judgement is not infallible. He

can make mistakes — in fact does. He cannot comprehend my plans. He allows himself to be guided by this or that preference." But faith answers: "The abbot is believed to act in the place of Christ, where Christ gives us a Solomon to take his place or a man without talent. To the eyes of faith, it is Christ whom the man represents." Then, when I have faith, I will say *Credo*, I believe. I obey this person, whoever he may be, because in him I obey Christ and I remain thus united to Christ.

These things I said to the staff worker and she understood and stayed. None of you desire to leave, I know. Your general training has already shown you something of this idea of obedience. But it is worth considering again.

However, there is another thing that I want to mention. There is something that should not be done even with the intention of utmost charity, or to get something off one's chest. This thing can tear apart the fragile, spiritual fabric of an apostolate, an order, the Church. That is to discuss the ways and personality of a superior with another. That creates deep wounds, and never should be done. They may not meet your expectations. They may have all the faults which you attribute to them and many more. But in criticizing them, we are guilty not only of tearing the seamless robe of Peter; but we are also guilty of sheer stupidity, or, perhaps, willful ignorance. We do not want to face the crucified Christ and endure the pain of imitating him.

You may gain a little emotional help by venting your gripes. But what have you really done? You have criticized a person behind his or her back. You might have sown the seeds of distrust and opened the eyes of criticism for someone who had been very trusting. To rob someone of his peace of mind is very sad. What did you accomplish? You have darkened your souls and have acquired deeper guilt complexes.

What are the real reasons why you are criticizing your superior? You don't like the job that she gave you. You feel guilty and hence angry that you have had to have had the obvious called to your attention. You are angry, ashamed, and humiliated to be reminded of your inadequacy. Your emotional babyhood wants its security, but it is also embarrassed by its need. You are depressed, moody and hostile, and so you hit back at a shadow — the person of the superior.

All the time, you are dealing with shadows. It is the voice of Christ who is issuing the orders. What we are actually doing is balking before God. That, my friends, is not a very healthy thing to do if you are seeking to reach the final goal — the Beatific Vision.

Lovingly yours in Mary,

Catherine

BETHLEHEM AND NAZARETH — OUR LIVES

December 17, 1958

Dearly Beloved,

"I salute you. There is nothing I can give you which you have not; but there is much that, which I cannot give you, you can take.

"No heaven can come to us, unless your heart finds rest in it today. Take heaven.

"No peace lies in the future, which is not hidden in the present. Take peace.

"The gloom of the world is but a shadow; behind it, yet within our reach, is joy. Take joy.

"And so at this Christmastime, I greet you with the prayer that for you, now and forever, the day breaks and the shadows flee away.

"Such is my Christmas gift and greeting to you."

These writings, taken from Fra Giovanni, A.D. 1513, are my gift to you. A Mass will also be offered for all of you. For one Mass is enough to restore the whole world. Its wealth should fill each heart to overflowing. Alleluia!

You all remember our chapel at Christmas. You know how I love every liturgical day of our holy mother, the Church, but especially I love her great feast days and amongst them are Christmas and Easter. During the midnight Masses in our little chapel, I shall, according to the custom of my people, humbly prostrate before the God who dwells there and pray for each one of you.

Again, I come in the Advent spirit of Holy Russia. It is the spirit of longing, of self-examination, of cleansing and preparation. I know my poverty and I realize how much I have failed you by a lack of charity. So I humbly beg your pardon and ask your prayers. If there is one in the Apostolate who stands in need of prayer, it is I myself. So remember me in yours. Let them be your gifts to my poverty and my need.

This is the time of year when we should realize how much like Bethlehem and Nazareth our lives are. How good God has been to make it so! Let us gratefully remember in our prayers, our Holy Father, Pope Pius XII, who put the seal of the Holy Spirit on this vocation of ours. Let us pray for our present Pope John XXIII, who is so interested in the lay apostolate.

However, not everyone is interested. As you know so well, there are people in our various communities, who have no room in the inns of their hearts for us. There will be many more. At one time, it seemed as if there was no room on the North American Continent for me and our little pioneer band.

Thanks be to God, we are still almost as hidden as the life of the holy three was in Nazareth. For who knows us? How few desire to know! Let us always wish to remain hidden in one way or another. For ours is the Apostolate of the alley-ways and of the lonely places of the world.

Let us be content to be misunderstood. Let us be content to be maligned. For aren't we small in numbers and in importance? Let us not worry about it. The Lord was very small in Bethlehem, and those who are small in him will some day be "big" before his Face; but not now. We still have a long road to travel.

Let us experience Bethlehem by cold and hunger, discomfort and poverty. Let us remember that when the Lord called us here, and his Mother led us through the blue doors, the call and leading was not to a life of ease, comfort and luxury. It was to a life resembling Bethlehem and Nazareth.

Let us remember that, at that blue door, we left all our rights.

All of us are paupers for the sake of a Child born in a manger, for the sake of a naked man dying on a cross. We should desire but one thing — to love so much that we become obedient to his most holy will even unto death.

Above all, let us enter the school of Bethlehem and Nazareth to grow in the one thing that matters: love. For after all, life is a dialogue for love, an encounter of love between God and us. With St. Augustine we should repeat: "Love God and do what you will." For if we really love God, then we will do only what he wishes us to do. Ultimately, we will be saints, that is, tremendous lovers of God.

Let us be done with human respect that bites so deeply into our hearts. Let us cease to be bothered about what people think, — and only worry about what God thinks. That is all that matters.

Since we are so little, let us learn, in that school of charity that is Bethlehem and Nazareth, the little things that make his charity great: kindness and thoughtfulness, which lead to death to self and growth in charity. Let us expect also all the temptations and doubts which will, like savage winds buffet us through the coming days of the New Year. Let us be ready in utter simplicity and faith. For aren't we the children of light? Shouldn't we expect the prince of darkness to unleash his powers against us?

Do not be afraid, little flock. For through the darkest storms and the coldest winds, over paths surrounded by steep cliffs, God's grace will be with us, and that is more than enough.

Let us also grow in faith. Most of our problems are due to lack of faith. We always seek to apprehend by reason, the strange ways, the unsolvable mysteries of God. This cannot be done. We must walk in faith, love in faith, and have our being in faith.

The ways of faith are dark, and we must accept this darkness; but it really isn't darkness at all. In faith we know that the darkness is allowed by God himself. He is like a thousand suns, and we must look at him without any sunglasses, and this is blinding to us. We think it is dark, when actually, we have been walking in the blinding light of God's love for us.

Yes, let us be humble, poor, without rights. We must be ready to go where we are sent, ready to live with what we have. We will make our home in Bethlehem and Nazareth, now and forever. Let us pray for a faith that bridges earth and heaven, and let us learn to love a little more every day. Then I know we shall have a holy Christmas, and a holier New Year. Then will all our days be Christmas-like and new in him. Then "our youth will be renewed like an eagle's."

These, and many other thoughts come to me as I think of you, for my heart is filled with love. My prayer for you is always the same: "Lord, May they know you better, love you more, serve you always. May they persevere unto the end in their humble and glorious vocation which you, in your mercy, have given to them. And in the end, may they see your Face. May you hold them in your arms, and may they hold you — the Child — in theirs!"

Lovingly yours in Mary,

EXAMINING OUR CONSCIENCES

January 9, 1959

Dearly Beloved,

Greetings to all of you, and a Happy and Holy New Year! May it be filled with charity, order and peace. May the Wise Men bring you the great gift of wisdom and growth in the vision of the whole.

Today, as we have been putting away all of our "little" Christmas decorations, I want to write to you about *little things*. In the hustle and bustle of work, little things are apt to slip into the background. If they do, a whole edifice might crumble, because they are important. A grain of sand can stop the machinery of a huge factory. Yes, little things are important. So I would like every house, every member, to examine his or her conscience about little things.

What about talking too much at night before going to bed,

and in the morning when getting up? It seems to me that because our Apostolate is an Apostolate of talking in many ways, we should always cherish not only inner silence, but at certain times, silence of the tongue as well. Is it asking too much to have five minutes of complete silence before the lights go out, so that people can compose themselves for sleep (which is but a preview of death)? We should recollect our souls and place them in God's keeping for the night.

Is it too much to ask that the first moments of the morning be given to God again through silence of the tongue? In that way we allow the Lord to receive the first fruits of our waking.

Another "little thing" we often disregard is time. Who can say how much of it each of us has to use for God? Who of us would want to meet the sad eyes of Christ when, at the judgement, he will show us the time we could have used for the salvation of souls? Each human act has redemptive value whether dusting a shelf or feeding the hungry.

Wasted time, idle talk, inner and outer disorganization, the disregarding of simple rules (like putting lights out and being punctual at meals) all these are little things, but oh how they corrode a house, and change its spirit. How quickly tensions, irritations, backbiting, and flaring tempers follow in their wake. It is of such small things that I wanted to talk to you. We, at Madonna House, are giving more time and attention to *little things*. We are more and more realizing that they are the very essence of sanctity and spiritual formation.

I beg you, at your next meeting, to openly discuss any failures in those little things. We have no chapter of faults, but once in awhile it is good to examine our consciences together in these matters. Let your next meeting be on little things. Let everyone speak freely, humbly and simply. Check your consciences on the following things: Are you punctilious in observing all the rules of your houses? Are you thoughtful of everyone and everything around you? Do you talk too much at night or in the morning thus distracting others? Are your lights out at the time appointed? This is very important for it means mental, physical and spiritual health of the individuals in a house. Do you plan carefully the jobs you are given to do, especially if it involves one or more persons besides yourself? Do you return all tools to their proper place after you use them? Is your house tidy and clean at all times?

I leave the rest of the examination of conscience to you. Let me hear of the results.

Lovingly in Mary,

ARE WE TOTALLY SURRENDERED?

April 15, 1959

Dearly Beloved,

Our chapel has changed. You have heard that we have received a most beautifully made wooden crucifix. It is one of the most realistic that I have seen. The corpus is of life size.

When you walk up the stairs and turn towards the tabernacle, you feel that you are at the foot of a hill. You realize that you must walk to the summit where he is crucified even though your body shrinks from the thought. The crucifix is the central focus of the chapel.

When you kneel quietly, the whole chapel will whisper to you "Look up! Look up!" You will see through love all the matters of life. You will hold the vision in the chalice of your heart like heady wine. You will see and hear how much God loves you; for there before your eyes, very vividly, is the price he paid for you. It is written out in the eternal love letter of the crucifix. Below, in the tabernacle, he abides in the Host — God and Man — your food, proclaiming silently his love for you.

At Christmas, the chapel will sing and rejoice in the portrayal of the whole story. There will be the Baby in the manger, the soft song of Love's Beginning. There will be the immense crucifix, the passionate song of his love, redemptive and all-embracing, and all-healing love. There will be the tabernacle where the Lover waits for the beloved throughout the day and the night. Here, within four humble walls, your vocation is spelled out for you as it is in every chapel.

You, like Christ, must incarnate yourself, in utter simplicity, humility and seeming weakness, into the daily stream of life. You must witness to the Incarnation in the marketplaces, the slums and palaces of the world. There you must reenact in your own person Bethlehem and Nazareth.

What does it matter if you *feel* inadequate? What does it matter if you think you are not contributing too much to our Apostolate? What does it matter if you think you are a sinner? Don't dwell on it. Take it for granted. We are all sinners. So do not impede his grace in your soul by dwelling on your poverty. We are all paupers before him.

Dwell instead on the incomprehensible mystery of his choice of all of us. Who are we? We could symbolically paint a picture of ourselves very much like the mural you have in Marian Center* of Christ among the destitute poor and rejected ones. You could put us — the lay apostles of Madonna House — in the line-up. You could paint us as women and men dressed in worse rags than the ones in the mural. You could give each one of us the modern posture of dejection. Some of us would look exceedingly untidy (we do at times; it would be realistic!) Some of us would be bowed down, round shouldered, some of us too thin, some of us too fat. Our faces would be filled with the lines of emotional tension and tiredness, disfigured by the dirt of our sinfulness and inadequacies.

Then, standing in our midst, lovable, tender and understanding, we could paint Christ in the full beauty of his mature manhood, offering his Heart to each one of us who came into the line-up as beggars covered with the dust of all the roadways of the world.

Should this really have happened, would we not offer our hearts in return, and, like Magdalen, love him passionately, and fall down at his feet and kiss them. We would forget all about ourselves, and remember only that he calls us unto himself to occupy a very special place in his Heart.

So let us be done with self-examinations. Let us think only of

*The name of our house in Edmonton, Alberta.

him. We can find him in the reality of everyday life: first, in our brothers and sisters with whom we dwell; in those whom we serve; and in the fathers of our souls — the priests who direct us or live with us.

Each presents to us a waiting Christ. How long are we going to make him wait when he desires with a passionate desire to elope with us *now*? Are we going to talk to him about anything else but love? We shouldn't.

Let us state this in practical, twentieth-century terms: The time has come for all Madonna House members to *stop taking and start giving*. If we really examined our souls, we would see ourselves as little babies with mouths pining for the breast of the mother, or for the milk bottle. We are yelling our foolish little heads off for the milk of attention, tenderness and understanding of our directors. Like babies, we want to latch on, to be held, to be cooed over, and have lullabies sung to us. We refuse to *give, give, give*. We want to *take, take, take*!

If we examined our souls, we would see that we make Christ wait day in and day out. We spurn the gift of His heart because we are immersed in small problems of self-centeredness and selfishness: Does our spiritual director or our local director understand us, love us as we would like to be loved? Do they approve of us? Do they uphold us and clarify for us every step of the way? We do not want to walk straight and free like adult men and women; we want to continue to walk in a baby harness, always aware that there is a hand at the other end which will not allow us to fall.

Another problem is: How do the other members feel about us? We think other people are inconsiderate, that our brothers and sisters don't understand us; that they should pay more attention to us, care for us more. In the spirit of the world, we are still greatly affected by the likes and dislikes of people and situations. We are still in the infantile, emotional state of children. Within these two areas are contained all the difficulties and problems within the Apostolate.

We are called to exemplify Bethlehem, Nazareth, the public life of Our Lord, his passion and crucifixion, his death and resurrection. Also, like him in the tabernacle, we must be available to everyone in the tabernacles of our souls and hearts. Did Our Lord latch onto things selfishly or self-centeredly? I don't think that even his enemies could say that of him. Can you say it of yourself? Our time is now. We must stop taking. We must start giving maturely as adult men and women should. This year should be one of deep searching of hearts, souls and minds. I humbly advise your directors and yourselves to come together to clarify that one theme. I suggest that you begin by sitting down and evaluating first, how deeply you are living your own apostolate, and secondly, how your apostolate is fitting into the vision of the whole.

My heart is sorely afraid that you are living in a deadly routine of work, equating work with prayer alright (as equate you should), but satisfied just with the work accomplished. My heart is sorely afraid that you evaluate yourselves and your apostolates by action more than by spirit. Action should be the fruit of the spirit; but it should not be the essence that replaces the spirit. Open your eyes and ask yourselves: What is your contribution to the spirit of Madonna House? What is your contribution to the spirit of your house? What is your contribution to the spirit of those whom you serve? You are witnesses of Christ, ambassadors of his glad tidings, apostles of his Gospel. You witness by breathing, by being. A saint reveals Christ "by the way he walks, and sits, by the tone of his voice, by the expression of his eyes, his posture, his sleep." Do you?

Think of the impact of thirteen year old Saint Agnes on the rough crowd of pagans! Think of the faces of Saint Vincent de Paul, Saint Catherine of Siena, of Saint Peter, and Saint John the Baptist, Saint John the well beloved. Think of any saint. Should you have met them, you would not, perhaps, have recognized them as saints! But you would know that you had met a personality who made an impact on you. It may have been a powerful impact or a quiet one, or an impact that affected you only later on. However, you would know that something unusual and wonderful had happened to you.

Do you have that effect on other people, and especially on each other? Search your hearts. Meditate deeply on the vision of your apostolate. Yes, the apostolate to the Brothers Christopher includes smiling, being kind, washing dishes and serving meals. All our powers of intellect, knowledge, prayer, identification, imagination, should go into these actions. But do you believe firmly and passionately that your *greatest* contribution to the apostolate of the Brothers Christopher, and all other apostolates, is your *union* with Christ? Are you offering yourself up for these people in an interior sea of love hidden from the sight of men? In each of those people you should see the passion of Christ more clearly than you do on this Good Friday on which I write to you.

These are the things which must now be clarified; for I confess to a weariness that is almost beyond endurance at the attitudes prevailing in all of you. With Christ and the Psalmist, I feel wounded a thousand times over: "How long, O Lord, how long will you be deaf to my supplications? I cried to you from the very depths. Miserere. Miserere."

It is said that, in its ultimate, patience is martyrdom. I am coming to believe that this is true. This October 15th, I'll celebrate thirty years in the Apostolate. For a human being this is half a lifetime. It is little to give to God, granted, but those are a lot of years. It comes to me as a shock that I am the only one of the original pioneers left.

Why did the approximately 350 people who passed through Friendship House during twenty-one years of its existence, not persevere? It is not for me to judge; but one thing I know: one reason why they did not persevere is that they were still more interested in taking and failed to give totally.

Patiently, I hope, I weathered the storm, with all its pain, sorrow and near annihilation. We entered a new phase of becoming a Pious Union, with a clear-cut understanding that those who come here would give their lives in total surrender under the evangelical counsels. Christ still asks me for the martyrdom of patience. Years are accumulating, as years are wont to do. I am coming to the evening of life. There is an urgency within me. I do not mind. I know that with the grace and my co-operation I will endure this martyrdom of patience until I die.

Passionately I have taught you (or tried to teach you) in season or out of season, the road to Golgotha. Like St. Paul, I think I have preached to you Christ and him crucified. In the darkness of a Good Friday, I ask myself: When will you begin to give and cease to take? Not because I matter, nor because my patience is strained thin. That is not important. But what is tragically important is that you are making Christ wait! As St. Paul says, you are still children and have not yet grown up.

The world is trembling with hate and anger against God. Souls are dying everywhere. The living dead are walking the earth. Hungry men and women are stretching out their hands to you. You are part of the army of lay apostles that Christ, through his Vicar, is raising up in this world in order to restore it to him.

He calls you to bring clarity to the confused, understanding to the bewildered, to feed hungry hearts and to give drink to thirsty souls, and to help restore the dead to life. But you continue to take. Before this sea of his pain, you act like little children, refusing to take responsibility, latching onto one another and onto your directors, wanting to be guided every step of the way, afraid of the slightest bruise, fall or pain.

Yet I know God has entrusted you to me. Though I lie battered bruised and bloody from the martyrdom of patience, my love for you as a flame, burns higher. I realize more and more that I do not matter; only *you* matter. I am willing to decrease so that you will increase. So, on this Good Friday, the parched, dry and cracked lips of my soul once more cry out to you: God thirsts. ''Sitio!'' he says. How long are you going to be busy about all the unimportant, the childish and immature things of life? When, O when, will you arise and offer him to drink of the cool waters of your love — the total gift of yourself in service and in love to others?

I want you to concentrate on one word this year: Love shares all things with the beloved. How much do you share the burdens and joys of your local director, of your brothers and sisters, of those whom you serve? Sharing means being able and willing to step with someone through life. Let the word *share*, therefore, instead of take, be like a knife that slashes through your self-centeredness.

Arise! Be about your Father's business! Share Christ's life from Bethlehem to Easter! Share it with every human being whom you meet, starting with those who dwell in your own houses. Then, and only then, will you have a glorious Easter.

Christ is risen, Alleluia! Alleluia! Verily he has risen! With an unshakable faith, in flaming love, and in the martyrdom of patience, I believe that this Easter will be a glorious one for you, if you begin to understand the one thing that matters: loving and

sharing the life of Christ, your Beloved, as *he* wishes it to be lived and shared.

Yours in the Resurrected Christ,

Catherine

OUR SCHOOL OF LOVE

April 21, 1959

Dearly Beloved,

Today, I would like to discuss growth in the spirit, which also includes growth in accepting responsibilities. It would be a mistake to think that when we leave Madonna House for a mission, we have completed our training. Training continues until we die. The school of love graduates its pupils only when they become one with Love Who is a Person; and Love is God.

So we graduate when we die. Until then, we are always learning. This is an important lesson, and one has to have a deep understanding and appreciation of it. Therefore, when we go to any foundation, we simply go into another class, as it were, another year of our school of love. Our growth in love and responsibility must be constant and unflagging.

In the missions, there constantly arise situations that re-arrange responsibilities, such as a superior's going away for some reason. Another member may be temporarily in charge of a house. In such a situation, every member immediately will have more responsibility. Thus, they are called to grow more in love. The temporary superior receives that intangible and beautiful thing that grace is, to do the job.

All must remember that *to govern is to love*. So what really happens is that the permanent superior finds one person more ready to love the other members. This person will have to show more growth in humility, will power, judgement, faith, hope, and especially in *charity*. It will be very easy to find out if he or she is doing well and growing in love. The peace of the house will show it. Peace is the infallible fruit and yardstick of proper directing. One will never have to wonder.

This principle also applies when the permanent superior gives different responsibilities. If the members would understand that they have the grace for a new task that the director gives them, they would be less tense. Let us face it: *without God we can do nothing*. So let us shed our desire for approval. Let us shed all personality clashes and all the thousand little human weaknesses that impede our flight to God and get cracking on whatever we are given to do.

Frankly, the impression I receive, dearly beloved, from your letters is that you are still full of emotional problems. Oh, you are much better than you were, but have you ever said to yourself: "Okay, so I have some emotional problems. So have many others. Some are laboring under much harsher circumstances than I. Mothers, fathers, children, priests, teachers, students, and nuns — all have their share of emotional problems; but the world goes on and so do they. However, I have received tremendous help in Madonna House which they didn't receive. I have graces they don't have. So let me believe that the remnants of my emotional problems, which will gradually disappear, are the cross God meant me to carry for the time being. Let me straighten out my cross a little and carry it generously and keep going at a steady pace. If I did that, I could give at least three quarters of my attentions to the present task, which is to love God by serving him in whatever responsibilities are given to me. It is time I grew up. If you reasoned like this, much unnecessary tension, misery and personality clashes would be avoided.

Speaking of personality clashes, frankly, I cannot understand them. So Y doesn't like X. But Y has been trained at Madonna House to know that, in the natural order, "like" is a word that belongs to the emotions, and "love" is a word that belongs to the spirit. So not liking a person does not mean that you do not love him or her or that you wouldn't try to make life easier for that person. This may be very difficult emotionally. Remember St. Therese and the nun with the rosary. And remember the words of Christ that we must love our enemies.

Surely no member of Madonna House is an "enemy" of another. That is inconceivable. All of us are brothers and sisters. Do you mean to tell me that you *hate* your brother and sister, that you don't love him or her? No. I can imagine your *not liking* them emotionally, but you must love them spiritually.

Otherwise, pettiness will enter in, and the seamless garment of Christ, which is the Apostolate, will be torn into shreds. Don't tell me that we have less respect than the Roman soldiers who played dice for it. I won't believe it!

How do you expect to grow in wisdom, grace and sanctity, if you are forever annoying others with your moods and tensions?

Honest to goodness! I could get very disturbed by all of this! But I love you too much to really get annoyed.

Another point, that I would like to discuss with you very seriously, is the matter of temptations against our vocation — this wavering between being married and celibate. This is a very dangerous thing. Of course, temptations come. They are our "tests". God permits the devil to tempt us so that we can gauge our own strength, and be promoted to the next class, which is nice. However, if we are going to give in to temptations, or let them worry us, make us unhappy or discouraged, then we are not passing our "examinations" very well, are we?

Let us look at it this way: You believe with a great certitude that your vocation is to Madonna House. Over and over again I have explained that your supervisors would never have accepted you unless they felt sure of your vocation. Their own immortal souls are at stake in these decisions. I, for one, do not propose to go to hell for you, or anyone else! No one is indispensable to our Apostolate. If you didn't have a vocation, the Apostolate would get along without you very nicely. Sometimes, we go through hell to fight for your vocation. When I think of all the hours of *talking* with each of you; when I contemplate how many lectures you have heard; when I think of all the people you have met and of all the travelling you have done; all the care expended on your physical health; I am just wondering if you realize that all of this has been done because your superiors are *convinced* of your vocation. Therefore, they haven't spared anything to prepare and train you. Would they have done this if they doubted your vocation? It would be good for you to stop and consider everything with some common sense and intelligence, instead of allowing spring fever and your emotions to help the devil. He, frankly, doesn't need any help.

Now, I want to present a rather tragic fact for your consideration. The truth must be told once in a while, and sometimes, rather brutally (a la B). It could very well happen that your superiors have a very thorny problem to solve. God, theology, and the Holy Roman Catholic Church, without a shadow of a doubt, clearly and brutally state a fact that we do not think enough about, i.e. "The personal good is subjected to the common good." So it is possible if you waver too much, if you are constantly moody, difficult and create too many problems for the house, that you might be asked to leave with your vocation wrapped around you like a mantle. An

116

Apostolate can endure laggards and troublemakers only so long. It affects the health of the other members putting on them too heavy a burden.

The directors, confronted with such situations, sooner or later have to dismiss people, as much as we love you. We shiver at the thought of doing it. You ruined your own vocation and affected the common good. Do you ever consider the common good, brothers and sisters? A few of you do.

I quote here from a letter which brought tremendous joy into my heart and the heart of the other directors:

> I see daily before my eyes the crucifixion of my director as she follows his way. Since I behold this with my very eyes, I come to the realization that *your* cross is, at present, beyond my comprehension. If daily we could only keep before our minds and hearts, the fact that our directors are living sacrifices, how joyful and exact would we be in carrying out their wishes.

> I cannot help but believe that the pain of Christ must be assuaged, not only in his poor, but also in his faithful directors. What causes this pain: the directors love God so madly that they suffer from the puzzling fact that we have everything and are so reluctant to *give*.

There is much more in my heart, because I love you so much and pray for you often. I beg God to kill your selfish self and to resurrect your real and beautiful self. I love you so much. I hope you can read between the lines how much.

Lovingly yours in Mary,

ZEAL AND HOLY RESTLESSNESS

April 27, 1959

Dearly Beloved,

There is one of God's gifts that is seldom discussed, but it is wonderful to have. Teachers of the spiritual life tell us that it is one of the gifts of the Holy Spirit given at Confirmation. It is called *zeal*.

Somewhere, I read about a saint who was possessed by a "holy restlessness." I like that expression. I think that it applies to me. I think that a writer of my biography, in years to come, may well apply to me the words of the Scriptures: "The zeal of my Father's house has consumed me."

I cannot rest because I see the pain of Christ so vividly. I see the tears of Christ so clearly. I hear always the cry of Christ (or was it a moan, or a whisper?) Sleeping or waking, my ears resound with the word "Sitio!" "I thirst!" I see Christ waiting, waiting, waiting — a Beggar for our hearts, for the implementation of our vocation. He is waiting — a Pauper at the crossroads of everywhere.

At times, it seems that I am a runner, called by God to bring souls to Golgotha. By his most holy will, I am called to teach them how to love him. My work, it seems, is to bring them to Golgotha at twelve o'clock on Good Friday (and to me, every day, in a manner of speaking, is Good Friday). Here, they see him dying for love of them; and from the cross teaching them how to love. I myself must run back to get more souls. That seems to be my life; I am a runner for love's sake.

That is why I am always reevaluating the Apostolate. When necessary, I change or add something to our techniques of training. That is why, for thirty years, I still repeat the same simple truths that lead people to God.

Often, I feel very guilty. I cannot comprehend that adults, after being in the Apostolate for several years, can still say: "Catherine, this is unclear to me. I wish you would clarify it." It is difficult for me to realize that some of us have not yet understood the essence of the spirit of the Apostolate: *Charity* and *peace*. They have not as yet comprehended that love spends itself on little things, first for one's brothers and sisters, then for the world at large — little *things* like seeing what has to be picked up, like cleaning a stove, like being on a job with one hundred per cent concentration, because one loves.

However, the fact remains that this is so. I feel guilty at not having trained you better. Perhaps this is untrue. So I begin to examine that training again. Because I love you so passionately in the Lord, I listen to the voice of love in my heart, and ponder the many ingenious ways of expressing the same thing over again. Love gives me the courage to keep starting over again for what seems to be the millionth time. Love does such things, you know. As you see, there is no end to such evaluation.

However, all of this, at the moment, seems very easy compared to a situation that has me stymied. My ingenuity is running low, though my love grows; and I can say that I am almost frustrated at times. The reason for all of this is you, my dearly beloved. When you went through your training, either I did not train well, or time was limited because the pressure of work was so great. Whatever the reason, our number one problem today is not the new class. It is the seniors. Not all of them, thanks be to God, but alas! many of them. You puzzle me and keep me awake at night. You are my rosary of external self-examination. Your names become beads in this rosary which I hold before me. I try to figure out where have *I* failed? Where have *you* failed? Why aren't we all on the wavelength of God?

The answers come to me slowly and I could sum them up as follows: While you went through your training, there wasn't much time for a constant follow-up. Then the needs of the Apostolate were so pressing that your training time was also a working time. We had endless bees, and the pressure of the work was immense. Organization: Though I was a good organizer under the circumstances, and spent myself unceasingly, nevertheless, often you or the Apostolate suffered from lack or organization. Emotional problems: I would say that these are enemy number one, often affecting your absorption, comprehension, and cooperation in your training. I think that this problem is still number one. Background: In many cases, your home was responsible for a lack of formation. It failed to give you a broad, Christian vision. Often the school did not teach you very much and a great deal of what you learned had to be unlearned. Frequently your church or parish did not help you very much. You were taught the sacraments which are precious and wondrous, and some catechetics, but you received little to make you a whole person. You belong to a pluralistic society. This means that you have not lived in an all-Catholic civilization. So in some ways, you have been mal-formed since the moment you took your first breath. Taking all these obstacles into consideration I must admit that I am still baffled by the fact that I must still be teaching the ABC's of our vocation to seniors. I would welcome any letters of yours that would shed light on the situation. We would truly be thankful for my heart is open to receive your help.

I am possessed, as I told you, by holy restlessness. The zeal of my Father's house is eating me up. At the moment, you are my Father's house. I am willing to be eaten up, to give you of my substance, and I am willing to lay down my life for love of you. Show me how I can do that so that you do not keep Christ waiting; so that he can drink the cool, clear waters of your zeal, your love and the implementation of your glorious vocation. So that you will dry his tears and assuage his pain.

Tell me, dearly beloved, any suggestions, any ideas that you have on why so many of you are not get "cracking" in the Apostolate for Christ's sake.

So much has been poured into you that it is almost frighten-ing. How can I help you? Let us have a dialogue. It is so vitally important, so terribly needed in our days. We are on the verge of a great growth, but it will be stillborn unless we all wake up and really start loving and doing for the Lord. Our time is now. Let that sink in deeply. Help me make this training center what it should be. Help me to train you in the Lord's spirit. For this I exist. For this the Lord has made me. Do not allow me to fail him. My dearly beloved ones, I count on you. You are my right hand. You are the pillar of strength on which I lean. My need of you is inexpressible. Please help me!

In the immense charity of Christ,
Lovingly yours,

THE SPIRIT OF MADONNA HOUSE

May 30, 1959

Dearly Beloved,

In this letter, I will clarify and synthesize something you are forever asking yourself and us: "*What is the spirit of the institute?*" I suggest that you copy the definition I give, keep it in your prayer books or missals, and meditate on it as often as possible. The immensity of this simple definition will open its riches to you daily if you approach it reverently and prayerfully:

> The spirit of Madonna House Institute is the beautiful and awesome spirit of the Gospel applied to daily living, without compromise. The spirit of Madonna House Institute is one of childlike simplicity. The spirit of Madonna House recognizes that the *duty of the moment* is expressed in hourly and daily needs.

> The spirit of Madonna House Institute is that the wish of the superior is, actually, the expression of the most holy will of God for us, second by second, minute by minute, hour by hour, day by day, week by week, year by year, until eternity!

> The spirit of the Institute is the spirit of little things done extremely well, with the exclusive motivation of the love of God.

This, dearly beloved, is it. It will take us a lifetime of prayer and practice to understand the height, the width, and the depth of this definition. There it is for all of us to see, to ponder, and grow into. Copy this. Like St. Francis's original constitution, it barely takes up a quarter of a written page

Let us try to review a bit what all this means. To live by the Gospel, without compromise, means to live the life of love. But to love means to die to self and live for others. It means to follow Christ's footsteps from Bethlehem to the tomb. This means to ask oneself, perhaps a thousand times a day, "How would Christ act, think, or feel if he were in my place — if he were I?"

To be childlike means not seeking to evade Calvary. The greatest problem in our Apostolate, and I guess in the Christian life, is that many times in our lives God gives us the grace to catch a glimpse of his reality — Someone Who loved us first. We must respond to that love by *loving him back*. This is what our faith is all about.

Childlike simplicity is this: not evading the Cross but being crucified on it and dying to self. Only thus can we love him back. So away with all the tortuous arguments and intellectual and spiritual rationalizations! The stark fact is that love is walking the straight line from where we stand now to the Cross. Love means not deviating one iota from the direct and shortest path between myself and Calvary. *This* is childlike simplicity in its most fundamental form.

To recognize the *duty of the moment*, as expressed by the needs of the Apostolate and our superiors, is to fulfill our vocation to the 9th degree. The motive for the fulfillment can only be *caritas*; for, again, this means death to self with a vengeance. The fruits will be *pax*. *Pax-Caritas* written on a cross, several lines on a quarter of a sheet of paper. There you have your vocation spelled out for you, personally, in God's primer of love. For he is truly the giver of your vocation and the Founder of our Institute.

Think about what I have written, dearly beloved. Discuss, read and meditate upon it. That is all there is to our vocation, but if we live those few lines to the hilt, there is no doubt, whatsoever, that we shall see God and be saints.

Lovingly yours in Mary,

POVERTY, HUMILITY, AND UNITY

June 20, 1959

Dearly Beloved,

Today I want to talk about our spirit of poverty.

Our constitution clearly states that any member can own and administer property. By property is meant:

(1) Money in a bank account.
(2) Money in stocks and bonds or other securities.
(3) Real Estate and income therefrom.
(4) Income from business that is managed by the family or by a trusteeship.
(5) Acceptance of any kind of inheritance in any of the above forms.

By administering is meant that any member of the Apostolate may sell stocks and securities, accept inheritance and invest income.

However, at the same time, our constitution clearly states that not a penny, of any holdings or savings accounts, may be spent *without the permission of superiors*. Therefore, our promise of poverty involves the *use of material goods*.

Here the Lord has provided us with a tremendous opportunity of practicing, not only the virtue of poverty, but many other allied virtues: humility, utter trust in superiors, childlike simplicity, deep spiritual awareness of details, great delicacy of conscience, lack of even the desire to get out from under all of this, and utter detachment from the pride of and desire for possessions, and detachment from the desire for independence.

Let us review these points a little. Let us start with humility: to be poor, one must be humble. This is why the poor will inherit the earth, for they are meek and humble like Christ. It means that one is going to be truthful too, for humility is truth. There will be no questions about *reporting* to one's superior even five cents given by a relative or friend.

It means accepting the word of that superior, regarding the

use of it, with childlike simplicity, openness, trust and *caritas*. It means repeating these acts of humility every time one receives anything. To do so, trust, the fruit of love (in this case for superiors), must be the handmaiden of humility. With this child-like simplicity should go great delicacy of conscience.

Let us take an example of this: Some members of our Madonna House family may be receiving one dollar a week or more from their friends or relatives. He or she might report this to the superior and ask permission to buy a record for the house. That does not mean that one can *presume* to buy a record *every week* for oneself or even for the house.

This also means that every time one receives *anything*, one comes humbly, with childlike simplicity, trust and love, asking what the superior wishes to do about it. If it is money, it could go to the common kitty, the vacation fund, or for a Mass. The full spirit of poverty demands a joyous acceptance of that decision. If that is lacking, then one should discuss the matter fully both with his superior (for one might become a scandal to the house and to others), as well as with his or her own spiritual director. Small as it may seem, it is a breach of the flaming spirit of poverty that should animate us. We should desire to bear its yoke fully for the love of Christ and our fellowmen.

To sum up the true spirit of poverty in our Institute, I would quote to you, dearly beloved, the words of St. John of the Cross: "The spirit of poverty consists in desiring nothing. . . . . Then one can joyfully accept all that one has and is given. . . . ."

To apply this saying of St. John to us, we do not, for instance, analyze or worry about our daily lives in the Apostolate. We do not discuss at all why one house is very nice, while another is very poor. Dearly beloved, you should not even desire another house's *poverty*. One can also make a god out of material poverty, instead of serving the *Lord* Who was poor.

No, we accept all that comes to us for the glory of God, with holy, joyous indifference and detachment. We strive to desire nothing and to accept what we have as coming directly from the hands of God, and to be joyous should he take it all away. Everyone agreed that this is the true definition of poverty accord-ing to the spirit of Madonna House.

The next question is a very important one. It concerns the role of men in the Apostolate and their relationship to women superiors. As I understand it, you gentlemen feel that you have a call to this vocation together with the women. Our twenty-nine years of history prove that it can work, provided you yourselves do not cut off your nose to spite your face with these constant discussions about women superiors, and "male" and "female" work. If you continue in this way, a simple thing will happen, and it is good for you to face it squarely: you will be separated canonically.

For instance, let us imagine this separation happening at Madonna House, Combermere. Obviously, the first step would be to build a completely separate training center for the men. It would have their own kitchen, chapel and recreation room. True, they would continue to work with the women. They would arrive around 9 a.m., work until 11:45 a.m. on maintenance jobs or what have you, and depart to their own premises for dinner. This "performance" would be repeated in the afternoon, then they would go back for their supper. That will finish the "common day". They would eat, recreate and pray together in all-male splendor. Their contact with their sisters in the Apostolate would be confined to work, because definitely they would be doing men's work, so their contacts would be reduced to a quick "hello" and "goodbye". The women, of course, would do likewise, and enjoy only each other's company and no one else's!

Now for the discussion of "male" and "female" work. Right away, you are confronted with the fact that the male also is a domestic animal, and there is nothing demeaning, nothing unmasculine about doing such things as cooking, sewing and nursing. Cast your eye upon the world in which we live, and in whose sorrows and joys we are supposed to share. In the most glamorous and expensive restaurants, men are the waiters. Waiting on table has deep, Christian connotations. The apostles themselves ordained deacons to wait on the tables of the poor and at the Eucharistic Feast, called in the early days, *agape*. This was their great privilege.

The best tailors are men. Even in the world of women's fashion, the great names are male not female. The best cooks are men. The best bakeries employ men, not women.

As to the point of being subjected to a woman, I think that you gentlemen are exaggerating the matter. After all, if this Vocation is for men and women, then the obedience that you render to your superior, young or old, male or female, is that of a son to his mother, or a daughter to her father. Superiors share in the grace of fatherhood and motherhood and to govern is to love.

Could it possibly be that the same objections that you have against obedience to a woman would still be there if the superior were a male? Could it be that, as yet, you have not completely surrendered your will to God and therefore, have a great difficulty surrendering it to any human being, whatever the sex? I am not judging. I am just asking. The answer will be found in yourselves, by speaking with God and your spiritual director.

One thing I point out to you very forcefully: if you continue to discuss, argue and object to the setup that you have now; if you fail to realize the source of the arguments about work being "male" and "female", then you will get what you are asking for — a totally separate Apostolate. Such discussions will tear apart this beautiful, new Apostolate, which unless it is lived in its fullness, will not be what God wants it to be. But if you discuss it constructively, with deep charity and objectivity, and cease to bring up arguments which are on an almost completely emotional level, then there is a chance that the vision I have from God and for which I fought the good fight for twenty-nine years, will be implemented forever.

It is up to you, dearly beloved. All I want to bring to your attention is the fact that there is a lot of loose talk unsupported by fact about this profound question. It is an emotional and immature approach. Also, the expression of your personal opinion to outside priests and bishops is dangerous for my vision which is the essence of the Apostolate.

All I want to say, is pray and think much, but say little outside the Apostolate. Discuss the matter constructively among yourselves, keeping in mind that you might *get* what you seem to wish, but which, in the long run, is not, perhaps, what God wants you to have. Because this is such holy ground, take your shoes off and walk softly. Walk in prayer and *caritas* for you have an awesome responsibility.

Lovingly yours in Mary,

ON MUSIC

June 1959

Dearly Beloved,

Today, I want to write about music, and its effect upon our emotions, minds, and souls.

It is very difficult to judge music effectively. Like all art, music is subjective. It will affect people differently depending upon their educational, cultural and social backgrounds. The history of music within a culture, as well as our own individual talents, plays an important part in our own music appreciation. Whether we are tone deaf, or have perfect pitch, will also influence our sensitivity to music. Memory plays a great part in the effect that music has on people. Certain pieces are associated with sad or joyful memories. One can often guess people's ages by the music that they select. All of these things can be taken into account on deciding what is good or bad music for the Apostolate; but these decisions will not always be easy to make.

All of the arts are apprehended through the senses. Painting comes through the eyes, music through the ears, and drama through them both. Music, passing through the senses, affects our emotions, minds and souls most forcefully. It has an immense power. Like all arts, it may lead us to hell or to heaven; may help to free us from earthly things and lift us into the realm of the spirit, or dash us into a literal hell, and surrender us almost completely into the hands of the devil. After the first World War, a piece called "The Black or Blue Sunday" had such a diabolical effect. It resulted in wholesale suicides in Europe. There are pieces of music that are used now as an accompaniment to the Black Mass by men who have lost all semblance to a human being and who, in an orgy of sensual desecration, openly worship the devil.

Man's dehumanization at the hands of the Communists, has been helped by the music of composers who sold themselves into the hands of evil powers. Wars, the sacrifices to Baal, the human sacrifice of Youth in the Persian and Indian Empires long ago, were all accomplished to the tune of music.

Music has sung of heaven and hell ever since man was created and began to sing. On the other hand, music accompanied the peaceful, pagan worship of God, as they understood him. What we call spirituals expressed the hope of the Negro slaves in the United States. Church music of early Christian times — Gregorian Chant and Eastern Rite music — lifts our spirits faster than any jet plane or rocket. Music is a stairway on which we climb into the presence of the All-Holy. We have sung of God in beautiful tones, with longing, hunger, joy and fervent prayer ever since we left Paradise.

Between these two extremes, music has expressed the infinite variety of types, and bestowed knowledge of things unseen. It has opened mysteries, painted sound pictures of love, passion, disappointment, happiness, goodness and evil. This is its creative function.

However, where there is good, there is evil; where there is day there is night. Music has been vulgarly prostituted to appeal to the lower emotions, and has made people addicts of sounds that fostered forgetfulness and catered to dreams that should not be dreamt. Such music has led only to one place — the street of broken dreams. It has perverted youth and dehumanized everyone. It has destroyed the image of God in man and left him bereft of reason, living through his senses only, like an animal.

These few words should help you to understand that in a lay Apostolate dedicated to the restoration of the whole man to Christ, music plays a tremendous role. It can be a "novice master" leading us to God, and a tool in the restoration of the whole man to Christ.

When I was in Harlem, some of the music was "classical". I do not agree that all classical music is good. "Geniuses" have written music for the Black Mass. Music can be "classical" in its horror, in its perverted beauty. Geniuses have written music that stimulated the mind; they have put our history to music. Some of it is good, some of it is bad. The label "*classical*" applies to many kinds of music, and does not always mean it is good.

When I came to Harlem, the youth especially, were drugging themselves with sensual music so as to "forget their pains and sorrows." What was I to do — I who was dedicated to the restoration of the whole man to Christ? Ban that music? Of course not. All I could do was to substitute better music, appealing to the music appreciation of the Negro people. I did so. Within nine years, there was an immense change in the youth who came to Friendship House. In order to affect that change, I had to determine what music to substitute and how to present it.

I will not go into a lengthy discussion of why men and women dedicated to God should be very careful of the music which they select, nor do I wish to discuss what should already be clear in the minds of superiors: that they are custodians of one of the most beautiful gifts in this world for molding people's emotions, minds and souls. Music can also help them to restore the world around them.

In selecting music, ask yourselves the following questions: Does this music arouse in you thoughts and emotions that lead you away from God? Does this music lead you into an escape from solving your problems? Does this music lead you into a web of forgetfulness of the cross as exemplified in your daily life? Does this music render you almost soulless for a moment or two, and lead you to that forgetfulness, and to a dreamy life that cannot be yours? If your answer is yes to any one of the above questions, it is the wrong music for you. But if it arouses in you a greater understanding of the beauty of God and his creation, and brings you closer to God in any form, then it is good music.

There is a depth in these two paragraphs that I want you to meditate upon. Next time you make your music selections, examine your consciences on these points.

Lovingly yours in Mary,

Catherine

ALL OR NOTHING AT ALL

July 10, 1959

Dearly Beloved,

Today, I want to discuss with you a very serious theme: vocations. It is time for us to consider the meaning of this important word. As the Apostolate grows, and experience accumulates, it is necessary to define the vocation of Madonna House more clearly.

A vocation is a call from God; on this we all agree. Its final clarification rests upon our being accepted by a superior. The Church, ever watchful, extends the period of probation, in our case, to almost eight years.

There are many reasons why a superior may dismiss someone during this time. Ill health is one of them. But with rare exceptions, a dismissal usually indicates that a person has been unfaithful to his vocation. What do we mean by being unfaithful to one's vocation? The answer stares us in the face. We behave in a manner which so affects the common good that, with sorrow in their hearts, the superiors must face the issue and dismiss that person. There is a theological and dogmatic law of God that *the individual good is subject to the common good.*

Have you ever projected yourself, at least in imagination, into the pain and suffering of a local director, or a director general, who is faced with this situation? Bending backwards in charity and mercy, they try to do the impossible: they try not to take this final step. But they are powerless before the free will of a person who insists on continuing to be unfaithful no matter how much is done for them, and no matter what the price.

There is much loose conversation in the Apostolate these days about *caritas* and mercy. Alas, even among senior members the words mercy and love are not yet fully understood.

Let us take, for instance, the imaginary case of a member who is bent upon doing his own will, and inwardly refuses to render full, open, trusting obedience to the superior. Can you count the hours that it would take, and has taken in some cases, to show this person the error of his ways?

In your estimation, should a superior, busy with the common good, and the works of the Apostolate, consume an infinite amount of time pointing out the obvious to a person who supposely has the promise of obedience?

What about this endless rationalization that goes on in the Apostolate? What about his refusal to face a very simple and obvious truth: you have come to this Apostolate to become a saint; you have a vocation to this particular Apostolate. The whole gist of your vocation, its heart and soul, is to accept completely, without holding anything back, the ways of this Apostolate. You have not come to change it. You can't. Those who have tried to do so have regretted it.

If an Apostolate exists with the approval of the Church, as ours does, it is then God's will. Thus anyone's rationalizations, gripes, discussions, interpretations are not directed against the superior, but against God, who in the final analysis, has instituted this particular Apostolate. Woe to him who fights God! Twice woe to him who dares, through word or deed to destroy the Apostolate by distorting its true nature in anyone's mind. He is trying to kill a work of God. He will not succeed, but the wrath of God will be upon him. Beware of it! These are extreme cases, I grant you, but they have happened in the past. Let us see that they don't happen in the future.

There are also other ways of destroying the Apostolate and one's vocation. There is the refusal to grow up emotionally. There is no reason for you to fail to grow in this way. You have been given more than many other people — certainly more than young people receive these days in preparation for marriage.

Consider for a moment the broad approach to emotional health which has been given to you, the courses you have benefited from, the individual attention of myself and your local superiors. Extreme care has been taken of your physical health. Priests have endeavored with infinite patience, to attend to your emotional, psychological, and spiritual needs. Without fear of a rebuttal, I dare paraphrase the words of Christ: ''Have you wanted anything?''

Later on, further opportunities for professional or intellectual training will open before you. All of this is given by the grace and goodness of God and his Blessed Mother, not by the superiors as such. We are only human beings, representatives of Our Lady and her Divine Son, from whom we also receive all that we have and are.

So I repeat: How long do you think that we should bear with immaturity, argumentativeness, moodiness? If you were a superior, how long would you put up with emotional immaturity that affects the common good? Well, I will answer that question for you: it wouldn't be very long; such emotional immaturity is a definite and clear sign that you are spoiling your vocation. This is ultimately between you and God. However, we do not have to endure indefinitely the effect of your actions upon the common good. This is my conclusion. If you consider it prayerfully before the face of God, you will understand it is the only conclusion possible.

God has chosen me. I might be a dung heap, and probably am; but who is there living who dares to question the choice of God if the Church Herself acknowledges it? The only thing that can be said in my favor, is that I have laid down my life for it. The results, among other things, are you — the members of this now, religious family of whom God is the Father. When you are admitted to this Institute, you are admitted to a vocation which comes from God, and of which I am the custodian.

Nothing is going to be changed about his vocation, not because it is mine, but *because it is God's*. You have to accept all of it, or you have to leave. There is no middle way, and there can be no compromise. All of you are in good mental and physical health. Your little emotional problems don't amount to a hill of beans, so you are able to face the naked truth as I have put it down on this piece of paper.

It was necessary that I should make everything crystal clear. I cannot have the individual good come ahead of the common good. Whether or not you can live up to this mandate which is being so clearly expressed — is between you and God. However, I am quite certain now that it is *all or nothing at all*. Should people persist in not realizing this, let them not be surprised if they receive a notice of dismissal. I still am custodian of the spirit, and it is my duty to watch over the common good.

This might sound harsh, but it is not; for love and mercy go with justice, God is perfect love and perfect mercy, but he is also just. That is why we shall be judged before him. That is why there is a hell, a purgatory and a heaven. If we persist in being untrue to God, and hence to ourselves, insisting upon our own way, not his, then we must accept the fact that love and merecy will render a just judgment.

I love you as much as a human heart can love anybody, and my compassion truly is boundless. Compassion is but another word for mercy; but I realize that love is just. If I were not just, then I would not truly love or be truly compassionate.

In his infinite mercy and justice,
Lovingly yours in Mary

THE NATURE OF MAN AND WOMAN

August 3, 1959

Dearly Beloved,

Today, I should like to discuss the nature of man and woman. Recently, we were most fortunate in having Dr. Voyer* give us a lecture on this important subject. I should like to share some of his ideas.

He first spoke of the *nature of man*. Man, he said, represents the will of the Father — in fact is a reflection of God, the Father. What God the Father is to all of creation, man is to his family. It is through God the Father that he receives the fecundity to be a Father, and to beget children. Because he has received this privilege to co-create with God, he is called father.

As a father, he must provide for his family. What God does for the universe man does for his human family. God provides for eternity; man for a short space of time. Therefore man expresses the will of the Father by *being* a father. To be a father, he must be a creator, and a provider. He leaves the home and returns to it bringing not only food, but new views for a better life. He seeks better ways of serving and loving God and sanctifying himself and his family. Like God the Father, he is the protector, the final authority and the head of the family.

To be all of these things, he must be strong, stable and in full control of his intellect, will and emotions. He must be strong enough to allow the rest of the family to lean on him. Since God the Father is love, mercy and tenderness, so man, must possess these virtues in a great measure. His very virility is always expressed in that love, that tenderness, that mercy and that understanding.

Because of this important role, he must be guided first by faith, then by reason. He must also be meek with the terrible strength of which Christ spoke so beautifully: "Learn of me, for I am meek and humble of heart." If he abdicates any one of these

*Dr. Voyer was a well-known Montreal psychiatrist and a good friend of Madonna House.

virtues, he will not conform to the nature of man, will not express the will of the Father, and will not pass on the Word to his family as he should.

You might think that this applies only to the vocation of marriage, but this is not true. These same traits of tenderness, strength, the ability to provide, protect, and cherish, and the possession of a deep faith that illuminates reason so it is in union with the will of the Father, must also be the characteristics of any man embracing celibacy. His fecundity will not be lessened by his celibacy, but will be channeled into the fatherhood of souls.

Thus, in our Apostolate, the men will be spiritual fathers to many, whom they will cherish and feed with the example of their strength, meekness, humility and simplicity. They feed them too with the fruits of their manual and intellectual labor. They will also be protectors of the women. They will carry the heaviest burden of the Apostolate which is to make a pathway through the jungle of the marketplace so the women can follow and walk by their sides.

The nature of the woman is to bear the children of the man and to mother them. She is eminently fitted to be a helpmate and companion to man. She provides a deep and profound intuitiveness and interiority which is contemplative by nature, and her motherhood which should flower into the making of a home. She functions emotionally, but in a more spiritual sense of the word. She clothes the Word of the Father with flesh so that children can understand. Thus she repeats the work of Mary, into whose womb the Word descended and was clothed with flesh.

Again, the nature of a woman who has embraced celibacy, has the same characteristics as the married woman. She clothes the ''word'' of the Apostolate in a more living ''understandable'' flesh than man can. She too, receives her fecundity from God the Father through the priests of the Apostolate, and bears children of her spirit even as men do of theirs.

You might, at this point, raise the sixty-four dollar question: If this is so, theogically speaking, then how is it that, in our Apostolate, women direct men? I would say that this happens often in life. Children of both sexes are directed by a Mother and Father. Our Apostolate is men and women working together even as a family is. If the nature of men and the nature of women as we have been discussing it, is lived out in our Apostolate, it will grow invincibly strong. Let us remember that Christ was subjected to

Mary for many years of his life, and that often the men of our Apostolate will follow this same pattern by being subject to a woman too.

At this point, Dr. Voyer, who has had many dealings with sick youth, made an interesting observation. He traced the emotional sickness of adolescents and young people to their father's abdication of their fatherhood. Because the men rejected the responsibility of their fatherhood, women rejected their womanhood. Examples of this are: the pegged pants of modern girls, the flat-heeled ballet shoes, the untidy hair, the sloppy sweaters, all of which reveal a rejection of their femininity. He went on to state that menstrual pains, as well as emotional binges, stem from the woman's rejection of her sex. She definitely did not want to be female. This particular monthly event reminds her of it. Why does she resent being female? Because her particular father did not accept his manhood, hence he was not an expression of God the Father to her. With adolescent boys, this took shape, sometimes, of the utter inability to pray the great prayer of Christ: "Our Father". He had patients who could not do it, and who rejected their sonship of God because their father was not a real father.

Much food for thought in all this, friends, is there not? Think it over.

Lovingly yours in Mary,

SHARING SOME INSIGHTS

August 22, 1959

Dearly Beloved,

I would like to share a lecture given to us by Dr. Odenwald, the psychiatrist.* It was very good. He spoke on neuroses and showed us, with a great clarity, how neuroses are caused by the ignorance of parents. The greatest insight that he gave to us, in my estimation, was this: if the neurotic would consider his anxieties and depression as the permissive will of God, he would cure himself. He must look at the symptoms of his neuroses as a cross shaped by the very hands of Christ and placed by him on his shoulders. He should seek proper medical help for the cause of his neuroses, but, in faith, he should bear the symptoms *simply* and *joyfully*. With this attitude, the symptoms should disappear, and in disappearing, help to eliminate their cause.

Dr. Stern* in two lectures, had given us the two principles which animate the world: male and female. He said that the female principle, and hence the woman, is a mystery who moves with the forces of nature. Her menstrual periods come monthly, even as the phase of the moon. Pregnancy takes nine months and cannot be hurried. Nature has its own rhythm in the feeding of the infant at the breast and in his growth. The woman, therefore, is passive and attuned to nature. She is the guardian of all that is natural and moves as nature does.

The male element, or the man, by nature, must delve into mysteries of all kind. His nature is to penetrate, conquer and dominate.

When man complements woman and woman complements man, there is peace. When the male element dominates, as it does now through intellect and technology, and the intuitive, myste-

*Dr. Odenwald was a well known psychiatrist in the United States.
*Dr. Stern was a famous psychiatrist in Montreal.

Both were good friends of Madonna House.

rious, female element is in the background, civilization is threatened with annihilation.

Dr. Odenwald said that one of the greatest tragedies, psychologically and spiritually speaking, was the "emancipation of woman". Women sought to compete with men on equal basis — as it were, to ape men. The result was the breaking up of women's oneness with nature and with God. It unleashed the destructive conquering and intellectual principle, which wants to master science for science's sake, and make science a God instead of worshipping the God of science.

He also said that such women are apt to beget feminine men and masculine women, and that the disorder within the woman is so great that civilization is threatened with a catastrophe as we are well aware.

He then pointed out the reason why there are so many women in Madonna House, is that the feminine principle must be restored in the world, and we are doing that here. The work of the Holy Spirit, he said is to restore the balance of the sexes.

Having those great men here helped everyone but especially me. They brought a fresh stimulus to Madonna House and they also gave me a postgraduate course in psychiatry.

Lovingly in Mary,

FEAR AND FAITH

September 26, 1959

Dearly Beloved,

I have been thinking about fear — about its place in our spiritual lives. There are good fears and bad fears, and both have to be faced. The first needs to be nourished, and the second vanquished. Scripture tells us that "perfect love casts out all fears." To live by these words is the beginning of true wisdom, and growth in "perfect love".

However, today I just want to discuss, in the light of the Apostolate, the thousands of fears that impede our peace of mind, break up our sleep, and weaken us both spiritually and emotionally. Human fears are born of weak faith, and in an inability to abandon ourselves to Divine Providence.

There is the very human fear that women have of evil men who walk in the night. There is the somewhat emotional fear of cockroaches, and other crawling things. There is the fear of drunks, the fear of the dark, unlighted streets, and the fear of sex perverts.

You and the young people who come to Madonna House talk with a lump in your throats about the young martyrs behind the Bamboo and Iron Curtain. Stars come to your eyes. This also happens when Charles de Foucauld and his Fraternities of Little Brothers and Sisters are discussed. One begins to think that this would be a greater vocation, than Madonna House.

You love to hear me talk about the old days of Harlem and Portland Street when we had bedbugs, and when the Communists threw stones at us and fought us. I told you also about when Flewy's collar bone was broken, and when a stone hit me in the temple and I bled. There are stars of vicarious identification in your eyes when I talk about the prostitute who held a revolver to my head; about one-eyed Joe with his razor held two inches before my eyes; about my being held up one night in Toronto by two guys who had shared supper at Friendship House only a few hours before. Many of you have been heard to say, "Gee, it is dull around here, now! All of the excitement has gone out of life!"

Has it? Aren't there many of you in Madonna House and in our missions who lie awake at night listening to footsteps outside? Aren't you nervous about prowlers, and terrified of rape, or just of people who might break in?

Why those fears? Isn't God the all-powerful and almighty Father? Haven't you gone there out of love for his Son whom you serve in the poor? Don't you wish, at times, that you could live in greater poverty and simplicity like the Fraternities of Charles de Foucauld, with less furniture to clean, less floors to polish, less clothes to care for?

Why don't you face the reality of identifications with the

poor, which is so much at the heart of the spirit of Madonna House and its foundress — a simple reality of cockroaches, bedbugs, and other unpleasant insects? Many of you might not have them, but some may. You, of course, are privileged in that you may buy things to kill them. This you should do for the sake of health and cleanliness. But perhaps some time you will have to live in such quarters where you will just have to endure these things. The poor have to live in places where the whole house and neighborhood are infested with rats, mice, and other things which cannot be eliminated. How far does your identification go? Do you deal only with pleasant superficialities that give you a glow of righteousness and a halo of imaginary sanctity? I hope not!

Identification with the poor! I think I read to some of you about the latest foundation of the Little Sisters of Charles de Foucauld. They went to live in a sampan. This is a flat boat the Chinese used to carry their goods to market. On the deck, in one corner, there is a room or two for the family. There is little transport these days so the boats have become very old. They are now the dwellings of many refugees in China. They are moored at the entrance of Hong Kong near old, dilapidated quays or waterfronts. The Little Sisters of Charles de Foucauld bought a boat and they live on it. It is moored between other ordinary Chinese sampans.

The police of Hong Kong rarely go there, for they know that poverty and despair breed criminals. They are only there if they are searching for a major criminal, and then they go not in twos or threes, but in tens or twenties. It is truly dangerous ground. Murderers, prostitutes, and perverts become bestial due to this poverty. Young women have worked among these dregs of society, unprotected and alone for the love of God. They are peaceful and without fears, I hear. "Perfect love casts out all fear." They seem to possess this love. They are from various countries and none are over thirty.

That is faith! We have gone into those dangerous places guided by holy prudence, which is the fruit of love. It is this love which drives us, and which drove the Little Sisters to their life on a boat. This love proves that we, being in the state of grace, have within our souls, the Indwelling Trinity, Father, Son and Holy Spirit. Where the Trinity dwells, there also dwells Our Lady of the Trinity. We have our angel guardians to protect us, our patron saints, to look after us, and the Providence, love and care of God to protect us. "For my Father, Who is in heaven, has counted every hair of your heads." Do we believe this, and believing, act accordingly, and sleep in peace, not listening to any footsteps, not wondering or worrying, oh ye of little faith?

When I went to gather information for the book *Dear Bishop* every one of the bishops, Bishop Sheil especially, understood that I was going into the type of danger that we are discussing, for I was going into the dregs of the large cities. Bishop Sheil told me all that I have just told you. Although I knew it anyway. However, it was a benediction to hear it from his lips. Then he added: "Moreover, Catherine, have faith also in the theological truth that there are angels to answer your calls and protect you. By angels, I mean the seraphim and the cherubim, angels and archangels, powers and principalities. When in danger, call on them, especially Saints Michael and Gabriel and your own angel guardian, and they will come tumbling down — a power beyond your understanding." Do *you* call on them? If not, you should. Call, and sleep in peace.

A year or so after we opened the Chicago house around 1941, two young Grail girls, twenty blocks away, in the darkest part of the Southside of Chicago, opened Blessed Martin House for neglected Negro children. It was a large storefront, and they had their apartment above it. One night, a man entered, terrorized them, and raped one. The second one finally found her voice to scream and the intruder fled. Both girls were in their mid-twenties. The police and the priest came. The girls were rushed to the hospital and given treatment. Cardinal Stritch visited them. (It was the talk of the town, as you can imagine.) He asked if they wanted to close the house. Both, with tears in their eyes, begged to return, and to live as before, without protection. He was very edified, and allowed them to do so. When they returned, the parish priest reported over two hundred conversions because of their courage.

We dream dreams of being martyred in China, or of being confessors to the faith. These are good dreams. But let us enflesh them with love in the reality of the moment.

So let us be at peace and sleep more soundly then we ever did before, in utter love, faith and trust in Divine Providence. We must remember that the difference between a confessor and martyr is that the confessor is one who has been hurt for Christ's sake, but has not died; a martyr is one who has died. Maybe God is putting some of us through the novitiate of being confessors to the faith before he allows us to be martyred.

It would never do to lie awake, to be nervous, to be upset and tense about things like that, for the aim of our Institute, is *identification with the poor*. The poor have to face these things all of their lives.

So let us not only dream dreams of glory and wistfully wish that we had been part of the "good old pioneering days" of Friendship House and Madonna House. Let us be pioneers in faith, love and trust. Let us pioneer in having that perfect love that casts out all fears. We have no right to waste the hours of sleep that refresh us because of the lack of faith, trust and love and silly little fears that don't amount to a row of beans. No, we have no right to do that, for we must sleep well to work well for the Lord.

Yes, I wanted to talk to you about fears. Here is a little poem to close my letter and help you examine your conscience about all someone has said:

> Courage does not lie
> Alone in dying
> For a cause. To die
> is only giving.
> Courage is to feel
> the daily daggers
> of relentless steel
> *and go on living*.

Lovingly yours in Mary,

CORRECTION AND CRITICISM

October 10, 1959

Dearly Beloved,

Greetings! For a long time I have been promising myself to write you a letter on the difference between correction and criticism.

Why should such an idea come to me? Why should such a theme suddenly appear in a letter? If you were to think for a moment, you would realize that this theme has been just begging to be clarified for quite a while. One of the graces that God gives to those whom he places in charge of others, is the grace of timing; and I feel That now is the time to discuss correction and criticism.

Let us take the example of correcting young people these days. Emotionally disturbed people come to us wounded by ignorance, scientific and social upheavel, and by the psychological effects of the endless wars going on in the world. These crises pollute the very air we breathe with tensions and stresses. They create insecurity in everyone.

Yes, people come who are tense, and who have a host of unresolved emotional problems, creating within them a self-centeredness that staggers the imagination. Yet they also come with a desire to give themselves to love and to the love of neighbor in one of the hardest Apostolates. For Madonna House demands maturity of emotions, and of the mind and soul. It demands the ability to make decisions, to take responsibility, to get rid of unnecessary fears, and to realize that we are the carriers of Life, of Truth — Christ — in a world gone mad with fear, confusion and much ignorance.

We have realized that, because of all these factors, the first year of formation is often a wasted year, as far as any spiritual or academic progress is concerned. We have proof of this. Over and over again, many amongst you have begged to listen a second time to the many lectures. A year later, you realized, as we did, that what you "learned" the first year barely penetrated because of your unresolved emotional problems. Because of the self-centeredness, you were incapable, in most cases, of absorbing what was given to you. The mental hygiene lectures were especially difficult for you, because they touched you deeply. Due to a very natural and normal ignorance of what makes a person tick, you fought inwardly and emotionally (and often with deep hostility in some cases), the very knowledge which would set you free from the prison of emotion and self. No wonder abstract, academic thoughts just flitted in one ear and out the other, without leaving much impression. Now, you began to realize that if you had not come to Madonna House, your life could have been pretty tragic in many ways. For whatever vocation you would have chosen, could have been in danger of being wrecked by those unresolved emotional problems.

But God was good to us all. We now realize that the first year must be spent in solving, in resolving, and in eliminating these emotional blocks which practically everyone who comes to Madonna House has.

This is especially clarified for us this summer when three great psychiatrists stayed with us, each for a week, and gave us so generously of their tremendous knowledge. They confirmed the data we had gathered about you, and emphasized again and again the need for clarification on this emotional level. They said that we would waste our time and yours by giving you a heavy curriculum before resolving these emotional blocks. For only after these are resolved can you really absorb teachings.

With this long introduction, we return to timing and the difference between criticism and correction. People with emotional blocks, who are therefore, supersensitive, confuse these two words. They see criticisms as knives of arrows directed at them personally. Because of their subconscious feelings of guilt, inadequacy, and inferiority, they violently resent criticisms and corrections. Only emotionally mature people welcome both.

Let us examine these words:

correction means to straighten out, to make strong, to help eliminate faults of character, of posture and of soul. It means mostly to make straight, make well, strengthen.

criticism is an intellectual exercise that helps people arrive at better, sounder results — a better book, better behavior, and so on. It keeps government alert. Literary critics prod writers to give their best, for the authors know that they'll be getting intelligent criticism from others. Without criticism, people would get into a rut.

Negatively speaking, criticism can be classified as nagging, uncharitable, faultfinding. Thus, if you examine the true meaning of these words, you will see that they are good words, but to an emotionally disturbed person, they are often hurtful.

Now, let us take these words from another angle, a spiritual angle — the one that interests us so much in the Apostolate. Here we are, people definitely called by God to a definite vocation which embraces the state of perfection as a lay person. What is perfection in the mind of God and of the Church? It is *caritas*, of course. Our faith is a love affair between the soul and God, in which God loved us first, and we love him back because we have been created to do so. We have been created to love and serve him in our neighbor, so that we might enjoy union with him in the Beatific Vision for all eternity.

What must we do to get there? We must become saints. Saints are perfect souls without blemish. How do we become souls without blemish? By obeying the commandments, poverty, chastity, and obedience. This means getting rid, not only of mortal sin, but of habitual venial sin and all of our imperfections as well.

We do not realize *all* of our faults. Most of us think that we are better than we are, easily excuse ourselves, and see ourselves in a rosy light. So the first thing we must do in order to fulfil our destiny (and in our case, our glorious vocation), is to find ourselves a spiritual director, who will relentlessly point out our failings, especially the ones that impede our eternal salvation. In our words, we must seek someone who will *criticize* and *correct* us constantly, in the right sense of these two words.

In the natural order of things, when there is no special vocation, the Lord uses life itself as the novitiate. Some people become very holy in this novitiate, if they listen to the voice of God within them; if little by little they are obedient to the duty of the moment in their particular state of life, and perform that duty exclusively for the love of God. Alas, such cases are rare on the whole. One reason is that most people cannot criticize nor correct themselves, and therefore, have not been liberated from their emotional prisons.

In the case of those called to a consecrated life (and these are the lucky ones), he gives another human being who represents him — one who has been tried in the vocation and chosen to lead others in it. Such people are duty bound to correct every little fault of those entrusted to them. Unless they do so, they will go to hell, which, of course, none of them want to do. If they don't correct, they will be lacking in *caritas* for those whom God has placed under their care.

Because so often in the past you have been corrected without love, you do not yet fully understand the difference between *correction* and *criticism*. Criticism, a negative sense, (the sense you are most accustomed to in the world), is often done with an intent to hurt. Constructive criticism, on the other hand, is a fruit and sign of deep love and friendship.

Constructive criticism can be directed to improve such things as politics, government, the condition of a family, the work of students or religious life. Such then, is the nature of criticism.

Now let us look at *correction*. One type of correction is that which comes from someone in authority who has special grace to do this: parents, teachers, superiors, and employers, spiritual directors and parish priests. Should you come into a position of authority, then it will become your duty to correct others even though you yourself will always be under spiritual direction.

There is another form of correction — *fraternal correction* which is from an equal to an equal, and it is another fruit of charity. Someone does or says something that is against the Spirit of the Apostolate. A member who observes this should gently and charitably correct him, and show him the error of his ways, for the betterment of his soul.

Now what should your attitude to correction be? Again I remind you of the words of Thomas Merton regarding superiors: A superior must be worthy of being a superior, but no human being is worthy. Only Christ is worthy. He knows that. That is why he is *in* every superior. So when all is said and done, you must grow in *faith*. Pray constantly for that growth, for it is not easy to see Christ in human beings on all levels of our Apostolate, especially in the temporary superior of a given job. However, that is what you must do: grow in faith and pray for the faith to always see Christ in your superior. This requires emotional maturity, an open heart, mind and soul. We must pray for the grace to even *welcome correction* because it leads to union with God.

Why have you been called to this vocation? To become saints. You have many helps that other people, even those who are walking the road to sanctity with giant strides, never dream of having. First, and foremost among these means is correction by superiors, and your cheerful, humble, intelligent acceptance. Without correction you wouldn't go to heaven, and you might go to hell.

So you must pray for grace to obey and follow advice punctiliously. Only then will Christ grow in you. You came for that. Why resent it? Your superiors would be greatly at fault if they didn't correct you.

In our Apostolate, constructive criticisms are most welcome; we welcome, for instance, constructive criticisms on ways and means of performing a task. We are glad to hear constructive ideas about your training; about articles being written, about how to communicate among us better. All of these things are constantly open to intelligent, constructive criticism which can help the growth and the health of the Apostolate.

We are certainly against nagging, faultfinding, criticism. This tears the fabric of charity.

This has been a long letter; but it is important that you who are growing in maturity should be open to, even glad of, correction and indulge only in constructive criticism. That is why I devoted a whole letter to this topic. Unless we understand these two concepts, charity might die amongst us.

Lovingly yours in Mary,

AWAITING THE DESIRED ONE

November 26, 1959

Dearly Beloved,

Today, I want to discuss the meaning of this wondrous season that we are entering: Advent, the days of expectation, of awaiting the Desired One.

I ask myself: Do we really desire the Lord? To desire something is to be constantly absorbed in that desire.

The other day, someone asked me a tremendous question. She said: "Catherine, why is it so difficult to understand love? You tell us that you *love* us. I see that you do, that you spend every waking hour in service. I feel your love everywhere; I go into the dispensary and I realize that you begged for all these drugs. Because of you, there is a nurse to look after me. I know that you begged for money for the farm, for the seeds, for fertilizers. Because of you, people came to run that farm. I know that everything that I use here all comes through your loving care by your begging.

"I realize that every morning you notice our tiredness, or our well-being and act accordingly. I know that you place us in jobs best suited for us. All this I see, plus the fact that you, the priests and Mr. D.* are always available. These should be proofs of love enough for me. Yet, I don't believe, *emotionally*, that this is real. So I'm looking for what's behind the racket. My emotions tell me that it is impossible for a human being to be like this. I have never known that kind of love. I feel it is all a dream, and so I'll wake up."

I tell this story to show how we human beings often act toward God. I told this little volunteer: "Yes, I understand this. You have never known what love is, in the reality of your young life, and so it is hard for you to see the face of love." Doesn't this same story apply to us? It seems to me that it does.

We, in the Apostolate, who have received so much more than this volunteer, have *we* finally recognized the face of love? The

*Edward Doherty, husband of Catherine.

real answer to that volunteer would be: "Oh child, how could I help but love you, since in your face I see the Face of the one my soul desires above all."

This should be our lives — our Advent, the expectation of the coming of him whom our heart loves, first in each other, and then in those whom we serve.

Recently, in various discussions, several points have emerged. We have come to the conclusion that the following is a blueprint for sanctity in Madonna House:

To realize that Madonna House is an Apostolate of *little things well done for the love of God.*

This Apostolate will not be implemented unless we *trust* and love our superiors.

Next, this trust and openness must extend to *one another.* Eddie* is writing a book. Recently, he read a chapter to us. He described how a life composed of little things can lead to immense things. Briefly, what has my life been for twenty-nine years? It has been composed of answering letters, working in the library, sorting, training, filing, organizing. Little, little, little things done over and over again, often the same things even to answering the same little questions everyone asks. Few ask new questions! Yet, when we look back, these little "bricks" one placed on top of the other have built eight houses, and the impact of the Apostolate is felt far and wide.

At Marian Centre, we are engaged in humble tasks such as washing dishes, writing thank-you letters and working in the clothing room. Yet, someone from Edmonton recently passed through here and told us of the impact that Marian Centre has on the city of Edmonton.

At Stella Maris House in Portland, Oregon*, we answer phones and doorbells, mimeograph endlessly and file constantly. We cook and listen to people — all little things, really. Yet, one of the priests there said: "It is fantastic to think that four young people in love with God can affect this city so much!" Yes, we live a life of little things, and big things come forth from that littleness.

But just the doing of these little things well is not enough. At this holy season of Advent, let us go deeply into our hearts, minds

*Edward Doherty, husband of Catherine.

*For a number of years, Madonna House had an active house in Portland and later a Prayer House but both have been closed.

and souls. Let us clean house, and make a loving manger for the Christ Child into which he can be born in all his splendor.

One thing that can prevent this is looking at the world from the narrow cell of self. I suggest that for this Advent that we remove from our vocabularies, from our conversations, our thoughts and, if possible, from our dreams, the sentences: "I feel," "I want," and "I would like" and replace them with: "What does *God* want of me?" I can truthfully say that if this change of attitudes, took place, life in the Apostolate would really take a giant leap toward *pax* and *caritas*, and hence toward happiness and joy.

I confess that I shiver a little when someone says: "Catherine, I *feel* I'm still worried about my vocation." "Catherine, I *feel* this is too much for me." "Catherine, I *feel* that I would be better off in some other department, some other house, some other place." Don't you think, dearly beloved, that the time has passed for you to worry about your vocations; to worry about what you are doing or where you are? Feelings do not matter. They are a cross we must carry. It won't be a very large cross. So let us stop thinking about "what I want", and begin to think what "God wants". If we did, we would be so much happier, and our Advent would be glorious.

Another point I should like to mention is time. Time is the most precious thing that has been given to us. Our own language recognizes this. You can *waste time, use time properly*, have a *good time*, have a *bad time*, and you can *redeem time*. It is something very precious. Are we aware that this time is a gift of God? We have already given God our bodies in chastity, our wills in obedience, and our desires for comfort, in poverty. But are we now going to think that we still *own time*? That would be foolish, would it not? Yet, many of us still think that time belongs to us. We forget that perhaps, the next minute we may be dead. God, alone is the Master of time. We have received it from him, and we must leave it in his hands.

What does this mean for our daily living? It means that when we walk through the blue door of Madonna House, we have left all of our rights outside, including the right to our own time. We are not entitled to days off. There is no time off from God. If some time is given to us to attend to our needs, we thank him for it. If it is given to work for him, we thank him for it. We must not be clock-watchers.

If we are employed commercially, we should be the first to be on a job and the last to leave. We do not take a worldly attitude to our work wherever it may be. We do not departmentalize, as the world does. Charity has no boundaries. No one can say in the Apostolate, that I'm not going to answer the telephone or the doorbell because I'm working in the office or the kitchen. Nor can anyone say I will answer so many bells and let others do the rest. No, we will answer them all, for we are in love with God, who is in that lazy nurse and in the patient who needs me. The same applies to all of our houses.

Yes, let this Advent be a *journey inward* for all of us. The time has come to really implement little things done with great love for the sake of Christ. Then our minds, hearts, and souls will become a lovely manger in which the Lord can be born, and a wondrous place where he can grow to full stature. When he does, we shall know happiness supreme.

Lovingly in Mary,

AWAKEN! BE MINSTRELS OF LOVE!

December 1959

Dearly Beloved,

Greetings, and a holy Advent to you. May you go deeply into the heart of this holy season. As you do so, you will enter the immense, flaming heart of the Christ Child whose Birthday is fast approaching. When you reach his heart, then everything that is not of him will fall away like old, worn-out garments. You will be filled with him and become like him. Your life will be a fire that will renew the earth. He who dwells in the heart of God is aflame with love, and sets on fire everyone he touches.

I imagine you listening to the reading of this opening paragraph. There might be some amongst you who will say with a weary sigh: "Here is our Catherine again, starting her Christmas letter to us on a dramatic, Russian note!" Some will like it, and some won't: but because you love me, and I know that you do, you will bear with me. To those who do not always like "dramatic openings," I'll put the same thought in good, everyday Americanese or Canadianese. It will go something like this:

I wish you a good Advent which means we go deeply into the significance of this liturgical season. The word *advent* means *coming*. Whose coming do we expect? The answer is simple: *Christ's*. This very simplicity is awesome.

If he comes, then we who call ourselves Christians, especially we, who have dedicated ourselves to be his followers, should make ourselves ready to greet him. Are we ready? Have our hearts really touched his heart in the sense that we are forgetting *ourselves* more and more? Are we remembering to love, and obey no matter what the emotional cost? Are we finally succeeding in making a cross of our emotional problems? Are we putting it on our shoulders ready to go to Bethlehem? Are we walking the path he has laid out for us — the strange path of the monotonous, little duties of every day, that could become gifts more precious than those of the Three Wise Men?

What are these little things? Here is a short list: dishwashing, filing, running from one meeting to another, answering doors and telephones, dealing with uncouth or difficult people, facing hopeless situations in schools or catechetical centers. Yet, all of these could become a cascade of precious gems, of gold too heavy to bear, of grains of incense that would cover the earth, *if only our hearts touched his Heart, and generously opened themselves to being loved by him and loving him in return.*

Now that I have explained myself in plain language(!), my Russian heart craves to resume the language of poets and minstrels. I give you a little poem that I wrote last night. It also speaks of Advent and about how I think of you and love you. It may help you to realize what I mean.

Is Advent a time of waiting — a time of
learning to sing lullabies?

But where to go, and where to learn to sing
songs to God, a Child?

Is then Advent also a time of walking on
pilgrimage to learn how to sing songs to
the Holy Child?

Or is it still-time, faith-time, time spent
awaiting some holy minstrel to come my way?

Lo, what is this, and who is knocking in the
dark night upon my door? Oh! It is only a tree
branch heavy with newly fallen snow.

The hour is late and I am sleepy. But the
wind is high, the knocking louder. I'd better
go to shake the branch loose of its heavy load
of snow.

Oh! night of wonder! The wind is singing a melody
of peace and joy. Its harps are trees snow-laden.
And tender bushes changed by cold into a million
bells that keep ringing lullabies the wind composed
to Christ the Child.

Awake, my soul, and listen. The Mother sends
her Spouse to teach you this Advent all the
Christmas songs you wanted so ardently to sing to
her own Son!

Yes, it was a little poem that I wrote last night, but it has a
deep meaning for me which I rather clumsily try to pass on to you,
my dearly beloved spiritual children everywhere.

I see you as musical instruments perfectly attuned to the will
of God, and becoming a beautiful symphony. This music pene-
trates places where the only other sounds are the voices of angry,
frightened people who do not know God and care less about him. I
think of you as minstrels, learning to sing lullabies to Christ the
Child. I think of you as notes in this beautiful melody of the Holy
Spirit. I listen to these notes one by one, hoping and praying that
each will be clear and true. The notes of your songs are your daily
work and your attitudes. I pray that no sour notes ever enter your
songs to the Christ Child.

I think of you as young trees and bushes adorned as brides
and bridegrooms for a wedding feast, adorned as only God can

clothe nature and the people who love him. I see you attuned to the Holy Spirit, the Great Wind, the ineffable Composer of the right songs that the Holy Child likes to hear.

I see you cherished by his Mother, who waits for you to come and share not only her Christmas joy in the stable of Bethlehem, but her whole life, so hidden and wonderful. It is she who has called us to imitate the lives of the Holy Family in Nazareth. Theirs was a humble and hidden life, composed of ordinary little things, but oh, how well done, and with great love!

Lately, I have been possessed by a holy impatience. As I always do in Advent, I've been praying frequently to the Infant, asking him over and over again for one grace; growth in faith for all of us. Because growth in faith means growth in love, humility, obedience, patience and joy. Growth in faith means growth in openness and trust with directors and with each other. Oh, it means so much — this request of mine! It means that our Apostolate could become a *hallway of heaven*, another Bethlehem, another Nazareth.

However, I know that in order that this take place, all of us must go through Golgotha. So I pray that we may each joyously accept the cross that God has prepared for us on the hills of love. Growth in faith means that we will understand the mystery of God's words: "He who loses his life will save it." Growth in faith also means an understanding of the vision of the whole of the Apostolate. It means to comprehend that we have been called to this lovely, hidden, simple and ordinary vocation in order to set the world on fire with the love of God.

I believe, with a flaming belief, that this is possible. I believe that we, weak as we are, filled with neuroses and self-centredness, can and will set the world on fire, if we pray and love enough. For God is never outdone in generosity. So at eventide before the Infant in the little chapel, I pray ceaselessly for the implementation of this vision. His love impels us.

Did you ever think how fortunate we are to be able to bring gifts to Christ the Child in the Brothers Christopher,* in the Mexican children, in the men and women who pass by our windows, in all whom we contact. It truly doesn't matter where, for the Christ Child is in everyone, and God has given us the privilege of welcoming him in so many. So let this Christmas be a

*The word used by the Apostolate for the men who came to us in need.

thanksgiving lullaby that wells up from our hearts to Christ the King.

He touches us daily in Communion. We must be like the loaves of bread that he blessed and broke. We must multiply ourselves around his cribs so as to make up for those who are not there. Many are there, but he is lonely for those who are not. Realize, dearly beloved, we *can* multiply ourselves if we love enough!

So, on the threshold of this new year, let us try to begin anew. Let us carry the cross of our emotional wounds on our backs. Let us really begin to live in him, for him and through him. Truly he is worthy of our love. Nothing on earth or in heaven matters except God. See how he comes to us in a wooden manger, proclaiming his love even before he can speak our language. Notice the wood in the manger. How he loves wood! He chose it as a Crib, and then he chose to work with it as a carpenter. Finally he died on wood. All this for love of us!

Christmas is at hand. Since we are poor in worldly goods, Alleluia! Let us bring him our hearts purified from the cross of self; hearts that at least try to understand his love for us. Let us have only one passionate desire — to love him back personally, in every human being we meet.

For the forthcoming Christmas of 1959, and for the new year, as yet unborn, I pray that you receive this passionate love, this flaming desire to set the world on fire for him. During this Advent, may your souls be awake, listening and attuned to the songs the Wind will compose for you to sing.

Lovingly yours in the Divine Child,
the Holy Spirit and in Mary

CONNECTING PHYSICAL THINGS WITH SPIRITUAL TRUTHS

January 14, 1960

Dearly Beloved,

This morning I had one of those inner shocks which come to me once in a while and envelop me in a mantle of fear and trembling before the Lord. Yesterday, Alma, my assistant, asked my permission to gather all the clothing which had accumulated in the Madonna House basement. This morning there was literally a mountain of clothing and miscellaneous articles, plus a barrel of footwear. There were also quite a few handicraft items. And alas! An all too familiar scene was once more reenacted during the meal. Item by item, things were lifted up for ownership to be declared. What was so tragic about it all was that the majority of offenders were not younger people, but seniors and juniors.

That is when the mantle of fear and trembling fell upon my soul. It seemed to me that I was lying prostrate before the Lord, and that with a sad and severe countenance he was saying to me: ''Behold, you have failed to teach them two things: the relationship between such thoughtlessness and sanctity, and the relationship between tidiness and penance which restores my world to me. You share in the guilt regarding their offences against the spirit and promise of poverty. As regards their seeming indifference to constant teachings, their callous and semi-joking attitudes, I will deal with them personally.'' So, instead of scolding or shouting or dramatics, I simply asked everyone to pray for me, that I may better show them the important relationship between good order and the restoration of the world to Christ.

How in heaven's name can an apostle of Madonna House develop the sixth sense, that empathy and sympathy so necessary in dealing with the untidiness of a thousand wounds in human souls, if they cannot take care of coats, shoes and miscellaneous articles that they leave lying around so easily? How can they heal the whole person — a work to which they have dedicated their lives — if they did not realize the connection between untidiness and poverty? Their life is that of restoring order to the world for Christ.

Letters come from the houses concerning the lack of awareness of little things done well *for the love of God*, that is daily *living lifted up into the heart of Christ*. At best, it seems as if we have been concentrating on efficiency, but neglecting its supernatural foundations.

Everybody says that our premises are in good physical order. Our day has an orderly routine. Most of our members are efficient in the natural order. However, I sense again and again that my application of the Gospel to our Apostolate, has become rather distant, academic teaching that is not too well remembered.

In examining my own conscience, I find many failings, but, on the whole, it seems to me that my voice is really tired and hoarse from constantly repeating: "Wash dishes for the love of God." "When you serve at table, whether it be for the Brothers Christopher, or the family, do it quietly and efficiently." If you learn to serve that way, and connect serving to the supernatural order, you will grow greatly in wisdom and love, and you will be a light shining in the darkness of the world. The light of your loving service will lead people to God.

I would like you to reread *Friendship House*, not because I am the heroine of the story but to remind you that eighteen people returned to the sacraments because I served them in a lousy cocktail lounge. This grace came to them, of course, from God, but through my gentle, loving service. They connected my love with God and returned to him.

Where did I learn to connect physical things with spiritual truths? That would take you to another book, *My Russian Yesterdays*. My father and mother gave orders to the servants to announce every hobo as Christ. My parents never let us forget that every task, however ordinary, was of redeeming, supernatural value, if done out of love.

Then again I think: why should I give you my poor, sinful self as an example when you are surrounded by marvelous books about the glorious saints of God? Many were canonized by the Church because they had the "vision of the whole" — that is they perfectly and constantly acted out of love.

The word I painfully seek today in order to bring before you the very essence of our humble Apostolate, is *awareness*. It's an important word, a glorious word, and a holy word. To be aware means to be recollected, to be *all there*. Where? Before the Face of God. It means that we arise in the morning, aware that this day is given unto us to grow in love and grace and wisdom before the Lord. It means that we realize that once again we have been given a little piece of time between two Masses to gain or lose the Beatific Vision. It means to realize that we have one more day to spend in the school of the love of God, and that if we waste it, we may not go to hell, but we will go into the painful refinery of love — at the terrible school of love — purgatory. In order to enter heaven, we must be lovers. We must learn love either here or there. Not to learn it at all is hell.

I have been thinking a lot about all of this during the past three days while I have been occupied in tidying up the recreation corner in the basement. My task there has been to sort games. Again the reason for this sorting was love. I wanted to give all those who live in Madonna House easy access to the fascinating games which Our Lady in her gracious kindness sends to us, but which often can only be afforded by the rich. This involves hours spent in the tiresome task of counting playing cards, and checking that all pieces of the games are there. Well do I know, dearly beloved, the intense discipline, mortification, and penance that such minute and boring tasks entail: sorting buttons, separating safety pins from straight pins, sorting in the clothing room, and working in the library over small and painstaking details. Yes, for thirty years I have learned the immense and ineffable lessons of love in the school of infinitely small details.

You dream of great deeds. Everyone, these days, reads about Charles de Foucauld. Many have a starry-eyed look. They wonder if they shouldn't become a Little Sister or Brother of de Foucauld. But, when I listen to their conversations, I want to cry. Not one of them stops to think what a heroic life he really led. He lived in a little hut in the blistering desert, with its cold and searing nights, amongst strange, primitive human beings. He saw his whole life as a failure but still remained faithful to God's strange call! He rose and offered Mass, then spent a whole day doing small things. All of this means hanging on a cross for years instead of hours, but nobody seems to be aware of this. Most just see the romance of his life, not the reality.

Right on our own doorstep, and in our midst, stands Christ. If only you listened, you could hear him! He says: "I do not even ask you to watch one hour with me in my agony; I simply ask you to get out of bed when the alarm rings. I do not ask you to be smitten on your cheeks nor to be spat upon; I just ask you to take correction (which you deserve), humbly, for love of me, with an open heart and mind, and a willingness to change. I do not ask you to be bound to a post and flagellated with leaden whips. I simply ask you to do every task that is given to you with total recollection and thoughtfulness.

"I do not ask you to hang naked on my cross; but I ask you to deepen the spirit of poverty in the care and use of my created things. I was stripped naked; why can't you strip your soul of your self-centered thoughts and begin to see such things as cups, dust cloths, food and clothing with deep reverence. You can do this only if you strip yourself naked of self-centeredness and connect everything — work, walking, sitting, sleeping with me.

"I haven't yet asked you to hang on my cross with me; but I will, if you prepare yourself in the way that I mentioned above. Remember, unless you hang on the other side of my cross, you cannot share heaven with me. Without the cross, there would have been no resurrection. The key to heaven is my cross; when will you understand that?"

Today, I fell asleep at 3:45 a.m. Around 2:00 a.m., a sad, mournful tune was going round and round in my heart and head: "Lord, when will they understand and implement the connection between your luminous truths, love, and switching off electricity taking care of clothing, realizing the significance in all these acts?" I fell asleep hearing that.

I have been thinking much lately about our vocation. It seems to me that Nazareth is the hidden, little village to which we have to go and live there with the Holy Family to become whole again. It is there that we will learn about the *little things* that we always *talk* about, and always *say* must be done perfectly for the love of God.

Yes, there we would learn about the little things and how to implement what we are talking about. It seems to me that each one of us is going to stay right in Nazareth until we do. That is our novitiate. Then, if we have made the first step, and learned the essence of our vocation, then one day God will say to us: "You go to Pakistan, and there show them my Face by healing the sick as I did in my public life. It is now time for you to share." To another he will say: "Go to Marian Centre and there do what you have seen my Mother do, day in and day out — housework, cooking, scrubbing, and washing dishes. Show them her face so that they may know her and that she might also lead them to me.''

To another he will say: "Go to Arizona or Texas and teach my truths by word and example. It is time that you showed them my Face." And to another he will say: "Go to Portland and show them the Face of your Lord who made everyone. Show them the Trinity. He who has seen me has seen the Father, and to him the Holy Spirit will come." And to yet another he will say: "Go to the Yukon and live there the perfect life of Nazareth. Show them the Holy Family, especially God made Man out of love for them."

It seems to me that he will say this to all of us. Then someday, he will call each of us to himself and talk to each one once more. This time his words will be very simple and brief, and go something like this: "You have been with me in Nazareth. Before that you came to Bethlehem (but don't remember that because you were very small when you were baptized). From Bethlehem you came to Nazareth, and from Nazareth I sent you to share the public life. Now, it is time for you to share my passion. Come, follow me through the joys of the cross."

Thus do I see our vocation. Do you see it in that way? You write me wonderful letters, and in Madonna House, we have inspiring talks. Yet, I confess that I am worried, because I have to be concerned about these things. God placed you in my sinful hands. I cannot die, then, with the thought that I have left something unclear, or that I have not implored him to give me words, if not of fire, at least words that you will understand. So when I see him at the first judgement, I can truthfully say, "Lord, I have tried."

You see, this is the *essence of our vocation:* to connect an ordinary and seemingly boring life with its repetitious details, with Love Who is God. Then the boredom vanishes, and a day spent in sorting buttons is glorious. Then a day at the typewriter, when your back is aching and your mind reeling with tiredness, is a day that has redeemed many souls; how many, God alone knows. We must have that awareness and make that connection. If it isn't made, it is a wasted day. What a horrible and a tragic thought that one of the most precious gifts of God, *time* has been wasted.

One of the local men left his farmhouse to go to a baseball game in Barry's Bay confident of the future; but at 3:00 p.m. he was dead in a car accident. Do you see the preciousness of time? You don't know how much time you have.

Oh, dearly beloved, try to understand my halting words. They come from a sea of pain. Believe me, I can't sleep these days, concerned as I am about where I have failed in all this. If you know of any way I can better help you to make this connection, I implore you to tell me; but if you think I have done what I should, then look into your hearts. Awareness is a terrible responsibility before God and man.

Whether you realize it or not, you yourself will be judged on how you passed the blueprint of God's Mandate on to the future generations in Madonna House.

If I have failed to do it, woe is me! Teach me. Help me remedy any mistakes I have made and in my blindness, do not see. But if the fault is *yours*, then for God's sake start correcting it. It is a terrible thing to fall into the hands of the living God. I am truly serious about the above.

How could I not be serious about all this when, from all sides I hear, see, feel and touch this non-connection that is constantly being presented to me — the non-connection between awareness, thoughtfulness, recollection and the implementation and restoration of the world to Christ.

Tell me how are you going to restore the world to Christ — the tremendous world of souls — if you have to be told daily (if not hourly) that the boxes in the left-hand corner of the hallway should be taken every morning to a certain place? How are you going to restore the world to Christ if your workshops or the clothing room, or the dishes, or the kitchen reflect the disorder of your souls?

How can you be aware of the world of souls if you are not aware of the fact that, when it snows, it would be a good idea to shovel a path and clear the steps? How are you going to restore the world to Christ if you are doing the minimum required — the letter of the law — and never plunge into its spirit?

In a word, Christ is waiting for you to become aware of him and of the Apostolate that he has confided to you, by becoming aware of the connection between brooms, dishwater, letter-typing, tidiness, and the restoration of the world.

Dearly Beloved, when, when, is this going to happen?

Lovingly yours in him,

EMOTIONAL PROBLEMS

December 2, 1960

Dearly Beloved,

One thing became evident at a recent convention of the lay apostolate. It is the fact that, in all lay apostolates, emotional difficulties present the greatest problem. I did not need to go to a convention to learn that! But it was interesting to see my own ideas confirmed. The last *Canadian Register* carries the full statement of the conclave of American Bishops. They say that we are in the mess that we are in because we have ceased to assume personal responsibility for our behavior and our lives.

I do not deny that all of the emotional problems must be tackled on a natural level, but I have come to the conclusion that the real answer in all of the apostolates, and especially in ours, is prayer. Though there are many reasons for us to be disturbed in our times, nevertheless Satan, who is always on the alert (and most brilliant, as you know) isn't just sitting back and letting such an opportunity go by. To further his tragic ends, and to confuse us more, he simply uses what already exists to create even greater disturbances. We should be on the lookout for him too without being disturbed. And the best lookout is prayer.

I have been thinking much about Christ and about love. There is a book about the Gospel of St. Matthew, which tells how Our Lord sent his apostles out *two* by *two*. He did this so that they might learn to love one another first. It would have been utterly useless for them to try to love the world and preach the glad tidings of love, if they did not first apply that Gospel of love to themselves, *totally with no holds barred*.

Now, in our Apostolate, this is not taking place I am sorry to say, and I would like to discuss this most vital matter, for upon your loving each other depends the true spiritual success of our work and the restoration of the world to Christ. The first two points which I want to take up are: the terrible need for approval, and departmentalization.

Let us take the first point. Because as yet we do not really love one another, because we still seem to be in the infantile stage, or shall we say in the 12 to 16 year old stage, we equate love with constant, unwavering approval. Can you imagine what burden this places on the directors of the houses? Their acts, their moods, their silences, their words, are analyzed and reanalyzed by the others. This places an intolerable burden on the tired shoulders of the directors who already bear so much responsibility. These poor directors can never be themselves. If they talk to someone an extra five minutes longer, others wonder why and feel *insecure*. In ordinary language, this is called *jealousy*.

Thus, the merry-go-round of constantly seeking approval begets worry and hostilities. These, in turn, beget depression and all of it begets guilt. Psychosomatic symptoms often arise: headaches, backaches, diarrhea, vomiting, dizziness or constipation. What certainly does manifest itself is a lack of concentration on the job, a repetition of faults for which one has been corrected many times, slow-down in work production. All of the above results in tension in the house, affecting everyone. When one person is laid low by this vicious circle, someone else has to pick up the work left undone. This results in overtiredness and disorder.

In the meantime, Christ in his Mystical Body waits at the doorstep of his beloved's heart — pauper that he is. There is no room for him there, for the heart is cluttered with disturbing emotions. He said to St. Paul: "My grace is sufficient for you." No one seems to believe that it is so. That is why I say that prayer and turning one's face to God is the real remedy.

If we think it over, dearly beloved, isn't it foolish to seek the approval of others, when the only approval we really need is the Lord's. It is his approval that we should seek constantly and with great eagerness. Faith assures that he loves each of us unto death. Every crucifix shouts this. His immense Heart is big enough to encompass us all.

How foolish it is to seek the approval of a passing shadow! Tomorrow the "important" director will be somewhere else, and another will take her place. It might be *you*! How would *you* like to carry the burden of their childish need for approval? Meditate on that!

This competition, this need for approval, the resulting tensions, miseries, disorder and slow-downs are bad enough, without strange and rather ugly problems entering our apostolic life. One problem is *departmentalization*.

You know that I am the custodian of the spirit by the will of God, sinner that I am; and I must admit I am filled with holy fear at the thought of our living in departmentalized cells. I want to cry out, and I feel a just anger rising in me, like the tide of a sea. If anything can kill the spirit of charity, it is creating departments that are sacrosanct, departments that cannot be touched. It is frightfully and jealously guarding one's authority over a two-by-four department of some sort that was originally set up for the sake of tranquility of God's order. This is to plunge a knife into the very soul of our Apostolate.

This has to stop! Sure there are departments in Madonna House and its missions, organized to create order. However, that does not mean that a head of a department should be as a sensitive hothouse flower; that she should jealously stand guard over her tiny prerogatives. This strange attitude that is developing here and there in the Apostolate must stop, or there will be no Apostolate!

There is no such thing as "my department". We should not hear, in the Apostolate, remarks like this: "I'm in charge of this; don't meddle with it, or "I started this, and I thank you to let me finish it," or "Why are you barging in? I was told to do this. I don't need your help. Thank you." There are a thousand variations on the above theme. Nor must there be resentment if someone offers some ideas about another's department. Nor must there be any anger, anxiety or depression, when, out of charity, someone comes into a department to help out when things get tough.

Arrogance, touchiness, uncharitableness, pride, have no place in the Apostolate, and people who exhibit these qualities will not remain long in charge of their departments. No matter how efficient they may be in a given task, the havoc they bring to the Apostolate and the sins against charity that are committed, are tragic. The avoidance of uncharitableness is more important than all of their efficiency.

I am sorry that at the beginning of Advent, the joyous season of preparation for Christmas, I must write such a letter, but write I must; for I am sad and disturbed in my soul. I hereby ask everyone in the Apostolate to really examine his or her conscience as to how the authority of Christ you have been given through me is being exercised.

The directors have enough to do without being bothered by this "leprosy." Let us clear it out of our Apostolate once and for all. If you want to kill the Apostolate, and thereby hurt Christ's plan for the restoration of the world, you cannot choose a better weapon than this: to go around parading your authority or your touch-me-not attitude, which is the child of pride. I demand a spiritual attitude toward your care of a department.

Unless we are humble and lowly like Christ; unless we remember that there are no such words as "me" and "mine" in the Apostolate; unless we remember that the person in authority today, may be without authority tomorrow, and that in Christ, there are no greater or lesser positions, our hearts will not be ready to receive him at Christmas, and make a manger in which he can be born and where he can rest.

Lovingly in Mary,

PEACE — THE FRUIT OF LOVE

December 21, 1960

Dearly Beloved,

The Peace of the Lord to you! The peace of the Child in a manger. The peace of the woman and the man sitting close to him. The peace of the Holy Three be with you — the only peace worth having. I wish you peace because peace is the fruit of love, and I know that you possess love because you possess God.

I wish you peace because we live in a time of *unpeace*, and we must remember that when we wish one another peace, we do so in his Name who said that he gave it to us not to keep for ourselves, but to give, first to one another, and then to everyone we meet. The more we give of his peace, the more peace-full we ourselves become.

The only way to give his peace is from the chalice of our hearts, a chalice fashioned of *caritas*. Then our peace will be fruitful. It will fall like a benediction on all those to whom we give it; for it isn't our peace which we give, but the peace *he* gave us. Everything he gives and everything he touches is holy and healing beyond our understanding.

The peace of the Lord I give to you, because I love you very much — how much you will never know until you meet him. In pain, in joy, in tribulation and darkness, in light and gladness, I have given birth to you in the Lord. You are precious to me beyond my ability to say. So I will not even try, but simply say, "Carissimi, I love you with a great love."

The peace of the Lord I give you, because I love you very much. Because of my utter poverty, I have nothing to offer except that which he has placed in my poor, human hands. So I give you the Lord's peace, the Lord himself, a Child in the manger to have and to hold always.

Learn of him, for he is meek and humble of heart, and you will have peace everlasting; and you will have love everlasting, if you hold him in your heart forever.

In him, lovingly yours,

Catherine

PLUNGE INTO THE GOSPEL

January 25, 1961

Dearly Beloved,

I have been praying very much that all of you might acquire the spirit of Madonna House, for unless we all have it, we are laboring in vain. In order to have our spirit, we must truly empty ourselves of all our preconceived notions, and plunge into the Gospel of Christ *with the accent that he has so specifically given to me for our own Apostolate.*

The more I live and watch our Apostolate grow, the more I see that we have difficulties among ourselves and in our houses where there is a sort of inward rejection of this accent. We put limitations to our surrender. We say to God, ''Yes, I will live that life, but with a great deal of *my own interpretation of that accent.*'' That is a dangerous thing for the collective well-being of the Apostolate. Think about it.

Lovingly yours in Mary,

ART — A UNIVERSAL LANGUAGE

February 11, 1961

Dearly Beloved,

Today, I want to talk to you about art. But before we enter into any discussion of art, let us clarify something about Communists. In 1944, when my book *Friendship House* was published, I wrote that Communists were infiltrating every part of the intellectual world of the United States and Canada. Since the beginning of 1930, I have been saying this. As you know, at that time I was considered obsessed with the idea of Communist infiltration, and I was eternally greeted with that stock phrase: ''Oh, it cannot happen here!'' Well, it *did* happen here. American and Canadian citizens now know what Communism is capable of doing.

Obviously, the Communists would not bypass such a powerful means of influencing people as the arts and not only the graphic arts such as painting and drawing, but the dramatic arts — theatre and movies, TV and radio. They are concerned with all the arts because consciously or subconsciously, art in any form affects a human being deeply. So it is a known fact that Communists have infiltrated all of the arts.

It is important for the lay apostolate to have a proper approach to art. And here we are discussing sculpture, painting, drawing and architecture. Before entering into any discussion, a few principles have to be established. One of the first principles is that art is a highly individualistic expression. The artist paints what he sees and feels, as he sees and feels it. This is very important. A special talent has been given by God to this individual. This talent is like a prism through which one's art radiates in a highly personalized way.

However, though highly individualistic, all the types of art that we are discussing never fail to reflect the society and the times in which the artist lives. Thus Gothic style of architecture was born in the medieval times when men of Western Europe were deeply Christian, and all their thoughts turned to heaven as their everlasting home. In that style, with its lofty spires and immense buttresses, they expressed the longing of their souls. In the same way, the Byzantine style of architecture with its round cupolas, expressed the more simple way of the East which took nature as it found it, and supernaturalized it.

In every age and place, there have been great artists. They painted what they saw, felt and lived. Those paintings, no matter to what era they belonged, were enduring art. They still affect people — even people who know nothing about art — when they take time to look and meditate on what they see.

The same can be said of modern art. It too, has its geniuses. Also every era has its mediocre artists in the true sense of the word. They are the ones who confuse us. Their paintings have good colors and sometimes good lines, but they are not genuine art. Something is missing from them, and instinctively we reject and rebel against them. This is because, fundamentally, they do not tell us anything. This always has to be taken into consideration when looking at or discussing art. For this, one does not have to be a connoisseur. One just has to be a human being. True art always speaks to us in one way or another.

Let us consider a few simple ways of approaching art appreciation. To begin with, art, like swimming, must be approached *gently*. Some there are who believe that the best way to teach swimming is to throw a person into deep waters and self-preservation will make him swim. This is a brutal and silly way. The best way is to let the person get acquainted with water slowly in shallow spots; then gently and lovingly, make him feel secure in the arms of a good swimmer. Then we bring him very slowly to deep waters and swim next to him. Then he will develop, not only the joy of swimming, but will come to love it.

The same applies to art. It is useless to decry modern art, and be ecstatic over classical or medieval art. People react to art in their own fashion. Art appreciation like swimming, is a very gradual experience. Knowledge comes slowly, because much ignorance and prejudice must be overcome.

Let us take Madonna House. When I first came to Combermere, always remembering that the Apostolate endeavors to restore the whole person, I definitely tried to introduce art as well. I hope that I did it gently. On the shelves and walls of Madonna House I put any statue or picture that any of the members, visitors or local people admired. Some of the statues were gaudy. Man of the staff and visitors admired them. Slowly, in the midst of the ugliness (for to me it was ugliness), I began to introduce one or two good statues. I did the same with pictures.

I finally made the supreme sacrifice of giving my beloved collection of art books, gathered over the period of a lifetime, to Madonna House. People began to look at the pictures. A friend used to visit often. She would stop and look at the good statue and say: "Gee Catherine, I like this statue better than this one. I thought that I liked the other one better, but now I have compared them, I don't like the first as much." Yes, here was art education. By putting a good statue next to a gaudy one, I let people make their own comparison.

Some of you will remember the day when a few of our members suddenly expressed themselves and said: "Catherine, when are you going to take that horrible, gaudy art off the shelves?" That was a great day for me! It happened seven years after I began the displays — a short time really, for some art appreciation to grow in people's hearts, minds, and souls. So we took the gaudy statues down, and today this art appreciation is still growing.

Art appreciation cannot be hurried. It is very personal. It grows with the growth of the individual. The main thing is to be exposed to good art. That's why members of a lay apostolate must visit art galleries, and keep on file various art reproductions. They can be found in our current magazines. Then periodically they can display these pictures. This is a very important part of the Apostolate, and must not be neglected. When money is donated for the personal use of members, occasionally they could use it to buy a good piece of art.

We here in Combermere are introducing art more and more. It has now become a tradition to make a display of art with Christmas themes during the last week of Advent. The same is true of Holy Week when we display themes of the crucifixion and passion of Our Lord.

Why should the Apostolate be interested in art? It is because art is a universal language that the missionaries of the Lord must learn to speak. It will also speak to us. The primitive art of the Eskimo and of the Indian, of Africa and of the East, and art in our own country will tell us much if we are open to it and appreciate it. It will tell us much about the country, the nation, the thoughts and feelings of those people whom we have come so lovingly to serve. It is another way of dialoguing — a powerful way of coming together in the depths of the human spirit.

Art also enlarges our hearts, for art is beauty, and Beauty is God. God speaks to us in the beauties of nature. All art stems from that speech. Therefore, art definitely forms a part of the growth of the lay apostle's growth in love and in knowledge. It is also one of our means of reaching more deeply the souls of the people we want to bring to God.

Is it any wonder then, that Communism wants to infiltrate art by emphasizing what is mediocre? They don't dare attack the real artists and real art. They emphasize what is poor, mediocre and unhealthy.

There is much room for healthy, positive discussions about art. I invite you to have such discussions, but approach the subject of art gently, lovingly, and sensibly. Let your discussions be fruitful.

Lastly, pay attention to *symbolic art*. God speaks to us in nature and through many other things in symbols. Modern man has lost his understanding of symbols because he is divorced from God and nature. Let us return him to both.

Lovingly yours in Mary,

Catherine

CLOTHING AND THE NAKED CHRIST

February 1961

Dearly Beloved,

This time I want to write about poverty. Poverty is an inexhaustible virtue. Since we have a promise to practice it, we should never cease to meditate upon it, and pray to God to perfect us in it. We should ask Mary to share with us her ways of practicing it. We should discuss it and examine ourselves again and again (especially as the years go by) on how we practice it.

I am afraid that in Madonna House Apostolate there is a place where we expose ourselves, unnecessarily, to a sin against poverty. That is in the clothing room. It might easily become an occasion of sin for those who work there. Mind you, I am not suggesting that it is an occasion of sin for everyone always. No, but it might become an occasion of sin to some people. Women especially, go through periods when they suddenly feel a need for new, exciting clothing. And often, "just the very thing" comes into the clothing room at such a time.

It must be remembered that clothing has deep, psychological overtones, as all of us realize when we deal with youth. Some come from fairly poor families. They never saw such nice clothing as they are handling now. Others, on the contrary, are from wealthy families. They have been used to the best. They may have a fixation on spotlessness and perfection. Each is tempted in different ways, and we are aware of this at Madonna House. This awareness must also penetrate our other houses. The directors must be on the lookout for such things. For one must always be on guard in the matter of poverty. The devil hates that virtue, and will connive to tear it apart wherever it is practiced well.

Being the brides of a Poor Man, the Pauper Who, during his public life had nowhere to lay his head, and died naked on a cross, one wonders why even a shadow of a temptation should penetrate the mind of anyone against this holy, joyous poverty that was a close companion of your Beloved. But we, being human, with the shadow of original sin upon us must fight these temptations which do come to us. We must fight them relentlessly with all the powers of a loving, dedicated heart and soul.

But oh — the paradox of the Gospels and Christianity! We also must look neat and pleasant. We have to bring souls to God and so we must identify with the people whom we serve. Only the ingenuity of love, and immense and passionate love of God, and the help of Our Lady can achieve the solution to this paradox, to this contradiction. There are many such seeming contradictions in the Gospel. Naturally, in choosing clothing, the spirit of poverty must always be present. All have to be watchful about this spirit, for an abundance of very nice clothing may become a temptation against poverty.

The same temptations exist for those in charge of the tremendous volume of clothing that comes into our houses. So many lovely things come! And here, another point must be considered: the best should go to the poor. They have so little of it. By succumbing to this temptation, we literally rob the poor of the beauty and joy that could be theirs. They are God's beloved creatures. Surely they deserve the best.

Every three months, everyone should check her clothing and see if there is anything she could do without. Lent is the season for all kinds of ingenious mortifications, and this is one of them.

The more we see Christ drawing closer to the flagellation post, the spot where all of his garments were taken away from him; the more we see him approaching the bleak, rough cross where he was crucified naked; the more we are reminded of the destitution of his birth, the more we should examine our consciences on the practice of the virtue of poverty. True detachment of heart is nourished by the ungreedy eye, and rooted in the love of Christ the Pauper.

Lovingly yours in Mary,

(signature)

MEEKNESS AND REJECTION

February 22, 1961

Dearly Beloved,

During this most holy season of Lent when we prepare for the death and resurrection of Our Lord, I would like to share with you two little words which came to me during Mass. I have been meditating upon them for they are very profound. Did you know that words dealing with God in any way have great depths which often do not reveal themselves immediately? Like all the things of God they open the doors of their beauty slowly and gently, revealing their full meaning only to those who persevere.

These two words which came to me are *meekness* and *rejection*. At first glance, they seemed to have little in common. As the days went by, a pattern emerged. Those words grew, intertwined separated and came together again. I want to prayerfully and lovingly share with you two words. I hope that this may help you as I have been helped. For I love you so very deeply, and one of the proofs of love is serving those whom we love by sharing what has been meaningful to us.

Meekness: I have often meditated upon meekness. It is a virtue that has always attracted me. I love the Beatitudes where meekness is truly extolled. "The meek shall inherit the earth," said the Lord. He also said: "Learn of me for I am meek and humble of heart."

Previously, all of my meditations on that beautiful, gentle but strong word dealt with *non-retaliation*. Somehow, they all related to the words of Our Lord: "If you are smitten on one cheek, turn the other." I connected that word also with Dorothy Day, the Quakers, and the pacifists. Once I witnessed the great power of meekness.

It happened during the early days of Friendship House in Toronto. I was returning to Friendship House one evening, when I saw a preacher giving his pitch on the corner of a slummy street. He was surrounded by quite a large crowd of very poor people. There were many Brothers Christopher* there (these were the Depression years, and people had little to do but stand around and listen to whoever wishes to talk to them.)

Being always interested in anyone speaking of God and the things of God, I stopped to listen. I liked what I heard. This evangelical preacher was talking of all things about peace and love. He spoke forcefully, with a flaming faith.

In his audience was a hulking, big brute of a man, slightly worse for liquor, but not drunk. He interrupted the preacher abusing him in no uncertain terms. The preacher continued to speak. His voice grew gentler, and a kind, little smile touched his face and lips, and gave a lovely light to his plain face. The big man became angry. He opened the palm of his hand and gave a resounding smack to the cheek of the preacher, who was a slight man. The preacher fell from the soap box on which he had stood, onto the dirty pavement. He must have been quite hurt because he rose painfully. Slowly he stepped onto his box. His face was dirty and slightly bloody. There was a big, red spot on his cheek. He smiled a sincere and loving smile, and turned the other cheek to the big man saying: "Brother, here is my other cheek, for I love the Lord, and I love *you* in the Lord. He said to turn the other cheek to him who smites you. So here *is* my other cheek."

There was dead silence. The big man suddenly crumpled and fell to his knees before the preacher weeping bitterly. I felt a cold shiver running down my spine, for I had witnessed the terrible power of meekness that Christ spoke about. As I looked over the faces of the motley audience, I saw many who were furtively wiping tears from their eyes. That night, the preacher, whom I got to know very well later, reaped a great harvest for the Lord. So

*Term Madonna House has always used for the homeless men it serves.

you see why it is that I have associated meekness up to now with *non-retaliation*.

However, this Lent as I meditated on that word, things changed. Another word came to reveal the depths of meekness, and that other word was *defenselessness*. Suddenly, on the screen of my mind, I saw the defenseless Christ during his passion. It is said that "he was defenseless as a lamb led to the slaughter." So I saw that meekness and defencelessness go together. What did that mean to me, personally? Why should those two words come to me in this Lent of 1961? I continued day after day to meditate on this.

Suddenly I saw light. We are always on the defensive — you and I and most of the world. We always have our guards up. We always have shields, bucklers and masks not of the Lord's making, but of our own, to protect ourselves from real and imaginary threats or attacks.

Ours is a century of neuroses and psychoses. Slowly, the Christians of the world have been drifting away from God, until finally they have cut themselves off from God completely by becoming atheists. People without God easily become neurotic and psychotic. From such mental conditions, stem the fruits of the devil — fears, confusion and insecurity. So, as the atheists grow, the devil obtains more of a foothold. The stench of all that is evil spreads in ever widening circles until everyone, even the believing people, are affected in one way or another. Because of this tragic situation of the world's soul, all of us are somewhat confused; all of us are frightened of threats and attacks from everything to the "A" bomb, to our next-door neighbor.

I too, am on the defensive, emotionally speaking. It is not too noticeable to the untrained eye, and, until now, perhaps, I did not pay too much attention to it myself, but many of you sense it.

Remember the times when you and I had our private counselling conversations? I would not take time to listen to what you had to say. Because you were emotionally blocked you took a long time to say what you had to say. Seemingly impatient, I would rush in and tell you that I knew what you thought or felt or hoped, and proceeded to solve (or think I solved) your problems. This didn't always happen, but sometimes it did. Naturally, you reacted violently. You became more hostile to me. Well, today, I know why I did that. I was defending myself against your hostility.

At such times, you were a threat to me. It didn't matter that I was a nurse, that I understood that I was only a symbol, and that your hostility was directed against one or both of your parents. Those were the days when I was exhausted, humanly speaking, from the huge waves of hostility that constantly beat against the shores of my person.

I certainly was not defenceless before you. I defended myself on such occasions *from you*, my dearly beloved, unconsciously or semi-consciously. Each one of us has experienced many of these situations. However, today with new insights into *meekness* and its gentle attribute, *defenselessness*, I understand better.

What you and I must do is to become truly *defenseless*, and identify ourselves with Christ the Lamb. We must allow ourselves to be led to the thousand slaughters that will fill our lives in the Apostolate. We must be meek and defenseless as Christ was. We must expose ourselves (at least I know that I must) to all the hostilities of others in peace and in love defenselessly. I must not defend myself by a thousand tricks of the trade, but lovingly expose myself, even to my own subconscious. Then it too, will be cleared of all its undergrowth by Christ the Lamb.

We must not justify ourselves when unjustly accused, for this too, is part of that defenselessness of Christ. Do you see, dearly beloved, how a little meditation on meekness leads not only to non-retaliation, but also to love of enemies? It goes deeper and deeper. It leads to the positiveness of a holy defenselessness that strengthens ourselves and brings peace to those who attack us.

According to the custom of my people in Lent, I humbly bow before you, and ask your forgiveness for all the past defenses that I have put up against you. In faith and love, trusting in the grace of God, I certainly will attempt the impossible: that is not to use any defenses against you in the future.

Such was my meditation upon *meekness*. But a few days later, during Communion, the Lord sent me another word to think about: *rejection*. This puzzled me again. Now what had the word *rejection* (which belongs to the textbooks of psychiatry) to do with God and me? What did it have to do with Lenten meditation? I confess that it puzzled me for quite a while. But one Friday in the great silence of the Lord in St. Kate's, (for you remember that Friday, these days, is a prayer day for me in the desert, or *poustinia*, as the Russians called the desert) I began to see light. Rejection belongs to the passion of Christ too. In fact, it belongs to his whole life. Let's briefly consider it.

St. Joseph, when he found out that Mary was pregnant, and he had not known her as a husband, would have rejected her had it not been for the angel's message. But rejection of Our Lady would have also meant the rejection of Christ — the fruit of her womb.

The innkeepers of Bethlehem rejected the Holy Family's need for shelter and hospitality. Because Christ was still in Mary's womb, this was a rejection of him also. We know, for a fact that the Pharisees and the Sadducees with the exception of a few, rejected him completely. That must have been a terrible pain for Christ.

One day when he was proclaiming that he would give his own flesh for the life of the world, many of his followers rejected him publically, saying: "Your sayings are too hard. We will not walk with you anymore!"

There was Philip who was constantly rejecting the words of Christ by asking silly questions. (So many of us still do!) I think that Christ was touched to the quick by this rejection on the part of his beloved disciple, for he scolded him. The momentary rejection of Peter made him terribly sad. But what the rejection of Peter did to him — a rejection sealed with a lying kiss, only his Father knew!

When he went to his home town, Nazareth, the people there rejected him violently and were going to stone him. After all, he was "just the son of Joseph, the carpenter!"

In Gethsemane all of the disciples slept, instead of watching with him during his tremendous hour of great agony. Love shares. Sleep is a rejection — a non-sharing. It must have added to his agony for he said: "Couldn't you watch one hour with me?"

From the time that he was arrested in the Garden of Olives, to the time that he was nailed to the cross, rejection accompanied him. He was rejected by the very people he had taught and healed. Yes, rejection, like pain and loneliness, were the shadowy companions of his whole passion, and indeed of his whole life.

This rejection by his own Jewish people reached its intensity as he was looking down from the cross at the mob surrounding the Hill of the Skull. How many familiar faces he saw amongst those who were laughing and taunting him, saying, "If you are the Son of God, come down from the cross, and we shall believe in you." Perhaps, amongst those present were those who had witnessed the resurrection of Lazarus and many other miracles. Rejection became a terrible, bitter sea for the pain-filled eyes and mind of Christ.

One of the deepest, human rejections must have been the slight of the small group under his cross, consisting of his mother and the holy women, *but only one of his apostles*! Judas was dead, but where were the ten others? Stop here, for a moment, and think of the depth of that rejection. These were his very own beloved apostles with whom he had walked for three years, and to whom he had given himself so generously!

Finally, the supreme (seeming) rejection that tore out of his parched, painfilled mouth and lips those terrible words, "Father, Father, why has Thou forsaken me?"

I began to see that *rejection* was a word that I had to meditate upon if I wanted to enter the passion of my Beloved. I also saw more. I saw the tremendous love of Christ in a new light. It is said that he was like us in everything but sin, and that he knew and experienced all that we in our humanity have to know and experience of pain and of sorrow. It stands to reason that he would experience the feelings of rejection also so as to help us in our neurotic, psychotic century. He wanted to help us understand, and to overcome that terrible feeling of *rejection* which is so neurotic, so deadly and life-shattering.

I began to see more clearly than ever that Christ is the High Priest, the great Teacher, the great Physician. He is also the great Psychiatrist, who teaches us, and heals us, not by psychiatric sessions as human psychiatrists do, but by identifying himself with us in love and in empathy. A brief perusal of the Gospels shows us that he was often rejected by others and how he dealt with it.

So, dearly beloved, here we are. Most of the problems facing the Apostolate on the emotional level, have to do with the mind-searing soul-searching, violent emotional threat that results in so many psychosomatic symptoms. It can be summed up in one word: fear of rejection.

To put it another way: we seek approval from people who matter. We crave it and hunger for it because we equate it with love. Rejection almost means *death* to us — a sort of living death, filled with loneliness. *Rejection* means aloneness, pain, sadness.

It means being unloved. It is, in fact, a hell on earth — a living death.

We are on the defensive constantly. We are afraid to reveal our true selves. We are abysmally frightened to be open, to trust, to communicate, lest people who matter find out our true selves and reject us. With this fear come feelings of inadequacy. Being afraid of rejection, we are unable to see or accept ourselves as we are. We cannot love ourselves and therefore are unable to love others.

Thus, the feeling and fear of rejection, and the putting up of defenses, constantly places us in a straight jacket — a prison of fear and a thousand other emotions. The results of this is that we are half alive in the reality of living, unable to love, yet desirous to be loved and accepted.

Gently, Christ comes to our rescue. He comes with two words: *meekness* and *rejection*, showing us, I think, that if we are truly meek, we shall be defenseless and exposed. A defenseless person is a trusting and meek person, a person full of faith, with the heart of a child to whom belongs the kingdom of heaven. People who are defenseless are open to all of the pain and thrusts of the knives of other people's words, glances, and deeds, because they are strong in faith and strong in love; because they don't retaliate, nor defend themselves; in a word, they are meek. They are not hurt for the sharp arrows of words and deeds bounce off the shield of meekness and fall at the feet of the attacker and the attacked.

From their hearts and souls, streams an almost unbearable light, for they are truly Christlike. The light of Christ shines forth from them unimpeded, and envelops the attacker with its gentle love, and illuminates his soul and heals him.

From this it follows that meek and defenseless people who practice this virtue for Christ's sake, will never feel rejected, because they are anchored in Christ. What is more, they realize this and feel secure. They have walked with Christ through every step of *his* rejection, and have seen how meekly, forgivingly, and lovingly Love Itself dealt with rejection. If they ever were neurotics, dearly beloved, by following Christ now, they are healed, and they heal others.

Such was my meditation for the Lent of 1961. Lovingly, I

share it with you, praying that the humble and rejected Christ may make *you* meek, defenseless, and hence secure in his Sacred Heart against any rejection.

Lovingly yours in Mary,

Catherine

SEE NO ONE BUT JESUS

March 20, 1961

Dearly Beloved,

I have been thinking and praying very much about you. I am especially asking the Lord for one gift for you: that you have the grace to see no one but Jesus!

What exactly do I mean by that? I mean, of course, that if we, emptied of all things that are not God, constantly repeated the words of the blind man, "Lord, that I may see," we would begin to see everything transformed. Everything would slowly acquire its real meaning. This transformation would happen because God would hear our prayer. He would touch our eyes with the finger of his grace and the spittle of his love, and we would begin to see the whole of creation, especially people, with *his eyes*. Therefore, we would also see *ourselves* differently. Slowly we would begin to understand that wherever we look, whatever we see, it is always Jesus.

How does that work in our everyday life? You are washing dishes; you are silently repeating that prayer, "Lord, that I may see," and lo! *you see*! What do you see? You see the same dishes, but now they have become very important. You concentrate on washing them *well*. You watch the water; you don't allow it to become too dirty; you dry the dishes perfectly. In a word, you discipline yourself for Love's sake. But you do more. You begin to see that these little tasks, performed with great love, are truly the coins for the salvation of the world. You see Christ standing by you gathering the fragments of your self-discipline. You see him joyfully and happily using them for souls.

You are annoyed by the thoughtlessness of others because you see *with the eyes of Christ*. Through his grace, you begin to see that one way of combating the selfishness and thoughtlessness of others, is by your own unselfishness and thoughtfulness. "The saint preaches by the way he walks, by the way he stands, and by the way he picks things up and holds them in his hands." Is there a more powerful sermon in this world than the sermon of example? If so, tell me about it!

Someone asked me to explain my letter on meekness and defenselessness. That particular person felt a need for further clarification. She wanted to know when to stand up and defend God and the things of God. She thought that, perhaps, it would be good to write to me for that clarification.

To me, the yardstick here is quite obvious, and it is this: Any attack by anybody, anywhere, anytime, on *yourself* is met with gentle silence, and an utter lack of justification. As regards yourself, you are defenseless and meek like Christ. But any attack on *God* and the *things of God*, or the Apostolate, or any other person *except yourself*, is met with a kindly, yet firm and unshakable defense. That is you defend justice and charity everything and everyone pertaining to God *except yourself*.

Frankly, I was a little surprised at this question. It showed me once more that you folks are very complex. You are always willing to discuss a lot of God's truths, academically, but for some reason, you seldom want to go to the heart of the matter — which is the shining, clear words of the Gospels, which we are pledged to live without compromise in our Apostolate.

Let us together try to cut through the underbrush of confusion, fears and hostilities, that still reign in our hearts. Let us try to see more deeply the shining path of the Gospel. Our consideration then, I think, will be very fruitful, for these are the things that really matter, aren't they? They are going to make our lives in the Apostolate fruitful, and God wants our vocation to produce fruits. So let us begin to prune the tree of self together. I shall learn much from your letters. I need a lot of pruning too. You will learn likewise. For wherever two or more are gathered together in His Name, *there he is among them.*

Lovingly yours in Mary,

THE CENTRAL POINT OF OUR FAITH

March 22, 1961

Dearly Beloved,

Christ has risen! Verily he has risen!

Our century has forgotten the central point of our faith — the resurrection. The proof that Christ is the Second Person of the Most Holy Trinity, God and man, lies in the glorious mystery of his resurrection. The Divinity of Christ was not proved by his life, not even by his death. It was proved by his resurrection from the dead. The early Christians believed firmly in the resurrection and because of it many were converted. It has brought ineffable joy to all generations of Christians. Our hearts can only sing: "Alleluia! Alleluia! Alleluia!" It seems that that short, beautiful word alone can express the awesome joy, gratitude and love that is in our hearts.

But his resurrection contains another mystery of his promise: his second coming, the *parousia.* Oh, if only we lived in the expectation of the parousia, as the first-century Christians did! Then our lives would be filled with that tremendous inward expectation of love which is dimly symbolized in the human love of two young people on their wedding day.

If only we could live awaiting the Bridegroom's coming as people who are passionately in love! Then, meaning every word of what we say, we could exclaim with King Solomon the beautiful lines of the Song of Songs: "I sleep, but my heart watcheth!"

Then, the *kenosis* that we have been writing about would be so completely understandable, so eagerly embraced, and so constantly practiced, that it would become the warp and woof of our lives. We could understand that by emptying ourselves now, we would be preparing to be filled by our Beloved, not only in this life, but in the next as well. We would understand also that by emptying ourselves, we would be bringing other souls to him. This is the only suitable gift that a human bride can bring to her heavenly Bridegroom.

Easter, the final proof of God's love for us! Our joy, our salvation, our hope, the *exultet* of our souls, our pledge of his second coming, of the *parousia*! How rich are we. How God overwhelms us with his gifts on this glorious Easter! Let us meditate upon it. Let this blinding light open our eyes and penetrate us with its power and joy. Then we, too, will be resurrected in Christ, leaving the old man in the waters of baptism and coming forth *totally Christ's*. *Kenosis* is a constant reminder of our baptism. Let us embrace it, because through its darkness and pain we too will come forth from the tomb of selfishness and self-centredness into the eternal light of God's love.

Christ is risen! Verily he has risen! Alleluia! Alleluia! Alleluia!

With a heart full of love and joy, I bless each of you with my motherly blessing. A Mass for your intentions will be said for each house during the Easter week.

LOVE AND KENOSIS

March 31, 1961

Dearly Beloved,

Once again it is my Friday in *poustinia*. Only it is not just *a* Friday; it is *Good Friday*. A great joy floods my soul — a joy I wish to share with you. Today is *Love's Day*. Today God has shown us how much he loves us by dying on a cross. He has shown us how much we must love him and one another.

Reread, at this point, the words of Christ at the Last Supper. Do not be in a hurry. Pause and read God's words from the Gospel of St. John.

Now that you have read it, try to remember how many times Christ repeated the word *love*; how many times he asked us to *love one another*; how many times he repeated so gently yet so strongly: "A new commandment I give unto you, that you love one another." He told us that he was the way to the Father, the Father who created us, who so loved us that he sent his beloved Son to redeem us. Christ spoke of the Paraclete, the Holy Spirit, the Spirit of love and truth who would make clear to us the truth about love.

Today as we celebrate the death of Christ, we are celebrating the awesome proof of his love for us. The resurrection will be the final stage of that proof — the proof of the fact that it was the Second Person of the Most Holy Trinity who became incarnated and died on the Cross.

But today is *Love's Day*. There is sadness and sorrow for his pain. I know that there is a desire to share in that pain for love always shares. Above all, there is joy beyond expression; joy that mounts in a crescendo, like the waves of a sea lashed by the winds. Gratitude that surpasses human understanding is present too. God loves me! Now I know with absolute certainty that he does! Now the door to paradise is open once more and I can, if I love him back, be one with him for eternity.

This paradise, this kingdom of heaven is mine *now* if I wish it. He will go to the Father to prepare a mansion for me, but will also stay with me in the Blessed Sacrament. I can be united to him in love and communion now! Joy like a flame — a bonfire — rises in my soul, and bereft of words, I sing an endless alleluia, the only word that comes to the speechless ones in pain or in joy.

Just think, dearly beloved, we are his! He chose us especially to be all his! On this lovely day, let us try to understand the immense joy of our humble, hidden vocation. Let us begin to realize that it is indeed a *vocation to love*; to love one another first, and then to love everyone else.

The words at the Last Supper are addressed to us asking us to love one another in the loveless marketplace. He asks this so that people in the heat of the day and the cold of the night could see his love for us, and ours for him, and for one another; so they could share its warmth. That is our humble, simple, glorious vocation!

In this connection I want to speak to you of *kenosis*. This is an emptying of oneself, of stripping oneself, so that Christ may grow in you, and that you may show him to the world and lead others to him through the stripping, that emptying, so as to be filled with him. This is the *truth*: we must be *kenotic*.

Let us go more deeply into that word. Let us examine the word *stripping*. If we look at it in the light of Christ's love in the light of the joy his love gives us, if we think of his mercy, then the stripping becomes joyous too. The hands of his grace, which alone can bring about this stripping and this emptying, are gentle and loving. He will make our desire for *kenosis* bloom like a flower of exceeding beauty. He will behold these desires, this flower, with love and the sun of his gaze will open the flower unto its utmost beauty and richness.

Slowly he will show us that flowers were created for the fruits of the tree; that the trees remain sterile unless, petal by petal, the flower dies and becomes the fruit. Do you remember how gently the petals of apple trees and the cherry trees fall to the ground? How much pain does the tree experience at their falling, at this stripping of themselves? How lovely becomes the pod, the apple or the fruit of the rose. How we watch the maturing! To a soul in love with God, to a soul for whom Good Friday is *joy*, this *kenosis*, this emptying, and this stripping will come gently and easily depending upon the intensity of the desire to possess and love God.

A room suffers little when being emptied of all things to be cleaned and made new for a special guest. If rooms could feel they would sing a song of joy. We *can* feel. Let us sing a song of joy on this *day of Love* who makes all things whole, and whose gentle hands would not crush a bruised reed. Under these gentle hands, our *kenosis* will be like the falling of flower petals in the spring. They fall to make room for the fruit of the holy tree the cross; they fall for Christ our Love, by whom we are so beloved.

Let us rejoice, alleluia! God loved us first. Christ came to prove this. Alleluia! Now let us love him back in joy and in gladness, and love one another as he and the Father love one another, Alleluia!

Lovingly yours in Mary,

OPENNESS TO OUR SUPERIORS

April 6, 1961

Dearly Beloved,

As time goes by, I begin to realize more clearly that being Director General means *training, training, and training* again. What, exactly, does training mean? It means many things. It means forming, shaping, teaching, clarifying and imparting knowledge in many different ways.

In an Apostolate such as ours, training has a very definite goal. The people who are being trained are brought to the Apostolate by God, who says to the directorate: "These are my beloved ones whom I have especially selected to go forth to witness to me, and to restore to my Father that part of the world to which I will call them. I bring them to you to be trained in the spirit of the

Apostolate of Madonna House which I have begotten through you. Pass this spirit on to them in its fullness.

Those of us to whom he has entrusted this tremendous task must use all natural and supernatural means to pass this spirit on to you so that you, in turn, may carry the flame both into the marketplace and to the generations yet unborn. These letters are one way that this formation in and the passing on of the spirit of Madonna House spirit must be done. As I realize this more and more, my letters are becoming more and more numerous. They are my last will and testament to you.

I think the reason for the increase of these letters is also the increase of my love for you. With God, the impossible always happens. Had you asked me last year if I could love you more, my answer would have been, "I don't think so, for my heart is so filled with love for you that it is brimming over." But lo! An hour passes! A day goes by! A month vanishes; a year is gone, and I find myself loving you more. There is an old saying that fits this state of affairs: "I love you more than yesterday, less than tomorrow." This means, of course, that I will love you more tomorrow.

However, true love not only grows daily, not only shares joy and sorrows with the beloved, but often acts as a surgeon's scalpel making wounds only to heal the whole person. It is like a farmer's pruning knife, cutting out dangerous growths. Love always is patient. It clarifies and teaches endlessly never tiring of repetition. In a word, love is what St. Paul, in his hymn of charity, says it is. I suggest that you often read that marvelous epistle; then love will truly show its face to you.

It may sound to you (as it sounds to me) that I am like an old wornout gramophone record, repeating and repeating the same truths to you who come within the sound of that hoarse and wornout record! Yet, I cannot stop. I must proclaim the *Good News* that God loved us first, that he emptied himself for love of us, to save and redeem us, to bring us to a life of union with him here and hereafter.

Nor can I ever stop repeating that we must love him back, that we must empty ourselves, that we must allow him to fill us, so that we might reveal him to others, so that they too, may love him and be united to him. *This is the essence of our Apostolate. This is its goal. This is the spirit of Madonna House!*

Thus, I come to the subject of this letter. I want to continue to speak of *kenosis* in terms of openness — *especially openness to our superiors.*

Openness begins with faith in the tremendous and mysterious ways of God who wished to be present in this world through his Spouse, the Church. The Church was founded on a man called Simon who became *Petrus* (the Latin word for "rock"). He was a sinful man who denied Christ three times. He was impulsive, rash, and at times, a proud and conceited man. At least he was like this before Pentecost, before the resurrection. On *this* man, God built his Church. He continues to build it on those to whom the apostles have delegated their authority — bishops, priests, and superiors of all kinds.

The first thought that comes to me is that the choice of God would not have been the choice of man. Right from the beginning of Christ's ministry we see that the person whom Christ chooses does not have to be a saint, nor even a very pleasing personality. He or she can be full of weaknesses. Perhaps God chooses that person to reveal to us his glory and his mercy. But who knows the mind of God? He chose Peter and gave to him the power to bind or to loose. Here, we are in the face of a tremendous mystery of faith which we have to believe as Catholics. This mystery extends down through the centuries impenetrating the very fabric of the Mystical Body of Christ, the Church which we are.

So here you are, faced with Father Callahan* and myself. He, of course, is clothed with all of the powers of the priesthood, but still a man. Even I, in all my weaknesses, sinfulness, inadequacy, am also clothed with Christ *in my office.* Incredible mystery! in my office *I am he.* This also is of faith.

In the exercise of our responsibilities it is impossible to direct unless, through the openness of every member, we have the knowledge which will enable us to balance the common good of the Apostolate with the good of each individual. It is that balance which leads to sanctity which it is our duty and responsibility to maintain — the balance of mutual charity and peace. Only if we know completely the state of affairs in each house, can we train, direct and form for the Apostolate according to God's will.

Have you considered the terrible responsibility that I, for instance have before God? Do you realize that in my sinful hands, through the most holy will of God, lies the fate of many people? I

---

*The first priest to join Madonna House. He was, therefore, the founder of the Madonna House priests.

have a bounden duty, on which depends the very salvation of my soul, to lead you to the cross and to sanctity; to lead you to God the Father through Jesus and Mary according to the spirit of Madonna House. Dearly Beloved, how is it possible for me to do this if each one of you is not open? Tell me, dearly beloved, how can I lead you to God if I do not know?

At this point you might well ask: "How is it possible for you not to know?" Well, let me give you a few instances: you might have a problem such as fear of authority; you might have a fear of disapproval; you might have a block against the realization that you are dealing with God and the things of God; you might have wrong ideas about loyalty and disloyalty.

None of you are that sick emotionally (or you would not be here) that you cannot make a cross of these fears and praying for faith, meekness, defenselessness and obedience, shoulder that cross. For the love of God, for the love of your vocation, for the love of your brothers and sisters in the Apostolate, *open your heart* and tell me about those fears. With the grace of God, with the help of the priests, through prayer, fasting, mortification and the little psychiatric knowledge that I possess, I might help you to overcome those fears. By helping you, I might bring more peace and *caritas* into your house, and to all those whom you serve and meet. Stop and think: by being closed up, you not only harm yourself, but you harm the very Apostolate that is your vocation — a tragic thought isn't it?

It might be that you have a superior who is *just what the doctor ordered*. She understands you and is always ready to listen. You have finally found a kindred soul. You are afraid that you will not love her, if you talk to me about her. No, talk about your director to me if there is a need to do so. You may want to praise her or to tell me something about her which confuses you. Often people have a very mistaken sense of loyalty which is at a high school level. You think that there is something disloyal in talking to a higher superior about a subordinate one without first telling the latter. It is an attitude of fair play carried over from the playing field.

There is much confusion in that sort of thinking. There is an unconscious judgment of my attitudes. Your thinking goes something like this: "I don't have to tell the B* about my superior, nor do I have to discuss my problems with my brothers and sisters. It

*A community nickname for Catherine.

won't be fair play; it will be snitching. I don't want to talk it over with the others either, but if I have to speak of it, I should begin with them. The B is apt to misjudge the whole situation. It is so difficult to explain things by letters.'' We can rationalize these things so easily while problems accumulate. The Apostolate does not function to its full capacity. Christ is sad. Christ is waiting.

The truth of the matter is quite different. I am an intelligent woman; I have been in the Apostolate of letters which contain problems many times heavier than any one of you will ever have, thanks be to God!

I try never to judge hastily. I love all of you with a flaming passion of love. Love is kind. I am aware of the mercy of God to me, and I am desirous only to give mercy. Who am I to be harsh? I try to love, to have a heart full of charity. Give me the benefit of the doubt! I understand much more than you think I do, and I can read in between the lines. Also, I often know you better than even your parents do. Give me the benefit of the doubt. You will be closer to the truth.

If it seems strange to you that I praise myself, believe me, dearly beloved, it is humility that prompts me. To acknowledge the graces of God is not to praise oneself, but the Giver of the gifts. This is humility and this is truth.

Moreover, Canon Law, which expresses the mind of the Church, and hence the mind of Christ, expresses great tenderness. The language of Canon Law may appear cold, but the heart of it is warm. It is full of love and compassion. Canon Law stipulates that in the case of any confusion or difficulties between the little ones of Christ and their superiors, these little ones may have recourse to higher authority with the light and joyous hearts, and with the Church's full approval. If they are not satisfied with their superiors, the Church, like a mother, provided access to ever higher authorities even as far as the Pope. The Church is jealous, both of her beloved children and of God's justice and charity among his children. She sees to these attributes — that they have full sway.

It may be that you do not wish to be open, meek and defenseless, because you do not know, or do not believe as yet, that Christ awaits you with love and understanding in the major superior. But also you may not wish to go to your major superior because you are satisfied with your subordinate in too human a fashion, as I suggested in the previous paragraph. This subordinate understands you, and you are content with a human being instead of God. Your way to God is through your major superior, but you don't want to go higher; it is so cozy where you are. It might be cozy, but it is dangerous to tarry with human beings when you are on your way to God.

Whatever your reason may be for being closed to me, consider the *Apostolate*. Your superior might not feel well; you may not tell me because you feel that it is not your place to do so. However, the superior might be so ill that her illness distorts her ability to think or to write. We might learn about her illness too late. Hiding her illness is no way to express your love for your superior. Your love must be strong and clear and without fears and full of truth. Your one desire is to love the Apostolate and to do what is best for it. If you do not confide in someone you may have an emotional upset that will blow you into a "hurricane". Again the Apostolate suffers.

I am also interested in that part of your spiritual life which deals with the little things done well for God. Write to me about that. But here, pause and think. If you write to me about your brothers and sisters and their faults, be sure to mention how you provoked them, how you dealt with them, what was *your* role in the incidents that you are discussing. Let that letter be fair and square.

If you ever think that I ask you to *spy* on your superiors on one another, perish the thought! Then you do not understand what I mean by openness, meekness, defenselessness for the sake of Christ, for the smooth running of the Apostolate. Then you are off base. I can distinguish that type of letter from the letter of a person who is opening her soul to me in order to grow in sanctity and the love of God. Then I can start pruning you who are a tender shoot on the vine of the Lord.

No, I do not want any spying, any snitching, any tale-bearing. God forbid! That is not what I ask. I want openness. I want a passionate love of God and of the Apostolate. Such love, as Thomas Merton says, is not afraid to reveal its own weakness to its mother in the Lord. Such letters humble, simple, and truthfully state the facts as they are. The writer is ready to accept the consequences whether they are joyful, or painful.

God, Church, Cannon Law, common sense, and a desire to grow in sanctity, should motivate you to be open. I hope I have made myself clear. If I have confused you in any way, begin now to be childlike, and simple as doves. Ask me directly and I will try to clarify your problems.

While I am on the subject of superiors, I want to speak about priests. It seems almost unnecessary for me to repeat to you what you have heard from the first day of your arrival at Madonna House. We treat priests as we would treat Christ; we go to them as we go to God, the Father. We listen to them as though we were listening to the Holy Spirit, for they carry the most holy and awesome Trinity. To be afraid of our priests is the height of foolishness. To say that we will not go to them because *they are busy* is to rationalize the truth. No priest of Madonna House is ever too busy to listen; nor is there anything to fear, because they love us.

Just stop to think of the suffering, the pain, the difficulties, the problems they underwent to become priests of Madonna House. Stop to think how they are always ready to help us, to listen to us.

True, our priests are men; they are human beings. But does this have any bearing on the most important thing that matters to us — *our immortal souls*? Woe to the person who forgets the priest in the man. They will not see the face of God. Our priests are holy in thousands of ways that we cannot even fathom; we are so blind. To criticize them, to even dream of arguing with them in matters that are completely under their jurisdiction, in matters pertaining to their priestly life, is to incur the anger of God. Christ not only dwells in them, *but is them*!

To allow the imperfection of a man to cloud our intellects and infect our emotions is to be downright foolish. Stop and think: half of the world would welcome a priest with shouts of joy, weak and sinful though he be. It would be better to perish rather than to judge those good priests whom God has led, through so much suffering, to Madonna House Apostolate! We will never be able to thank the Lord of Hosts enough for our priests.

I tremble before the incomprehensible goodness of God in sending them. I know well the hell and desert that an apostolate can be *without them*. What would any of our houses be without our priests? Even though you are going away from Combermere, you have our priests at the end of an air mail letter, or telephone. You have their interest, their prayers, their love, their suffering, and their Masses. You have been given so much, that it would seem to me incredible that you would dare to look at them and see the tiny, little motes in their eyes, not realizing that, in doing so, you blind yourself with the biggest and most dangerous beam of all.

One more thing I want to tell you. Your priests of Madonna House and priests, in general, act as sort of psychiatrists for you out of the goodness of their hearts. It is out of a superabundance of their charity that they do so. So every time that they listen patiently, to all your emotional problems that you often exaggerate to get attention, fall on your face before the Blessed Sacrament and thank him for their immense charity. Often, though exhausted themselves, they listen to all of your problems. At this point of your development, you could easily fashion these problems into a cross (it wouldn't be a very big one) and carry it behind Christ. It would lessen the burdens of our priests.

This doesn't seem that if they wish to listen to you, you should not go to them. By all means do, but be grateful and understand that this is an added gift of their charity which by no means belongs to their ministry. Be sure to thank them and be grateful to God for it. Never regard it as your right. It is an unexpected, incomprehensible gift of Almighty God through them.

Don't forget to pray for our priests always.

May Christ, the High Priest, bless you and keep you, and give you sight that you may see, and seeing, may understand.

Lovingly yours in Mary,

192

ARE OUR FRIENDSHIPS GOD-CENTERED?

May 16, 1961

Dearly Beloved,

For a long time letters as well as personal inquiries have come to me about *friendship*. Many wanted to know the spirit of Madonna House on this all-important subject.

The more I thought about it, the more I realized that these questions stemmed from a confused, Jansenistic, and puritanical attitude. I realized too, that this area was sort of *terra incognita* (an unknown land) to our modern youth. I sense also some tricklings concerning *particular friendships* coming from various religious houses. Nobody knows exactly what a particular friendship is. Everybody wonders, at times, if he has contracted a "particular friendship."

Let us think a little about friendship. Christ said in a beautiful and heart-warming sentence: "I will not call you servants any more; I will call you friends." In another situation he spoke of a hungry person knocking at the door of his *friend*, and asking for a loaf of bread. Even though that "friend" didn't answer at once, nor open the door, the man persevered, until his friend opened. Christ, in many ways, calls us to a *friendship with him*. He, Who is the Author of all that is perfect and beautiful uses the word *friend* and *friends*! often. So, in itself, friendship cannot be wrong. God wants it to be among us as a gentle, joyful and quiet companion.

I could, of course, answer the problem in one sentence by saying that true friendship can easily be defined by analyzing its goal. If you make friends with someone for your own ends, or as an end in itself, it is a wrong kind of friendship. In fact, it isn't friendship at all. It is latching onto someone for your own selfish purposes.

If, on the other hand, you become friends with a person in order to help each other to God; if you become friends in a mutually give-and-take spirit, then it is a good friendship.

Perhaps, this is too simple a way of stating it. I will quote

Father Voillaume of the Little Brothers of Charles de Foucauld and his fraternities. He is their director general and has just written two extraordinary books: *Letters to the Male Fraternities*, and *Letters to the Female Fraternities*. The only tragedy is that they are in French. I am reading them slowly. It is amazing how our spirits dovetail.

He states that he receives many letters from both fraternities about this question of friendship. He states that it is a difficult question and he has asked Blessed Martin de Porres (The letter is written in Peru) to go to each member of the Fraternities and help him or her to understand what true friendship means. He goes on to state that the question posed can be summed up in this manner:

Have we not renounced the sweetness of human friendships when we entered our vocation? Must we not be detached in that sense? Isn't it wrong that friendship, even supernatural friendship in Christ, often clothes itself in one human face and rests on a natural foundation?

He continues:

Why do you ask me this when you know that the *caritas* that stems from the heart of Christ into our hearts should lead us to a love of one another full of friendship. We communicate our love for one another even as we receive Our Lord in Communion. Our Communion with Christ should translate itself into daily living with great joy; into intimate collaboration, and into a life that is really brotherly and sisterly.

Our friendship with Christ should incarnate itself in our humanity and spread to others. Indeed, we should be friends with one another, for only people in love with God can be true friends to one another. it is the friendship of Christ that unites us, and the human expression of that friendship must grow and grow and unite all of our brothers and sisters in the Apostolate. We are members of one another, and we must recognize the human face of our personal friendship with Christ.

This applies to each one of us even if, in the natural order, we might not all be congenial.

Christ asks us, in fact, to be friends with every person who comes across our path. But we must remember that in order to be friends with one person or with many true friends, that is, our hearts must truly be detached from themselves. It must be a *humble and generous heart that is truly capable of friendship*.

True and holy friendship cannot exist in reality *unless two people have something to share*. For in friendship there is constantly a mutual *giving and receiving*. In the Apostolate, friendship is holy *if it leads to the deepening of the spirit of our Fraternity, and to leading each other to God*. It must *lead to the constant widening of this circle of mutual friendships to include more and more members of our Fraternity*, until a given house overflows with this type of true and beautiful friendship.

So speaks Father Voillaume. I don't know what I can add to this. Yet I must try. For the members of our Apostolate are full of fears and emotional problems, and in a way of speaking, do well to mistrust themselves. "Particular friendships" is a rather obsolete label, yet it has a modern reality. So let me speak in modern language.

If you call friendship the latching onto one person because you are lonely and "no one understands you", because you want to gripe to someone about many things; or because you find something personally agreeable in a given person and you want to enjoy that agreeableness all by yourself, you are on the wrong track.

If, on the other hand, you want to be friends with a certain person because he or she has something to teach you, and you hope you can teach him or her something, then it is a wonderful friendship. If, as Father Voillaume says, *you have something to share mutually* (and who in our Apostolate does not have *God* to share?) it is a wonderful friendship. (Who in our Apostolate does not need to grow in the spirit of Our Apostolate and in virtue and holiness?) If these are the motives that animate you, I repeat it is a wonderful friendship.

Examples: You find in your house a person who likes painting as much as you do, or one who enjoys reading together even as you like to do, or you both like nature and walking. There is nothing wrong about forming a friendship to share these common activities. But always remember that two people can never be a *closed circuit*. They must be open, always ready and eager to include someone else.

There are some amongst you who question physical expressions of friendship. For example, you wonder why some women always need to put their arms around others when they talk to them. There are many who are not used to that kind of friendly, physical demonstration. It takes all kinds of people to make a world.

Sometimes, people who put their arms around their friends have had very little physical loving in childhood and yearn for it. On the other hand much depends upon race and nationality. Italians and many Eastern people are, generally, very affectionate people. Men of these cultures embrace each other, and the girls are forever holding one another by the waist and putting their arms around each other. On the other hand some people such as Mohammedans and Hindus, never touch each other.

Questions that arise: Why does it bother a person to be touched? Why do others need to touch each other? These are profound psychological questions, but on the whole, the answers do not matter very much. It doesn't really matter whether or not people touch you. These things are more cultural patterns and mannerisms than anything else.

However in an Apostolate such as ours, these physical signs of affection are better restrained. In Canada and America it is not a custom, but if we go to countries where it is a custom we submit to it gracefully. But let's not make a mountain out of a molehill. There are moments when such physical signs of affection between the same sex are perfectly normal; in times of distress or special joy, they are a natural expression. So let us accept them as they come, but let us not indulge in them unnecessarily in countries where it isn't the custom.

So I end my letter as I began it. Friendships should be the natural outcome of *caritas*. To know if it is a right or wrong friendship, one must consider its goal. Is it "I" centered, selfish? Is it *God-centered* and hence unselfish?

In our day and age *particular friendships* often mean homosexual tendencies. We are an enlightened generation, or should be. We must be on the alert to note such an accent. But frankly, in the Apostolate this is not even discussed, because homosexuality is a sickness, and would soon be recognized by the directorate. Most of the Maudlin friendships that arise among youth here are simple due to immaturity. Such relationships cannot be called friendships; they are childish attachments because of insecurity and other emotional factors of which the directorate is constantly aware.

Often neurotic people come into our houses and simply latch onto us. Such people should be immediately and simply discouraged by being told directly and frankly that in our Apostolate such *latching on* is not encouraged because it is psychologically bad for them.

To sum up: friendship is part of *caritas*, part of the Madonna House spirit. It is unselfish, open and open towards one another, sharing common interests and all that is good. These are characteristics of friendships which are encouraged by our Apostolate. A friendship may begin with two people, but it should never stop there.

Lovingly yours in Mary,

APOSTOLIC VACATIONS

August 3rd, 1961

Dearly Beloved,

There are several topics which I would like to discuss with you. The first one concerns vacations.

Let us understand each other very clearly regarding this matter. It is true that we feel that you should have a vacation (two weeks a year) in order to have a change, and in order to fulfill the obligation of *caritas* towards your parents. You go to visit your folks because you love them and they have a right to your presence periodically.

However, you must never forget that for an apostle the Apostolate comes first. In fact, a member of an institute totally dedicated to Christ under the counsels of perfection, obviously cannot ever take a vacation from him.

So your vacation is really a re-creation of yourself, a re-collecting of yourself in Christ, with his help. Therefore, you cannot look at your vacation with worldly eyes as you used to do. Others can just let go of the routines of their day, but not you. Especially is this true in matters of behaviour, inward attitudes, and the fact that you really do not take a vacation from Christ nor from the Apostolate.

This does not mean, of course, that you cannot change your routine. Discuss the matter of your prayer life and your daily schedule with your spiritual director or with your director general. Then follow the advice which you receive. They will probably allow you to alter your routine, but let them be the judge of it; for then you will have a real change and rest. It will be under obedience and therefore God's will.

After the first year at Madonna House your vacation should be geared to enriching yourself with new knowledge in order to serve God better. There are many ways to obtain the knowledge that would benefit you and the Apostolate, and help you to grow.

Investigate various summer courses. Mosaics, weaving, silk screening, all kinds of arts and crafts are available for short periods in the summer. A week or two of taking such courses would be a beneficial change for you, and would help you to see another facet of God's infinite mercy and tenderness. Moreover, it would help you to become a more efficient member of our Institute, a better servant of Christ. I cannot begin to enumerate all of the courses available to you that you might take.

Consider the Apostolate. If at all possible, members of the Apostolate should take their vacations in other houses so as to experience the other rooms of Madonna House. It would enrich your understanding of *the vision of the whole.*

With due preparation and consultation, and with the full understanding that you should pay for the trip by begging or using your own money with permission, you should consider the possibility of trips to Europe or the Holy Land. Travel is a tremendous cultural and spiritual experience. It will enlarge your vision of the whole Church.

A retreat for a week in some quiet spot for those who are especially on the go, and in the public eye all the time, is another wonderful possibility. Here, people can plan to catch up on their spiritual reading, and have time for meditation and contemplation, while giving the body a well-needed rest.

When going on vacation be fully aware that you have left father and mother behind and are only going with permission and out of love for your parents. Don't revert to the spoiled darling type, and let Mama and Papa fuss over you. You are there to serve.

You are not there to miss Mass, the Divine Office, and spiritual reading. These are part of your life wherever you go. Even on vacation Mass should still be your first concern.

Nor can you spend carelessly any money which you have received. You are still under the obligation of holy poverty. For instance, if there is a choice between a taxi or a bus, you take the bus. You do not go on a binge of buying records nor books, even though your parents have given you money to do so. You have to remember that nothing can be bought without permission either on vacation or off, or at other time. You are subject on vacation to the same rules as you are in Madonna House. You must carefully figure these things out ahead of time, and make sure you have the permission or presumed permission, in the spirit of poverty. You always have to show the face of poverty to the world.

If you are invited to a good, steak dinner, accept. This is the bounty of God. If you are offered a drink, taste it. But have the spirit of holy poverty there too. If you are invited to go to a show or to the theatre, be sure it is a decent performance, because you always have to give a good example, don't forget that. Needless to say, women of the Apostolate should not frequent bars, cocktail lounges, and beer parlours unaccompanied by their friends or relatives. If you go to these places, then do not wear the cross outside, but inside. The only time to wear your cross in such a place is if you are on God's business.

Don't spend your time watching TV all day. Take walks, go to museums, look at art. If you are interested in rocks or a craft, and you are in a city, make sure that you find out all about your hobby in the many places that are open for learning. Try to locate books about your craft. Remember an apostle is always an apostle — at home, abroad, on a vacation. Your mind is always on the alert seeking ways and means to help the Apostolate.

Try to visit the sick or shut-ins whom you know. Also, wherever you find former member of the Apostolate, make a point of contacting them. They are still the living history of your

Institute. Meet them, talk to them, find out about the early days of your Foundation. They will not always be available, and you are missing out in not making contacts with them.

I have tried to show you what an apostolic vacation is like. It isn't lolling around, doing nothing, and indulging in all one's whims. That would not be a vacation. That would be a sliding backward in the spiritual life. I beg of you, not to engage in endless activities, wonderful and apostolic as they may seem, such as addressing various youth groups, seeking out your old friends to tell them about Madonna House. It is a pitiful state of affairs when members of Madonna Houses come back more tired from the semi-social round than when they went. Surely, they are not fulfilling the basic idea of re-creation, of rest in the Lord, and of recollecting oneself.

Once more I repeat that the expenditure of money is guided by permissions, and the spirit of holy poverty. Remember you are a member of an Institute and you will be judged by your actions and behaviour.

I beg you to mediate seriously on this matter and if you do not understand, feel free to ask questions.

Lovingly yours in Mary,

P.S. Many should consider a vacation to Madonna House in Combermere for the renewal of your spirit and for getting in touch again with the source of your vocations.

ARE WE STEALING GOD'S TIME?

August 28, 1961

Dearly Beloved,

As you know, I love each and everyone of you very deeply, but I must admit that I am concerned about several things.

I think that, by and large with a few exceptions, the majority of you have reached a point where you must lay aside psychology and begin to implement the deep, spiritual training which you have received.

With the exceptions of those few who still need counselling (even they will benefit by making a cross of their emotions while they are being helped), the rest of you should begin to examine your consciences not so much on psychological blocks, hostilities, guilt etc., as on pride, selfishness, self-centredness, and a lack of charity. We cannot constantly remain children, or keep blaming our emotions for a lack of spirituality.

Each of you is perfectly aware of his or her personality problems. Therefore, there is very little to add. Now you have to face the reality of life. Understanding yourselves better you can do so much more easily. For example: if your emotional difficulty has been hostility against your parents, which you transfer to anyone in authority, then begin to concentrate on charity, humility, and self-forgetfulness. If your pattern is guilt and fears, then think of faith and trust. So on down the line. Pray much about this.

We must truly face reality head-on these days. We are living in dangerous times. We have solemnly promised before the Blessed Sacrament to be poor, obedient, and chaste. We have promised also to bind ourselves as members of the Madonna House Apostolate which means that our duty is first and foremost to become perfect. We cannot remain eternally in the realm of our emotions if we are going to reach that goal.

We have to understand that if we do not practice the counsels of perfection to the best of our ability, we will be judged by Almighty God, not only for positive failures, but for sins of omission. A dedicated lay apostle who fails to work at his or her own task spiritually, hinders God's message for the Apostolate. The Apostolic work which should be done promptly, obediently and well will remain undone. People whom we could reach will remain neglected. This is a responsibility before the Lord.

Have you ever considered how much of God's time is stolen in the Apostolate by pouting, by self-pity, by personality clashes? So much wasted and "stolen" time which could have been used to grow in grace and wisdom and love.

One psychiatrist here expressed a very important truth in the course of his lectures: "Many very honest people, who wouldn't think of stealing anything, not even a safety pin, *steal God's time constantly!*''

It is frightening to think of these things, dearly beloved, especially against the backdrop of a world poised once more before the abyss of a war that can lead to annihilation. So much wasted time, so many years gone by, so many of us still wallowing in our emotions without trying to overcome them, which we could easily do. None of you are that sick! If only we held onto the cross of Christ, so that some day soon we might lift it high for men to see so that they can see and embrace it with love. Truly at times I am frightened at the slowness of our collective growth, the pain that the directors at every level have to go through.

I have been to one of the best clinics in the United States. They found that all is well with me physically, but that I was under a terrific stress and strain. What was the stress and strain? Well, some of my psychiatrist friends told me that my stress and strain is you. I wish to lay my life down so that you may become saints and my body reacts to this stress and strain. The priests and I all blame ourselves for not giving you enough. When we examine the results of your years in the Apostolate, and the fruits thereof, we come to the conclusion that we should give more. And we try, until we fall flat onto our faces, for we have nothing more to give.

What do you yourselves think? Have we given you too little, or have we given you enough, and you haven't taken it or implemented it? I am neither judging nor accusing. I am just stating facts and asking a question. May I have your answer? Before you answer me, please pray about it. Rest assured that if my very life were needed to make you stop acting as children and start becoming saints, I would gladly give it.

Lovingly in Mary,

LIVING BY THE SPIRIT

September 4, 1961

Dearly Beloved,

Here is a meditation which I made on the Epistle to the Galations. (5:25-26; 6:1-10).

"*Since we live by the spirit, let the spirit be our rule of life.*"

Let we consider the words of this wonderful Epistle in relation to our daily life in the Apostolate.

We have been brought together *to live by the spirit*, so how else could we live — we who have been chosen so especially by the Lord; for the Lord has said: "I have chosen you. You haven't chosen Me." We must accept in deep faith and joy the fact that we belong, through the mystery of his choice, to those chosen few whom he means to live by the Spirit of Love — the Holy Spirit. Why did we come here except for this? Consider our lives minute by minute, hour by hour, day by day, as a stranger would if he were allowed to observe us for a certain time, would he say that we always lived by the spirit?

I leave the answer to you. I simply suggest that the topic is worth much prayer and deep examination of consciences. It is time to realize that your eternal salvation depends on the answer. If those who have been especially chosen by God to live by the Spirit don't live this way, then what will happen to them?

"*We must not indulge in vain ambitions.*"

Are we completely free from any *vain ambitions*? Do we get upset when we do not have our own way? Do we have the ambition, even deeply hidden in our hearts, to do *our* will instead of God's? Do we have the desire to be *promoted* to the small, key positions or our humble Apostolate?

Do we want to be "in" on confidential matters, to be specially close to the persons in authority so that we would be a little "higher" than the next member? Do we measure the jobs given to us by worldly, instead of divine standards? Do we consider that collecting garbage, cleaning rooms or toilets are *beneath our dignity*, that we rate better jobs? Do we boast of the talents or special knowledge that we have? Do we seek the limelight, (insignificant as it may be in our Apostolate), and are we shattered emotionally when we do not get it? If we haven't left behind that type of ambition, we walk in pride. Need I tell you what happens to proud people? If you are in doubt, read the Gospel concerning them, but read it on your knees.

"Envying one another and provoking one another to envy".

Do we jockey for positions? This is still part of ambition and begets envy. This is probably why St. Paul put envy after ambition. Do we always wish to be right, so that others may envy us? Do we engage in arguments so that others might be proven wrong or ignorant? This is an inverse form of envy. He who loves is open to another's point of view. In the spirit of humility, he is even willing to let the other fellow appear to be right in all that does not pertain to faith and morals.

Do we belittle our own talents and virtues with a Pharisaical tongue because fundamentally we envy other people's virtues, and hope that if we make little of our own, he will exalt ours. Do we envy others by thinking that we could do a much better job if we were in their positions? Do we not see every little concession given to another person, and envy it? Envy is a deadly sin.

"Bear the burden of one another's failings; then you will be fulfilling the law of Christ."

This is a stark sentence. It bites deeply — or should — into the heart of any person chosen by God *to walk in his Spirit*. How do we measure up? Are you bearing one another's failings and thus fulfilling the law of Christ? Or is the clash of personalities one of the greatest obstacles to sanctity? Personally, I think that next to the dangers of envy, this clash is the crux of the majority of the problems that beset our Apostolate. As Father Callahan said: "Unless we love one another first, we will not be able to love a more distant neighbor as we should." Hence we will fail in the task the Lord has allotted to us, our part of the restoration of the kingdom of God on earth, which is the kingdom of love!" To bear one another's failings is to really love. Do we? Again I leave the answer to you.

"The man who thinks he is of some worth, when in truth he is worth nothing at all, is merely deluding himself."

After all that you have been taught on poverty and kenosis, is it necessary to comment at all on this flaming line of St. Paul? Surely by now you know that of ourselves *we are nothing and have nothing and exist moment by moment by the mercy and love of God.* Why then, is it that we put such a tremendous worth on ourselves, that we are forever hurt when someone does not recognize our worth? If we just understood the simple truth that we are nothing, then whole Epistle would become part of the wrap and woof of our lives, and we have the peace of the Lord dwelling in us.

"Everyone should examine his own conduct."

If we really did that, then we would walk in wisdom and in grace. We would be able to fulfill the last sentence of that Epistle:

"Each of us then would have his own burden to carry."

We would not weigh others down with our burdens but would stand ready to carry theirs too if necessary. We would *practice generosity* to all, but especially to our own family.

Besides this Epistle, I recommend that you read the 29th Chapter or the Book of Proverbs. This is what I read:

"The man often rebuked but stubborn still: suddenly, irretrievably, his fall will come."

I leave you with that sentence for a meditation.

Lovingly yours in Mary,

POVERTY WITHOUT COMPROMISE

October 10, 1961

Dearly Beloved,

Once again I must write to you about *holy poverty* and remind you of her beautiful face. With a deep sadness, I have to call to your attention that unless you accept her in all of her beauty, austerity and joy, you will be untrue to your vocation. Being untrue to that vocation means being untrue to God who was born in a stable at Bethlehem, lived in a very poor home in Nazareth, and who died naked on a cross for you and me.

Compromise with Lady Poverty is impossible. For she walks in truth, fortitude and with a flaming courage that faces the realities of God without any compromise. She abhors them and will have nothing to do with them.

Unless we accept poverty completely, we will never understand obedience and chastity will veil its face. We will be like sounding brass and tinkling cymbals. We will be abhorrent to the Lord of Hosts. We will profess with our lips that we have embraced Lady Poverty whereas in fact, we have not done so. That is hypocrisy. How do you think that God who is truth, looks on the face of hypocrisy? Reread that part of the Gospel where Christ talks about it so sternly: "You hypocrites, you whited sepulchres, etc. . . ." Reread it and examine your consciences.

You might wonder why I am writing a letter like this now. The reason should be very clear to some of you. You have, by now, realized that my letters are usually written because I have noted somewhere in my spiritual children, a *deviation, a compromise with the spirit of Madonna House* which the Lord has entrusted to me. I have been guarding this spirit with my very life for thirty-one years and, without exaggeration, I would die for it in a second.

Our Constitution states that our poverty concerns the use of things. So may I remind you to reread the part of the Constitution that deals with these matters! May I remind you again, and I hope for the last time, that you are bound to report to your immediate superior every item that you receive from anyone. When I say everything, I mean a spool of thread, a pin, money, be it one cent or a thousand dollars. Nothing is excepted or exempted. All must be reported to your superiors.

If you keep anything, be it ever so tiny, you sin against our Constitution and our promise of poverty. Let this be quite clear to you, and there are no arguments on the subject. There is no compromise. This is it, and be sure that you understand it. I have a sad feeling that this particular part of our Constitution is ho-hum, and not too well observed by some people. I may be mistaken, but I want to bring it to your attention once more.

If we allow a tiny chink no bigger than a pinhead to enter into the essence of our vocation, it will take only a few minutes for Satan to create a big opening. Then pride, greed, compromise, and other demons will enter the soul, spill over into the house where this happens, and break the bond of charity. That place will be like a desert that yesterday was flowering, but is now devastated by the hot blasts of hell.

An apple was such a small thing, but look where it led mankind. Let us be watchful, dearly beloved, and let us stay close to poverty. It will teach us charity, obedience and chastity, and above all, it will reveal to us the fullness of the beauty of the face of the poor Christ.

Lovingly yours in Mary,

A MEDITATION ON JOY

November 16, 1961

Dearly Beloved,

Lately there has been much discussion in Madonna House about joy. During these fall months one group is preparing for Advent, and another is studying the vows. At present, they are studying the vow of poverty.

When people really seek to come close to Christ, the Holy Spirit is with them, and they begin to understand more clearly things that at first they saw "as in a glass, darkly." One result of this close study of the Word of God was the desire to seek more clearly the meaning of joy.

At first people took many books from the library thinking that perhaps they could find the answer to that elusive gift of joy. But little by little they discovered that one cannot find love, joy and hope in books. Joy, especially, eluded them. So they left the books alone and began to talk about joy, which brought them to the word *sharing*. This led them to the word *love*, and this led them to the word *family*. So they had come to some very important words along with joy: family, love and sharing. They discovered that joy was the fruit of love, which creates a family. Love created the family of Madonna House. Love created the great family of the Mystical Body. Love and family foster a sharing of oneself which creates openness, defenselessness — in a word, kenosis.

Someone gave this definition of joy: *Joy consists in possessing what one greatly desires to possess.* At this point everyone is asking what is it that one desires most to possess. I put that question to you also: What is it that you desire most of all at this moment? Suppose you try to answer this for me and then, perhaps, you too will realize, as our group is beginning to realize, that maybe you have no joy because you desire the wrong things, the possession of which does not bring a real and lasting joy.

In the meantime we are reading a book called *Work* by the Cardinal Primate of Warsaw, Poland. It is a terrific book. I suggest that you all read it. We read a chapter called "Cooperation" which speaks of love and sharing. I got into a little discussion with some people here about their wrong attitudes to work.

The kitchen, for example, seems to be a frightening place — a place one has to "go through" as one would study mathematics or geography and then be done with it. I told them that we should see those tasks as challenges which are interesting and add to life's experiences. Working anywhere fosters sharing and adds to growth.

I suggested that they consider such a simple thing as the fact that while some were cooking, others were doing their laundry for them. This very morning someone had swept their dormitory. The nurse in the dispensary had been sorting out medicines and making the sick bay comfortable. The librarian was even then busy sorting and organizing books, lists, and what have you, so that they would find it easier to obtain the needed books for study.

So here is *sharing*. They are cooking for those who are working for them. Here the idea of the family is developing;

everything is based on love. Why are we here? Because God has loved us and has called us in his love to be his very own, and to cooperate with him in the restoration of his kingdom.

The realization of his love for us should be *great joy*. Supreme joy should come to all of us especially through the Mass. One of the commentaries before the Mass recently was: "We are now going to be one in love with Christ," meaning that we will literally be one in *caritas* with the Lord of Hosts, by partaking of His Body and Blood. What a unity with God and among ourselves should come forth from this oneness in love! Sometimes it moves me physically. I tremble at the thought. Joy floods my heart until I am drowned in its singing waters. Such are the ideas that came out of our discussion of joy.

And now I want to share with you some of *my* ideas of joy. They are personal, I know, but I love to share them with you, for I love you truly and joyously, though many of you do not realize this.

First, I want to look at joy as generally understood by the world. A woman feels full of joy when she gets a mink coat. This is a very "synthetic" joy. We say we had a good time, a joyous time, when there was a lot to drink, superficially pleasant company, some flirtation for the young, and lots of noise. This, in the estimation of many, is a good time. That is all connected with *sensual* enjoyments. But is that a joyous time? How soon all of this fades, and how quickly there is nothing left!

Joy is very quiet. It is like a light that shines in the darkness. It is connected with hope and with love. It is full of wonderment. To give you an idea of my joyous moments — the first occurs when I wake up. I have the habit of saying, even when I am half asleep, three words: "Jesus, Mary and Joseph." And then, when the bed is still very warm and I am half awake, joy comes to me every morning with the incredible thought that here God has granted me another day to love him and to serve him.

True, simultaneously, other thoughts come to me from the devil and from my own humanity and emotions too. They creep in like shadows over the shining light of my joy. They whisper: "Look, you are going to have a whole day answering letters that always contain the same problems. You are going to have to be in four places at once. The library is waiting to sort and classify books, and they are in a hurry. Don't forget the slides that you have to do — mounds of them — so that the future generations, as you say, might know the history of the Apostolate. That jewelry that everyone thinks you like to sort out for the poor is also waiting. And remember the heavy problems of the houses that have to be dealt with.''

So on and on and on. The whole weight of the day and my office creeps in through those whispers, but joy smiles. I know that I don't have to face all of those things at once, that these too are works of love for Christ's sake, that all I have to worry about is doing the duty of the moment as it comes to me, with love and enthusiasm for Love's sake — for Christ's sake.

The next moment of my joy is when I cross the bridge from my island to Madonna House. Nary a day nor morning passes but the scenery is different. Rainy days, misty days, and even the dark mornings of the winter — all have a beauty of their own, as if God were saying, "Here, child, is joy, the joy of my creation. Since you are mine, I share with you all of these gems from my bountiful hand."

Then my joy is complete when I am at Mass and I receive Communion and become one with God. I cannot describe this. You who have never been a wife twice, and marriage is a holy state. But were I asked if it is the supreme state of loving, I would answer, "NO!" It is a pale reflection of the unity, love and oneness that a human being can have with God at Mass and Communion. Nothing equals that! I'm not saying that this happens to me every morning, for perfect joy doesn't come to us on this earth. But it comes often, and is as perfect as my finite nature can expect.

My other moments of joy come from the *enthusiasm* with which I greet every new task. It baffles me that there is, or can be, a lackadaisicalness, or indifference, about the little jobs which we do. To me, each one of them is a challenge. Satan may whisper to me of the dullness of my forthcoming day, but I must admit that most of the time he whispers in vain.

To me, your letters are not a chore; they are a challenge. It is joy for me because when you give me your confidences by turning to me with your problems (which I may have answered many times) they are always new, because *you are unique to me and always beloved*. I would not be telling a lie if I say that I put my whole intelligence, my love — my whole being — into answering your letters. No matter how many times you write, I am always *enthusiastic about answering*. I might be tired occasionally. But that does not matter: *You matter*.

In the natural order I am not particularly fond of sorting jewelry, but I bring an enthusiasm, a joy to the work that is like a song, a light within me. As I handle that jewelry I see the gladness of people receiving that jewelry because they are getting something pretty for the Birthday of the Lord. Many people have so little of the special things that we take for granted in life.

The gardener comes to discuss her work. My mind leaps with enthusiasm because we are creating beauty for Our Lady's altar, for the visitors and for ourselves. The library is in need of clarification and reorganization. In the natural order it is a tedious job, but one that arouses my enthusiasm as soon as I begin it. I see my dreams coming true — youth learning the depths of the Word of God at Madonna House.

I never forget — and this is the essence of my joy and enthusiasm — that everything that we do will eventually lead souls to Christ. This is happening while we are doing the duty of the moment, joyfully, and lovingly. Already God accepts that for other souls.

Everything can be a dreary chore. It can become light and joyous if one looks at it, first in the natural order, as an experience and perfection of oneself, and secondly in the supernatural order, as being done for God, Frankly, I cannot imagine why people look at things negatively instead of positively. I could go on for pages and pages, telling you about my enthusiastic interest in every aspect of the duty of the moment given to me by God.

I've been sculpturing lately. I made a little set of figurines which came out of my meditation of Friday. I made little, clay islands with a little tree, and figures bending inward; they are figurines of self-centredness. I made several figurines like that and put them on a piece of wood. They represent members of Madonna House, each an island, each turning his back to the other. Kitty-cornered to this I put a figure of Christ, standing with outstretched arms. In my imagination, rays came from his hands; trying to make each person turn around and look at one another and love one another, and share themselves with one another, becoming a family instead of a collection of individuals in a house; but he was not succeeding. No one was turning around in my little tableau. No one was trying to build a bridge from himself to another island.

Often people talk to me about the difficulty they have in

loving. Or someone may say: "Why doesn't love grow amongst us?" I answer: "Love, Christ Himself, stands before the doors of our hearts twenty-four hours a day. He greatly desires to enter. But our hearts have doors with latches only on the inside." Oh, Christ knocks with his graces, but we turn a deaf ear to his knocks because we are afraid that if we let him in, he will ask too much of us. Love and joy are the fruit of faith, sacrifice, and pain. True joy does not come to people who are self-centered, and who view the world only from the way that it affects *them*.

So Christ stands outside and knocks. He has given us free will, and he doesn't violate that gift by forcing himself in. Until we allow Christ to come in, we will not be able to love one another. First we must love him and *surrender to him willingly, and let him take total possession of our souls, then the rest will follow*. That is my answer to those who say that there is no true love in a given house or department. How could there be when Love stands outside waiting? If Love isn't present, joy cannot be there either.

However, you will not bring Love there by reading books nor meditating about him. The yardstick of your love is with what enthusiasm, completeness, and thoughtfulness you do your duty of the moment. It is all so very simple, and *we* are the ones who make it complicated in order to escape the one thing which we fear above all: *to surrender to Love in the daily, ordinary, little things and duties of the moment*.

Temptations to quit — to leave — come to many of us. Temptations must come. They are the examinations of God. The more sorely you are tempted, the stronger you become. For Christ knows that you can fight these temptations. Christ permits them to happen to you in order to strengthen your will. He knows that you can fight these temptations for he has given you the graces.

I myself have had about twenty such violent temptations in my life. To those who have such temptations I say, with deep understanding and true knowledge, "Fight them by staying close to a priest. Be careful and watchful!"

Each of you might be in the position that I was in. One of our great temptations to leave — mine and Eddie's — was when we came to what seemed a dead-end street — Combermere. You know the history of our Apostolate and you know the deadness that we encountered in the first years here. First one of us, then the other, would want to leave. We could so easily say to ourselves that we had done enough for the Lord, and we were getting older, and it was "Okay to live our own lives." But we fought the temptations, and we stayed, and Madonna House and its many missions are the fruit.

Suppose we had left and then died. All of you and the many missions that were in God's heart would have been shown to us when we met Christ and looked into his face. Can you imagine how sad his eyes would have been? Try to visualize the fear that would have possessed us at that moment!

Each of you who is tempted now or in the future, imagine the picture of your particular judgment. Try to understand this terrible, awesome thought, that *on your perseverance, your surrender, your stability, depend many, many yet unborn souls, and that you will be answerable for them before God. He has called you to this vocation.* This is an awesome consideration!

Yes, joy is quiet. It is composed of enthusiasm, holy wonderment, understanding the inner challenge of things, and relating them to the Lord of Hosts, the Tremendous Lover. Joy is quiet, a constant song within one's heart. Joy is a light to one's feet in the darkness, provided that we walk the path of the little duties of the moment, which are nothing but the bloody footprints of Christ that he has traced for us on the sands of time, so that we may be sure to follow without losing our way.

Lovingly yours in Mary,

ADVENT — THE DAWN BEFORE THE DAY

December 4, 1961

Dearly Beloved,

Advent, the season of penance, is with us. It is interwoven with dark colors and bright colors. It reflects the life of a human being as it wends its slow, painful journey to the parousia, the final advent of the Lord of Hosts, the tremendous Lover.

Advent is the time of expectation — the dawn before the day. How many generations waited in the darkness of the Redeemer, the Promised One of the Father who was to come?

Advent is a short season, but it is the long road of a soul from Nazareth to Bethlehem. It is such a short distance as we in North America are accustomed to thinking of distances. Yet, it is a road into infinity, into eternity, having a beginning, but no end. Advent is, in truth, the road of the spiritual life which all of us must take if we wish to get to heaven. It is the place from which we must start if we do not want to miss the way. We must start with a fiat that reechoes Mary's *fiat*. A fiat that each of us should say in the quiet of our chapels preferably at eventide when all creation is still.

I sit quietly in the absolute silence of St. Kate's, broken only now and then by the fan in my oil stove. It has a high-pitched song of its own. I realize daily in greater depths the inescapable fact that each one of us must echo the *fiat* of Our Lady. Unless we do, the Apostolate will come to a standstill, or just crawl along instead of walking with the giant strides of love as planned by God.

There are nights when the word *fiat* beats against my tired brain like a million hammers hitting copper gongs. I ask: "Have I myself said that *fiat* completely and irrevocably?" If I have, what must I do to teach *you* to say it too? Then the darkness descends upon me with doubts about my own *fiat*. I see that I am such a poor example to you, and that is why you hesitate to reecho Mary's *fiat*. I do not judge the motives nor intentions of any of my spiritual children, but I cannot close my eyes to the fruits which are perceptible.

Beloved, I am not censuring, criticizing, correcting, or

teaching you. Prostrated in the dust before your feet, I am simply imploring you to look squarely at Love's Coming during the Holy Season. Try to face, at least a little bit, that it is Love — Love Himself Who is God — Who died for you and me, coming to prove once more his love for us.

Let us then arise, shake the sleep out of our eyes; the sleep of our emotions running amuck; the sleep of indifference; of tepidity; of self-pity; of fighting God: Let us arise from that sleep with its dark nightmares and be off on that journey to Bethlehem. But let us understand that Bethlehem is our own souls, our own hearts, and our own minds. What kind of a birthplace are you and I providing for the Christ Child? Is the straw shiny and golden and clean? Is the manger solid, and will it hold up under the weight of the Child? Are the animals quiet, scrubbed, brushed? Have we made the doors of the stables of our hearts secure against the cold winds of apathy, selfishness, indifference, so that these cannot penetrate? Is the dry wood of our sacrifices, our penances, our prayers, ready to be lit to provide warmth in that cold stable?

I am trying to write about Advent. I am trying to share with you my thoughts, but words escape me. How does one plead for a dedicated soul to be more dedicated? How does one teach the bride of Christ to love him and all those for whom he died? How does one teach the bride of Christ to love him and all those for whom he died? How does one sing about Love's coming into our midst? How does one describe a little word like *fiat*, the word that would make a joyless house joyful if said with one's whole heart?

Dearly Beloved in Christ, I think I shall write no more about it, for if there is anything that I feel more than *my own* abject poverty, I do not know what it is. It seems to me that I have run out of words. As I look at myself, what is there left to give, and what did I have to give that was my own? So all I can do is to implore Christ to wake you up, to blow the sleep out of your eyes, to set your feet on that journey from Nazareth to Bethlehem, to explain for you the *fiat* with all the immense depths of its meaning, and to bring you unto himself, the Child.

Advent, the coming of Love. Behold he comes in the womb of a woman. You will catch your first glimpse of Love on the straw in a stable. Emptying himself, the Lord of Hosts, out of love became a Child; and we who are so poor cling to our rags as if they were diamonds.

No, I don't think I have much to say, except that I love you with a love that beggars the imagination. I will try to beseech the Lord to teach you to say *fiat*; because there is really nothing else that I *can* do.

May the Lord find in your house a warm resting place on Christmas night. There are so few resting places left for him in this world.

Lovingly yours in Mary,

WHEN THE CROSS UNVEILS ITSELF

December 6, 1961

Dearly Beloved,

At times all of us are tempted to leave our vocations. We are tempted especially on the days when the period we have promised to serve God at Madonna House has been fulfilled.

This is one of the most profound and common temptations that beset people in all forms of dedicated life. Once the excitement of the honeymoon has passed, the cross of any vocation unveils itself daily more and more; human nature, often assisted by the devil, desires an out.

But where can we go to escape the cross? How foolish and pitiful are our attempts to escape! When once we know that our vocation is the will of God, and we try to run away from it, all we do is to add to the cross that God has given to each of us. We make our own crosses of frustration, guilt, and many others which slowly, like weeds, clutter our lives. We decide that we will love accordingly to our own will and not his!

When the temptation to leave the Apostolate comes, let us remember the Scriptural quotation: "Lord, to whom shall we go? You alone have the words of eternal life." As I travel across the years, I witness all the time this desire to *escape*. As recently as a couple of weeks ago, I listened to the mother of four children telling me, with tears in her eyes, that she belonged in a convent, that she had made a mistake in marrying. She went so far as to petition a bishop to let her do this. Thanks be to God, I think I was able to show her the foolishness of her ways, and she departed with a more peaceful heart.

I have known nuns, as I am sure you have too, who very legitimately, and with the permission of the Church, left their convents after a long dedication to that life, only to wander disconsolately through the ensuing years. Some married, and one of them said to me: "Yes, I am content in a general way. But oh, Catherine, what a fool I was to exchange the love of God for the love of a man!"

However, all of these stories, I know have little influence on the minds, souls and hearts of those amongst us who are beset by the temptation of leaving the Apostolate. It is a deep temptation, one that I have undergone many times in Harlem, Toronto and in Combermere.

When this temptation besets you, dearly beloved, whoever you are, be sure to write immediately, or talk it over with your spiritual director. Write to me too. Do not be ashamed. Desolate are the days and hours when we live in those temptations. They must be fought, and we need help to fight them.

Remember the story which I tell you about our Bishop Founder, Archbishop Neil McNeil of Toronto, who when I told him that I wanted to leave, that I couldn't take the rap any more, bade me to get a crucifix off the wall. When I did so, he told me to look at the other side; then he asked me for whom did I think it was reserved. I reluctantly answered: "For God's friends." He quietly went on saying: "Child, do you want to abandon the cross, and leave God alone there? Do you truly expect him to be happy about that? He — who is so lonely? So few want to share this place with him." These words of the old and saintly prelate pierced my heart and helped me through all the years of the Apostolate.

The temptation to descend from the cross of God's choosing to leave him alone, to escape the pain, is natural. But we are Christians and we have a supernatural destiny. Think of Christ when your temptation comes. Think of Gethsemane and what would have happened to you and me if he had given in to the temptation to leave the Garden! An impossible thought, and yet one which we might well contemplate.

Oh, dearly beloved, where can I find the words to tell you of the tragedy of giving in to that temptation? There aren't any words to express it. It is such a deep and tragic denial.

There isn't one of you who wouldn't be very angry and disappointed if a friend of yours had made *you* a solemn promise and then had broken that promise as if it were a twig. You must confess that you would be highly indignant. There would be no admiration in your heart for that person. We do not think well of people who break their promises. There is something sacred in even an ordinary promise that is solemnly and firmly made between two human beings. We have no respect even for a business concern that does not keep its promises.

But for some unknown reason when someone amongst us departs, especially before his or her promise time is completed, we have an entirely different attitude, or at least, *seem* to have. Everybody seems to be very tolerant and "charitable" about the situation. We should be charitable. Our Christian faith urges us to love and pray for sinners but never to condone the sin. Let us keep things straight before the Lord. Let us not allow our emotions to cloud facts; but most of all, let us pray that we are all faithful to our promises.

Lovingly yours in Mary,

LEAVING ONE'S VOCATION

February 3, 1962

Dearly Beloved,

It is time to clarify the whole question of leaving one's vocation.

Each one of you knew before you came to Madonna House what I would call some special facts of life. Unless you were a very recent convert you were aware that some priests depart from their priesthood. Some leave to get married, some are emotionally sick, and there are many other reasons that only God and their superiors can judge. They may do so with their permission of superiors; they may do so without it. You have both cases. There is nothing to do in the first instance but be sad and offer prayer with much understanding, tenderness, and compassion. There is no need to be personally affected by it, except in the measure that one is affected by the sadness of God.

You are also aware that nuns leave both with or without permission. We have cases like that. Again, in both cases, all that is left for us to do is to pray and be compassionate and tender. Such things made God sad, as in the case of the rich young man, only in these instances his sadness is a little deeper.

All of you were quite aware before coming to Madonna House, that marriages break up; that people may ask their bishop for separation; that either husband or wife may petition for a legal, civil divorce, as a protection. In these cases remarriage is sinful. You all knew that, in some cases, marriages are annulled and then the parties can remarry. But just as there are priests and nuns who leave without permission, so married people often become divorced and separated without the permission of the Church.

We have statistics of marriage and priestly vocations that have ended with or without permission. Now we have such statistics regarding Secular Institutes and other lay apostolates. The latest ones that I am aware of are pretty low, stating that fifteen per cent will probably leave one way or another.

Human nature, clothed with the sacrament of the priesthood,

with the solemn vows of the religious life, or the sacrament of matrimony, or with the promises of a lay apostolate, is always the same; it doesn't change. God gave us free will in order to earn merits, in order to grow in faith and in the virtues. The Church is very realistic in the face of our free wills. Our human nature still functions under the shadow and darkness of original sin, even though the sin itself has been washed away by baptism. With sadness in her heart, the Church acknowledges these situations in her legislation. She dispenses religious from their vows. A Trappist can leave his monastery after the most solemn vows imaginable and become a secular priest. A nun can leave her convent after receiving an indult, and marry; so can a brother who is not a priest. The same realism and sadness with which the Church legislates in marriages, she now also applies to the lay apostolates.

You notice, of course, that in both sacraments, that of the priesthood and that of marriage, the Church does not dissolve the sacrament, because she can't; this is of God; but she grants a mitigation of its responsibilities and obligations. *This is always done with sadness on her part*, but with a realistic attitude towards human nature — its frailty and its needs.

If this is so, then why are you so perturbed? You knew about this before you came. I understand your compassion, your tenderness your lifting your voice in prayer for those who leave, for it is always sad to see a person reject a vocation. Nevertheless, I cannot comprehend why it should affect some of you so deeply. Could it be that you think to yourself: "Here, but for the grace of God, go I?"

I confess that that thought is quite legitimate. But far from making you depressed, it should make you alert and vigilant. It should move you to pray for yourselves asking God to make you more aware of the graces that he has given you, to help you remain in your vocation, whilst permitting the devil to tempt you against it, to help you to become stronger and to grow in faith. This dual concern of prayer for the one who leaves, and your greater awareness of your own need for prayers and God's graces, I understand. But I do not understand those who get depressed, worried and miserable. What I do understand is sharing the sadness of the Church, and God's sadness.

So let us be realistic like the Church, and know that we too have to face the sadness of the departure of some of our companions. The saddest person among you is myself, sad with the sadness of God and the Church. But don't let such things affect your emotions too deeply. Don't project it onto yourself. Thank God that you are here, and resolve to increase your prayers and awareness and alertness against temptations, against the devil. That is the proper Christian attitude to have.

Lovingly yours in Mary,

THE VIRTUE OF TRUST

February 24, 1962

Dearly Beloved,

Lent is approaching. On these great, liturgical seasons of the Church, my mind, heart and soul turn to you with great longing and love. I think that I can say with St. Paul: "I love you with a jealous love, guarding, praying and leading you to the one Spouse, Jesus Christ crucified."

To love is *to show concern*. I evidently love you very much because I am *concerned* about you day and night — and I do not exaggerate when I say *and night*. Many a night I stay awake thinking of new ways and means to tell you the Glad News that God loves you and that you must love him back.

It seems to me that I have been saying this ceaselessly for over thirty-one years. I must confess that to me personally, this glorious message is always new and always radiant. I don't know whether it is to you, but I hope so. May prayerful attempts at presenting this message be for you new stepping stones to deeper meditation in this holy season of Christ's passionate gift of his love.

I would like to share with you a discussion which we had about trust. For quite a while *trust* has been a problem in the Apostolate. I keep getting letters from you saying that you do not *trust* your local director, nor each other, nor even sometimes, God help you, your spiritual directors. This lack of trust exists throughout the Apostolate. I am greatly concerned about this, so I decided to bring this whole affair of *trust* out into the open. Our meeting began with cooperation and interest because everybody wanted to discuss trust. I asked, "What do you really think trust is?"

Definitions of the word were many. *Confidence* came put as a synonym. Someone said something about love being the mother of trust. Others thought knowledge was its parent, and so on down the line. So we decided to leave the word alone for a while, and to discuss the image which each had *of a trustworthy person.*

Very quickly the portrait of a *trustworthy* emerged. Its composite features were as follows: it is a person who understands and accepts another with all his or her faults; it is a person who is utterly and completely *reliable*, who would never betray the trust of the trust-giver. It is a stable person who never changes. It is a person who not only understands you, but loves you as you are. It is a person who has lots of sympathy and empathy. It is a person who has the interest of the trust-giver at heart.

Now let us put all of these descriptions together and take a look at this person to whom *you would give your trust: loving* no matter what kind of a heel you are; *understanding* you no matter how foolish or evil you might be; a person of *reliability*, prac-tically immovable in his or her stability; a person utterly *selfless* who had *your* interest at heart. This, my dearly beloved, is a picture of *God*, not of man! It was a startling revelation to the people present, to realize that they would only give their little, human two-bit trust to a paragon of virtue who did not exist, and that only God could fit their picture of a *trustworthy person*! Everybody was silent for awhile, and we pondered this revelation. I think that everybody realized that by demanding such an impos-sible creature, we are way off base. Then everybody asked the following $64 question to which not much of an answer was given: if we demand such perfection of others before we trust them, what about ourselves? Are *we* trustworthy? Have you, who constantly complain that you cannot trust others, have you reached this stage of perfection required by these people? *If you have not, then how dare you ask the impossible of others when you cannot attain it yourselves?* This realization hit everyone very hard. I hope it hits *you* hard and makes *you* think.

But we didn't stop there. We asked ourselves again the significance of the very concept of trust.

We discovered that trust was the result of the theological virtues of faith and charity. Then we asked ourselves the next $64 dollar question: *If I, an ordinary Joe or Jane, make such immense demands upon people before I trust them, how come God trusts me?*

That God trusts us is obvious. It began with St. Peter. No one here thought that he was the ideal image of a trustworthy person. He betrayed his Master and ran away when Christ needed him most. What about the other apostles *who were not there either*! In our estimation, would they all be *untrustworthy?*

From that time on, God has trusted every living creature. He trusts you now. You might tear his Mystical Body apart. You might wallow in sin, but he trusts you *until your very last breath leaves your body!*

We talked quite at length about all of this. Slowly, but inexorably, we came to this conclusion which I offer you as a meditation for Lent: To trust the *trustworthy* is not a virtue and does not pertain to the virtue of trust, any more than to love the lovable pertains to the virtue of charity! Christ distinctly said: ''If you love those who love you, what are you doing more than the pagans? I say to you love your enemies, and do good to those who hate you!''

The same saying of Christ can be applied to the child of love, *trust* and one can paraphrase the above saying: ''If you trust the trustworthy, what are you doing more than the pagans? I say to you, trust the *untrustworthy*, and your trust will make them whole.''

This then is the fruit of the virtue of trust: to trust the untrustworthy as Christ trusts us. I remember when a man stole all of our clothing from the clothing room in Harlem. I still gave him the keys of the clothing room the next day, and made him the night watchman without a single word of reproach. This eventually brought him back to the sacraments, and to leaving all the rackets which he controlled on 135th St. Dorothy Day did likewise to a man who stole all the cash ($25!) at the Catholic Worker. She fetched him out of some tavern where he was spending it, and made him treasurer! The man is still at the Catholic Worker, and some of you have met him.

This then is trust. Yet, let trust be your Lenten meditation: The fact that you mistrusted *even those in the Apostolate whom you know love you* will bring you to your knees. if you have mistrusted them, you have sinned against charity, the mother of trust.

Yes, dearly beloved, meditate on the virtue of *trust* during Lent.

Lovingly yours in Mary,

CURIOSITY

March 9, 1962

Dearly Beloved,

These first days of Lent have sent me and everyone else into the chapel to pray. Of course, prayer is not restricted to a place. Christ said: "Pray always." We should do so by offering our work, pains and our joys to him throughout the day. Everything can be offered to him as a love-gift if love for him rules our hearts.

In chapel one night I was meditating upon the word *curiosity*, and wondering why people are so curious about so many things that do not concern them. What is that inner compulsion which makes people want to know the details of every event, especially those concerning people "who matter?" It seems that we emotionally crave to know every little detail — what was said, when it was said, and how it was said.

Curiosity also wants to tear with its sharp fingernails (not caring how deeply it wounds) the veil of personal, normal reticence which surrounds every individual. There is something ''indecent'' about this, something terribly frightening, something that reflects the smouldering fires of hell.

Consider the whole newspaper world and its dissemination of news today. I think, perhaps that you are all influenced by this. When I took a course in journalism, I learned that there is such a thing as *yellow journalism*. This is the type read by the masses of people. I learned to my horror that this type of journalism does not care about hurting people as long as it is news. It gives the public the titillating details of sordid love affairs, murders, and what have you. When one thinks of the havoc which is left behind by *curious newsmen*, one shivers! I wonder how you would feel in the glare of the klieg lights of modern, yellow journalism! Imagine someone probing your private life with millions of people looking on.

In smaller ways everyone has a hunger for those horrible details about others. Amazingly, those same people would cry wolf the moment intimate details are revealed about *them*. We would be horrified if a priest broke the seal of confessional, or a doctor broke the confidences of a patient. Rightly so, for these are personal communications. However, we do not hesitate to listen to some person who, breaking all laws, prevaricating (if not actually lying) relates to us something about somebody in the community. People sit there, all ears, relishing the ''gory details.''

The person who is a gossip is well known to doctors. He or she is a frustrated personality. Often the person is a mousy creature who passes unnoticed, but actually craves to be the *centre of attention*, at the price of anybody's reputation. It is a pathological state. This person should be put into a mental hospital or at least led to a psychiatrist. The Church lashes out with knotted cords against gossipers as Christ lashed out at the vendors in the temple. It is the only sin for which the Church demands public restitution. The only way to restore a reputation is to publicly announce that it is untrue.

In one town at the turn of the century, the adder's tongue of the local woman drove an innocent girl to suicide. She was accused of being pregnant. Names were given and occasions mentioned. When an autopsy was performed, she was found to be a virgin. That cured the community gossip, but only for a week or so!

Decent journalism and decent people do not desire to have anything to do with this kind of "glorified gossip". The *Christian Science Monitor*, the paper which I read precisely for this reason, never mentions murders, divorces, or anything that pertains to gossip. The *New York Times* is very restrained also. Catholic papers also avoid this as every decent person should.

It is interesting to note that in civil law, one can sue a person for defamation of character, that is for gossip. In the Church one who listens to gossip, and confesses the sin, is given a stiff penance. That is because *listening to gossip is participating in it*. If there were no listeners, there would be no gossip.

Theologically therefore, *curiosity* is a sin against charity and justice, and the dignity of the person. All three are sins if they pertain to hurting anyone. This is food for thought.

However, I presume that none of you will participate in gossip; that you will always do what I try to do when people gossip. I have to listen, because I cannot stop other people from talking, though I try. However, if this is impossible, then I simply say nothing. This usually acts like a cold shower. Definitely I never show any *curiosity*. I listen with a bored face which at least stems the flow of the gossip. At the end of the story I usually try in some gentle, charitable way to minimize the entire affair. I try to say something good about the person, and gently to point out the evil of gossip.

So this is one of the many facets of the sin of *curiosity*. Below, I give a theological definition taken from a reference book on moral theology written by Tanquery:

Curiosity consists in the excessive desire to see, to hear to know what goes on in the world 'behind the scenes' as it were.

This desire to know is not indulged in order to derive any spiritual profit therefrom, but to indulge in our craving for frivolous knowledge.

To curiosity pertains also, the desire to know the future, leading to a host of mortal and venial sins such as teacup reading, visiting fortune tellers, astrologers, etc. These things are very dangerous because they constitute an aggression upon the rights of God Almighty, and are an attempt to wreck the confidence and trust with which man should abandon himself to God and his Divine Providence.

It is under the sin of curiosity that immoderate reading, especially of forbidden books, comes.

The brother of curosity is *avarice*. For curiosity likes to hoard, finger and play with knowledge thus acquired that is of a special kind and that only the furious hoard and cherish. . . . .

Avarice is curiosity extended to things. As the curious finger their bits of knowledge, so the avaricious finger their gold and silver; neither will let go.

The remedy for vain curiosity of which we are speaking here, is to recall to the mind that whatever is not God or a thing of God, is not worth winning, finding out about, being interested in, for all things 'pass away'; only God remains.

Wholesome curiosity is interested in God and the things of God. This means the natural world, its beauty, and the human institutions of the world which we are to restore. Above all, I (and I'm sure God too) would welcome your curiosity about how to become saints in doing the works of the Apostolate. Have curiosity about everything which leads to *caritas* and all the other virtues through which you are going to restore the world to Christ. *Here your curiosity should be unlimited.* To those to whom this applies I give a warning: your immortal soul is in danger if you indulge in idle curiosity for it leads away from *God*.

To such persons and to everyone I direct the following questions: What does it benefit your soul, your growth in sanctity, your development as a lay apostle, to know the intimate details concerning the lives of prominent people in your community? What *does* it really matter? Why *do* you want to probe into the lives of others?

Why do you want to know why Father X came to this house or that one? In Madonna House you were always "squashed" when you asked questions out of turn. Necessary information was always given to you here and will continue to be given in your houses. Do not seek to know by underhanded means or silly questions of idle curiosity, that which you do not need to know.

Frankly, I am somewhat angry, and I think justly so, that people who have been trained in Madonna House *not to ask personal questions from our visitors, indulge in this with those who come to their houses.*

This certainly does not bespeak that modesty of mind, the chief characteristic of which is to remain silent at the feet of God. I desire this sinful curiosity to cease, for it destroys the morale of a house as nothing else can. Those in charge of writing the news of the house do not need to know all the details of events. Suffice for them to put down that which is pertinent. Idle curiosity is a sin against the Spirit. Let no one in Madonna House be guilty of it as so many seem to be.

Curiosity is a sin of the mind, and stems from pride. It uses the illogical argument — pride is always illogical: "I am a member of this Apostolate. Why do they (meaning the authorities) keep so many things away from us? It makes me feel as if I did not belong, as if I were an outsider looking in."

When such idle thoughts come to you, ask yourselves just one question: How would *you* like to be the person under discussion? Would you enjoy being torn apart and put together again? You demand that we respect *your* lapses, *your* inner and outer difficulties, and you have a set of tremendous arguments in *your* favor. But you refuse to do *unto others as you want done unto yourself*! Ponder this, please, and may God have mercy on your souls.

Lovingly yours in Mary,

COMMUNION OF LOVE

March 12, 1962

Dearly Beloved,

Lent is with us and my thoughts turn deeply to the Lord.

I was looking at a book of art with reproductions of sculptures and paintings from the Museum of Modern Art in New York. One sculpture made out of wire and tin, shows a crowd, and each person is very thin and elongated, giving a vivid impression of loneliness. Each person (there are several in the sculpture) is standing alone. All have their backs turned to each other. Even their shadows do not blend. The name of this sculpture: *Loneliness*. Non-communication.

It all made me think of the terrible isolation in which the majority of our members live (and perhaps I do too). I cannot always reach you to help, though God knows that I try. It seems to me that on certain days I am really like the huge battering rams with which the medieval soldiers used to force open the gates of a castle. Yes, I seem to be that ram, lifting myself up, or being lifted up by the hands of God, trying to break down the doors, or is it the walls, within which you imprison yourselves?

Letters come to me from all of the houses, and whatever the letters are about, and in whatever mood they are written, they always reflect the loneliness of the writer.

True, there is an effort *to love* the other members. One can read between the lines and see some hidden hunger in each letter that reveals a desire to really be a community of people who have *communion of love with one another*, based on *daily communion with God*. But this is still an unfulfilled hunger. So from my vantage point I see people moving like shadows, each enclosed in the prison of self, unable or unwilling to escape.

I know that you have often heard me speak on this subject, so I will quote to you today some Scripture. You are all familiar with this quotation, but nevertheless, it is well to read it aloud as you read this letter.

Christ says: Then shall the King say to them that shall be on his right hand: "Come, ye blessed of my Father, possess you the kingdom prepared for you from the foundation of the world. For I was hungry, and you gave me to eat; I was thirsty, and you gave me to drink; I was a stranger, and you took me in; naked and you covered me; sick and you visited me; I was in prison and you came to see me." Then shall the just answer him saying: "Lord, when did we see thee hungry, and feed thee; thirsty, and give thee drink? And when did we see thee a stranger and took thee in; or naked and covered thee? Or when did we see thee sick or in prison and came to thee?" And the King answering shall say to them: "Amen, I say unto you: as long as you did it to one of these, my least brethren, you did it to me."

You know, of course, that Christ repeated the same thing, telling the souls on his left hand that they did not do all these things to him, and therefore, when they too, asked him, "When did we not do these things *to you* he repeated that they didn't do it to the least of his brethren so they didn't do it to him, and added those terrible and awesome words: "Depart from me into everlasting fire!"

Now, let us face the stark, frightening fact that these are the yardsticks of heaven or of hell. How do we love our neighbor? St. Paul expreses this love better than anyone:

"Love, charity, is patient, is kind, envieth not, dealeth not perversely, is not puffed up, is not ambitious, seeketh not her own, is not provoked to anger, thinketh no evil, rejoiceth not in iniquity, rejoices in truth, bears all things, believes all things, hopes all things, endures all things, and never falls away."

I suggest that you reread this Gospel and Epistle. Then the application that I want to make will be clearer.

Let us apply the Gospel first to ourselves as members of the Madonna House Apostolate. Here is what each member can say to the other: "I was hungry for your understanding, and you did not give me to eat, I was thirsty for communion with you and you did not give me a drink. I was a stranger and you did not take me into your heart. I was naked in my emotional difficulties, shivering in the cold and you did not clothe me. I was lonely in the midst of you, and you visited me not. I was in the imprisonment of my bewilderment of my fears, and you did not come to me.

Then take the Epistle. Let us realize that if we do all those things to each other only out of "obligation" or for any other motive except *love, caritas*, we will be like sounding brass and tinkling cymbals. If we could perform miracles, and yet had not charity, or let our bodies be burned at the stake, and had no charity, or distributed all of our goods to feed the poor, but had not charity, it *would profit us nothing and our martyrdom would be in vain*.

It follows from this that we must feed, clothe and give drink to each other in a given house with a great immense and flaming love. If we don't, then the house will be empty but our hearts, souls, and minds will be emptier than the house. We will be living lie-apostles who do not love one another, but profess before the world that they are lovers of Christ. No, on the contrary, they are walking alone in the dark night of their own making, without the light of *caritas*, which we must always remember is a Person, God himself. What do we gain if we profess to follow God, and yet are Godless?

Let us go further. Charity is patient. Are we patient with one another? Charity is kind. Are we always kind with one another? Are our motivations as well as our actions, constantly directed toward the good of another member? Is our conversation at table filled with "I", or is it directed toward the interests of others as it should be? Charity is not envious. Then why do we argue? Why do we want to have the last word? Why is it so important *that we should be in the limelight*?

Charity does not deal perversely. What about the countless justifications of our actions when corrected, our endless hair-splitting, as if there were no *First Station of the Cross*? But let us be honest, we rarely are like Christ. Usually when we are accused for purposes of correction it is *just*. Most of us do not receive correction well.

Charity is not puffed up. How about us? We must be very puffed up about our own worth to resent correction so much. We must think ourselves to be faultless. Doesn't that come close to pride?

Charity is not ambitious, meaning it is satisfied with one's lot, always joyous and gay. What about that burden that comes over us when we are contemplating another day in the Apostolate? Is it not our secret ambition to get out from under its monotony and routine? Our blind eyes never, or rarely, see its splendor.

Charity seeketh not its own. Is that true as far as we are concerned? Or are we always seeking ''our own'' in the Apostolate in one way or another?

Charity rejoices in the truth. Let us consider those corrections: do we rejoice in the truth of them and accept them with an alleluia in our hearts?

Charity bears all things. How about us? Do we bear the slightest contradictions? Do we really bear them joyfully?

Dearly beloved there is only one way to break down this loneliness and non-communication, and that is to love.

Lovingly yours in Mary,

THE STEWARDSHIP OF TIME

March 14, 1962

Dearly Beloved,

The graces and blessings of Lent are slowly penetrating me and constantly bringing *you* back into my thoughts.

Yet, I must confess that my great love for you is often tinged with a deep sadness. I know that you may say or think: ''Here she goes again pointing out to us what is wrong. Why doesn't she write some positive letters sometimes, and praise us for our efforts?''

Perhaps some day I will write such a letter. In fact, I could do so right now. However, I reserve such praise for my private letters. I feel that the Lord of Hosts praises you better than I ever could. I know that he often praises you by sending you graces beyond reckoning — clear consciences and his ineffable peace. *What would my puny praises be in comparison to these*?

On the other hand he has placed the Apostolate and its spirit into my custody. Night and day I am acutely aware of his *mandate*, especially now that I have crossed the threshold of my sixties and the sands of time are running out. This is the acceptable time to *pass on to you the spirit, the flame of the Apostolate*. So continue to bear with me.

Today I want to speak to you of the terrible sin of wasting time. Time is the precious gift that the Lord has given to us to earn eternity and the bliss of union with him. If we waste time, we will spend eternity in loneliness, for that is what hell is — ultimate, terrible aloneness!

We can waste time at meals. The waste occurs in our *conversation*. What are they about? God and the things of God, or the inconsequential chatter of self-interest? Do we carry on senseless arguments just to prove ourselves right, or to listen to our own voices? Do we enjoy consciously or subconsciously, the venting of our hidden hostilities on either one chosen *victim* or the whole group?

Mealtime is *agape time*. Agape means *love*. This was the name given by the early Christians to the breaking of the Lord's Bread, the Eucharist. They sat or reclined at a table as the Lord himself had done. *Mass* was a replica of the Last Supper. As yet there was no written New Testament. People passed on stories of Jesus and his teachings by word of mouth. All meals should be an *agape*, a time of love, a gathering of the family, of sharing, but mostly of *feeding body and soul with love*.

As I wrote to you recently, a psychiatrist friend, during his visit last week, told us of the psychological, as well as the spiritual, role of cooking. He said it was human love's way of *transforming raw material into edible, cooked food*. This is so fundamental to human existence that Christ by his love, transformed Bread into his Body, the immense Sacrament of the Eucharist. He went on to point out that our tragic century has begun to break this pattern of love. The transformation of food is done *for us* in factories, and at shopping centres, and thus becomes impersonal. All that a person has to do is heat it or eat it. Non-participation in the preparation is evident. Mealtime is snack time. Instead of large tables, counters are being built. Families eat at various times. The family gathering is breaking up. Psychiatrists say that this will lead to a real tragedy. Neuroses and psychoses will increase. We will be sick, sick people. But for us in the Apostolate, Deo gratias! meal times must and can be *agape time*. Is it? If not, why not?

When I say that we should have conversations at table directed to God and the things of God, I do not necessarily mean "pious" conversation. Life should be lived in God. Recreation is, or should be for us, re-creation. Any topics which interest us, since all things belong to him, come under my heading "God and the things of God". The topics, therefore, are unlimited, as God himself is.

But what is *not* of God? Well, snide remarks. A completely self-centered conversation. Gossip, unwholesome curiosity. Chit-chat that is without substance, and leaves everyone dissatisfied. We know when the meal has been sort of *empty* while everyone is physically *full*. What is the "accent" of the meal? There are undercurrents that make even digestion heavy, and arouse emotional hostilities. There is the pin-pricking that passes as mirth or wit for the uninitiated.

Do I have to draw a picture? I don't think so. Yet, I know from many sources (some outside ones, incidentally) that not all of your conversations at mealtime "are of heaven" in its broadest sense. Nor are your meals *feasts of agape, of love*. Each should pay attention to the interests of others. Topics should often be of *general, apostolic interest*. And since the concern of the Apostolate is life in the world, there should be plenty of topics.

I beg you, I implore you, to really take stock of yourselves in this matter. It may not apply to all houses, but to those whom it applies, I would deeply appreciate it if the directors would go into this topic thoroughly.

My love is saddened because *meal time* is not *agape time*.

In him who is Love,

Cathinnu

THE DEPTHS OF HOLY POVERTY

March 30, 1962

Dearly Beloved,

This is the time for clarifying the question of poverty. Poverty which is never static — always dynamic, is an essential part of the Gospel. It is only since the coming of Christ that poverty truly found her place in the hearts of men. She came from the heart of God, the God who was born in a stable and died naked on a cross.

The first impact that poverty makes on souls who fall in love with God, is a tremendous desire for physical poverty. One wants to be truly dispossessed of all the created goods that people crave with such a passionate hunger and greed. They have made these goods the yardsticks or symbols of *their status* before others, and one almost shivers to think *before God*. The soul falling in love with God, I repeat, first desires to dispossess herself of all these worldly symbols — these possessions that possess.

However, as time goes on, and one grows in the depths of love — as dedicated souls will — the words of the Gospel about poverty withdraw their veils, or sometimes just simply explode in your face, revealing new depths and understanding of the mystery. This is what has been happening to me and what I want to share with you. Slowly, as the years went by and the graces of God filled my soul, I began to realize that physical poverty, being dispossessed as we truly were in the early days of Harlem and Toronto, was but the kindergarten of God's novitiate of love. I began to understand that poverty would not grow unless obedience walked with her. For a soul must surrender not only its goods, but itself. Obedience surrenders the will of a human being, *truly his most precious possession*, becoming the crown of poverty and the footstool of charity.

Time went on, and more graces came, more words of God exploded in my face. As God led me to the high school, or maybe college, of his love, I understood that both poverty and obedience lived in the house of truth or humility! that the poor had nothing to hide, and therefore, if their poverty was offered to God, they lived in humility and truth.

Detachment and holy indifference had to be embraced also if one wanted to be poor: detachment from family and friends, indifference to heat, cold, kinds of food and living conditions. A deep detachment and true holy indifference would lead into the heart of poverty, the Sacred Heart of God. There it would be stripped naked of all attachments to created things and return to the world with a flaming love of all things now as a reflection of God himself — a love that sings his glory alone.

The implementation of this mystery of poverty into the reality of everyday life beggars the imagination. Now a cup becomes a creature of God, and is washed with great gentleness and reverence. Now a tool becomes a reflection of God's goodness, a means of extending his kingdom, and is treated in the same way as an altar vessel.

Now begging becomes quite simple, for identification with the Poor Man of Nazareth, who was also God, is almost complete. True identification with the poor is also profound and begging, the outward sign of this inward grace now becomes natural.

Beggars cannot be choosers. They cut their lives to suit the cloth, the gifts that the charity of others give them. They have nothing of their own and are so totally dependent upon *the providence of God*. This brings about an increase of faith and love for the Almighty. Now the Fatherhood of God, up to now a tenet of a somewhat, academic faith, becomes a reality of everyday living. Now the Gospel of the lilies of the field and the birds of the air makes sense! Now one truly is a brother and sister of Christ and a child of Our Father who art in heaven.

Begging kills pride, teaches simplicity, and makes faith grow and love prosper. It also identifies us with all of the poor beggars of the world who, personally and collectively, are Christ.

When begging is done not only for oneself but for others, then the fear of hell recedes. The terrible Gospel of the Last Judgement is the only criterion of love that God has given us. Now one feeds the hungry, clothes the naked, nurses the sick and give drink to the thirsty, and visits the imprisoned, not out of one's own bounty, which has been surrendered long ago and far away when we were in the kindergarten of the Lord, but now in utter humility, complete faith and love. We beg for thousands who are fed with the goods of their world. But, what is more, they are also fed

spiritual food because we voluntarily and totally identified ourselves with them and therefore brought God to them, crying the
Gospel with our lives and bringing the hopeless hope.

I hope that we will always beg in Madonna House. This is
why we beg, and I wanted to tell you about it.

In Mary, lovingly yours,

STABILITY — LOYALTY — DEDICATION

April 5, 1962

Dearly Beloved,

Recently we finished a training course and I gave the last
lecture on *stability, loyalty, and dedication*. Since we have so
many foundations, and Madonna House is training more thoroughly, I feel ever more deeply the need for these tremendous
virtues. They are like the foundations of a building. They support
our vocation.

Everyone, really, has trouble with these virtues in day-to-day
existence. So it occurred to me that I should share these lectures
with you. This year we began by defining each word. We searched
the dictionary and these were the definitions and our discussions
which flowed from them.

Stability: "State or quality of being stable or firm; strength to
stand or endure without alteration of position. Steadiness. Firmness. Constancy. A thing established as settled. Great firmness of
character to produce the above."

That is the definition given in the dictionary. Let us consider
it more closely. Stability is a state that demands strength to stand

without alteration of position. Think that over. It means that, in the Apostolate, you are not like a weather vane, or a child plucking petals from a daisy and saying: "This is my vocation. This ain't my vocation." Stability means that you are not always seeking to change your position, nor your state of life, always rationalizing yourself in and out of your vocation, or the duty of the moment, or the place where you are. It means the absence of daydreaming as an escape. It means facing reality, both in everyday life, and also the great Reality in which that life is lived — namely, Christ.

Stability suffers no changes, accepting what is because it stems from a promise. One has undertaken this promise with all the firmness and constancy that a human being can possibly produce. Stability means there is no change of position, no going back to what was and is no more, no looking forward to what is not yet, but standing unmoved and unchangeable in what is unchanging.

What a tremendous change would come over each house of the Apostolate if each one of you were truly stable in your determination to serve God alone. How many useless pains and sufferings would be avoided. How much discontent with oneself and one's state of life would not even touch us, emotionally speaking.

Oh, if we only had inner stability standing straight and still before the Lord in our minds, hearts, and souls, allowing our whole beings to serve him firmly and simply, as the duty of the moment calls us to do.

An apostle without stability truly cannot be one *sent by God*, the Unchangeable, the Stable, the Everlasting. Think that over. Apply it to yourself.

Loyalty: "State of being loyal. Fidelity to a superior. Fidelity to duty. Fidelity to love. Fidelity to a cause. Fidelity to a principle.

"Faithful and true to the sovereign, or to the country to whom one is subjected (the government thereof) unswerving in allegiance; enthusiastically and reverently attached to an idea, to a cause, or to a person. True to any person or persons to whom one owes fidelity especially to God, government, wife, husband, lovers, friend to friend. Always constant in that fidelity.

"Synonymous with loyalty are the following words: faithfulness, constancy, allegiance, fealty, homage."

Here again we have the definition of a dictionary. Meditate

on that definition. In itself it contains all the answers that a lay apostle of Madonna House could possibly ask about loyalty in the Apostolate.

Consider especially such words as *enthusiastically* and *reverently, faithfulness, devotion, fidelity.* Tremendous words aren't they.

Holy words. Powerful words. Now apply them to Madonna House, its directorate, to one another, but above all to God.

What would you think of an American or Canadian who was disloyal to his country? Would you like those people for your friends? Or consider a person whom you know, a friend of yours of old, in whom you have confided, who helped you through a tough event of your life, and from whom you expected full loyalty. Suddenly this person broadcasts your trials, tribulations and misery to anyone who wants to hear it. Would you consider this friend loyal to you? Examples can be multiplied indefinitely.

What about Madonna House? Do you realize that Madonna House is not created by man, but is the creation of God? Do not let your mind be obscured by the fact that people call me a foundress. You know enough about God. He can make stones speak, make fire burn without consuming, and he can raise the dead. Imagine Christ walking down the roads of Palestine and picking up the dead branch of a tree, laying it on the ground, and saying in a loud voice: "This is the cornerstone; let Madonna House arise from it!" Before the echo of his voice had died, there before your eyes would be Madonna House. Then he would call out again, and this time it would be a series of names, yours amongst them. To each he would say that he wanted that person to be a member of the Apostolate, and to each he would give the vocation with all the graces necessary. Consider, then, each one of us brought by God. The Lord didn't need to create Madonna House, but he desired in the mystery of his most holy will to do so. I am that dead branch that he picked up, or a pebble, or a gray stone or just a person — myself.

Disloyalty to Madonna House is disloyalty to God. Conversely, through the mystery of his most holy will, Christ is in the directorate. Disloyalty to the directorate is disloyalty to Christ. Disloyalty to one another is again disloyalty to Christ, for we are members of his Body. The disloyalty which caused the break up of Friendship House was not a disloyalty to me, but to Christ.

How can a member be disloyal to Madonna House and

therefore to Christ? Oh, so very simply. Disloyalty is a subtle thing. Often it is barely noticeable to the one who is disloyal. Would you consider it loyal to be more interested in your own affairs, than those of the family? To seek privacy when you should be with the family? To cater to yourself more than to the common good? There is a little word "but" which often acts as a wedge to disloyalty. For example in a conversation one might say: "Oh, Madonna House vocation is wonderful, *but*. . . . ." I leave you to fill in the rest.

Certain behavior on vacation or off the premises might be *disloyal*. I don't think that I need to fill in everything here, either, for one can be disloyal to Madonna House, therefore to God in thought, word and deed. It is a terrible thing in any way, to tear down that which God has built. God have mercy on the soul of the one who is guilty.

Dedication: "Devoted exclusively to the service of worship of a divine being or to sacred use. Set apart formally, seriously, *to a definite use, to a definite end, to a definite service*. To give oneself or to surrender by way of dedication. "Synonyms of the word *dedicated*: devoted, consecrated, hallowed.

Any comments are superfluous. I think I'll let you meditate on this holy word, *dedicated*! Yes, I leave it to you to ask yourselves: *Are you thus dedicated?* If not, why not?

Lovingly yours in Mary,

EATING FOR THE GLORY OF GOD

April 11, 1962

Dearly Beloved,

This is a letter on meals.

Christ revealed himself in many ways throughout his early life. Once he revealed himself to two of his disciples "in the breaking of the bread." We of this pitiful century have forgotten that every action of our day should belong to God, and that we glorify his name in everything we do except sin.

Of all things forgotten by us, the truly lost generation, is the breaking and eating of bread as a symbol of rest and re-creation. Eating is gathering together all the parts of ourselves that have been scattered throughout the day. We gather to be refreshed by the taking of food.

A meal is a *sacramental*. All the religious of mankind have used it as a symbol. Christ alone made it the very center of our faith, giving himself as the Food and Drink without which we lose our eternal destiny, the Beatific Vision, God himself. He said distinctly: "Unless you eat my flesh and drink my blood, you will not have life in you."

Yes, every meal is a sacramental. It should be prepared with love and eaten in peace, because its purpose is to strengthen us for the service of Love — of God.

However, all around us are the signs of our forgetfulness, of our own being *lost*. Some eating houses advertise "quick lunches." Another with mistaken pride, invites all to a "five-minute lunch." Even the house is now planned that the family eats at lunch counters. These may be more "useful" and occupy less space, but are cold and impersonal, and far, far removed from anything dimly resembling gracious living. Truly there was gracious living in Nazareth, for all things the Lord did were gracious.

Let us then begin all over again *to eat for the glory of God*, graciously peacefully, and joyously. No matter what the fare, let it be prepared carefully, prayerfully, *lovingly*, and to the best of one's ability, using what God in his great mercy has seen fit to give to each one of us.

Especially let *eating for the glory of God* be part of the Apostolate and of the Madonna House Family. It begins with "grace." Grace is a holy word that means "gift of god", "help of God". The graciousness of meals comes from God's *grace*.

The soft glow of homemade candles adds graciousness. Such soft light brings the peace of God's altar into the hearts of all around the table, which, in a manner of speaking, is an *altar* too.

It doesn't matter whether we use oilcloth, plastic, cotton or fine linen, as long as it is spotlessly clean. Cleanliness reflects the purity of hearts.

We will use whatever food we have, but let it be well prepared. Cooking is an art — the art of blending. It demands the cook's whole attention, *all of her love*. It is a visible sign of the invisible but every present grace of her vocation to love.

Knowledge begotten by constant training is needed in the novitiate of the kitchen as much as in any other novitiate. So part of the cook's vocation is orderly, and constant study. It would be a good thing if we would form a *recipe exchange* correspondence and write one another for tastier, newer, better recipes. It would be a new, tiny extension of growth of our lay apostolic family, and would bring together those who indeed, with all of their hearts, desire *to cook for Christ in others*.

Lovingly yours in Mary,

Catherine

GRATITUDE TO GOD

May 12, 1962

Dearly Beloved,

I want to speak to you about gratitude to God. I am often saddened by the obvious fact that gratitude to God for all of his goodness is not an outstanding characteristic in our Apostolate. I get letters all of the time filled with many negative attitudes. How rare are positive letters! Yet, if you really stopped and thought a little, instead of always acting on the emotional level, you would fall prostrate on the floor, weeping, laughing and singing with gratitude.

Consider, dearly beloved, the fact that God loved you first. You've heard enough about this, but somehow it hasn't penetrated. If it had, you would be gratefully and passionately loving him back. As yet there are few signs of it! Such things are judged by their fruits. Such love of God would be reflected immediately in your love of one another and in the family spirit. It would grow and grow in each house until it could be felt, touched and seen. It would be reflected in your true and genuine concern for one another and for all of your superiors. I pray to God that your letters someday, will be an outpouring of this realization — a beginning at least of gratitude and love.

But there is more. How many of us truly and constantly realize the bounty of God to us just speaking in the natural order? Does every member realize the bounty of God that daily allows us to live as many would not be able to live in their own home? Do we thank God for the medical care we receive, for our clothing, our food, and for our holidays?

I receive letters from people who were in accidents, or who suffer from sickness. One woman, mother of many children, broke her arm and wrote to me: "Only now do I realize what it is to have two hands, both of which I need so much." We walk; we have the use of our limbs, eyes, speech, hearing. Are we grateful to God for all of these?

But above all, do we realize the immense grace of our

vocation, that is a call from God out of the light of his mercy and the mystery of his choice? Do we ask ourselves breathlessly before the Blessed Sacrament, "Oh, Lord, why me, why not someone worthier?" And then pour ourselves out in gratitude? Or do we take everything for granted, and grumble and natter and mumble and complain and feel sorry for ourselves? Ours are tragic, apocalyptic and frightening times, and God is so good to us. Do we realize what we have? It is time that we should!

I fear with great fear when I see this lack of gratitude. Think about it, meditate about it, pray about it, do something about it! The time is much shorter than you think. *And our time is Now!*

May Our Lady open your hearts to gratitude, and may Saint Martin de Porres fan the fires of this tremendously needed virtue amongst us!

Lovingly yours in Mary,

CHARITY AND RESPONSIBILITY

May 19, 1962

Dearly Beloved,

I am having sleepless nights. They are not too bad. In the quiet of the night, with the world at rest, and the vigil lights burning before Our Lady's face in my little isbah,* I can think through more clearly the things that worry me about the Apostolate.

More often than not, they are not big things in the world's

*isbah — Russian for a log hut.

way of reckoning. They are little things; but Madonna House is an Apostolate of little things. When I begin to see many tiny straws flying in the wind, either here or in the missions, immediately that inner intuition of mine, that clarity of vision (or whatever you wish to call it that the Holy Spirit gives to foundresses) comes into play.

These intuitions usually come during the night. I had one of these sleepless nights lately. I have been worried about *one whole load of straws*, lately! The load, of course, is *charity*. That is strange! Each of you wears on your breast a silver cross bearing the words *caritas* and *pax*. One would think that just seeing the cross and feeling the words would remind you of this theological virtue which will remain with us for all eternity and, when all is said and done, is the only key to heaven.

I feel strongly that the bond of charity is weak in many, many hearts that beat in our Apostolate. Naturally, I will neither name the house nor the persons. That is not the point of my letter. Who am I to judge anyone in a particular way? There, but for the grace of God, go I.

But I want to remind you that although I am simple, poor, unimportant, and often give bad example, by the mystery of God's merciful choice, I am *the foundress of Madonna House*. This means, theologically, according to the teachings of the Holy Roman Catholic Church, that God has given me the spirit of Madonna House to plant, take care of, and nourish; *but above all to be watchful over, and to raise my voice about whenever that spirit is in danger!*

I know that if I fail, especially in being watchful over the spirit, my soul will be damned, and the work of God will die too. Therefore, dearly beloved in Christ, be not astonished when letter after letter comes to you on the spirit of Madonna House. I must always prune, tie the bent branches, be always watchful, loving, faithful to the mandate of God, and ready to deal also with the "unfruitful fig tree". The common good stands above the personal good. One rotten apple can spoil the whole barrel.

Not that we have come to such a pass, God forbid! But I must be watchful that every apple is wrapped in the tissues of charity, and placed in a proper temperature of peace and God's love; and I must watch over your response to that love.

With these preliminary remarks, I want to talk about a phenomenon that seems to be present throughout the Apostolate.

Not everyone in the Apostolate is affected by it. Those who are will realize that this letter is directed to them, and I hope that everyone will take care to make an examination of conscience about it.

Throughout the Apostolate meetings take place weekly or bimonthly from the reports that I receive — for I receive a copy of each meeting — I note that the corrections and problems discussed are so repetitious as to be disheartening. They are always the same problems: untidiness, not picking things up and putting them where they belong, lack of thoughtfulness. It seems that we come together to hear those problems, agree that they are bad, agree that charity is good, and proceed to do exactly as we did during the week before.

·   In some cases there is a snail's progress; in others none whatsoever. The meetings: bickering, arguments, lack of manners, impoliteness, personal cleanliness, oh, a host of various difficulties, individual and collective. Two weeks later, the meeting minutes mention the same problem again! Nothing has improved. In God's name, why not?

One repetitive item that amazes me is that some have developed a strange habit. Let us say that they are in charge of something as small as keeping a holy water font filled, or as important as keeping order in a classroom, dormitory, or the office files — name your poison! The exhausted, tired and depressed director (and who is the director who is not depressed by these repetitive meetings?) reminds the members, privately, publicly at meetings, and everyday in between, let us say, about that holy water font. The person caught red-handed says, ''I'm sorry; I have forgotten!'' This is said perfunctorily, without conviction. There is no sense that the apology is heartfelt, that the person realizes that she has sinned against the virtue of obedience, that she should immediately see her spiritual director or go to confession. Her disobedience may not have been a serious sin — that is for the priest to judge. But depending upon her reactions, the state of her soul may be in danger. But I am not judging that part of it.

May I ask those of you who act like that, do you consider it justice and charity? Don't you understand what you are doing to the Mystical Body of Christ to your own house, to your own group, to your own mission and to the Apostolate? You are nullifying its works and merits. You are performing your obedience in a sloppy way, damaging the morale through not having holy water in the font, through untidiness in the dorms, or through your bickering and argumentativeness that tears the Mystical Body apart.

Those who know that these corrections apply to them should begin to think seriously about them, becuase I know that Christ is tired of this neglect, and I certainly know that I am.

No, it is not enough to say that you are sorry. It is not enough to add that silly, meaningless word, "I forgot." You had better remember! For if the holy water font is forgotten long enough because of your thoughtlessness, lack of concentration, lack of dedication, lack of surrender, for all these are involved. In that "forgetfulness," you are fundamentally untrue to your promises, and in a pretty bad way. This has to cease.

I don't think that there is one amongst you who can accuse me of a lack of patience, a lack of concern, love and empathy toward you. I don't think that in any way I praise myself when I say that most of you female members have, at times, received literally *operas* from me instead of letters. I have explained to you every point, answering all of your questions, gently, lovingly, and tirelessly; and I will, of course, continue to do so, for I try to live St. Paul's Hymn of Charity as far as our relationships are concerned.

But I have to also be vigilant and watchful over the spirit of Madonna House which has been entrusted to me by God. There is a moment where the justice of God and the concern for the common good must take over. It is part of perfect charity to see that the whole does not suffer from one or two individuals.

So let us understand one another. I do not ask for miracles of sanctity over night. I know that human hearts are slow to change, and I know the patience of Christ. But I ask you to behave as Catholics, as Christians, as lay apostles dedicated to restoring the world. To Christ. I ask for good manners at all times, especially with priests. There is a slackening there which reaches me now and then. One person, after Good Friday ceremonies, permitted herself to correct a priest as to his way of unveiling the cross.

Who in hell does she think she is? Not a single member of Madonna House must permit herself to ever lift her voice, criticizing, correcting a priest in his performance of his liturgical duty on the altar, in matter of faith and morals and in his *magisterium*. This is inconceivable. When I heard about it, I was literally fit to be tied!

Nor do I want a casual attitude towards priests, a familiarity that breeds contempt. A respectful familiarity is something else. I want no arguments with priests on the above-mentioned points — no asking where he was or what he did; no talking back as if you knew something about faith, morals, theology, and scripture. I want you to show good manners towards priests as you have been taught in Madonna House; rising when a priest enters; serving him first; laying out the red carpet treatment for him any time when possible and needful. I needn't repeat to you all of these things; you know my attitude to them. I want these things implemented everywhere and at all times.

I repeat: I do not ask for miracles of sanctity overnight, but I expect you to behave as Christians, Catholics, lay apostles who are dedicated to restoring the world to Christ. *This begins with the restoration of yourself!*

This restoration begins with such little things, remembering to put holy water in holy water font, keeping a dormitory spic and span. Above all it is realizing that saying: "I am sorry; I forgot," does not end the situation between you and the director who is correcting you. I want you to know that the correction is only the beginning of that situation. I have asked the directors, henceforth to inform me about each person, if after three corrections on the same subject, he or she has not put all of his or her faculties into implementing the correction in the reality of daily living. Enough is enough!

The Apostolate is not a game. Eternal life is at stake, and I want to explain one more thing. You think that you can get away with a lot of emotional basis, because during your stay at Madonna House you had quite a dose of the science of psychology, and a little psychiatry. But you also had a dose of *religion and mental health*.

Recently, a psychiatrist friend was here. He was telling the priests and me that in his experience in psychiatry, those patients did well who not only cooperated with him, but understood that emotions, in the long run, are still subjected to Christ, the great Psychiatrist, and the rules of the spiritual life still apply to neurotics.

I suggest that all of you read *The Hidden Face*, a new biography of the Little Flower that will literally set you back on your heels. Here was a saint who, while lying on her deathbed, told a nun who was taking care of her to remove a potent medicine from her table, as thoughts of suicide were still with her!! The thoughts might have been there, but the implementation was not. It is a good book for you to read.

So I end this letter of sadness, the fruit of my sleeplessness and in night prayers for you and the Apostolate. I beg and implore you not to hurt Christ the way you do through those thousand little things about which you are so careless. I beg you to begin to realize in depth that you are *dedicated lay apostles of the Lord*, and that you hinder the restoration of the world to him by your utter disregard of the *little things that are so immense*.

Lovingly yours in Mary,

P.S. As regards charity: Don't you see, dearly beloved, that you not only wound but cut charity into pieces, crucify charity all over again. You do this when you are rude in your manners, rude in speech, rude in tone of voice. You do it when you snap at each other. You do it when you use smart and sarcastic techniques on one another like disdainful silences which wound and shout louder than words. Refusal to reply to a simple question is like a slap in the face of another. Do you consider that this is prompting charity, or crucifying it? There is only one thing I have to add to this: If you *crucify charity, then remember that charity is love and love is God, and that you are guilty of crucifying God.* May he have mercy on your soul!

PREPARING FOR PENTECOST

June 6, 1962

Dearly Beloved,

I cannot let the tremendous Feast of Pentecost pass without writing to you about the Advocate, the Consoler, the Father of the Poor, the Holy Spirit, the third Person of the Most Holy Trinity.

Who is he, this Holy Spirit? Pause for a minute. Try to shut out all the noises within and outside of you. Try with his grace to catch a tiny glimpse of the intensity of the Father for the Son and of the Son for the Father.

So awesome, incomprehensible and passionate is the love of the Father and the Son for one another that it becomes visible, as it were, and begets the Third Person of the Most Holy Trinity, the Spirit of fire, the Spirit of Love.

I wrote once in Advent that the pure of heart will hear the clear sound of a donkey's bells, if they listen. He is a holy donkey because he is the donkey who carries the Mother with the Lord in her womb.

Now again I say, listen with your hearts and your souls. Listen with an ear attuned, with expectation, desire and love, and you will hear the coming of the wind of the Holy Spirit. This wind is mightier than any tornado. He comes with a speed that cannot be measured. Yet he is as gentle as the evening breeze, swift, immense, harmless to nature and to man. Not only is he not harmful, his passage brings light and warmth, peace and wisdom. He is bringing fortitude, longanimity, charity, faith and hope — all the gifts and virtues that are his to give.

If you try to love God, if your faces are lifted up to his Face, if your mind, heart and soul seek him instead of your own self and your own will, you are bound to hear the approach of the mighty wind. Blessed are they who do hear, and I fervently hope that you are amongst them.

Why does he come? Haven't you already received him in Confirmation? Hasn't he made you once and for all a lover of

Christ — a solider of the Lord? Hasn't he prepared you already for all of the trials to come, even to martyrdom?

Yes, he has done that; but like God the Father and God the Son, the Holy Spirit knows our weaknesses. So, sent by the Father through the Son, he comes every moment of our lives to help us to become saints, lovers of God, for he is the Sanctifier.

He comes to console us. Who is there amongst us who does not need his consolation and fortitude to face another day in the Apostolate with love and not with the selfishness that kills?

He comes to make clear through the gifts of piety and counsel, the verities that Christ taught, and that we are so apt to forget or rationalize away. He not only comes with these gifts so that what we have learned through one gift we may pass on through the other. For true love is like that: it desires to make the Beloved known, and the Holy Spirit helps us to do that.

Father of the Poor, of whom we are the poorest, he comes to make us rich. Do not be discouraged when we speak to you of being poor. Rejoice! When we speak about our poverty, we speak theologically. While we creatures of God are poor because we have nothing of our own, at the same time we are rich because we are created in the image and likeness of God. Above all we are rich because God loves us.

Thus, we are both poor and rich but we certainly need the *Father of the Poor* to make us see how rich we are. So *he comes*.

During a discussion about the Holy Spirit, someone asked me what wisdom is. For a moment I was lost for an answer, but the answer is so simple that I was astonished that anyone should ask. Wisdom is the simplicity of love. He who really loves God and others as they should be loved is wise! He is not wise with his own wisdom, but with the wisdom of God who always comes to dwell in a soul which has so died to itself that it offers him space to dwell in. If God dwells in you and acts in you, how can you fail to be wise? To acquire wisdom, all you have to do is to die to self.

I have many more thoughts on the Holy Spirit, but perhaps I write too much. I have deluged you lately with letters but perhaps you do not realize that they are not so much letters, as a cry of my heart. I love you so much and, like St. Paul, I am jealous for you and I want to lead you holy and unspotted to God. My love wants to lead you to true happiness, notwithstanding the fact that at every step I meet with nothing but reverses, indifference, and certainly few results. But then again, this judgment might seem harsh to you, negative, and depressing or even unfair.

Here is where the ability to communicate comes in. What do I mean exactly, that I meet with few results? Do I mean that any act or word of mine can change any one of you, can bring you closer to God?

The general answer is *no*!!! In theology the answer would be a partial *yes*, because it teaches that the grace of God often comes to us through others; that each of us can be a channel of grace for others.

But this is not exacty what I mean. I must be a channel of grace for you, not so much through *my words* but by being a clear channel for the *words of God* that he wants me to pass on to you.

What then, do I mean? Again words fail me. Maybe I am a poet. Maybe my Russian mind doesn't work like yours. But I doubt that. I think that all human minds are similar. But often I see in pictures — pictures that break my heart because I love *you* and I love *God*.

I see you, *his chosen ones*, your hearts filled with gratitude, your minds (when not clouded by emotions) understand well *the infinite amount of benefits you have received from God through this Apostolate.*

But I see you also drawing a line, limiting how far you will go towards God. There he is standing in front of you with his arms open, waiting for you *to surrender, to throw yourself into his arms, to stop doing your will and to begin doing his.* However, there you stand before some imaginary line that you have made yourself, and you won't move any farther. Why? Who can tell? Who can judge? Certainly not I. All I can do is pray and continue to try to help you and to be patient. This is what I truly try to do.

But of course I am inadequate. Every person has a free will, what then?

The answer is *the Advocate, the Consoler, the Enlightener, the Gift and Virtue Giver, the Father of the Poor.* He and he alone, can *move your will.* So let us prepare for *Pentecost.* Remember, in the life of a Christian, *every day is a pentecost.* Every day the mighty Wind comes, if only we call upon him. *Every day the tongues of flame descend upon us if we realize our need for them and desire them with a great desire.*

So this humble, little letter is good for any day of the year, for every hour, every minute, and every second. God love you!

Lovingly in Mary,

(signature)

HAVE WE UNDERSTOOD REAL JOY?

June 19, 1962

Dearly Beloved,

I have been meditating upon *joy* and asking myself why we have so little natural, spontaneous joy amongst us. There should be a natural joy among us penetrated by the thousands of graces God sends us throughout the day — a joy that shimmers and glows like a waterfall flirting with the sun.

I was asking myself why do we have so little, truly supernatural joy — the kind that radiated from the saints and made the humblest task a glorious adventure and changed every day into a challenge of love?

That is not to say that we do not laugh, that we don't have our moments of relaxation and simple joys, that we haven't grown tremendously in appreciating things that only a few years ago might have seemed too simple or childish for us to even notice.

I remember in the early days of Madonna House when the only ice cream available was in Barry's Bay* and only on certain days. Since we were poor we couldn't buy luxuries; but one of our visitors happened to go shopping and brought ice cream for everyone at Madonna House (when everyone meant five people). We hadn't had ice cream for months, and it was such a treat! What

*Barry's Bay — is a town about twelve miles from Madonna House.

everybody takes for granted was an extraordinary event for us, and we licked our plates and laughed joyously!

A picnic is another joyful event. Being alone with the family (as much as we like visitors) and having a cozy evening together can be a rare treat. But the abiding joy of the Lord that smiles and laughs and sings that we have little of. For what is inward and true will always radiate outward. It is this joy that is less visible amongst us.

It seems to me, leaving all emotional problems aside, that we really haven't met and fallen in love with Christ yet. So many amongst us are still fighting their vocations. Many still want to have their cake and eat it too. In a word, many amongst us have not yet understood this secret: *the cross is joy*!

It is because we fight the cross that *the joy of the Lord is not within us*. I can be really tempted to say; "Oh, foolish people, why don't you embrace the cross, for this is the way both to eternal joy, as well as joy in this world of tears".

We are foolish, for we imagine that we would have joy somewhere else outside of Madonna House. We dream of states of life and places where there is no cross, forgetting that there are no such places. They are figments of our imaginations, the misty stuff of which dangerous daydreams are made.

Perhaps this is the reason why a lack of enthusiasm reigns among so many of us. Perhaps this is also the reason for a "slow-down" in our gestures, in our walk, in our work. We sometimes drag ourselves through the day istead of walking about *our Father's business* with bouyant, joyous steps. How different our steps would be if we were going on a date! What a whirlwind we would be! Or if we were working for big money, how careful, efficient, alert, awake we would be on the job.

I can just see a socialite, planning, arranging, bustling about the preparations for that party that will bring to her all of those "important people" whom she wants so much to meet in order to climb the social ladder.

Or I can see an ambitious, junior executive studying nights, and moonlighting in order to have enough money to have the proper clothes. He hastens to acquire outward polish, inward knowledge and bones up on etiquette. No effort is too great and time to him is certainly precious. The urgency of "getting ahead" fills him with energy, enthusiasm, and speed.

However, for God, we move slowly, like shadows across a

screen. The telephone might ring. We think: "It is nothing but another request for information." "It is nothing but another donation for the hungry and poor." "It can wait."

Joylessly we go through our day. Dutifully but slowly without haste, acting somewhat half-heartedly, our hearts are not in our jobs. Filled with self-pity boredom and doubts most of the time, we are dreaming about doing something else or being somewhere else.

We certainly do not live up to our complete potential. The incentive appears to be very small: "It is only God! It is only the things of God! It is nothing exciting, nothing worthwhile hastening for." At least that is how it appears from where I sit. In so many of you there is no "oomph", no joyful life in God, no understanding of the immensity of your task and its urgency.

Throughout the Old Testament, Yahweh urged his prophets to *hasten*. In the case of Moses he would brook no delay. Moses had to go to Pharaoh *this minute*, no matter how he felt about it, it was the same; it was the same with Isaiah and with all the other prophets. Hasten! *And bring the words of Yahweh to the people of Israel!* This urgency seems to have been the theme song of God the Father in the Old Testament.

His Son, Jesus Christ, was even more emphatic. I suggest that you make a study of the Gospels and for the fun of it (though it isn't fun at all, really) count how many times the Lord of Hosts used the word "haste". I am afraid you will be extremely surprised.

Do we really *hasten about our Father's business? Does the zeal of Our Father's house really eat us up? Do we think about God and the extension of his kingdom day and night?*

That, in truth, is the sixty-four dollar question that each of you alone can answer. On this question hinges the salvation of the world, the tempo of our Apostolate, and our spirit of joy! Love and love alone can achieve this hastening process. Love and love alone will bring joy.

We literally change under the impact of wrong "loves". Believe it or not, there are distorted, tragic, frightening "loves" that are the very opposite of *Love who is God, who is a Person.* This is *caritas* that we all should be filled with, and would be if only we let him enter our hearts.

Take for instance, an avaricious man and his love for material goods which isn't really love, but a caricature. What agonies will he not endure! What long journeys he will undertake to gather that for which he has given his heart! I need not proceed with more examples. People have murdered and risked their lives to achieve the goals toward which their wrong "loves", their tragic, perverted attachments impelled them.

But for him who is love, for him who so gloriously, tragically and painfully died for us, for the God of our fathers, for the Love of our hearts, for the Salvation of our souls and nations, for the Mighty One, for the Beloved, for him we do not propose to die. In fact, for him we don't even hasten our steps as we go about his business!

"No. He should be satisfied with our slow, reluctant and bored service. We don't see him. He is so far away and intangible. Why bother?" At least, that is the impression we often give. Can there be joy in that kind of attitude? In that kind of apostolic life? It is as if such a person was reluctant and halfhearted. If this is our attitude, then, of course, there will be a lack of real supernatural joy.

Lovingly yours in Mary,

Catherine

THE ROMANCE AND IMMENSITY OF LITTLE THINGS

June 20, 1962

Dearly Beloved,

Some time ago the whole house had a long discussion. We gathered in Eddie's* room, and the conversation drifted to the big

*Edward Doherty: Catherine's husband.

topic of *little things*. So here is a staff letter coming to you to remind you again of the little things that are so important.

The first thought that comes to me as foundress of this place is: for reasons that I will never fathom (since it is a mystery of God until I see him), he touched me and said, "Come".

You have often read how I discuss my vocation as a stupendous adventure. Let's begin with that. I was just breathless when God called me. Thirty years later, I am just as breathless when God calls me. Thirty years later, I am just as breathless as on that first day when I realized that this vocation had come to me.

Okay, now get the picture of a young woman realizing that God has gloriously called her, although at the time she was responsible for a child, and a lot of other things. One gift that I have had since childhood is a great faith. Faith is a gift from God. You can pray for it, but you can't *grow* in faith unless he gives you the grace. It is a free gift from God. Knowing what he was going to do with me, he endowed me with a very strong faith.

Now as I look back, and as I look at you, I think maybe you, if you were a married woman without a husband and with a child, would have hesitated. If a call like that had come to you, you might have hesitated because you are Americans and Canadians, having a lot of possessions. I don't know. Maybe you would have done what I did and just said, "God, I don't understand. Now it is up to you to remove the obstacles."

So he removed them through a bishop.

Then, when I received the permission, I took the plunge. That is, I took my son and "yanked myself" into the slums. I consider this one of the "little things" because I keep repeating to you this poem: "Lord, I throw at your feet my life and sing that I give you such a little thing."

For there before my eyes is a crucifix — to me, living, breathing, full of wounds, and saying to me, "I love you, I love you." When I compare my life with that crucifix, then my whole life is nothing. So to begin with, I consider that the gift of my whole life from the day that he called me to the day that I am speaking to you, is *a tiny little thing* in proportion to what he gave me.

Now, is that clear — what I call a "little thing?" I think that we misunderstood each other right here. Understand that, for me, my whole life is as nothing to give — I wish that I had a thousand lives to give him. Then you will understand why I consider it to be a "little thing."

Now if I consider that my life is about as big as a thimble, then what is *in it* is still smaller, isn't it?" I sing and sing that I throw at your feet my life — such a small thing." If I consider that my life which I throw at God's feet is such a small thing, then what is inside cannot be bigger than the whole, can it?

I am a poor woman. I wrote a poem. You don't read my poems much, and probably they don't mean too much to you, for the language is symbolic, but some day you might understand them. I wrote a poem one day in which I said:

> I am nothing
> A beggar
> Covered with wounds
> Lying upon
> A thousand roads. . . . . .

Meaning that I am nothing, that I am the least of all, and that I can't offer him anything. But he touched me.

> But you came
> My King,
> And touched me
> With your hand,
> And I arose
> And I followed you. . . . . .

He touched me — a dirty, unwashed, no-good soul. I am not deprecating myself; I am a marvelous creature. I have been created in the image and likeness of God. But we are all sinners, *and when I say that I consider myself a sinner, I mean it!!!*

So, what can a grain of sand, who is a sinner, do for God? Little things. I am in Friendship House. Everyone in the place is calling me names. Priests do not believe in what I am doing. Only one lonely bishop and two spiritual directors believe in me. Day in and day-out, hour-in and hour-out, I hear, "Look at that woman! She probably sleeps with those hoboes."

But I consider this persecution a "little thing." It is the tiniest of little things to be persecuted for twenty-one years out of thirty. I consider it very little to offer to God!

So I talk of little things. Probably to you persecution would be something very big. I am so small, so unworthy. I have only one life to throw at his feet, and it is so *small*. He gave me *his life*. And he is God.

So I ask what can a little person do who tries to love God tremendously? And I answer, everything: from putting the lights off because of holy poverty, to refraining from changing clothes every five minutes because there is a clothing room, to being indifferent to food, to going where God calls you.

Now here again, let us understand one another for I do not think that we do. First, remember that I have a personal relationship with Christ. To me he is real; is in this room. Besides my faith, I have a vivid imagination. He is *real*.

So, there is a knock at the door. Someone calls for my nursing services. No matter how tired and exhausted I am, *I know that it is God knocking! I literally see his hand with a wound.* (I don't mean in a vision, but in my imagination.)

You pass by and whisper, "B, may I see you today?" So unless something more important intervenes, something that he also wants, I will talk with you.

My day is directed simply by the needs of the Apostolate. I weigh those needs. Should I dictate three hours or four? For you it is simpler, and I envy you! You know his will. You know it clearly every second of the day. How lucky you are! I have to make decisions. Fortunately, if I am confused, I have Father Call to tell me what to choose.

But once I know God's will I am going to try to do it perfectly. My heart swells and I say, "This also, Lord, for love of you." I know very well its redemptive value. Do I speak too symbolically?

Another example: I have empty hands. At night I consider that I have to bring something to the altar for tomorrow's paten. What can I bring? I can bring a thousand buttons well-sorted with great love, understanding full well that because of my attention these buttons have redemptive value. I can bring hours of conversation with you. I can bring many letters with attention to details.

This faith comes from a tremendous, personal understanding that God is *real*, and *my tremendous Lover*. He has first given his life for me. In the face of that gift I am like one who is bereft of my senses! I go around gathering every flower so that I can bring it to him. It is his will that directs the gathering.

In March I shall speak to the Medical Association — the

psychiatrists — and I'll be a "big shot," quote unquote. They will meet me at the train; they'll make a fuss over me. They'll put me up at the biggest hotel. "This is the great Baroness de Hueck, the celebrated lecturer of the United States, the author of books —" Now to me all of this is exactly the same as doing the buttons! There is no difference.

Writing these books, is a little thing for me. You read my books they have been written piecemeal. I have never said to myself, "Now I will write a book." I would only do so if Father told me: "I want you to take three hours every day and write a book." Then, I would try to write a book. But I don't need three hours to write a book? Why don't I need three hours? Because I write what I live. I don't need any solitude, reference books or anything else. I write only what I live. I couldn't write a story, a plot, an essay, if you paid me!

Why do I write as I do? Because I love. It is so simple. Any one of you could write to your girlfriends about your boyfriends. You went out with your boyfriend and you are writing your best friend about Joe. You become eloquent, because you love Joe! And you, who ordinarily cannot put two words together, will write or scribble six pages to your girlfriend about Joe!

So that's what I do. It's so simple. That's what I want you to do. Yes, even writing books is a little thing.

So to me, life is all little things. Thoughtfulness. Fr. Cal says to me, "Katie, I don't want you to talk to anybody in the morning; you have low blood pressure and you feel, shall we say, a little upset." Then I try not to talk in the morning. I obey him. If I disobey him, I go to confession.

But sometimes this combination of tension and low-blood pressure in me creates a quick retort. Well, then I am really sad, because I feel that this is a "big thing". Sin is a big thing. Anything connected with sin is a big thing, because it hurts love. Everything else is very small.

It never occurs to me that you can possibly separate anything from love. That is why I keep pushing the priests, almost impolitely, to connect daily life with poverty and reverence. I have no right to do that, but I do so unconsciously. The words are out before I can control them. I must work on that. As I told you I am a sinner!

For example, I will speak of cups, because you seem to have an aversion to washing dishes. If you have this attitude that this is a beautiful, little thing that you can give to God, then washing a cup becomes an adventure. It is this sense of adventure glory, and joy that you lack.

I have lots of fun. I might be terribly tired, and the job might be monotonous but I will make it interesting for myself. For example, many of you saw the terrible monotony of the library work down in the basement before Christmas. You saw that I was sometimes tense, and sometimes, perhaps, a bit sharp, for which I was sorry. Nevertheless, I kept thinking, "Gee, this is wonderful! Generations of our members are going to benefit from this." Again a little thing to give to God. Now, do you get the picture, or are you still missing the point of what I mean by "little things?" The whole of life is a "little thing" which we throw at God's feet and sing and sing. Every little thing should be done perfectly, completely connected with God, for otherwise, it ceases to be interesting. It has no sense and no being.

There is great freedom in this. You don't have to "smile" doing the little things. The very fact that, in your hearts you enjoy doing them will radiate in your eyes, will show forth in your concentration.

People come here for summer school.* Why do you think that they come here? They come to see human beings throw their lives at Christ's feet and sing that they bring him such a small thing. They touch us, and then change in some way, or receive graces from Christ.

This is your Apostolate. If you go to Marian Centre, and wash dishes, the whole of Edmonton is changed. For Edmonton *is* changed in quite a big way because Marian Centre is there.

Whitehorse, Yukon is changed because of the presence of Maryhouse! By doing those little things you radiate love, and *that* is the Apostolate.

Both the talented ones and those who have no particular talents all contribute to the restoration of the world to Christ. *It is not what you do that matters. It is what you are. If you have understood* the romance and immensity of "little things," then you will restore the world to Christ. You will be an adventuresome, joyous glad, simple, and humble light by doing little things. They will become big because they are touched by God and done for him.

Now, have I explained what the "little things" are, or are

*Madonna House formerly had a summer school of Catholic Action.

you still confused? How is it possible to live this life as a vocation, unless you connect every gesture and breath with God? Unless you have an awareness of every lamp that is lit unnecessarily? Unless you pick up everything after everybody and after yourself, especially, so as not to burden your brother? Unless you are completely *in every little thing* with your whole heart, your whole soul, your whole mind, this is not the vocation for you. Go elsewhere, but wherever you go you will certainly have to do little things. Try to do them without love, and see what happens. But doing little things with our whole hearts is our vocation.

Maybe sometime you will be a great professor in a university. But then, you will be utterly indifferent to being a professor. You must neither refuse anything to God, nor ask anything as far as your vocation is concerned.

Christ is a piece of bread that the priest carries, and you, too, are a piece of bread that is carried on the wind and word of your superiors. You are another Christ, glad to go anywhere, and glad to do anything, always considering everything so very small, because what he gives you is so very big.

The smallness is always in relation to God, but the hunger to return to God is immense. The only "big thing" about you is your hunger to love — to be and to do — for God.

Is that clear? It's so simple! Of course we must also do "little things" well in our personal relationships. How else are we going to learn to love unless we love one another? What is the use of going to learn to love unless we love one another? What is the use of preaching and talking about Christ, unless we are Christ to one another?

It all hinges on God as Person, on the sense of adventure, the sense of call and on the three lines of this poem: "Lord, I throw at your feet my life, and sing and sing that I give you such a small thing."

That's all. Once you get that picture, you've got the whole thing. It's possible that you might not be called to this life. However, once you are in it, then you know that you are called. Then, it is your vocation, and you have to accept and act accordingly. You cannot just connect a "little" with God; you must connect completely.

But if you are not connecting completely, go and seek help. It can happen. Emotional or other kinds of problems might sometimes obscure the realization of your vocation. Go and seek help from God, and from those who can give it to you. You *have* the vocation. This means that you must live the life sooner or later. That's what I mean by "little things."

There is also the cross. I should speak about that also. I cannot visualize a love story with God without a cross. To me, the cross is *the thing*! I desire it, I accept it, and I ask the grace never to fear it, because one day I shall know its joy.

You may think that I am just talking through my hat. But again, as God is my witness, I look at the cross as the marriage bed of Christ. I desire union with him at the price of being crucified. Then my soul cries out, "Where are the nails? Where is the hammer?" even though my flesh flinches. Of course the cross is there. When I talk about the cross I think that you misunderstand what I mean. For me the cross is the key to him whom my heart loves. Without the cross, there is no Easter. Unless I lie on my cross, I can't see him in heaven. But I must lie on the cross that *he* made for me, not the one *I'm* making for myself.

This is all so clear to me that I, quite naturally, talk to you about the cross. However, I am beginning to think that for you the cross is something heavy. Something that you wish you could throw off, something that you have to carry, but you do so without joy.

God embraced the cross because he wanted to. For this he was born! For this we are born — to lie on it with him. I literally mean the words that I say, but I don't think that you understand me. That's why you have a problem with "little things."

Does that make sense to you? Do you understand how I think and feel about these things? You may disagree with it or not understand it, but this is what I mean by "little things." If you wish to be in this Apostolate, you have to come to this understanding with the help of the priests and myself, and afterwards through my writings. For this is your vocation. This is what he gave me. I'm passing it on to you.

When somebody says to me, "Catherine, I don't think that I can take a lifetime of these little things. It's excruciating." I want to weep. It's a failure to understand our *faith*. The same person, whoever he or she is, will have a lifetime of other little things that will be just as excruciating.

However, never think of your vocation as a lot of monotonous "little things."

Think of it as the glory of the cross. Measure the "little

things'' against *his bigness — what he has done for us.* Try every minute to put a little grain of sand before the altar, and before you die, you might have a mountain to offer. It is so simple!

Lovingly in Mary,

THE FAMILY SPIRIT

August 29, 1962

Dearly Beloved,

Today I want to talk to you about our family spirit. It is so vitally important to our Apostolate, that all of you must cooperate towards achieving it. This is especially hard to do in the larger houses where the very size of the place militates against close physical presence.

Of course, your directors try to see that you have the opportunity to be together some time each day, and on various other occasions. However, the family spirit does not depend only on physical closeness. It can flourish even under such adverse conditions as separate rooms. In Harlem, we lived not only in separate rooms, but on different streets, but our family spirit was terrific!

The family spirit begins and ends with *our loving one another.* Love will forbid any withdrawal from the others. Love will compel each *to be concerned about the other.* Love will teach you not to speak constantly about yourself, but to be interested in the others.

Yes, the family spirit begins and ends with everyone loving one another. Then everyone will be watchful over the whole Apostolate and especially about the following:

1. *Conversation at table.* Conversations at table reflect the state of everyone's mind, heart and soul. They are an important part, therefore, of the family spirit that spills over to all of our guests.

This does not mean that we cannot discuss our daily affairs, or laugh over little incidents that were funny. For surely during a day something funny happens to everyone. If you are very much at peace with God and others, then even "unfunny" things become funny, and can be shared with others. You have finally acquired the ability to laugh at yourself instead of others, which is a great step forward toward emotional health and sanctity.

Laughter has been given to us by God to relax us, to sing him a song of joy. The devil hates laughter, and he wants to snatch it away from God. So he tries to use it as a harmful thing by provoking some uncharitable joke. For example, he urges us to tell an unpleasant truth in jest.

Yes, love will be watchful over table conversations. Love will direct much of it toward the spirit of Madonna House, toward God, toward spiritual matters. In general the discussions will be about something worthwhile, instead of a silly, wasteful spouting of words that really make no sense. An argumentativeness has no place in our conversation. A sullen silence that is felt by everyone is a sort of withdrawal from the general conversation and has no place either. This too is a break in charity, and therefore, in the family spirit.

Let us remember that a meal should be agape — the breaking of bread in love, reminding us always of the Eucharist and the Last Supper. If we remember this, then we will act accordingly, and no injunctions from me will be necessary.

2. *Argumentativeness and rationalization.* Nothing breaks the family spirit, the bond of charity, as these do. We already discussed arguments at the table. One person always has to say that a thing is white when someone says it is black, and vice versa. It is not just an intellectual matter; they just want to put their own ideas across.

There is another argumentiveness that will kill charity and the family spirit. It is the argumentiveness of members towards the director.

Let me give you an example of a director asking a favor: "Please X, you are going this way; will you take this parcel for me and leave it such and such a place?'' X doesn't feel like it, so she begins a long argument why it can't be done. She should have said; ''Of course, I will do it,'' for obviously taking a parcel from one room to another will not delay anyone that much.

People show that kind of argumentiveness when they tell the director or another person how to do a job, knowing all the while they have no better way to offer.

I have been the recipient of that sort of argument practically all of my life. You old-timers know that I am a specialist in files, outlines, and office work. However, I can remember the time when some of you gave me powerful and unnecessary arguments which delayed our work for God. What a waste of time, and what a breaking of the family spirit of charity, obedience, and especially common sense! It leaves nothing but bitterness in the heart.

Another type of argumentiveness maintains that ''I have to do it now.'' It is the old song, ''Give me Five Minutes More.'' When the director insists that it is lights out, there is no time now; a torrent of arguments comes forth taking up even more time!

I don't need to give you many examples of how you ''rationalize'' your actions, but I will give you one.

In one house a rule was made that the tape recorder could not be used without permission. Here is how one person got around it. She came to a priest who was giving a retreat in their house, and the retreat was taped. With an innocent face she asked the priest (who didn't know the rulings of the house, of course), if she could listen to his tape as she had been on kitchen duty during that particular talk. The priest naturally gave her permission. So she went to listen to the tape and being unfamiliar with the machine, broke it. That's how the whole thing became a public affair.

Now what did that person do but ''rationalize'' her action. She knew very well that she couldn't use that tape recorder without permission. She was probably hostile to that rule, and probably didn't have the spirit of obedience and family unity. She probably said to herself: ''I will ask permission of the guest priest to hear his tape. I obviously cannot hear his tape without using the tape recorder, so I guess that will give me permission to use the tape recorder.'' That's rationalization!

If she had the family spirit, which is, of course, a spirit of obedience and taking care of the things of God, she would first have asked permission to use the tape recorder; second, she would have asked someone to start it for her; third, she would have asked permission to use the tape.

If you are truthful before God, you will find that you "rationalize" things at least ten times a day. Don't! There won't be any family spirit left if you do.

3. *The little word, "but."* A strange little word with which to break the family spirit, but oh, how powerful! Especially when it is used deliberately, then semi-deliberately to undermine the morale of a house.

It also undermines the authority of all superiors, and ultimately that of God himself.

Let's take another example. The house has had a staff meeting. The tired, wearied director, bowed down by a thousand responsibilities after much prayer and consultation, has finally taken the bull by the horns, and once more for the 100th time, he or she is explaining the spirit of Madonna House in relation to some happening, some difficulties, some problems common to our spiritual family. The meeting goes well. The members seem to be participating, and the director gets a glimmer of hope that *maybe this time the point has sunk in.*

It's evening recreation time, and the members are sitting around the table going over the meeting. Someone who hasn't gotten the point, alas! begins the conversation: "That was a good meeting and So-and-So was really terrific. . .*But*. . ." And with a few sentences one member sows in the minds of the others, doubts, hostilities, tensions, anxiety and a host of questions that needn't have arisen.

That is how a little word of three letters can smash the family spirit in two minutes. It can do more than that. A member is given a task to do. Listen to "but. . .but. . .but. . . ." There are so many *buts* in the conversation that it almost makes one cry!

The replies go like this: "But look, I have to do this. . .this." "But look, I haven't finished this. . .this." "But one moment, don't you think it would be better to do it this way?"

The little word, *but* is the very soul of argumentiveness and rationalization. Used in this way it is better left out of your conversation. You can bring it in when someone praises you; then you can say, "*But* you don't know me. . .I'm not as good as all that." Then it will be in its proper place!

4. *Withdrawal.* If anyone would like to deal a final blow to the

family spirit, then *withdrawal* is the way to do it. It is very much like being an executioner beheading a person with an axe. The blow is fatal.

There are three types of withdrawal: physical withdrawal, inward withdrawal, and a combination of two.

By *physical* withdrawal, I mean a person reading in bed every night in a dormitory, never participating, or participating very little, in the goings on of this relaxing period of the day. Or a person may lie there with eyes open, but saying nary a word, and not participating. This would be a type of *inner* withdrawal.

Then there is the person who stays by herself during recreation under the guise of doing some project. It is well to do projects, and at times, you have to do them by yourself, but it is better not to do them by yourself; it is better to do them together.

Let us say that you all have different interests in a given house. One person is reading at a big table in a common room. Another is studying her cooking lesson. Someone is whittling, another embroidering, another is modeling with clay, and still another is repairing watches or sorting rocks. All of this can be done in one room around a big table. Each house, no matter how small it is can have a corner for such projects.

There may come a time when a certain craft would demand a few days of working alone, with a kiln maybe, or something like that, but it would be a rare occasion.

Most members are bound by holy obedience to write letters to their superiors. You could write these letters together. That may be asking a lot, but maybe it can be given some thought.

The ingenuity of love is the essence of the family spirit. It should flow from each member into the common treasury of love. Each person can think of other ways of "togetherness." There could be: game nights, bull sessions when the things of spirit are discussed, impromptu, and easily. There might be musical nights of listening to good records and discussing them.

Academic studies, in all of the houses should be together. I don't have to mention picnics and various other outings which you have already.

However, the inward withdrawals, which are so deadly to the family spirit, can take place at all of these gatherings as well. A rigid face, a closed heart, a withdrawn mind are felt by the group as a deep wound in the Mystical Body which they are.

Here, let us remember St. Francis of Assisi saying: "Let not the darkness in your heart darken the sunshine in the hearts of others.'' Yes, withdrawal has many faces. It is a subtle weapon of the devil. Let us be on our guard against it at all times and in all places.

There is another type of withdrawal that I hate to mention also. It is about the person who does not *do his share in common gatherings.* As an example I can cite picnics when one or two people carried only a salt or pepper shaker from the picnic basket to the table and didn't do a single stroke of work as far as packing things in the car, helping set the table, or helping in the thousand other little chores that go into a picnic. In some cases, it is known that people wandered away or played ball together, while the rest prepared the lunch. Then, nonchalantly the selfish ones, the withdrawn ones, came to eat the work of others' hands.

Such people deserve the name of parasites and drones. If such behavior continues, they may be overtaken by the same fate that drones in a beehive meet. In case you are not familiar with bee-keeping drones are *thrown out* of the hive!

5. *Monopolizing Conversations.* There is the type of person who has almost a compulsion to be the center of attention, to yak, yak, yak all of the time, and always about themselves, their achievements and their competence. You will recognize them by their constant use of the words, ''I'', ''me'', and ''mine''. They don't belong to the family yet, either in spirit or in fact. They consider their department to be *exclusively theirs.* You will hear them talk about ''my department'', ''my classes'', ''my patients'', ''my laundry'', and ''my sewing department'', ''my'', ''my'', ''my''.

They sin exceedingly against the family spirit. This is selfishness and self-centeredness which is dangerous for their souls and the collective soul of Madonna House. That conversation must be squashed immediately, not only by the director, but by everyone to whom it is addressed in private or in common.

Remember the beginning of this letter: *The essence of a family spirit is the love of each member for the others.* To love is to be concerned about your sisters and brothers. It is especially to be concerned aobut the ultimate salvation or sanctity of the members of your spiritual family.

It is here that everyone of you must act, not only the director. Each must be vigilant about what breaks the family spirit. It must be pointed out to people that they are self-centered, egotistical, and that they must substitute the word "our" for "mine".

If you hesitate, you will be guilty before God of a lack of charity, and a lack of concern. The family spirit bites deeply and demands much of you. Don't hesitate to spread it. For unless we have a family spirit, we will not have an Apostolate.

Lovingly yours in Mary,

Catherine

THE WEAPONS OF THE SPIRIT

October 1, 1962

Dearly Beloved,

"The terrible difference between Christian hope and the world's fulfillment has never been more starkly pointed up than at this Eastertide. While the Church sings alleluias exulting in the triumph of life, the world prepares for death. . . ." This was a *Commonweal* editorial for April 8, 1955.

The words of this editorial were like a sharp lance that entered my heart and made it bleed slowly with the bloodless blood of my wounded spirit.

I looked back over the long years and heard myself speak in a loud voice, vibrant with an urgency that overcame its foreign accent — a voice burning with a desire to warn, to explain, to alert my audiences to the shadows of that death which were so utterly invisible to them.

I am neither a prophetess nor a seer. I am just an ordinary woman. But I belonged to that vast army of refugees from

Communism which now has grown to such immense proportions. I loved Canada and the United States with a passionate love, and a gratitude that cannot be put into words. I longed to repay, be it ever so little, the immense debt that I owed this part of the world which had given me welcome, shelter, citizenship, understanding, and friendship. In a small measure I would try to do this, because, having become a lecturer on the many platforms of both countries, I had access to many ears.

What did it matter that my words had a foreign accent? Love speaks in all accents. What did it matter that being unfamiliar with the platform, and never having studied public speaking, my words at first were halting, and my sentences not too well formed? Love speaks through all words and all ways.

Thirty-three years of lecturing are now behind me. And when I try to remember their content, I do not have to strain my memory, for all of them had but one theme! I called upon my audiences to wake up from their sleep of complacency, and to examine their consciences, to open their eyes, and to see that the makings of death were all around them — cosmic death! The death of a world! I did not know anything about nuclear weapons, nor did I foresee, in any way, all of the other ''isms'' that have since reared their heads in our tragic world. All that I knew was that a diabolical force was loose in the world; that it fed on the sins of omission and commission of Christian nations and peoples; that its name was Communism; that it was an idea, and that bullets do not kill ideas; only *better ideas* can kill them!

I knew too, that we Catholics held in our sinful hands the fullness of truth; that each one of us was an apostle of this truth; and that we had to restore *ourselves first*, and then the world, to Christ, or perish!

I knew also that poverty, social injustice, greed, selfishness in low and in high places, hatred, and prejudices were the fodder that fed this force, and that the love of God and neighbor, hunger for justice, poverty (of spirit, at least), chastity, and the living of the Gospel by those who publically proclaimed their allegiance to it, were the answers to this doctrine of despair, of the absolute void, and of degradation.

I called for a true armament *with weapons of the Spirit*. And, because I had *seen such* ''death'' with my own eyes in my own land, I said that unless we Christians armed ourselves with these weapons, we, and the world we know, would be destroyed.

My lectures began in 1923. The *Commonweal* editorial is dated April, 1955. The "death" which I spoke of in symbolic and realistic terms, is upon us. We have nuclear weapons; so has the enemy. The barely visible shadow of the twenties has become the dark, stygian night of the fifties!

And still, in the infinite mercy of God, there is time to arm ourselves with the weapons of the Spirit. With an alleluia of gratitude for the redemption, of which Easter is an exultant proof, we must, this fateful year, resort to the sackcloth and ashes of repentance. We must examine our individual consciences, turn our faces to God, and heeding the voice of his Vicar, begin to arm ourselves with the weapons of the Spirit. They alone can win for us the victory that our small numbers and our frightened hearts barely dare hope for.

Let us live the Gospel. Let us show the world that Christians still love one another. Let us begin to be our brother's keeper in the full personal, social, national, and international sense of the word. Let us begin to learn how to love, so that, if need be, we may learn how to die of such love for our friends. For greater love hath no man!

If we do this, darkness will become light, and death will become life.

Lovingly yours in Mary,

INTELLECTUAL LEARNING AND SPIRITUAL WISDOM

October 1, 1962

Dearly Beloved,

Somewhere along the road of my apostolic life (I don't know where or how), I have acquired several, strange reputations. One was that I was, and still am, opposed to any intellectual, academic, or professional formation of the members of the Lay Apostolate. The other was that I dislike social workers, and professional training for social work.

"She is," they say, "utterly completely and absolutely against degrees. She functions on a somewhat emotional level of 'caritas only'."

I am quite used to being credited with many ideas and notions which I never had. It has never bothered me. But now I think that I should clarify things. The Lay Apostolate is growing. We are becoming quite a large family, and members of a large family should get to know one another. How to do this has always been a problem considering the great distances that separate many of us, and the immense work load which all of us carry.

It seemed to me necessary to explain some things about myself, not in a spirit of personal justification — God forbid! — but to clear up any misunderstandings and bring us all a little closer together.

I had better begin at the beginning with a statement that may startle you: I am *not at all* against intellectuals. I am, believe it or not, an intellectual myself! I have gone to a university. I have some degrees. I have even studied philosophy and theology. I speak quite a few foreign languages. These include English (which is a foreign language to me — a Russian!) I am a nurse. I have studied psychiatry. And I am the author of six books, several pamphlets, and innumerable magazine and newspaper articles.

I believe firmly in *academic and professional training for the members of the lay apostolate*. Both God and the people whom we have pledged to serve, especially the poor, deserve the best in every way. Lay apostles certainly must be as wiser, or wiser, than the children of the world. Intellectual formation, therefore, is a "must tool" for the Apostolate and for the apostle.

I would like to tell you a story or two from my own life. In Europe no one sought learning for the sake of degrees, nor for an open sesame to the world of commerce business, and money. Knowledge, generally speaking, was sought for the sake of knowledge. Degrees were never mentioned. Nor were they considered the passkeys to heaven, but an added responsibility to be used for the glory of God and for the service of others!

I remember my father blessing us for grade school, and throughout the years. "May the Holy Ghost overshadow you, child, so that you may understand that all knowledge must be used for the glory of God and the service of our fellowmen."

True, intellectual learning demands a stern discipline that goes well with spiritual discipline.

In 1930, when I began our first foundation in Toronto with the poorest of the poor, I realized that I would have to use every ounce of my academic, intellectual knowledge with great love and delicacy. I had to "fold the wings of my intellect," as it were, for an infinite time; perhaps a very long time. For in such a milieu in the midst of a terrible depression and incredible, human misery, there would be no time whatsoever to satisfy the hunger that fills the heart of one who has put her feet on the path of serious learning.

Neither would there be time nor opportunities to enjoy the company of other people with intellectual interests. I realized clearly that I was called to give up the joys of a normal, intellectual life for Love's sake, for God's sake!

What I did not realize was how terribly hard it would be; how intolerable it would become! I would lie awake at night and desire with a flaming desire, time to spend with people who study, think, read, discuss. *But there was neither opportunity nor time.*

The endless lines of the naked and hungry, the lame and the halt, were ever present eating up time far into the night. I seemed to have become a child in kindergarten. Yet I was an adult, hungry for intellectual companionship, for books, for study. There were so many new experiences that needed evaluating.

I spoke about it to a learned, holy priest. I told him that I did not think that I could stand it for very long. His answer was simple: "Catherine, if God who has given you your intellect wants to suspend its use for awhile, or even forever, won't you say a loving *fiat* to his will?'' It was not easy. Only with the help of God's grace was I able to say that *fiat*.

Many years passed in my ''kindergarten state.'' I used daily all of my knowledge for the service of the poor. It seemed to me that I was standing still, never learning anything new. Then, suddenly, the Lord seemed to smile and I was catapulted into lecturing, writing, studying, exchanging thoughts with others. It was then that I understood that I had been through the highest school of learning — *God's School of Love* to understand that if we give up our intellect to God, at his request, he will return it to us cleansed of all that is not of him. And our secular and spiritual knowledge will become new and powerful in him.

I am opposed to sending the members of our Apostolate to higher schools of learning *before they have gone through a total fiat, before they have joyfully laid aside intellectual pursuits for the humble tasks that demand love, detachment and humility, especially from modern man.*

When filled with this love, detachment and holy indifference, then they will truly *mean* their fiat. Then, their intellectual learning time has come! They will never make the mistake of thinking that intellectual and professional knowledge and degrees are pass-keys to human hearts. They will know that *only love* is the key. In understanding this they will become *truly wise with the wisdom of God, not of men.* The rest will be added unto them.

I seriously fear that to lay great emphasis on academic learning and degrees, can be dangerous to the Lay Apostolate. Spiritual formation should come first without loading the individual with a heavy study program. In Madonna House we feel that at least two years are needed for this spiritual formation. Then one is ready to go forth and seek such knowledge as will add to his apostolic efficiency.

I do not dislike social workers or social work. One of our men, even now, is getting his B.A. in order to enter a school of social science. What I often fear, in this field, is that ''scientific objectivity'' may blot the face of humanity for such an academically trained social worker. I fear that the ''client'' will replace the person, and hence God. But I love social sciences and social workers, who are handmaidens of the Lord.

To me one has to be the Lord first, and for this one has to go to the School of Nazareth! Only then can one *do* for the Lord.

After that one can go to any school that can make your love of the Lord shine more clearly.

Have I clarified my stand? I wonder! I believe, too, that people without *specialized knowledge* can serve the Lord. That does not mean that I am filled with emotional sentimentality.

A great many humble and tremendous lay apostles of the Lord had no degree!

Let us put first things first. The rest will follow.

Lovingly yours in Mary,

ALMSGIVING

October 1, 1962

Dearly Beloved,

The Word was made flesh and dwelt among us. The Uncreated became man for love of us. The *Word of God* walks among us, and yet millions in our dark and fearsome days "know him not." However, not only the fate of our own world and civilization, but also our life eternal depends upon our knowing and loving him. *It is, therefore, the acceptable time for us, the children of his light and his love, to make him known.*

We can do this in many ways. The simplest and most direct way is through almsgiving. Not only can we give money, food and clothing, (not all may be able to give these), but we can give the alms of words which we all need.

All of us possess these alms. All of us have them to give. The need for such alms is *everywhere*.

However, like all other alms, words must be given lovingly,

gently, thoughtfully. To be able to dispense the alms of words, we must be one with *the Word*, and on the way to dying to self and living in him. One must try to see with his gentle eyes, think with his clear-sighted mind, try to love with his burning heart.

For alms given without love, without compassion or graciousness, or deep understanding, bring hurt and pain, and do even more damage than indifference and coldness. Without these we prostitute the very act of giving.

But when, watchful and alert in the cause of Christ, we see our neighbors as Christ sees them. Love will give us understanding. It will enable us to read the signs of hungry minds, numbed hearts, frightened and lonely souls, and broken bodies. Love will enable us to hear symphonies of pain and hurt, fear and near-despair that life and the prince of evil play, with endless variations, on the strings of people's emotions.

Everywhere, the ministry of love — the alms of our words can be exercised.

Do you see that lonely and sad child? Have you a moment to spare to give him the alms of a few little words? They will bring light into a darkness that should not be there. Making friends with a lonely, lost or unloved child, be he poor or rich, is to bring Christ to him. Take the child into your heart. Those who do, take Christ into their hearts. And surely he will reverse the process in eternity by taking *you* into *his* heart!

Do our eyes really see? Are we not blind to the thousands of little signs that exist in our own family? Father is a little greyer, a little more worried, a bit more silent. Mother is more tense, often with eyes that reveal tears. Sister or brother is sharper, thinner, less pleasant, more withdrawn. Maybe this is the beginning of tragedies.

Is our love watchful, ready to give the alms of gentle, key words spoken in time which may keep a door from closing? A gate may be opened allowing light and love to flood the depths of minds beginning to doubt the very existence of love.

Are we convinced that we are our "brother's keeper?" Do we understand how far this "keeping" goes? Business associates, friends, fellow workers, strangers who cross our paths now and then, our whole work-a-day world — *all are our brothers and sisters* whom we must cherish in the Lord.

A smile and a pleasant word about the weather given to an ill-clad poor person in a public conveyance, or to a stranger within our gates, might mean the difference between his hatred of all that we stand for, and his understanding.

For example, with regard to foreigners in our midst, clearly annunciated words, spoken slowly, lovingly, with a smile of encouragement, are rich alms. Here especially, the alms of our words can change the fate of our nation. For this stammering, shy alien, who barely speaks English, may tomorrow become the leader of hate and revolt, and may do untold damage to minds, souls and bodies. And this all because *no one took time to give the alms of gentle, understanding words when these could have been food and drink to a hungry and thirsty stranger*.

The sick may be tiresome at times in their self-centeredness, in their urgency to take us through every step of their domain of loneliness and pain, pain through their halting, rambling, repetitious speech. How are we to console them, bring them back to the realm of God's light and love, show them the treasure that can save worlds of souls everywhere? We can teach them to offer that loneliness, those pains, to Mary, the treasurer of God! How else but through the alms of our comforting words, and our patient, interested, unflagging care, can they learn the importance of offering everything through her?

The forgotten, the unwanted, the lost, the rambling alcoholic, the neurotic, the borderline "psychos" — would they be what they are if someone had given them the alms of words when they so desperately needed them?

Such words of love, understanding, compassion, patience, and help are oils that sooth the burning wounds of exhausted minds. They are cool waters that quench the thirst that almost kills them. They are food that nourishes a starvation resembling that found in concentration camps. Words are often keys that open prison doors. They are so easy to give, yet so often withheld.

Alms of warm, kind words are like a mother's lullaby to the unwanted and the elderly who often have a hungry loneliness. These words bring peace and joy into joylessness and unpeace, make crooked ways straight, and people feel wanted and loved again.

The pariahs of our modern world the "bums", the panhandlers, the prostitutes, and those in prison — what about them? Who has the time and courage to give them the alms of words, or the courtesy of an attentive silence?

Everywhere, at all times of the night and day, people cry out for the alms of words. They cry silently not even knowing why they cry. Yet they *do know* that they are desperately hungry and thirsty for love and friendship.

But love and its flower, friendship, are God, for God is Love, and God is the Word, and he clothe himself with flesh for love of us!

Let us then lovingly show him to our brothers and sisters expressed *in the thousand ways of love's ingenuity, but especially in the alms of loving words*!

Lovingly in Mary,

WHY WE BEG

October 1, 1962

Dearly Beloved,

For almost thirty years of my life in the Lay Apostolate I have been asked again and again, "Why do you beg? Aren't there less difficult, less humiliating, easier ways to finance your Apostolate?"

Perhaps there are, but I have only one answer to this question. It is so simple that it is difficult to understand. It goes like this: We of the Apostolate beg *because we are in love with a Beggar who is God.*

Love does such things; it cannot resist doing so. Those of us who fall passionately in love with God feel impelled by faith and love *to imitate him, to identify ourselves with him, to become one with him, to be poor like him,* depending daily on utter trust in our

Beloved and his words: "Behold the birds of the air, the lilies of the field! Go, sell all that you possess. Take up their cross and follow me!" ring constantly in our ears like heavenly melodies.

Our eyes always see beautiful images etched against our minds, our souls, and our hearts: a woman, a man, a stable, a Child being born; a man standing against the hills of Galilee telling his hearers, "Foxes have holes, and birds have nests, but the Son of Man has nowhere to lay his head." Another image: a day in Palestine, another hill, a flaming sky; the same Man, now stretched out and lifted up on a bleak cross, crucified for love of us. He is crucified naked; he is utterly poor. To prove that he was in love with us, and to save us, he died a pauper! These are the melodies that we hear constantly. These are the pictures etched in our minds. My heart almost breaks at this hearing and seeing.

But there are other reasons for becoming beggars. He wants us to depend upon his providence, to trust him to move the hearts of others to help us.

Poverty, chastity and obedience are our gifts to God. Through them we surrender all of the wealth we have so that we may enter naked into the kingdom of charity, enter naked into his Sacred Heart, even as he entered the tomb naked and crucified for love.

After we have surrendered ourselves, what is there left for us to do *but to beg*? We have nothing of our own. We must beg as he said we should, and be content with what we receive.

We live with utter trust in his divine providence. When we pray, "Our Father who art in heaven . . . give us this day our daily bread," we mean just that. Not the bread of tomorrow, nor the bread of the day after, but the bread of *today*.

If all of us were earning a living, we would still have to beg, because it seems that the more we love, the more we deny ourselves, the more people we find to help. The sea of the lame, the halt, the blind, the hungry, the disturbed, the sick, the homeless, rises and rises around us. There is no organization existing that could earn enough to fill those needs. God alone can do this!

But people say, "This is not rational." Nor is nature. This is where the supernatural comes in, and faith bridges the gap. Faith is a slender but strong suspension bridge which carries my flagging spirit across the chasm of the impossible.

And lo! the impossible becomes reality! Money comes in!

Another step is taken. Another house is opened. Another need is filled.

However, there seems to be just one condition for all of this, and that condition must be observed or nothing at all happens. It is this: I or someone must beg ceaselessly, with an unshaking faith and a fiery certitude in every word of God, but especially in his *"Ask, and you shall receive."*

That is why "Restoration" comes to you with many articles, and even a letter stating our urgent needs! *I beg, we beg, because we are in love with a divine pauper who begged us to be beggars for love of him.* How can we not beg when we see the Divine Pauper on a crucifix!

Another most excellent reason for begging is to give other people the opportunity to acquire great merit. For graces are poured upon those who pour out their money, their time, their talents in acts of charity! If nobody begged, who would give? If nobody gave, how much sadder the world would be! How much more the God of charity would grieve! Remember the words of St. Paul, "God loves a cheerful giver." Maybe he loves a cheerful beggar too, for it is the beggar, don't you think, who makes the giver!

Lovingly yours in Mary,

THE ESSENCE OF LOVING

October 3, 1962

Dearly Beloved,

Today I would like to talk to you about the very difficult subject of inward surrender. It seems a bit nebulous and it is, and it is difficult to find words to express it. However, I must try, because we must begin to understand what is asked of us or we shall fail in our Apostolate. This we cannot do, because we would fail God who counts on us to restore this tragic world of weary and tired souls to him. Souls who are so in need of God that they are dying of thirst without realizing it. They seek him in the darkness of their days and in their nights which are sleepless and fearsome.

So we cannot fail. We will not fail because we have his grace and the help of his most Blessed and Beloved Mother, the saints and our guardian angels.

Let us consider this inner surrender of ours. It is the essence of loving. Let us say that two people marry. If they do not have this essence of loving, if they do not surrender inwardly to one another, their union is a prostitution of true marriage and true love.

If a man and woman surrender only their bodies, they haven't surrendered anything, and soon there will be satiety, and following that a dislike or even a hatred of one another. The marriage will fail as so many marriages have done.

The same holds true of religious life. People can wear the habit and all of the trimmings. People can live in silence, fast and mortify their bodies, and *yet not be surrendered inwardly because they are always* seeking to do their own will instead of God's.

The same is even true of priests. The outward trappings must signify an inward surrender. Only when this inward surrender is present does any dedicated life reach its fullness and glory.

The same applies to us and our vocation. Surrender, I said, is the essence of love. Surrender means doing the will of the Beloved. It is using that ingenuity of love, and that inner intuition of love to anticipate the will of the Beloved.

To do the will of our Beloved, the Most Holy Trinity, is the perfection of love in Madonna House. A passionate desire to live the duty of every moment perfectly should burn within us like an unquenchable fire.

You might say at this point: "There she goes again talking about little things!" Yes, you are right. But by now you should *know that "the little things" that I talk about are immense.* They are immense because they deal with God and the things of God. They deal with the love of God and our love for him. What could be greater than that?

Let us face it. In the natural order we might have moments of excitement, but by and large, there is a sameness to our life. The repetition of our daily talks would not hold our attention, or our interest, especially since it brings us no tangible remuneration.

We are here in Madonna House only because of our love for God and his love for us. We are here because he has shown his great love by choosing and calling us.

How then can we utterly surrender? The answer is simple: We must strip ourselves of self as Christ was stripped on the way to the cross. Only in this utter and complete stripping of ourselves lies the real surrender. There is no other way. But how are we going to strip ourselves? Before God we are resplendent because we are created in his image and have his divine life, and at the same time, we are paupers who have nothing of our own. So the answer is simple and very concrete; we must become contemplatives. That is we must pray without ceasing.

How does one do that? Well, there are many ways of becoming contemplatives. The word "contemplative" simply means thinking intensely about someone or something of importance. It means being absorbed in a particular person or situation.

When we speak of our contemplation of God, it might seem to us that after Mass we forget him until duty brings us back to chapel. This is where the real work of a lay apostle begins — our Opus Dei. We must *work on ourselves* to frequently bring ourselves *back* to the contemplation of God.

There are many ways to do this. If at all possible, spend half an hour before the Blessed Sacrament in silent prayer during each 24 hours of the day. Then there is the recitation of the Eastern Prayer of the Heart: "Lord Jesus, Son of God, have mercy on me, a sinner." Some of our staff have tried it, and believe it or not, it works!

Another good way is to make the sign of the cross when you begin or change occupations. These are but a few ideas. You might have others. The time is at hand when our inner surrender must be complete. We must live in such a way that we see Jesus everywhere and in all things.

And let us examine our consciences well. Let us work on our faults and on our sins of omission. Let us be watchful over them so as to eliminate them. Let us try to practice perfect obedience, for nothing strips us to the bone faster than obedience. Nothing leads us more quickly to total surrender. Let us work on this too with deep prayer. Prayer alone will overcome our faults and emotional problems. Prayer alone will give us the courage to do what has to be done. Then we might at least begin to say in the very near future: "I live now, not I, but Christ lives in me."

Dearly Beloved, unless our obedience increases one hundredfold, unless we become contemplative, we will not begin to die to self, and we will not surrender. The work of God will be stymied, and this must not happen. The greatest tragedy of our era is *not to be a saint!*

We have to start on the way to sanctity no matter what the cost. Sanctity alone matters. It isn't what we *do* that is important, but what we *are* before God. I mean this with my whole heart, my whole soul, and my whole mind. I pray only one prayer — that we may become lovers of God and give ourselves over to him in a totality that knows no reservations. No matter what the pain, we must give ourselves to him joyously, passionately, as he gave himself to us.

Lovingly yours in Mary,

THE FABRIC OF FAMILY SPIRIT

October 17, 1962

Dearly Beloved,

I have been thinking very seriously about why it is so hard to achieve a real, family spirit.

Now mind you, I know that we do have a very pleasant time together, that there are many interests in common, that there is generally amongst us a great love for one another. But I also know that it is still fairly superficial. I want it to grow. As the Scriptures say and we should realize it in our lives — ''How wonderful it is for brethren to dwell together in unity!'' Meditate upon it.

What I am talking about is a deep and beautiful reality. I am not talking only of the best family spirit that is possible in a real, blood family, but I am talking about *the family spirit that should be amongst us because we belong to the family of God*!

Consider: God is our Father, Christ is our brother, and the Holy Spirit is our Advocate. The Triune God gives his own divine life; and Mary, our Mother and all of the saints are part of our family too. This oneness with the divine family, with the Church Triumphant, with Our Lady should be reflected in each one of us. We should love one another as God the Father loves his Son, so that from our love for one another the Holy Spirit would become almost visible to those around us.

This demands real depths from us, or perhaps I should say, this demands going into the depths of our spirit. It demands that journey inward about which I always write in my poems. This means constant concern for the other, and utter forgetfulness of oneself. It demands openness.

Now we talk much about openness, but exactly what do we mean by it? First and foremost, we mean not hiding our weaknesses, even our sinfulness from others. It is taken for granted that we are all sinners. One cannot live in a community without being aware of the little sins and weaknesses of one another. These have to be born with great charity. We must take one another as we are; but we must also help one another to overcome our weaknesses by kindness, by love, and by gentle, fraternal correction.

Openness also means that when we are really depressed, or in trouble of some sort, we share our troubles with one another, or bring them to our superiors, so as not to allow the darkness within us to blot out the sunshine in someone else's soul. We seek help from one another, and especially from our superiors quickly, so as not to endanger or tear the fabric of the family spirit. Openness also means sharing work of the Apostolate, and also our own interests, joys, and thoughts so that we become like open books to one another. Thus we come to know one another at our best and at our worst, and thus truly love one another.

The desire to be together instead of alone should grow daily in us. Can you imagine the Father and the Son wishing to be apart from one another? Can you imagine husbands and wives wanting to be apart from one another? Wherever there is true love and family spirit, *people want to be together*.

True, everyone, even husbands and wives, need solitude at times. But solitude is not withdrawal from the family. Solitude is going apart to be even more one with the family in love and prayers. For this, we provide the poustinia. For this, in years to come, we will give more and more time to pray before the Blessed Sacrament as our members increase. No, solitude is not withdrawal.

However, what we have amongst us *is* a withdrawal. Let me give you an example of this. There are a few minutes at night when you are all in your dorms. This is the time to really be together, to read together part of the Gospel, prepare for your meditation, or discuss some of the events of the day, or just to have a pillow fight or laugh and talk together. It certainly is not the time to curl up with your back to everybody, studying German, French, or what have you, nor to read your favorite detective story book or even a spiritual one. Nor is it the time to work on your embroidery. We have other times for handicrafts. This is the time for a real, human, family togetherness.

The family spirit shows itself in doing things together. We are now organizing handicrafts both as a recreation and for apostolic reasons. All of these things broaden your vision, your intellects, and your imaginations. Handicrafts should be done together.

For in a family people should share common experiences which build friendships and love, and help us to know one another better and to come closer together.

How beautiful it is to see a common room filled with the family of Madonna House! Someone is playing a game, someone else is embroidering or reading, a group, perhaps, is playing some good music and discussing it, or another group is just having a conversation in a corner.

Picnics, whenever possible, are another shared experience, another coming closer together. Walks through the city or the country are good, and help to preserve the family spirit.

The family spirit also consists in sharing simply, humbly and beautifully, news from home, the work of the day, knowledge acquired — everything that people who love one another like to share.

Yes, the family spirit consists in making a real effort to know one another in depth. It consists in being open to one another as we share our work and our play. It consists especially in being together and *being deeply concerned about one another*.

This is what I would like to see more of in Madonna House Apostolate. I worry, pray and think much about our not being together enough. You are together, and yet you are apart. That won't do. For we belong to the divine family of God, the Father, God the Son, God the Holy Spirit, with Our Lady for our Mother, and the saints as members of our family. None of these withdraw from *us*. But if we withdraw from one another, if we do not have this family spirit, that means we withdraw from them, and that would be a great tragedy!

Lovingly yours in Mary,

THE CHILDREN OF CHARITY

November 19, 1962

Dearly Beloved,

Though I have written to you quite often about good manners being the "children of charity," it seems that I must discuss a few things about these matters.

I want to mention one point especially. It is the terrible habit you have of *yelling* across rooms and down corridors. You all know that loud noises are plentiful enough in every house. You have all been taught, I am sure, in your childhood and youth that when you want to ask someone something, you go up to the person. Yelling startles everyone! In some lines of work this is necessary, but stop for a moment and consider that you are called to be saints, and saints *teach by the way they stand, walk and talk.*

One whose soul and mind are peaceful does not desire to yell across large spaces. But it goes more deeply than that. Often the reason that we yell is that we are too tired or too lazy to go and talk to that person. Yes, we have to take many steps in our houses. Did you ever stop to think that this is one of the best "steps" of mortification in our unmortified age? One good way of "dying to self." It takes effort to go to another person and speak in a simple, Christian way.

Yelling is the main "manners" fault of which we are all guilty. It irritates and makes miserable both the person yelled at and the persons within hearing. May I ask you a rather trite question? I think it is worth asking: Do you think that Christ yelled at his apostles or at the people? In the Gospels he lifted his voice *once*, when he raised the cords in the Temple. I think that we would all be shocked at the thought of Christ yelling. Nor can we imagine the Blessed Virgin yelling at anyone. It is so self-evident that they wouldn't. Ask yourself why you yell. It is a good meditation.

But there are other grave points of irritation that we are overlooking. Take loud singing by one person, even someone with a good voice. When people sing psalms or religious songs at the top of their voices, how do you think that affects people who have to listen all day?

Granted, there is nothing wrong in lifting your voice loudly in song if you are happy! But consider the other people in the house. Their moods might be different; they may or may not like the song you are singing. Singing loudly all of the time would annoy anyone, for there is a limit to good things!

There is another annoying situation: when several people are working together, and some seem to have a need to talk constantly. It is often senseless conversation. Often these same people tend to monopolize the conversation at dinner. Usually these good people have a compulsion to tell all that *they* have been doing. Almost unconsciously the pronoun "I" is very prominent in their conversations. Interesting as it might be to live with that sort of a person, it is not easy. They never seem to realize that they should also be concerned about other people, especially the shyer person who needs to be drawn out a little.

If this type of person lives in a very small house where some are not talkative, the agony they inflict upon others is beyond imagining. It is like a sharp needle entering the brain.

You see that the care and attention about all these "little things" form the very essence of the spirit of Madonna House. When they are done with an almost cruelty in their thoughtlessness, *showing a tremendous lack of love and concern for the others in the house, they have the power to lead us to hell instead of to the love of God*. Do not think for a moment that Satan is idle about the spirit of Madonna House!

Yelling across spaces, singing at the top of your voices, yak-yak-yaketing all day long in some corner when working together, monopolizing conversations at table thoughtlessly just to hear oneself talk, seem like only scratches on the body of charity. However, you keep scratching the same place long enough and you will have a deep wound. The morale of a house may well crumble under a loud voice, thoughtless singing, and constant yak-yaketing.

Also, we will not teach anyone love if we behave like that; if we don't teach love then we are unfaithful to our vocation. So you see how very much harm can be done by a lack of good manners.

Lovingly yours in Mary,

THE TRAGEDY OF CONFORMITY

November 28, 1962

Dearly Beloved,

One evening at Madonna House a man who was both an artist and a craftsman came to discuss the tragedy of conformity, which he lists as Enemy No. 1 of any artistic endeavor, and even of happy normal life. There were quite a few local people present as well as the women of Madonna House. He presented us with story after story of the tragic conformity that one sees everywhere amongst the young, the middle-aged, and even among senior citizens. He said that one of the most poisonous, most dastardly phrases that he knows — a phrase that kills initiative, talent and even thought in children and youth, a phrase that carries over into their whole lives, is that terrible sentence which so many North American parents use: "What will the neighbors think?"

Our speaker, a mild and a very polite man, said publicly, "To hell with what the neighbors think! Be free. Be an individual. Be adventuresome. Experiment, and above all, don't be afraid of the neighbors."

I thought about his words and how well they apply to the Apostolate. Alas! Since the majority of our members are of North American origin, they are very much bound by this tragic attitude: "What will the neighbors think?" They are conformists to the depths of their beings. This is what is responsible for so many of our emotional problems, because at the bottom of conformity lies insecurity and a sickly need of approval at all costs.

By now you are familiar with the tragedy of the organizational man who, though an adult, is asked to conform not only because of what the neighbor thinks, but because of what big companies demand. Many tests are made on each person who seeks employment. I was recently reading an article in a journal of psychology that said that all these tests are tragic, because they select for good jobs people who haven't any gumption, who will conform, who will not step out of line, who will accept the line the company lays out for them. Soon, if we do not watch out, this conformity will lead us to become men and women robots.

See how in the Apostolate you are still bound by styles. You are much freer than those around you, but nevertheless, there is little originality regarding hair-dos, or clothes. I don't mean only because you are getting clothes secondhand. You really wish to be like everybody else. You are still subject to the need for conformity.

But saints (and you are supposed to be saints-in-the making), are the most original, the most individualistic, the most adventuresome people in the world. Note as you get to know the lives of the saints how no two of them are alike. The Lord loves diversity in unity. If we can compare the saints to a garden of flowers in which he takes delight, I personally imagine that he would be very bored if the garden were all lilies, all roses, or all any one type of flower. The beauty of a garden is its diversity, its originality, and its individuality. So it is with the minds, bodies, and hearts of the saints.

I've been thinking lately that we are commissioned by God to bring that variety, that holy individuality, that human originality, that spirit of adventure, that desire for experimentation into a world that is becoming more and more robot-like in its conformity.

We must take the cords of love, and like Christ, chase conformity out of the temples of human souls — chase it in firmness and gentleness and love, but chase it nevertheless. Yes, before we can do this, we must smash conformity within our own minds, souls and hearts. This is a task for each person in the Apostolate.

Let us be adventuresome in the food of foreign countries to which we are going. Let us break the notion that we can eat only one type of food, and that any other will make us sick! Nonsense! Let's be adventuresome.

Let's be adventuresome in our appearance. Let us be adventuresome, individualistic and experimental in seeking out hobbies and creative outlets without which we perish, for it is one of our needs.

Let us be adventuresome, individualistic in proclaiming the truths of God. One must speak differently to kids on skid row and to undergraduates in a college. Let us become all things to all men without fear and trembling.

Let us be original in our sanctity, in our prayers, in our efforts to go to God. Let us share the wealth that we find with one another.

Let us plunge into the depths of God's love and come forth a new man, a new woman, with ideas and thought that will enrich the Apostolate by their individuality. Let us not be afraid to think and to seek answers to our questions. Let us be different, bringing forth the talents which God has given to each of us. Let us conform to one thing only: let us all love God daily more and more, together.

Lovingly yours in Mary,

THE CRIB — A CALL TO TOTALITY

December 20, 1962

Dearly Beloved,

All around us is the struggle for political autonomy, power and glory. New continents such as Africa and Asia are splitting up into smaller nations. The struggle for power among these new countries continues. Dominating them all is the struggle for power between East and West — between Russia and the United States. Every country seeks its own glory at the price of someone else's. As a result, the ordinary little people suffer in silence and pray and hope for someone who will come and truly set the world free. The tragedy is that half of the world doesn't know, and the other half has almost forgotten, *that the King has come in power and glory.* He came as a spring breeze, as a gentle wind in the summer comes to refresh us. He came as the mysterious whispers of the night when tree talks to tree, and grass whispers to grass, and flowers sing to flowers. He came in the dark of night, humbly, the Child of poor folks. He was born in a cave. His first human contact was the gentle hands of his Mother. His first sense impressions were the gentle whisper of the straw in which he lay, and the sound of the ox and ass chewing their cuds.

The only people who came to render him homage on that holy night were the humblest of the humble — the shepherds of Israel. The only mysterious signs of his heavenly origin were the angelic choir, and a strange light in the sky. The shepherds and the kings heard these angelic voices, and saw this wondrous star that had arisen.

How far removed is his gentle coming from our centuries-old wars and struggles for power which still continue. But make no mistake! The Child who lies in the manger, listening to the sound of the straw and the munching of animals, possesses all power and glory!

He has dominion over life and death and not a hair of your head falls but he knows it and wills it! Even as you read my words, your life lies in the palm of his hand! Nothing escapes his dominion, and his will reigns supreme over a thousand universes. Man prides himself on his discovery of space. But in the eyes of the Lord, a thousand universes are like a grain of sand. He has made all of the laws which have brought them into existence. They are created by him and are subject to him.

Yet it is the same Child in that manger, the same humble Carpenter of Nazareth, the same Man who walked barefoot in Palestine and died naked on a cross, who possesses all power and glory, for he is an eternal King, to whom nations and universes are but a footstool.

Note how he rules, the Just One. A bruised reed he will not break. A sinner before him finds mercy; gentleness shines in his footsteps; in all he does love sings its eternal song.

Dearly Beloved, on this Christmas Day, My heart goes out in torrents of love to each one of you. As I kneel before the Crib in the Madonna House chapel, I ask the Lord of Hosts, the King of Power and Glory, who lies before me — a little Child — that you might meet him in both guises. I ask that you might know the Child *and* the King, the Man *and* the God in one person. I ask that you might know him who has called you so specially to himself, who changes himself into a tremendous lover, and desires of you but one thing: that you might love him back by surrendering totally and completely to him.

If, by some miracle of God's grace, you were to find yourself transported to Bethlehem on this holy night, and Christ the Child were to ask you directly, as he did to Peter: "Do you love me . . . Sally, Dick, JoAnne, Joe?" What would you answer him? Could you answer like Peter: "Lord, you know that I love you?"

Or would you have to say: "Yes, I love you, Lord, thus far, but no further!" Or, "I love you, Lord, so much — and no more." "Yes, I love you Lord, but I find it so hard to grow in love." Perhaps others would answer, "Yes, Lord, we do love you!" But before you answer, you would have to be very sure that you understand what *he* understands by love: *a total surrender, a total consecration, a total dedication.* That's what he considers love, and that is what it truly is. That's how he loved us.

We are not kings, nor tribal chieftains, nor men and women of importance. Nevertheless, we seek to be kings and queens when we glorify our own wills and enjoy our own power. Let us beware of ourselves and let us implore Emmanuel, the Child, who is King of love, of gentle power, and of hidden glory, to teach us

the one virtue which will bring us to our knees before his face —
the virtue of humility, which is only another word for truth. In this
humility we can tell him that we love him and that we want to be
his completely; we can also humbly and truthfully beg him for the
grace to do so.

I will pray for this for each one of you for this year before the
crib, and then I will ask the Divine Infant for one special gift for
each of you.

This is my Christmas present to you. Pauper of the Lord that I
am, I have nothing but my love and prayers to give. They are
yours in their totality, because you are Christ's and he is yours,
dearly beloved.

I wish that the coming new year be a year of growth in faith;
for as you grow in faith, you will grow in love and surrender, and
that is really all that matters!

Lovingly yours in Mary,

SPIRITUAL DIRECTION AND THE HEART OF A CHILD

January 8, 1963

Dearly Beloved,

Throughout this beautiful, Christmas Season I have prayed
very ardently for all of you that the Infant Christ might touch your
hearts, minds, and souls with his tiny hands, and open them to his
own beauty, and to the realization of his need for you in his
Mystical Body!

I have prayed that you might begin to be Christ-centered, instead of self-centered. It is tragic to behold a world that makes Christ wait to receive our love! It is even more tragic to behold you still making him wait — you who have been specially called by his love of predilection to an Apostolate of his own creation, to his little flock of Madonna House.

Yes, this was my prayer for you. It might seem to you that I begin the year of 1963 on a rather sad note. It might appear a little negative to you. Some of you might say to yourselves upon hearing the opening sentence of this letter: "Here she goes again — our Katie!"

For all the words that I use, and all the seemingly new angles that I present to you, when all is said and done, come back to this sentence of John the Beloved: "Little children, let us love one another." I have nothing else to say, really, for it is the very essence of our vocation, our religion, and our faith.

But of course, there *are* angles that a loving heart (and I hope that mine is a loving heart) can, with the ingenuity of love, try to explain to its children, in order to spur them on to their total surrender, their total and inward dedication to the Lord of Love. Through your promises you have pledged yourselves to serve him through poverty, chastity and obedience.

There are several angles that I want to discuss with you today, and I will begin with the most important one. It is one without which surrender and dedication will continue to be slow, heavy and difficult, and will continue to make the tired, eager Christ wait. This is the question of spiritual directors.

One would think that you understand this, and I am sure that most of you do. You realize that through the Fathers of the Church God has made it clear to us that we need spiritual direction. All Christians, all Catholics, should make use of it. St. John of the Cross has said that "*only a fool directs himself.*" Especially should people dedicated to God seek direction. Through this grace they realize better their poverty and their weakness. We need a spiritual guide on the narrow road that leads to heaven. The devil delights in placing confusing signposts on our way, especially at our major crossroads.

Yes, I believe that the majority of you believe in spiritual direction. While at Madonna House you selected a spiritual director; but ask yourself, how close are you to him now that you are in the missions. As you all know, spiritual direction should continue via letters. It is vitally important to your growth, and to the growth of the Apostolate, that you should write to your spiritual director never less than twice a month. That holy man, that priest, *must know the state of your whole self mentally, emotionally and spiritually.*

Moreover, these confidentially written communications bring peace to your soul by the very fact that you have expressed yourself in writing. The great Spiritual Director, Christ, who stands behind your own spiritual director, already begins to bless you. Often without your realizing it, he gives the beginning of answers, and places a great peace in your soul, because you have been humble enough to write; because you have recognized your dependence upon the priest he has given to direct you.

Through spiritual direction you have taken the greatest precaution a human being can take against *pride*. Pride is the greatest enemy of a Christian, the one sure guide to hell. Pride is the devil's daughter, or perhaps even the essence of the devil himself. It was pride that made him hurl into the endless heavens his terrible, challenging cry to God: ''Non serviam!''

I know that there are some among you who, strangely enough, still question deep down in your souls the need of spiritual direction. Due to a spiritual sloth, you do not see the need for communicating the state of your soul to that other Christ. He is the person whom you have chosen with the grace of God to lead your souls to the green hills of the Lord, to that sanctity and life of perfection that you have promised so solemnly when you made your promise before the Blessed Sacrament. But to question the *need* of a spiritual director is to question God, the Church, and the popes themselves.

There are some among you who see a conflict between the ''independence'' that you have been brought up with, and the freedom of the children of God which comes through obedience to a priest. Somewhere deep down in your emotional and intellectual self, you rebel against submitting your will to that of another. You may sing the hymn: ''Give me the heart of a child,'' but you don't want the heart of a child. You want to be an ''individual,'' your own master. However you perceive this, dearly beloved, in reality it means slavery to self, to one's own judgment. In a word, it means pride.

Yes, I am making this letter strong, but let those to whom it applies take heed. This warning comes from the very depths of my motherly heart — from the heart of a foundress of a little Apostolate of God which can do great things if its members are obedient, humble, dedicated, and surrendered. And you understand that it is my duty to do all that is in my power to help you to become dedicated and surrendered.

In response, you might say that you are writing, or have written, to your spiritual director, but you have received unsatisfactory response, or maybe none at all.

I remind you not to let this disturb you, because what you are seeking is human consolation. It is nice to be consoled, but sometimes it is better not to be. In spiritual direction, it is *you* who have to reveal your soul to your spiritual director. In blind confidence, and child-like trust and complete love, leave the rest of the responsibility to him, knowing in faith, that his silences, his short words, and his seemingly unsatisfactory answers are God's way of teaching you. This does not justify ceasing your correspondence with him.

You have to understand the tremendous graces attached to your writing, even as they are attached to his silence or his short, concise answers. Remember that Christ, the great Spiritual Director, is standing between you and him. Once you have fulfilled your obligation, the duty of the spiritual director is to watch for the guidance of the Holy Spirit. Rest assured, if your letters need an answer, you will get it. But keep your soul in love and trust and confidence, and keep writing even if you keep writing surrounded by a constant void of silence. At the other end of your communication is a man who is another Christ, *who knows the state of your soul*. It is now *his* responsibility. All you have to do is to *enjoy* the tremendous peace and blessings that will come to you after writing. Spiritual direction is important to you and to the whole of the Apostolate, for on it depends our collective strength, dedication and surrender. For we are only as strong as our weakest link.

The second question that I would like to treat is the obedience that I have given to you *to write to me at least twice a month*. This is the only *holy obedience* that I have given to you. It is an obedience given according to our constitutions, and binds you officially to obey as you have promised to do.

There are some among you who have broken this obedience. Let me draw your attention to the fact that this is a serious breach of obedience. Once again I command you — a word I practically never use — I *command you under holy obedience to write to me twice a month*, no matter how distasteful or unpleasant for some individuals this task may be. All I ask of you is to write a few lines.

Sorrowful as I might be that this is all that you can write to me, I who love you so much, and sad as I might be that you want only to fulfil the letter of the law and not its spirit, still, I will be satisfied with those few lines, but they must come *regularly twice a month, please*.

There is a film entitled: "Four Families: A Comparison" which helps us to see our distorted, North American ideas of "independence." It depicts a Hindu, a Japanese, a French, and a Canadian Family. The Canadian way is in great contrast with the rest of the world. You will see the tragic seeds of your wrong ideas on "independence" which really is not freedom, but license.

Among Canadian and American youth, "independence" is quite early equated with having a key to the front door of the home and coming in whenever you please. When you begin to earn money, you consider yourself free from discipline, parental or otherwise. In a word you think that you can do what you want, when you want and as you want it. At least this is what is happening in Canada and the United States according to all reports on juvenile delinquency.

In the last month I have read a "sea" of articles on the decline of morals in Canada and the United States. We have been taught from childhood an erroneous notion of "individualism" and "independence." Truly a great hue and cry is being raised around these words. They are at the bottom of the emotional problems of our modern society.

A book by Jung, one of the great psychiatrists after Freud, has just been published. He states that after working in depth analysis for 45 years with people from all over the world, he came to the conclusion that the story of Genesis must be true. He said that mankind must have sinned against God, because in the very depth of every human being, no matter what his belief, there is a sense of guilt. He said that depth psychiatry would only be successful if the psychiatrist could bring about the reconciliation of the souls with God, or some Higher Power as the person understood him.

He goes on to say that especially the Europeans, Americans, and Canadians are a prey to anxieties and depression because they are not obeying the laws of their religion. Until they do, this world, dominated by Europeans, is going to be a sick world. This is only another (albeit scientific) way of speaking of the same surrender and dedication to the God of love that I have been speaking about as regards spiritual direction.

Those of us who are fighting for their wrong kind of "independence," and mistaken "individuality," are digging an emotional grave for themselves. God, after all, is the greatest psychiatrist. Obedience, openness, trust and love, are the essences and the fruits of the great commandment of love that God has given to us. We destroy ourselves if we do not follow that great commandment.

Take, for instance, obedience. It will not heal us, nor make us grow spiritually, if we must always know *why* we obey. Then it becomes an act of *reason*. Men "obey" in this way in business and in their ordinary loves. But it is not an obedience which is the fruit of love and of faith. With the heart of a child, full of trust and confidence in him who gives the order — and it is always *God* who gives the order through the superiors — you obey joyfully, immediately, without question. Then, and only then will the spirit of the law be observed; only then will poverty shine in the fullness of its beauty. The surrender of our will is the crowning of poverty. Such poverty gives love a footstool, a foundation on which to grow. That is the role of obedience.

Through such obedience the sense of guilt disappears, depressions are lifted, joy floods the heart, and life in the Apostolate becomes happy and fruitful.

I wanted to speak to you of these things, dearly beloved. With my letter goes my prayer that the ears of your souls, mind and heart be open to my humble, stumbling words about these great verities that alone can make us faithful. I wish you again a grace-filled, fruitful new year.

Lovingly yours in Mary,

UNCONSCIOUS SUPERIORITY

February 23, 1963

Dearly Beloved,

I have been praying for quite a while about this letter. It is not going to be an easy letter to write, but I want you to know that I do so with great peace, and with a tremendous love for each of you. I fully realize that most of what I am going to say concerns thoughtlessness on your part rather than any kind of malicious intention. I write this letter to show you how any kind of thoughtlessness hurts, not only other people, but some members of our own household as well.

I know also that there are times when a religious family such as ours has to come together and make a collective examination of conscience. So read this letter peacefully and attentively, making a point to remember and implement the things that I write about. Do not let it disturb you emotionally. Remember that whatever corrections I give you are given with a great love, deep concern, and a profound desire to help you and lead you to sanctity.

The point which has made me think and has caused me some anxiety before the Lord, is the persistence of a thoughtlessness concerning your conversations, attitudes, and expressions regarding *minority groups*. What I want to say may not exactly apply to every house. Some of you are not involved with minority groups. Nor does it apply to every person.

In some mission reports I hear about the ignorance of local people, the banality of nurses, doctors and governments, the lack of equipment and know-how.

The general point that I want to make here is not that these facts aren't true. The point of the story is this: if these mission lands *had* doctors, hospitals, medicine, well-educated people, etc., then our Apostolate wouldn't need to *be* there. The fact is that these people are *not* educated. The fact that they *are* poor, ignorant in matters that we of the Western world take for granted, doesn't mean that they haven't other tremendous qualities too numerous to mention; qualities which we could well learn.

It also stands to reason that we are there because, through the greed of the white man, through other political, economic, and colonial factors, these people were never allowed to become anything else. We go there to teach and serve them with grave humility and in atonement for all of this. Of course there will be a lack of instruments, knowledge, efficiency and equipment. I repeat: if it weren't so we wouldn't be there!

Nor does their ignorance permit us at any time to think any the less of them. In discussing these shortcomings with a horrible, white superiority, we show ourselves to be less charitable, less thoughtful, and certainly more ignorant than these gentle, humble people. Yet this attitude shows its ugly head now and then in almost every house.

Examine your conscience in depth as to your attitude towards the transients. Occasional, cruel jokes are made about them behind their backs. What would be the use of serving these people with a smile, when we harbor such things in our hearts and express them thoughtlessly in secret! The very fact that these thoughts are in our minds, that we *do* think that we are better than they — and who of us hasn't once in a while thought so? — already breaks the bond of charity and wounds our Apostolate.

What is our attitude at Madonna House towards the local people? Do we feel a superiority? Do we always talk about them with grave humility? I wonder.

What is our attitude toward Spanish-Americans, Mexicans and Blacks? Are there now and then accents of unconscious superiority and pride? Is there a division in our minds between us and them that is subtle, yet dangerous to our spirit?

I heard that in one of our houses someone said, "And do you know, you do all you can for them, give them the best, and they say nothing, or find fault and are not grateful." Frankly, this remark horrified me. That any one of you does anything for Christ in the poor and expects Christ in the poor to be grateful! This is either the epitome of stupidity or a complete misunderstanding of the whole Apostolate of Madonna House. Spiritually speaking, we should kiss the feet of the poor and be grateful that Christ allows us to serve them. If we have any other ideas about our Apostolate, we are way off base, and we have neither charity nor common sense. I would like to see that same person *open a conversation at the table about your thoughtlessness towards minority groups, towards one another and the directorate*!

I have said what I wanted to say. I leave the rest to the Holy Spirit, and to your collective examination of conscience. None of us can say: "Not guilty." Let us do away with this thoughtlessness and uncharitableness. Otherwise, the Apostolate will die.

Lovingly yours in Mary,

THE CLIMATE OF WORDS

March 14, 1963

Dearly Beloved,

During this Lent I have very specially prayed for and thought of each one of you. Whether or not you know it, you are very dear and close to my heart. When I say that I pray for you and think about you very specially during this Lent, I simply mean that I search my heart, mind and soul before God, asking him to give me new lights from his Holy Spirit, by which I can help you.

I have been thinking of the power of words. Lately we use the dictionary a lot, and we are discovering that words have tremendous power and also many meanings.

One day we came across the word "give." I asked the group to tell me, "off the top of their heads," how they would define the word "give" if they hadn't come to Madonna House. What did it mean to them? Generally it meant "to give of one's possessions or one's time to worthy causes, needy people, civic endeavors, or what have you."

Quite truthfully and honestly they all acknowledged that before coming to Madonna House, the idea of giving *oneself* was foreign to them.

We tried the word "authority" one day and found out that it was synonymous with "power and dominion over people such as representatives of governments and courts of justice have." Two words "power" and "dominion" stood out in the minds of everyone. The sum total of the discussion of that word was that *authority was someone who had lawful power and dominion over you mostly to hurt or to inflict pain.* An interesting reaction, isn't it? Not one person among the twenty-two or so thought of authority as benign, gentle loving, like that of a father or a mother.

It was another very revealing reaction of modern Canadian and American youth to words and images. We listen to beautiful sermons, go through a period of training on this continent that is unequalled, but what can we do when your ideas and concepts of words are so false and narrow? We are stymied. So it was a good idea to study words and their effect upon you.

Another word that we studied was "fraternal correction". The word "correction" itself seemed to produce a common reaction from almost everybody. First, it isn't a pleasant word. Secondly, everyone will accept corrections easily (even if they are not pleasant), as long as they deal with their *job*, because they all said that they are used to correction when working in the world. Supervisors correct, and one accepts this.

However, everybody acknowledged, with a few exceptions, that the moment that correction touched their inner person, trained in what they call "American style independence", immediately hostility was aroused.

No one understands the depth of the love a superior making corrections in Madonna House.

I found an entirely different climate of reactions when I substituted the word "restoration" for the word "correction". "Restoration" means correcting in depth leading a soul to sanctity, God and love. That is what you and I are pledged to do. The Apostolate is supposed to *correct the abuses of society and social organizations*, that is to restore them to the tranquillity of God's order.

You have been much in my thoughts, prayers and love during this Lent, and will continue to be, dearly beloved. That is why I take time out to share with you the thoughts that come to me so spontaneously and which deal with the training of your minds and souls — your restoration to God!

I am partly responsible for this restoration and I want to fulfill my part. I will always try to bring to you the waters of truth, but you alone can bend down and drink. I pray that you will.

Lovingly yours in Mary,

ON BECOMING OTHERS AND FACING OURSELVES

March 30, 1963

Dearly Beloved,

Greetings in the Risen Lord! I am wishing you ahead of time a happy, holy Easter and the joys of the Risen Christ, for Alleluia! he is risen! Verily, he is risen! Alleluia!

There are many things which I would like to discuss with you, but were I to do so you would have to leaf through a whole book. So I will pick up just a few points that kind of bother me at times and sadden me a little, without making me lose my faith and trust in you, but which make me ask the Lord for more understanding, fortitude and patience to bear with you, my beloved whom I love very much.

I wrote you a letter on identification with the poor, and it seems to have penetrated somewhat, but not very deeply. Some of you are still fidgeting, emotionally hostile, and inwardly uninvolved.

What am I talking about? Let us say that you have living with you a down-and-out, broken down, selfish, self-centered, not too clean hobo, who doesn't want to do a stitch of work to repay your hospitality. Just sitting there, he resembles a toad or a mushroom.

There are many ways in which you can face this situation. You can decide that it is a good Lenten mortification to bear with him. That will be good, but that is far from perfect.

The next step would be to realize what terrible handicaps this man may have suffered from the beginning of his life. Try to make the pilgrimage of *his* life, and ask yourself what would have happened to *you* if you had been in his place. It is not as hard as it seems, dearly beloved.

You see, you demand from us — your superiors, that we should always understand you, constantly help you and patiently bear with you, and be silent in the face of your outbursts — and all this without murmuring! This is what you ask from us and (though you may not say so), what you expect from each other. True or false? Look into the depths of your hearts and answer that question yourselves. If you ask *us* to make that pilgrimage into your lives, you should be able to do the same for the imaginary hobo.

That would be very good, but it still would not be perfect. It would be perfect if you tore open your guts, so to speak, opened your heart wide, and out of love truly *became* that hobo. Love, empathy and grace would help you to do that. You would become that hobo in your mind, and actually. This would be identification.

I used to weep in the night at Harlem. At times I could accomplish this identification with the grace of God, but I could not *become black*. This was a sorrow for me — a tragedy — would it be for you? At times like this, I clearly see Christ in my neighbor and you should too.

I don't mean that I see the face of the human Christ of the Gospels with long hair, etc. Christ is a spirit. The Russians portray the Trinity as fire, light and movement. This is as close as we can come to express the word ''Spirit''. How can we catch a glimpse of that fire, that love which is God? How can we catch a glimpse of that movement which is the creation and thought of God? *We can see Christ in our neighbor*, become drawn to that light, *that* flame, *that* movement. Then by the grace of God and the Divine Light that is in us, we can love that gross, lazy, good-for-nothing hobo for whom this *Light, this Love, this Flame, this Movement became incarnate and died on the cross. This is what I call identification in depth. Love alone can do that.* Begin to love with that love, or you will not be totally involved in the Apostolate. Don't let your emotions stand between you and that love, because love can cure all emotions.

Those of you who work in clothing rooms or who have dealings with the poor and troubled of all nationalities, with a tired priest, or with an upset girl from a good family must slowly learn this way of total identification. Only if you *become them* will you know their needs and be able to help them. How else can you know? You will only be guessing.

I know that this is deep stuff, but it is time that I showed you the depths. You have been on the shore long enough. The love of Christ is waiting for you to jump in and discover in faith how warm and lovely these depths are.

There is another point I want to take up with you! Why do you lack so much ordinary common sense? Why is it that you do not see tasks that are so obvious?

Why is it, for example, that after years of training in cleaning you still leave crumbs in drawers or on shelves, still don't clean in corners, still have to be taught how to sweep and to wash dishes? Do you mind my asking you why do you think that this is so?

I hate to touch on the topic of emotions again, because, frankly, I am a little fed up with it, but we have to discuss them. Love always is ready to continue loving.

The majority of you are fully aware of your problems, which can be summed up as follows: *You desire approval from the people who matter*. This is childish in adults. You realize this, why don't you work on it? You constantly have your emotional defenses up. Against whom? Against what? There is really nothing to defend yourself against in Madonna House except love. You are surrounded by security and love. So why such a defensive attitude when you know how to deal with it?

You are unhappy in your own self-centeredness. You know that you should be concentrated on others; that you should have a giving rather than a taking attitude. This knowledge should make you free. Why are so many of you still so bound? Some of you are aware that your eternal argumentativeness isn't making you happy. Your desire to have the last word and always to be right is making you feel guilty. Why not stop yourself before you begin?

Some of you hate corrections because you still do not understand that corrections are signs of love, leading you to God. They are like a good set of sitting-up exercises that will give you a lovely, spiritual posture. Yet the very ones who hate being corrected, are forever correcting others. Is there any sense in that sort of attitude? I wonder. Is it pleasant to be senseless and thoughtless? It is an unpleasant state to be in, I would say.

From the ordinary states we can go to more sublime things. It is high time that you understand what obedience is. Brought up as you were you have a wrong idea of independence. You are also under the illusion that by obedience in the Apostolate you will lose your identity and personality. Nothing is further from the truth. God, who respects the human, free will, would not maim, break or change your personality, since it is he who has invited you to live the life of the Apostolate under the views of perfection. If you stop fighting with the wrong weapons and stop long enough to think things out, you would realize that he lovingly called you to make your personality flower, to bring out your full potential and not to stymie it.

It might seem to you that I am approaching things in a negative way, but I am not. I approach them in the form of questions that I would like you to answer. I desire with a great desire *to make you think, which we don't do very much*!

These last days of Lent, and the forthcoming Easter are joyous times, even though they are serious and painful. It is the same with my questions. If answered rightly, they would bring you to a true resurrection, a true Easter.

So let us grow in love for one another and in Christ. For Christ is risen, verily he has risen. Alleluia!

Lovingly yours in Mary,

PRAYER, PANIC AND GOD'S PEACE

April 4, 1963

Dearly Beloved,

When the Cuban, Missile Crisis occurred, I shared some attitudes about what our behavior and attitudes should be in the face of such emergencies.

There was no denying that after the speech of the President the world was breathless awaiting the answer of Russia to the challenge. It was a suspended moment when the world, especially Americans, had to face the possibility of a nuclear war with Cuba's missiles descending in a fiery death upon Washington, New York, and other cities. It was a breathless, fearsome, and tragic moment.

But we must be prepared for these moments. To us they mean all that they mean to any other human being. It will be normal for us to have an ordinary fear. This is a legitimate, not an illusory fear.

However, we belong to him who is perfect love. Perfect love casts out all fears and makes human fears of destruction and death bearable with his graces. So for us, the first step in such emergencies is to come together in prayer . . . prayer for peace, prayer that the dark clouds pass, prayer for people to keep their sanity, and remember that God is with us.

After the collective prayer at Mass we should be praying individually all day for the same thing, beseeching and calling upon the mercy of God and his intervention in these affairs.

Those of us who are far removed from the scene of the conflict must then go about our business, which is the business of God, as we normally do in the days of peace. The greatest contribution that we can make is to go about the duty of the moment and offer it up for the same intentions as our prayers. At no time can we, the apostles of the Lord, show panic in the face of destruction and death, for many will rely upon us.

We should not have any fear of death since we have faith. Nevertheless, we must take every precaution to prolong our lives, and, of course, the lives of others. We prolong our lives, not for ourselves alone, but so that we may serve others should an emergency arise. At all times our thoughts must be of peace and love, and for others, not for ourselves.

We must also be prepared for those emergencies. It would be well to update our First Aid courses, so that we might be of better assistance to our neighbor.

Let us also be men and women of peace, bringing God's peace into the troubled and frightened hearts of others. During the Cuban Crisis a friend of ours was called by a panic-stricken friend. She asked her if she was going to stop a certain project because of the crisis. "Surely," the woman said, "you are not going to continue with nuclear war hanging over our heads!"

Our friend very calmly said "Of course we will!" and began to talk peacefully and quietly to the panic-stricken woman and calm her. So thus she was able to stop panic and fear in the heart of the mother of a family. We must do likewise. Let us truly remember that these are moments when we should bring peace to those who are so emotionally fearful that they can't think straight.

Let us never spread rumors about the crisis. Let us be truthful, but let us never exaggerate. Let us never pass on unconfirmed reports, but discuss only official information. Let our voices always be calm and quiet, our steps unhurried, the horarium of the day, whenever possible unchanged. Let our houses be refuges of peace and calm.

Let us stand ready to be of any assistance to our governments in the way of directing, helping with the organization of feeding or First Aid stations, and whatever else we are capable of doing to help. Whatever we do in public or in private, let us be efficient, peaceful and quiet. Let us be, at these critical times, men and women of constant prayer. Let us be ready to serve God and our neighbor without counting the cost.

If possible during these emergencies let us keep in touch with each other. If it is not possible, let us commend each other to God in complete peace, faith, confidence, and hope because of his love for us and our love for him, who is Lord of life and death.

Lovingly yours in Mary,

Catherine

THE TRANQUILITY OF GOD'S ORDER

May 3rd, 1963

Dearly Beloved,

Constantly those especially responsible for Madonna House are immersed in a travail of spirit. We are forever examining our minds, hearts and souls. We are always casting our nets far and wide gathering new knowledge concerning the lay apostolate. We try to keep attuned to the Holy Spirit who so vividly and clearly sheds divine fire on the Church today! A new pentecostal mind blows clear, fresh, heavenly air across the whole Church!

Daily we are becoming more aware of becoming the mother of the whole Apostolate (I use that word in its true sense of spiritual motherhood). "Headquarters" is a cold, dry word savoring of the business world. But think of Madonna House as the soul-mind — the heart of the Apostolate. It is also the training centre.

Perhaps a better phrase than "training centre" would be "formation centre." For indeed, we not only have to form souls, but reform human beings, we try to restore them and make them whole before the Lord so that they can go forth and restore this complex, ever-changing, secular, almost-pagan world to him.

I think that the priests and I, though older in years than most of you, are, in a manner of speaking, the youngest at heart, for we stand ready to change our ways of formation, our techniques, our approaches at the drop of a hat, if we realize the need for such changes in our fast-changing world. The ways and ideas of the Apostolate are constantly being clarified.

Because of your emotional needs for safety and security, you seek clear cut orders and a comfortable routine. Thus you are not as quick to grasp the need for this adaptation, this constant rolling with the punches of the world, and the needs of the world apostolate, but you are learning!

What I want to say is very simple. Whereas we should be pliant and amenable to necessary changes as the world and the Apostolate demand, at the same time there are certain normal and basic foundations in our Apostolate that we do not surrender. These basic foundations are vital "little things" which are really big and important. They may appear to you very irrelevant. You may say to yourself that, *of course*, all the things which I am going to say to you are done in your house. Yet years of training went into these things. So, I beg you all to re-examine your consciences about these daily little ways of living the ordinary life. The life of a family.

You know that Madonna House is distinguished among all apostolates by its family spirit. We are lay men, lay women and priests. We present to the world a real family. Family spirit means the love that the members of a family have for one another, and the ways that they live out that love in the little things of every day. It is of these little things that I want to speak in this letter.

One of the things which I have always insisted upon from the beginning of our Apostolate, no matter what the pressures of the work, no matter how tired we were, was immaculate order.

Each house has to be immaculately clean, not only in the obvious places, but everywhere. Every drawer must be in order. Every library must be dusted and in order. In a word, there is order in the obvious places, order in the hidden places, order in every corner of the house. By this I mean physical order: everything has its place and there is a place for everything.

The second point that I want to mention very forcibly is the question of meals. Your house might be of the poorest. You might have unmatching crockery because of your poverty. But I wish that all the tables for meals be laid out in grace, order, and beauty, and arrangements of the food be gracious and pleasing. I wouldn't want the food to be brought out in pans in which it was cooked! I want the table setting to be as nice as the poverty and simplicity of your mission can afford. I would appreciate it if you had on the table a statue of Our Lady or some saint, with some decoration — flowers, for example. Something that looks pleasant and cozy. The meals should be on time.

Kitchens must be immaculate and all the offices too. If you get behind in your work, I suggest that you get volunteer help. It seems almost ridiculous for me to mention the following, but I expect you to make your beds as you were taught in Madonna House. In a word order and tidiness should ornament the palaces of Our Lady of Poverty. These are the only luxuries that the poor can afford. We must set the example of order and tidiness.

You might wonder why I bring up these things. I remember, I must admit with deep sadness and shame, an occurrence that happened in Harlem when a wealthy lady came to Friendship House bearing a check of $25,000. At that time Friendship House in Harlem was under the care of a woman who was quite disturbed emotionally and didn't attend to this fundamental order. The place was dirty, untidy and cluttered. The lady looked at all of this, and without mincing words, told that director, "I am sorry. I was going to give you $25,000 for your work of restoring the world to Christ, but seeing the disorder in your house and its lack of cleanliness and tidiness, I will not give you this money. People who cannot keep their own house in order cannot help to restore order in God's universe or in human hearts.

Yes, tidiness, order, cleanliness, peace, graciousness and simplicity are fruits of charity and the tranquility of God's order in our souls. Disorder is the fruit of evil and cannot be tolerated.

It is so easy to let go of this and that little point, so that before you know it the whole basic foundation of Madonna House in this area is broken, and there is disorder in the heart, mind and soul. Please examine your consciences in this regard. Stand back and see how you can improve your attitudes in making your house part of the immense tranquility of God's order. It is vital that you should do this.

Lovingly yours in Mary,

GUARDING OUR SPIRIT

May 25, 1963

Dearly Beloved,

Lately my soul has been in great travail. I am constantly concerned about the spirit of Madonna House which, as you know, I consider a very special mandate of God to me — the Foundress. Madonna House, the spiritual family that God has deigned to call into being through so poor and weak an instrument as myself, is not for myself, but for others.

I realize that, until my last breath, I must do all in my power — and then try to do the impossible with his power and grace — to transmit to you that mandate, that spirit of our Apostolate which I firmly believe (and the Church evidently does too since She has approved of our constitutions), that God himself has given me this mandate.

Yes, my soul has been in travail again. Constantly I ask myself: "Have I transmitted to each of you that spirit in its fullness?" I ask: "Am I constantly watchful that that spirit is not being compromised by anyone?"

The time has come when I must trust the directors of the houses and the heads of departments to share this travail with me. They must constantly question themselves, even as I do. Each member must also question himself or herself but perhaps along a slightly different line: "How much am I interested in acquiring *the spirit of* Madonna House in all its immense and glorious height, width and depth?" All must question themselves very severely and deeply as to the slightest compromise with that spirit. Every compromise is a step towards mediocrity. The Pope says *that in our day and age, no Christian can afford to be mediocre.*

Of course, it is unthinkable that a specially chosen apostle of the Lord would even permit himself or herself anything that would lead to a compromise with the spirit of our constitutions. Leon Bloy stated a tremendous and awesome truth when he said *that the only tragedy for a Christian is not to become a saint.*

Dearly Beloved, let us face something very directly: God has selected me as an instrument to found a new Lay Apostolate, to form a new, religious family that the Church has taken into her bosom. But a person does not become a founder or foundress until, during his or her lifetime (or after death as in the case of Charles de Foucauld), God raises up followers of that founder or foundress, in the spirit that he has given. For he has chosen such people not to stand alone, but to bear, through his begetting, a new family in the Church.

It stands to reason, therefore, that he has called *each one of you individually* to this humble, glorious, hidden, new vocation of the Madonna House Apostolate. This means that, since the Church has accepted this vocation as a life of perfection under the counsels of poverty, chastity and obedience in the name of God, she promises that *if you follow the letter of your constitutions religiously and honestly your eternal life in union with Christ in Paradise is guaranteed.*

This means that each one of you *must stand alone face to face with God.* You have of your own free will made a covenant, a contract with God. You promised to live a life of perfection. So now *you* are dealing with the most important matter in your life — *your eternal salvation!* Your duty, therefore, is to be very concerned about knowing the spirit of Madonna House Apostolate. It should be of tremendous interest to you to really plumb its depths and scale its heights, because your whole immortal life, your eternity, depend upon it.

Yes, my soul has been in dark, travail again; but I don't mind the travail. It is a small enough price to pay for the souls that God has entrusted into my sinful and weak hands. I know that I can go only so far in this matter and then I must stop. The place which I am approaching is so holy that, even if I took my shoes off, I couldn't walk on that ground — the ground between you and God. On that ground each person must answer for himself or herself. Make no mistake, dearly beloved, this is an answer you must face either now or later. I pray that the Lord will have mercy on your soul!

I believe in openness and frankness. So I will tell you how it came about that my soul entered again into this dark night and the heavy travail. It happened very simply. I decided that I would be closer to the staff. So I began to dry dishes twice a day. I noticed what happened to leftovers from the special food given to those among us who have to gain weight.

People who have to gain weight often have very small appetites so often leave very nice specials half-eaten. I noticed that people were helping themselves to the leftovers. Yet, I have said that in the spirit of holy poverty such things should not happen. With imagination other ways could be found to use this food.

I noticed another thing: a freshly baked batch of cookies seemed to shrink very quickly. Not only the juniors, but the seniors would also help themselves. Cookies are special tidbits made for special occasions, and taking them was not in the spirit of poverty.

I kept quiet for a while and started investigating more deeply. If there were breaches of this type against the spirit of Madonna House, I told myself, maybe there are more. Little compromises often repeated lead to bigger compromises. Sure enough, I found that the reporting of gifts from home were not being reported as well as it should be. Permissions were often presumed with flimsy excuses such as that person couldn't find anyone in authority. My soul wept before the Lord.

I knew that I had never ceased to emphasize these aspects of poverty mortification and detachment. I sorrowfully faced the fact that after my death, it will be so easy to lapse into that mediocrity, to compromise inwardly and outwardly if someone is not super-vigilant. At this point I had to make what was a stupendous act of faith and detachment. I had to humbly lay into the hands of the Holy Spirit this Apostolate which I have borne in such pain, and which through so many years I have nurtured. At the same time I implored him to enter your souls. When I am gone *you* will have to bear the flame of the Spirit who seeks to consume within you all possibility of such compromise.

But now, while I am still living, I raise my voice and I will continue to raise it again and again until my last breath. I ask each one of you to make an examination of conscience and answer the following questions truthfully. *Remember that your eternal life depends upon it.* You cannot fail God, nor should you try.

Ask yourself: Do you choose the best things to eat, thereby giving scandal to others? Do you allow yourself coffee breaks without permission? If you do I wish that you would weep. In our times with millions of people going hungry, with our own Apostolate feeding the transients in many places, with your knowledge of the destitution and poverty in our own land, surely the spirit of detachment and bodily mortification should be a flaming desire in your souls. How soft have you become? How much do you compromise the spirit of poverty and of obedience? I leave this for you to answer.

In the measure that you compromise, in that measure you tear the Apostolate apart. There will be nothing left of it but a shell not worth having, and the face of God will be turned away from you. The strength of theApostolate is not in buildings or in works. It is in our reflecting Christ the Workman, the Pauper, the naked man who had nowhere to lay his head. It is to him that you will have to answer if you wreck the Apostolate. You will wreck it through these compromises even though they may seem to you to be very small things.

Yes, my soul was in travail, and still is; I guess it will be until I die. Pray for me as I constantly pray for you, that we may grow in the spirit of our Humble and glorious Apostolate. Our spirit is needed today as never before so that we might restore Christ's world to him. It is for *this* that he brought us forth from his own Sacred Heart.

Lovingly yours in Mary,

ALERTED BY THE SPIRIT

May 27, 1963

Dearly Beloved,

As you may have noticed, you receive letters when I am "alerted" by the Holy Spirit in regard to the very essence and spirit of our Madonna House way of life. It takes a little time for an ordinary human being to understand in truth and reality what ''the grace of an office'' means. The same is true of people who get married. It is not until later on that a woman or man realizes his or her vocation as a married person. I can testify that it took quite a long time for me to understand the very special grace of being *the foundress* of a new, lay apostolic family in the Church.

I now know (as much as a human being can) this mystery of the choice of God, of the pain, the sorrow, the joys, the labor that goes into responding to God's will and grace. I hope that I am becoming a pliant instrument in his hands. I always knew one thing very clearly from that very first day of our foundation, October 15, 1930: *God gave me some sort of mandate.* What it was in detail I did not as yet know. But what I did know was that I had to live and die for that mandate, which is today the spirit, the essence, the soul of Madonna House.

Sinner that I am, imperfect and weak as I am, I can say one thing in truth before God: inasmuch as it has been possible for me, and with the help of God all along the way, I have in truth laid down my life and I am still laying it down for this spirit of Madonna House. I hope to do so until I die.

However, let us understand this situation very clearly: I was able to do this only through *the grace of state of being the foundress*. Well do I realize, dearly beloved, the words of Christ: ''Without me, you can do nothing.'' Truly this applies *100%* in my case, as it does in the case of everyone in authority in the Church and our Apostolate.

I can witness to one of the tremendous graces of this state of being a foundress. God (the Holy Spirit especially) in a mysterious manner, *alerts the mind, soul and heart of the foundress to any breach or any attack upon that spirit.* This ''alerting'' comes in different ways, but it always does come.

I think that founders and foundresses, alerted by God, are especially watchful of the fact that Satan is always roaring like a lion, or sneaking around and whispering like a serpent. Truly they are watchful for his coming. They know well that the time of grace is the time of his enhanced attacks. He becomes angry when he sees anyone receiving special blessing from God, and growing in grace and wisdom. It is then that he wishes to destroy that person, organization or Order. I think that is what is happening to us now.

What form do these attacks take among us? I haven't been alerted to all of them, but I have been alerted to some recently, and there is no mistake about them. Some attacks have come to my notice and they all point in one direction.

What I note is a little, red thread of rebellion running through some of our members. Of course, I have discussed the matter fully here in Combermere, so this letter is predominately addressed to you in the missions; it is also addressed to you members, yet unborn, who will have the same techniques of Satan hurled against you. Those to whom and for whom this letter is written will recognize this rebellion in the depths of their hearts. Let them ponder and pray about this. Above all, let them realize that they are on truly dangerous ground. They had better stay close to God and to Our Lady, be watchful over their own souls, and be sure to write about these things to their spiritual directors. They are in danger. What is more, through them there is danger to the whole Apostolate, for we are truly as strong as our weakest link.

There is a wind that certainly doesn't come from heaven blowing here and there throughout the Apostolate, and it whispers ideas such as these: "Madonna House is becoming institutionalized." "There are too many rules to observe." "There are too many permissions to ask". "The director is only a community member in an executive position. Why can't we talk like equals?" "Why can't I argue if I find something to argue about?" "Why pick on me when somebody else gets away with murder?"

There are many more similar ideas being blown into the ears of the Apostolate by this unheavenly wind of rebellion. Let us examine them one by one.

"Madonna House is being institutionalized." By this people mean that Madonna House is becoming more like an institution, with a lot of dry rules and regulations, with a lot of "musts," and "does," and "don'ts." People feel that this is totally against the free spirit which they heard was prevalent in our pioneer days.

To this I answer very simply: "The free, happy, family spirit is here at Madonna House for the asking. It hasn't changed. If there are more rules it is because people don't seem to be able to function without them."

In the early days of our Apostolate when we were small, and I was with the family all of the time, whenever a question arose as to the spirit of Madonna House, I would simply answer: "What would Christ do in this case? We try to live by the Gospel." But the place grew bigger. Lots of people came with emotional disturbances and with their own ideas about running things. Because of our growth and the needs of these people I found it necessary to write outlines on the spirit of the laundry, the library and the other departments. The staff letters are my answers to the endless questions that arose.

If all of our members were totally dedicated and living the Gospel, I doubt that they would ask those questions; but because they aren't living the Gospels totally, these questions have to be answered. These answers were incarnated into what some of you call "rules and regulations", but which are actually the deepening of the spirit brought forth by your own very personal needs. Madonna House will become institutional only if the childish need for security demands it. It is up to you to preserve the free spirit of Madonna House.

But, on the other hand, you must realize that with growth, the constant clarification so needed by weak human beings trying to become saints will continue. Right now, Madonna House certainly isn't institutionalized. Those of you who think so, are rationalizing because you do not want to surrender to the total dedication that God demands from us in this particular Apostolate.

"There are too many rules to observe." Again, we are on the same ground. Rules are necessary for the tranquility of God's order in a closely-knit community where various dispositions, emotions, and ordinary human weaknesses rub shoulders with one another all day. You can see rules as fences that "fence you in", or as stepping stones to heaven. It is up to you whether you are obeying just a dry, dead letter of the law, or whether you are obeying with the flaming, joyous, glorious spirit of true holy obedience.

"There are too many permissions to ask." The Lord knows that, generally speaking, obedience is pretty easy at Madonna House. Yes, there are quite a few permissions to ask, because we must lead you to the cross. We must allow the nails of obedience to bite deeply into your hands and feet as they did into Christ's. If you don't understand this, then you don't have the first inkling of the purpose of obedience. You have to surrender your will, the noblest, the greatest possession that you can give to God. How do you expect to accomplish this surrendering unless there is some way provided? The permissions are those "ways" which teach you the virtues of humility, poverty, and dependence which constitute the essence of obedience. So I simply state here that you must be very observant of these permissions if you are to become real apostles.

"The director is only another community member in an executive position. Why can't we talk as equals?"

The question is not common, but it arose in one house, and so I answer it. For someone to ask that question shows that he or she has missed the whole point of Thomas Merton's letter which I have often read to you. He answers that question better than I ever could.

"No one is worthy to be a superior. Christ alone is worthy. Christ is present in every superior. The only thing that a superior must do is to be a channel of Christ's directing."

Thomas Merton says that the superior might be sinful, arrogant, filled with hostilities and anger. He agrees with St. Ignatius of Loyola that it is relatively easy to obey when the superior is a saint; but even if the superior isn't a saint, one must still obey him or her because *it isn't that person, but Christ in that person who is being obeyed.*

I have just discussed at length what is called the grace of state. This is the essence of the grace of state: Christ is realy present in that person. That is why we stand up for priests. It is because Christ enters the room when a priest enters.

That is why we cannot talk to superiors as if they were simply equals. One doesn't talk to the President of the United States as one talks to his brother; or to Queen Elizabeth as one talks to one's sister; or to a judge as one does to an uncle. Thus do we observe signs of respect even in civic society.

The directors in Madonna House have special graces from God to guide you as they do, for they have the tremendous job of leading you to sanctity, whereas you do not have the graces to do the same for them. So both in the realm of faith and the hierarchy of God, and in the human order of society it should be self-evident that there is a difference between people in authority, especially authority from God. The director is not just another executive. He or she represents Christ to us and we should act accordingly.

"Why can't I argue if I have something to argue about?" This question is quite superfluous and hardly needs answering. By "arguing" we do not mean here a philosophical, abstract, intellectual discussion peacefully pursued by a fireside! It is a desire to prove that one is right and everybody else is wrong. It is a desire to put across one's own ideas and one's own way of doing things. This simply comes down to the desire to do one's own will instead of God's. That kind of argumentiveness certainly shatters the bonds of charity, and what is Madonna House without charity? The Scriptures say that if you call your brother a liar you are in danger of hell fire. He who says he loves God, and doesn't love his neighbor is also a liar, and I leave it at that.

"Why pick on me when somebody else gets away with murder?" That answer is very simple: *judge not and you shall not be judged.*

I leave the rest of the answers to your own faith and intelligence.

I know this is a long letter. I know you are going to find it difficult to read through in one sitting. But you must read it, because the very life and soul of Madonna House Apostolate depends upon your understanding. God bless you. May the Holy Spirit enlighten you.

Lovingly yours in Mary,

OUR BODY PRAYS

June 28, 1963

Dearly Beloved,

I want to pick up on a few things which I have observed and perhaps have not been ready to clarify until now.

One of these things is the question of posture at prayer. I notice that many of you cross your legs or sit in a slouchy position when you are at Mass, or during the Office. Now a lay apostolic group should realize the awesomeness of the Divine Liturgy. These are your *official* acts of worship before Almighty God. Your posture must express outwardly what I hope you feel inwardly-reverence, adoration, worship, wholesome fear, and the realization that you are creatures before your Creator!

Therefore because of this realization, which I am sure that you have, you must participate not only with your whole mind, heart and soul in this act of worship and adoration, but express it with your body as well. Also you must be an example to our guests and visitors. It is truly a scandal for dedicated lay apostles to have sloppy manners during their worship of God.

It says in the Scripture, "Worship the Lord in holy attire." We all realize that we must look decent according to the time of day, and the day of the week. We should "dress up" for church — I hope out of reverence of God. Occasionally we might come in working clothes, but these must be clean, not torn — in a word "decent". I therefore beg everyone to see that this is done.

Regarding the bowing and other outward signs that I have taught you in Madonna House, you must first understand *why* you have been taught these Eastern forms of bodily worship. For many years my heart has been ecumenical. I am filled with a flaming desire for the reunion of our separated brethren with the Catholic Church.

I realized that teaching you these bodily ways of worship would be a very hard thing to do, because in Canada and America both clergy and lay people are so ignorant of the Eastern Churches. So I didn't begin to implement my desire at the very beginning of the Apostolate.

Naturally, my heart was drawn very specially to the reunion of the Orthodox Church with Rome. So you began to learn more about the Eastern Ways as Eastern Rite priests came to visit Madonna House, and especially when Father Raya became our associate priest. I began slowly to introduce you to these ways of the East, knowing that our missionary growth will bring you more and more into contact with Eastern peoples. They are used to worshipping the Lord, not only with bows and prostrations but even by dancing before the altar!

As yet we have not tried to teach people in Madonna House these extremes, but as our missionary activity grows, we will. However, there is a time and a place for everything. I am sure that you have not forgotten my constant injunction: "We must identify ourselves with the ways and customs of the people we serve." So evidently when you are in Canada and the United States and go to churches, you identify yourself with those customs.

I believe in the freedom of the children of God. If you are alone in the chapel, and you feel like bowing before a Station of the Cross or during prayer, I will not object. But at Mass and during the Office be guided by your director and the customs of the country where you live.

Another point which I would like to mention to everyone is that bodily postures at worship are simply part of the good order which I so often emphasize.

Lovingly yours in Mary,

LOVE AND PROFESSIONAL COMPETENCY

July 10, 1963

Dearly Beloved,

At all of the lay apostolic gatherings and seminars, one question always engenders very interesting, and, at times, very heated discussions: "What is the role of professional competency in the lay apostolate?"

No one could deny the need for every kind of professional competency in the lay apostolate. Competency and technical skills of all kinds should be one of the prerequisites of every lay apostle and lay apostolate.

However, *it is not the alpha and omega of the apostolate*. True, grace working on nature can, and will, with the cooperation of the individual, transform his whole self, including his intellectual and professional competency, into tremendous tools for any type of lay apostolate.

However, we must not over-exaggerate the place of professional competency. If we do, we will not only run into heresy, but we will be (if I may put it bluntly) acting "stupidly," not using the very gifts of intelligence which God has given us.

It does not take too much thinking to realize that if intellectual, professional or technical competency were the alpha and omega of the lay apostolate, then such outstanding saints as Catherine of Siena (who could neither read or write), Cure of Ars, and many others would be excluded.

In fact, a quick glance at the apostles of Our Lord, according to our modern standard of *competency*, would show that even though they were good fishermen and tax collectors, none of these "natural talents" were used by the Lord, nor was he interested in them.

The only thing that he said about St. Peter's competency as a fishermen was that he would make him a "fisher of men". In the natural order this must have been quite incomprehensible to Peter at the time. If he gave it any thought at all, it must have dismayed him very much. We knew something about catching fish, but he didn't have the faintest notion of what it meant to be a fisher of men!

If the question of professional competency ever became the yardstick of the lay apostolate, then the apostolate itself would be reduced in efficiency and in scope. It would die a natural death.

One can think of a most efficient, superbly competent nurse, willing to go to the ends of the earth to practice her professional "competency," but if she lacks dedication and love, her apostolic activity will be not only nil, but she will be a detriment to the Church, distort its image, and leave a bitter taste behind her.

This constant talk about this competency on the American continent is already annoying many of the members and citizens of the nations to which these highly trained professional and technical people are going. Our American-Canadian competency is seen by them as implying that "they haven't got what we got!" It implies that we are bringing them gifts from the hands of some Lady Bountiful called America and Canada. Thus, even before we depart on our mission of love, we are already judged and often rejected.

All of these competencies, all of this intellectual, academic, and skilled training is vitally important. *But, in my estimation, they are totally secondary. I would never dream of excluding from a lay apostolic team people with very little intellectual or technical formation.*

To me, spiritual formation and the training of the soul is of paramount importance. The formation of lay apostles in the two Commandments of love is, to me, primary. I feel that everything else is secondary to love. Even the knowledge of languages which sooner or later must be acquired (for love communicates) is secondary.

Above all, I would stress that this spiritual formation should be based on Scripture and liturgy and steeped in prayer.

The foundation of that training should be St. Paul's writings on charity, the Gospel of St. John, and the words of Christ. When Christ sent his disciples two by two into the world, he did not care if they were professionaly competent. He gave them, a blueprint of what a lay apostle should be. They were to be ambassadors of love, of the glad tidings, of flaming charity and of peace. They were to be ambassadors of God. I think that this "technique" of Christ, this blueprint of the Lord, should remain forever the blueprint of the Apostolate.

To overburden our tension-filled, emotionally unstable youth with a curriculum that would train them in various "competencies" is good, but it can be done only as a secondary part of the spiritual formation that I have mentioned.

I know from painful experience in the Madonna House Apostolate that an extremely competent teacher who has several degrees, who is a teacher of teachers, who loves her profession will be utterly inefficient in the service of the Lord, if she has not been given this primary spiritual formation. Her emotional and spiritual problems will be an obstacle.

In my mind, this is the correct order of formation: to form souls to be passionately in love with God, and hence with their neighbor, filled with love that will overcome all obstacles, and be able to communicate this love with or without professional competency. Professional, technical competency, but always as an adjunct, is a servant of love, but not the most important factor.

Love and love alone will change this world. We have many examples in the history of the Catholic Church that great lovers, really great saints, were not necessarily professionally or technically competent. Remember Benedict Labre, Matt Talbot and a host of others.

Let us not forget this in our super-technological, machine-dominated age.

Lovingly yours in Mary,

OUR LETTERS TO PARENTS

July 12th, 1963

Dearly Beloved,

It often happens that parents write directly to me or to one of the priests, either inquiring about the well-being of their children who have not written, or sending the children's letters back to us asking for explanations about their content.

Whatever your attitude to your parents might be, emotionally speaking, you realize that in justice and charity you owe them deep gratitude, love and respect, especially for the gift of life which sets you on the path to the Beatific Vision and to eternal life.

There are many more reasons than justice, love and gratitude why you should write but these are fundamental. God has commanded us to *love and honour our parents*.

However, another point must be made very clear to you. It is a theological truth and therefore a matter of faith and morals. No child has the grace of state to teach his parents, or to correct them in any way whatsoever. It is the parent who has the grace of state to correct the child. So please resist from instructing your parents in spiritual truths which you may have learned, because you are called to a special vocation. You have studied psychiatry but you are not qualified to teach it to anyone, and especially not to your parents. Don't permit yourself to analyze their relations with each other in the past that may or may not have affected you. All of this is out of the scope of your capability, grace of state, and knowledge.

You might imagine that you are doing all of this to "share with your parents" your newly-found knowledge. If this be so, then it can be said in a few sentences such as, "Dear Mother and Dad, I have had a wonderful course in mental hygiene, and have had the privilege of studying a few wonderful books in which you might be interested: (name them). That's all that you should mention along these lines.

You are not called to instruct your parents on liturgy, the use of the missal, or anything like that. The devotions of the older generation are pleasing to the Lord. Any indoctrination should be done by the priests who have the grace of state for all ages.

What every child needs, even in adulthood, is a dose of empathy, which is a fruit of charity. Imagine yourself to be your own mother. What would be your main interest in your daughter or your son? It would be primarily connected with their physical welfare, the way they spend their day. Are they comfortably housed? Are their little aches and ills taken care of? What is their food, clothing, recreation like? What is their environment?

They may be interested in the subject matter of your studies and you could list these, for parents are proud that you are acquiring academic knowledge, but you don't have to give them lessons!

You are doing a disservice to yourselves and to the Apostolate by not writing the right kind of letters to your parents from the moment that you begin your life in Madonna House. Be always sure to invite your parents to come and visit, for one visit to Madonna House allays most of their parental fears regarding your well-being. I beg you to take this letter very seriously.

Lovingly yours in Mary,

POVERTY AND MODERN VERONICAS

August 28, 1963

Dearly Beloved,

In this year of 1963, we of the Madonna House Apostolate are being led by the Holy Spirit, even as the Church herself is being led, to examine our lives as to how we show the *face of poverty* to the world.

Cardinal Lecaro, in his speech to the Second Vatican Council, fearlessly threw down this gauntlet of poverty to all the Fathers of the Church. He didn't mince words. He had no mental reservations, whatsoever. He didn't use casuistry or sophistry. No, in plain, blunt words, he asked the Fathers to go back to the poverty of the Founder of Christianity, even unto the shedding of all the princely trappings of the bishops. They were not, nor ever had they been princes *except princes of poverty, princes of peace, princes of love, followers of the Divine Pauper who had nowhere to lay his head. They were followers of a Carpenter who during his hidden life, though not destitute, by any stretch of the imagination could not be called a man with status. Although his daily needs were never totally assured, Christ was not destitute. However, he died naked!*

In our modern, secular world which worships Mammon — wealth, power, status, and above all comfort — how is the Church going to teach the luminous Gospel of Christ which calls us to detachment, poverty of spirit, and even *factual* poverty?

Yes! How *can* she teach poverty against this background of a world divided between the extremely wealthy, comfortable nations, and the hungry and destitute?

The only way she can do this is to become visibly poor herself in the lives of the men and women who *are* the Church — Pope, cardinals, bishops, priests, religious, lay people! Then and only then when she clothes herself in the good news will she be able to cry the Gospel, and bring the glad news to the world.

Slowly, inexorably, perhaps because of the Vatican Council, the Holy Spirit has come like a flaming wind, searing and burning away our puny, little arguments which for so many centuries tried to justify untenable compromises with the world. We of Madonna House are the Church too. We are also beginning to feel the fiery Wind who seeks to consume, to burn out of us any compromise. This Wind demands that we who work in the marketplaces of the world show the face of Christ's poverty in all its splendor. Then and then alone will people listen to the Gospel that we are trying to cry with our lives.

But, since the Church is human, we are faced with a crucifying dilemma. In a world moving away from God with the speed of a rocket, in a world that measures everything in terms of cash, in a world that equates success with wealth, power, and status, this secular world which is not living at all by the principles of the Gospel, is not ready to — in any way to concede that we should be allowed to beg. We desire to embrace poverty completely. We desire to beg the alms that our Apostolate in this modern world requires. For us it is a *privilege* to beg and receive alms for the works of the Lord.

In this society of ours no matter where one is, in a leper colony in Burma, in the hot rice fields of Pakistan, in the overcrowded, beautiful islands of the West Indies — *money is needed to perform corporal and spiritual works of mercy, that is to cry the Gospel with one's life. In a desert of hungry bodies, minds are incapable of absorbing the Gospel.* Yes, money is needed for modern missionaries, more so now than in times when the world was Christian and everyone — kings and queens, priests and religious, paupers and lords — all contributed to the spreading of the Gospel.

We have the words of the Gospel: "The children of light must be as wise as the children of this world." The children of light in the service of the glory of the Father must use the *good* means of the children of the world. They *have* good means such as efficiency, ingenuity and imagination, but apply them to the wrong goals. We must use them to cry the Gospel with our lives.

Groups such as ours can and do use many means to achieve the raising of monies for this holy and urgent purpose of preaching the Gospel in our modern world which has forgotten God.

Such groups beg as St. Francis did. Some work for a living. St. Paul was a tent maker. The rabbis of the Old Testament worked, and Christ himself was a Carpenter. Some groups have businesses such as the publishing and distribution of books. Some run grocery stores at very fair prices and make little profit. Some manage credit unions and cooperatives in poorer sections of the world.

There are groups who make their living running good movie houses. There are others who run art and handicraft shops where the products of their hands are sold at reasonable prices and their apostolate is an education for the people as well as a contact. Our secularist society forces us to raise money in an infinite variety of ways. People in our society do not understand their obligation to Christ living in the poor. How could they, since they know him not! They do not understand any more that unless they share their earthly goods with their brethren, they cannot enter heaven. So the lay apostolate in everything it is and does must reeducate society in this sublime doctrine of the Gospel. It must do this especially in the ways it is compelled to raise money for its apostolic ministry.

Madonna House, since its foundation in 1930, has existed solely on begging; it has been poor. Since 1951 it has been faced with a strange and mysterious expansion that can be attributed only to God. God is the giver of vocations, and vocations come to Madonna House. This demands an expansion of buildings, and the growing of more food. It is necessary to provide more money for the support of its constantly expanding missions. The missions increase because God wants them to, since a request for a missionary team comes from the bishops.

Madonna House continues to beg, but there is a limit to the begging capacity of any apostolate, though there is no limit to Madonna House's faith in divine providence. We will continue to beg relying on this providence. Nevertheless, we remember the prayer of St. Ignatius Loyola: "Pray as if all depended upon God, and work as if all depended upon you."

Therefore after much prayer and much agony of soul, and much fasting, as well as taking counsel with priest experts in this matter, Madonna House has launched a little business!

Yet it happened simply and quietly. To all of those who have watched its growth and its flowering the hand of God was visible. God speaks to us through *people, things and events*. He thus spoke to those of us who run Madonna House Apostolate. Yes, it happened very quietly.

When I accepted the invitation of Bishop Smith of Pembroke to start a rural apostolate, I understood, by the grace of the Holy Spirit, that in such a setting I would be able to train the future staff in the spirit of the Gospels more deeply than I was able to do in the urban centers which had been the novitiate to which God had lead me. In my family's way of life the Lord had already prepared me for this special type of training that I was to give. Slowly and prayerfully I began to understand this in the early days of the Combermere foundation.

He had allowed me to be born into a certain family, at a certain time of history, in a certain country — Russia. Russia was an agricultural country when I was young. My people were noblemen and farmers in the broad sense of the word. Modern civilization as understood today, had not touched the centuries-old ways of living in Russia which was close to nature and the earth.

Our estate was far removed even from railroads. With the exception, perhaps, of sugar, tea and coffee, we were self-sufficient. We had sheep, and we carded, wove and spun our own materials. True, expensive and artistic tailors made wonderful clothing for us, but they were handmade just the same.

We grew flax and processed it by hand. We wove our linen, sheets, pillowcases, tablecloths, napkins, towels and everything else.

We grew our food and processed it in the manner that today is preserved only in the remote areas of the North American continent, or in its museums! We made cheese and butter in churns which now sell as antiques at ridiculous prices.

Our religion blended with our way of life, and the liturgical year made sense to us, for it blended with the natural year. God was ever present. We knew much about nature and its ways. The earth taught us to understand the Gospel better. She opened her secrets giving us dyes for our clothing, food for our kitchen, medicines for our ills. We approached the earth reverently, knowing that it belonged to God, and was his creature.

Yes, looking backward I understood that the Lord had prepared me to restore modern man (on this most modern of all the continents of the world!) more deeply, more profoundly than I had been able to do in the urban centers. Perhaps also he wanted to make me realize how deeply man was wounded in modern society.

I began as usual, simply and humbly, and in utter poverty of means. I had little money, but thanks be to God, I had a great imagination and a clarity of his vision for this Apostolate. Yes, I began by cutting out from second-hand magazines, articles pertaining to crafts, art, cooking, farming — how to do things with few materials and much ingenuity.

These clippings I kept because of my dream dreamt in the Lord. Like all my dreams it came true. I went further. Long before there was even a place to store things, I begged the wherewithal so that some day I might implement the ways of old, blending them with the new. So when other members, whom I knew in faith *would* come, came, we were ready for them and for their "restoration". They can tell you themselves (and I hope they will), what awaited them, and how the farm and the handicraft, the food and the arts grew in Madonna House.

But the Lord helped me even more and sent me special graces. For some reason which I cannot account for today, I also collected strange things. I collected all sorts of antiques such as old buttons, old farm instruments — what modern people would perhaps call "junk". Years passed. One day I knew why I had collected them. God wished for two things; a museum and a little shop we call the "PX", but which I hope some day to call "The Madonna House Mission Shop".

That shop also started quietly when a cottage was freed for this purpose. It had a few shelves to display my "collection". Things sold, and the money thus earned was used for the needs of the Apostolate.

More donations came. It seemed to me that Our Lady became our buyer and sent us articles which other people wanted. True, it entailed much work. It demanded sorting, storage, patience, and time. We had time and patience, but if we hadn't had them, God clearly indicated that we had to *make* time and *grow* in patience which these "little things" clearly demanded of us.

The shop grew. Today on the third of August 1963, Madonna House and I stand crucified once again on the question of poverty; this time it is because of the business of this shop.

I have a deep, inner conviction confirmed by my spiritual director, that the Lord and the Pope not only permit, but seem to encourage, this method of raising money that blends so well with modern minds and is understandable to them. Yet, it must not only be a shop to raise money for the Apostolate and its missions, but also *an apostolate of contacts with those who will come as customers.*

At one time we took care of a hostel in Whitehorse. Because it was a government hostel, the combined salaries of our staff there were a great help to Madonna House.

But the Lord made us withdraw from this hostel. And now we are faced with ways of making money to make up for the loss of this income. Much prayer, I confess, has gone into facing this need. No matter where I turn, the answer seems to be that we should enlarge our shop, and a museum that will teach our staff to respect and learn from ages past. We will open this museum to the local people of this rural area of Canada, and to such tourists as might come; but at the same time, it will help the shop that will be located near it.

The children of light, as the Gospel says, must be as smart as the children of darkness, but for another goal! So we are confronted with the necessity (about which we are thoroughly confirmed), of opening the shop either by purchasing a suitable house which is available, or of building one. To do either we must beg as usual.

Once we have the premises, what is going to be our "policy" in running that shop? Here comes the agonizing question. Must we imitate the efficiency of the children of darkness? Must we use begged money to build the premises? (It will be some time before we have enough.) Even if we have enough money from the profits, should we use them, since all the profits belong to the missions? Should we purchase lovely boxes, following the "packaging idea" of secular business, or should we beg boxes and wrap our goods in second-hand bags that we have also begged? What shall we do?

Does part of our apostolate of the shop consist in a special apostolic salesmanship that bluntly and truthfully, yet humbly, tells the customer that the jars we use are begged baby food jars, or any jars that we can get, that we try to paint their covers the best we can, that we are still amateurs? Do we tell them that our packaging is poor because we are poor, that we do not feel that we can spend a penny of the begged or earned money for any trimmings because millions of people are hungry in India and we want to send every penny there.

At the same time we do not wish to sell things for high prices. This is an apostolic shop, when all is said and done, not another cold, business proposition where all is based on the profit motive. How far must we imitate the children of darkness in this venture that seems to be spearheaded by the Lord, approved of by his priests, and which has flowered now in my soul after much prayer, agony, fasting, thinking and searching?

What are the answers? These are questions which I ask of you whom God has called to Madonna House. Give me your answers, but before you do, pray!

This shop must be an apostolate. Our salesmanship must spring from a longing to show the face of true poverty to a world saturated with the love of money, comfort and power. We must show the face of poverty to the people whom the world calls "customers", and who expect worldly packaging.

Can we sell the goods that Our Lord sends us, and of which Our Lady is the buyer, packaged in a worldly way? Or must we package them in poverty and blazing charity? What shall it be? Or is there room for both?

Lovingly yours in Mary,

Catherine

P.S.

As I was finishing these few thoughts, my secretary contributed the following idea, which to me is very beautiful. It concerns the name of "Veronica".

Our first guest cottage was originally called "Veronica", because she is one of my favorite saints. I consider her a patroness of the lay apostolate, and I pray to her for courage. It took tremendous love, courage and faith for a young Hebrew girl to step into an angry mob and wipe the Face of One who was considered to be a criminal, and who had been subjected to derision, spittle, and blasphemous laughter.

He rewarded that courage by leaving the imprint of his Face on her veil. It is strange that the sign with the name "Veronica", (which means "true image") remained on the building. My secretary had the beautiful thought that it was fitting that it was so.

Those who sell, and those who buy in that shop, by those very acts, fashion, as it were, a towel or veil of their buying and selling. Both know where the money goes: the goods are sold to wipe the Face of the suffering Christ in the world.

Could it be that those who are engaged in those transactions will find the Face of the suffering Lord imprinted on their souls?

HIS GREATEST GIFT

September 12, 1963

Dearly Beloved,

I begin this letter to you in the name of the Lord, and with a heart full of sorrow and joy. I sorrow because a member of our Apostolate is in pain. Sorrow is human, for we are all human.

At present there are three members among us who are in pain. Alma, especially. Unexpectedly cancer was found in her body. She had to have very radical, very deep surgery — five hours and fifteen minutes on the surgeon's table.

My sorrow, I repeat, is deeply human for I suffer with Alma in my body, mind and soul. I sorrow also with two other members who are both in the hospital. But my joy is great! This may astonish you. Why a heart full of joy?

I am joyful because what appears to be the heavy hand of God upon our Apostolate is really his gentle touch. I would go further and say that it is his tender, loving touch. Or, as I have been trying to tell you all since the very first day that you came to Madonna House, pain and suffering — his cross — is *his greatest gift to us*. In so many words it means that he has found us unworthy to really be co-redeemers with him, to enter into his passion, and therefore to be sharers of his eternal glory, love and joy.

It also means more. It means that we can become saints, truly lovers of God, truly heirs of his kingdom. If we who have been touched by his tender, loving hand have been asked to suffer with him, accept his holy will joyfully, and offer ourselves, our pains and sorrows, our fears and our darkness for the world, the world will then receive God's light through us — incredible as this may seem!

Those touched by his tender, loving touch can become victim souls in truth and in joy. The apostolate of suffering is God's hurricane of love. Usually he sends the Holy Spirit of his love as a gentle breeze, as quiet, constantly falling sparks of fire. Then it seems to me that God, beholding the misery of the world, cannot contain his love any more. He descends upon certain chosen souls, the lucky ones, in large tongues of fire, as on the first Pentecost, desiring as it seems, with infinite desire, to make known his love to the world through those chosen souls whom he has so specially, so lovingly so tenderly selected.

I pray that they may see the vision of God's love for them, and see the immense, incredible, overwhelming apostolate that he has now entrusted into their hands. My heart as you see, dearly beloved, is filled with great joy that some of us have been found worthy to suffer with and for Christ in this particular manner.

Yes, they are the lucky ones, beloved in a very special manner. They are our priceless, suffering members. Let us remember that, while rejoicing that God has found them worthy, let us do our share in understanding their pain and sharing it. I know that you can easily do this as regards cancer and other serious operations, but there are other pains, more hidden, more subtle, more difficult to grasp. We call them by the generic name of ''emotional problems''.

Here we must walk very softly, never judging, always praying for understanding. People afflicted with this kind of pain have been especially called to remain in Gethsemane and share with Christ the lonely hours through which his disciples slept. A great honor, indeed! And one that we must understand, revere, and share to the best of our ability.

I thought that I would tell you some of the thoughts that came to me when I heard about this illness. The words of a director came back to me: ''The price of souls are high.'' Yes, the price of souls is high, dearly beloved, and you are beginning to get a glimpse of it. Be not afraid, little flock, the Lord is with us until the end of time.

Each of us will have the grace needed to pay that price. Let your hearts be filled caritas, so that we might have the peace of heart needed to share in the suffering of your brothers and sisters.

Yes, my heart is full of sorrow and joy, and now you know why.

Lovingly yours in Mary,

THE VERY HEART OF POVERTY

October 23, 1963

AN ANSWER TO THE QUESTION OF POVERTY
September 24, 1963

Dear Catherine,

We are waiting to get your letter on poverty. Really poverty has another face when you are in a land where extreme poverty is the norm. As one priest said: "It is impossible to witness by your poverty; No matter how poorly you try to live, they are always poorer. They cannot be impressed by your poverty because this is the only condition that they know."

We met the sisters of Mother Theresa who do a fantastic and heroic work; and, of course, their work is only among the poorest and lowest. And they themselves are very poor. This seems to be the main theme of their spirit. And we've talked about poverty among ourselves and with others and hear many points of view, but there are many things to which I do not find answers.

Is poverty something you use to "impress" people? Is poverty a goal, an end in itself, a way of life? How do you live poorly and not wear poverty as a sort of rich garment that hides your rags and displays your own virtue rather than God's love? Can we use poverty as a kind of stepping stone into people's hearts?

We've been hearing for months that we are here to love these people just because God loves them, that they too are his beloved children, and not because we want to convert them. If it is an unworthy motive for love, then it must also be for poverty. Is it realistic to try to live as poorly as they, that is, the really poor ones, to eat and sleep as they do?

This seems to be the heartache of many here, that they cannot really be one with these people whom they truly love. They will always be white, and the people brown. They have come from a background, environment which is part and parcel of them; it cannot be torn out or removed. But it is beautiful to see how much they try to absorb this culture and have absorbed it. As they say, they are "at home" here. We have much to learn from each of them. Pray for us.

Lovingly in Christ

A Staff Worker

October 10, 1963

Dear Heart,

Thank you so very much for your letter of September 24. I am extremely happy that you have finally arrived. But of this later. Right now I want to answer your letter asking me about *poverty*.

You will never know how happy your questions made me. Not only because I witness your growth in wisdom and grace, but because *only now can I begin to speak about poverty*. Yes, the key word is *begin*.

Now you too begin to understand the terrible frustration under which all returning missionaries live! In due time, you too will feel as they do, when you return home for a spell, or forever. Those missionaries have no words to express what they have seen, heard, smelled, what they have experienced so deeply in themselves.

Now *my own* frustration and spiritual sadness may become a little clearer to you. For I have seen the same poverty in my childhood and youth that you now see. What is more, I have experienced it in Russia. I know the gnawing hunger that makes one eat rats, cats, dogs, chew wood, and bless God for manure to suck! I know this poverty in my own mouth, stomach, mind and soul!

But I know more. I know the horror of lice eating one's body. I know the gratitude for having a warm spot to lie in even though one must have the almost stoic indifference of sleeping with crawling bedbugs! I do not know in my own body, soul and mind the life of the Hindus, but I have had the privilege and grace to experience for a while a few aspects of their life.

I thank God that you three are where you are, seeing what you are seeing, experiencing what you are experiencing. You are young, and because of your youth, yours are the voices that from now on, and for as many years as God has allotted you on his earth, will speak and shout in the wilderness of the minds of the future generations of Madonna House. Alleluia! Alleluia! Alleluia! that there will be such voices!

Now you asked some questions and I must try to give you some answers. But the answers will be a little simpler than before, because now you know several truths: 1) the physical poverty in the United States, Canada and Europe, as practiced by religious orders, is "kindergarten stuff". 2) You have also realized that your life at Madonna House really was only a "kindergarten", barely preparing you for the physical poverty that you have met in the East.

This is good. For now the time has come to understand that *poverty is not only a virtue to practice. Poverty is also a state, a way of life, the fruit of love of God, the key to humility which is truth*. God is Truth; this poverty is a short-cut to God. Yes, poverty is all of that.

One has to begin at the beginning. The beginning is to finally acknowledge *your own immense poverty*. Now you have to fully, deeply realize that *all that you are, all that you have, is from God*! From this follows that you have and are *nothing*.

Once you make this truth of your own poverty before God *the very marrow of your thoughts, your life, your love, your body, in a word, your very being, then you will become truly humble. Then you will walk in truth, walk in and with God*.

Here then, is your first gift to those whom you have come to serve, although their poverty is physical, *you can equal their poverty by acknowledging your radical poverty as a creature, your total dependence upon God*! The acceptance of this truth will make you truly free, free to love and serve these poor, tragic people. It will also make you free to love and serve God more passionately, more constantly, more totally. You will then be on the threshold of this many-faceted, infinitely beautiful virtue and attitude of heart, state of life, that is poverty!

But still, you will only have begun. I repeat you will be only standing on the threshold of poverty's dwelling.

The next step is having a heart wide open to grace! Now you will enter an unknown terrain, through which God himself will deign to lead you. All that you have to do is to be open to grace.

The moment you cross the threshold of the house of poverty you will enter the hallways of *obedience*. A hallway, generally speaking, is a place where people hang their outer garments — coats, hats, umbrellas and such. But this is also the hallway of faith. Nevertheless, it is just a place where you do leave your garments. Here you continue to become truly poor! You let yourself *be stripped* of your garments. There is a big difference between "taking off" and "being stripped". Here, in this hallway of faith and obedience, you will let yourself be stripped of your garments — *all of them*! This will enable you to stand even more naked before God, and before those people whom you are meeting in India's streets, and will meet again in many places.

Yes, you will be as naked as Christ was at his crucifixion. First and foremost, you will have to relinquish *your own will* completely, and do that of another. The more completely that you do this, the more completely, in a *mysterious fashion will you truly identify yourself with those poor about whom you have written. And what is more, by this very identification, unseen and unnoticed by people, you will heal those very poor whom you have come to serve.*

Yes, *obedience* will make you truly *poor*. You will have surrendered that tremendous, magnificent, incredible gift of God that each of us possess as a free, loving gift from him — *your free will*! Think of it! giving back to God the one gift that makes you most like him, the one gift that is truly worth giving to God, and giving exclusively out of love for him. You give it freely with the full consent of that same *free, magnificent, tremendous human will*. You offer him this gift also as a love-offering for those poor whom you serve. This is the most beautiful facet of that priceless diamond which we call *poverty*.

But there are other facets. Though we might have in one swoop, in meekness and simplicity, decided to be utterly stripped of our own will in the hallways of faith and obedience, being human we shall still have shreds of our erstwhile "garments" clinging to us. Every shred must be picked off and thrown away.

It is impossible for anyone to define, list, or categorize all of these shreds. Each one of these is of a different size, color and length. In each new situation shreds will change too.

Understand well this parable-like letter. The poverty of which I speak is an *inner state of soul*. For instance, one of these shreds might be a desire for comfort, oh, ever so slight; yet, this must be taken off immediately. Other shreds will be wrong attitudes which will begin forming in you. These have to be examined carefully, prayerfully, and dealt with accordingly lest they interfere with total nakedness, that total surrender. Thus life will be a continual *inner stripping* of yourself. It will never end until you enter into his eternal kingdom.

Perhaps now you understand better that *poverty leads to obedience, obedience to total surrender, total surrender to death to self; death to self, growth in the Lord and resurrection.* All of this begins *here and now* on this earth! This is identification with the poor; this is identification with those you will serve.

Your physical poverty is not too important. You will not be able to have too many comforts, but only the minimum without which your body, mind and soul brought up and fashioned by God's design in the United States or Canada, cannot survive. But keep before your eyes the poverty of the people which affects you so much, and which, in itself, will be a brake against any extras which you might momentarily desire.

So don't worry about it. I agree that you cannot, as much as you wish, identify yourself with the physical poverty of the people there. In any case, it won't mean much to them! In this sense, it is not a *tool of the Apostolate* as much.

God, as I am sure you are beginning to realize, demands a million times more of you! He does not demand your physical death. No. He demands your *death to self through the perfection of poverty which is obedience.* He demands also, death to self through the acceptance of a new life — its mores, its food — through a thousand "little things" that will come your way.

But above all, *he wants you to enter into the very heart of poverty. Then he will make your poverty a healing, beautiful tool of our Apostolate, which strangely enough will enrich Pakistan and the Church's apostolate beyond all of our dreams. What is more, the Mystical Body of Christ will grow there in a mysterious and holy fashion!*

The naked crucified One always knows his own, and he especially cannot resist the ones who strip themselves inwardly

*naked for him, and immolate themselves with him on his own cross
for love of him and the souls for whom he died.*

*Stripped in this fashion, dying to self, crucified through
poverty and obedience, walking in humility which is truth, you
will be able to feel what the poor feel. You will heal, console, and
bring multitudes to God. You will be truly poor in the full sense of
that glorious word, and hence truly rich.*

Lovingly in Mary,

LOVE LETTER IN BLOOD?

November 8, 1963

Dearly Beloved,

I have received many letters from our team in the East. They
raise many questions that haven't been settled or discussed
officially, so I am writing this letter.

The first question is a very simple one which seldom requires
an answer, except in extraordinary circumstances. However, it
takes on new and added significance there. It deals with — of all
things — our attitude towards animals! One of our team is a Third
Order Franciscan and Franciscans love animals, nature and
flowers very specially. That was a characteristic of St. Francis.

Christians are lovers of all of God's creations, which *if it is
theologically kept within the proper order of God's creation is
fine.* In a Moslem country, this takes on different dimensions.
Moslems consider dogs unclean animals and won't have much to
do with them. So stray dogs roam around. What attitude should
we have to stray dogs when they find a haven in a small, adobe
house in a compound?

The answer is one of common sense as well as theology. All of our "loves" must be orderly. If they proceed from God and are rooted in God they never go overboard in a sentimental, gushy way. Who of us doesn't feel slightly disgusted at seeing a spinster who has twenty cats in her house, lavishing on them the affection that is due people? Who of us doesn't get angry when we hear of some rich person endowing a home for cats and dogs when there are children orphaned and going hungry? You see what I am getting at? There is a right and orderly way to love cats and dogs, and there is a disorderly way which would be abhorrent to St. Francis himself!

Psychologically speaking, such a disordered love of animals shows that the person is in need of counseling! The reason that they withhold their love from human beings and lavish it upon animals is that animals do not talk back, cannot hurt them, do not cause them suffering and pain, and hence this isn't love at all, but an unhealthy caricature of what love really is.

Concerning foreign missions, I suggest that we keep away from having any pets. The expense of food; the fact that we may have to employ Moslem cooks who certainly don't like dogs; and because we may be breaking some taboo or other — all of this argues in favor of just keeping our own body and soul together and not having pets. If we have the slightest surplus, give it to hungry human beings, and not to cats, dogs, lizards etc.

Another perversion of love is to endow an animal with human *feelings*. This bespeaks, first of all, a lack of real knowledge of zoology and the anatomic structure of animals. Animals have a different nervous system from ours, and they don't suffer pain as we do. For example, a worm cut in two doesn't suffer any pain and may grow again. A fish caught on a hook doesn't "feel it" as we would.

The next aberration is refusing to kill any insect or rat in the house. These are a danger to health. Who of us can tell, especially in the tropics, which bug, spider, or what have you, is injurious to health? For instance, the bite of a black spider is deadly. Moreover, God subjected insects and animals to *us*, and it is only perverse sentimentality that would refuse to kill a mosquito or fly.

Joseph Labre was not canonized because he was full of lice! He was canonized because he was full of real love, humility and poverty in spite of being full of lice.

The second question asked by this team of ours was much more profound. It concerned *martyrdom*.

A Sister of the Holy Cross had been appointed to a very distant mission near the Chinese border. Last year war broke out there and many people especially Catholics were killed. Our team had a long discussion on martyrdom. It arose because the Bishop under whom that Sister worked had told the priests and nuns that although he wished them to leave because of the danger of death, nevertheless he gave them the choice of staying.

So the team wants to know what is *our attitude to martyrdom?*

It might startle you to know that when I read that letter, with that question, an immense joy flooded my heart. For what could be greater for a Christian than to be a martyr? Nothing on this earth.

Martyrdom is the greatest act of which we are capable if we accept it voluntarily and joyously understanding what it involves. What is involved? An incredible, mysterious event takes place: *we are allowed to mingle our blood with the Precious Blood of Christ*! God wrote his love letters *in blood* for humanity. Incredible as it seems, some people, (I think in the name of all humanity) are permitted, nay called by God, to write him a love letter also in blood in the name of all of us.

Another incredible result of martyrdom is that the Gospel which we try to preach with our lives suddenly comes alive to our executioners and to all of those who do not know God, or who reject him. It becomes alive, not for a day, not for a week, or month, but forever. For "*the blood of martyrs is the seed of Christians.*" The reward of the martyr cannot be described. God puts a seal upon our hearts at Baptism. We then seal our wedding with the Lord with our own blood.

But my next reaction to the letter was sadness, for few are worthy of being chosen for this final confession of faith that changes the face of the world. Yes, until recently so few of us have been found worthy to die for the faith. Nazis and Communists, strange as it may seem, have been instruments of martyrdom. Who knows but that the Second Vatican Council, the fresh air that is blowing through the whole world because of Pope John and Pope Paul, is due to the blood of those martyrs which has been shed in concentration camps and labor camps.

However, I brightened up immediately, and joy flooded my

heart, for I realized that marytrs are not selected on their personal merits, but through the mystery of God's merciful choice. It is hard for me to believe, much as I passionately desire to do so, that Madonna House may have its own martyrs; but I will not deny that we may have if God so wills. I hope that I have made it clear to all of you that the very thought of martyrdom for myself or for any of our members sends my heart a-dancing and my soul a-singing with joy. I'm sure that it does yours also.

But now enters the solemn and austere virtue of prudence. Whilst holding firmly to all that I have written above, I know and realize that it is my duty — the duty of the directorate of Madonna House, and also of each director in the missions — to approach every situation that may led to martyrdom with prudence, spiritual and intellectual foresight and deep prayer. This is the moment and time *"to be as wise as serpents and as simple as doves."*

First of all, we must be directed by ecclesiastical authorities, i.e. the Bishop of the diocese. If he commands departure of all religious personnel, including lay apostles, then the problem is solved for us very simply; we pack and go for without exception *obedience is always better than sacrifice.*

If the bishop or religious superior in the mission territory gives his personnel a choice, *then a choice it must be* — a personal choice of *each individual.* Let us say that the director wishes to leave and one of the other members desires to remain. In this case, there is a second point to consider: the decision of the director. If she wishes to leave, *she can also command in holy obedience that the others leave with her.* They will have to obey on the same principle that *obedience is always better than sacrifice.*

If the director decides to stay and the others disagree, they must be given a choice. (It is presumed that there is not any time to communicate with Combermere.) Then the director may stay on and send the others away. For martyrdom must be embraced freely.

Here I want to note that if a person expressed a desire to stay, she is, as it were, a martyr by desire. It is so considered in heaven, even though under holy obedience her desire was not able to be actualized.

To sum up: martyrdom by desire is open to all of us; It is especially efficacious, spiritually speaking, when there is a real possibility of martyrdom. But at all times this desire must be subjected to holy obedience.

A director who wishes to stay, and send away the others who do not wish to do so if he or she is sure that the others will ''make it'' without his or her help. If there is a doubt on this subject the director cannot stay. Her first duty is to the others. If all are the same mind, one way or another, then of course there is no problem.

Have I clarified anything? I hope so. I know full well that I have placed on the director, as well as upon the missionary team, one of the heaviest burdens of decision that could be placed upon human beings. However, I am not worried, because I know one thing, and I know it with a certainty of my holy faith: *that at that moment of decision the Crimson Dove, the God of Love, the Holy Spirit, will cover you with his flaming wings and send his seven gifts to you in depth*. I know also that if you choose martyrdom, he will bring you such graces through Our Lady's hands that you will know joy beyond description or understanding.

If you choose retreat, he will help you to go safely where you have to go, because it would be he who would have helped you to make that decision, and because it is the will of God for you then to forego the quick martyrdom of death for the slow, white martyrdom of life.

Therefore, cease arguments and discussions on martyrdom until you see in the distance its beautiful face. Amen. Alleluia!

Lovingly yours in Mary,

THE LAVISHNESS OF LOVE

December 12, 1963

Dearly Beloved,

Humbly with a heart full of love, I come to you with empty hands, having nothing to give you but my heart, and I fervently hope, a life spent in your service. For to love is to serve. To govern is to serve doubly. I bring you also my constant prayers which are a part, oh so large a part, of my loving and serving.

Once again it is Advent — Christ's mystical, mysterious Advent has come, reminding us so vividly, so beautifully, of his first advent in time.

I know that you are all meditating on this mystical, mysterious Advent that recurs so miraculously every year. *Even while he is coming, he is also with us in many guises*. He is in the tabernacle. Incredible Love that he is, he could not separate himself from us. Even though he has ascended to his Father, he also remains!

Not content with this proof of love, he walks among us in his priests. There is only one priesthood — that of Christ. But like the hosts he multiplies himself in the men we call priests so that they can feed us with the Bread of Life — himself; so that they can dispense his sacraments of love to us. He is with us in all priests but especially in our Madonna House priests. How immense must be his love for us! Daily he performs a miracle of love greater than the one that he performed for the Jews when he multiplied loaves and fishes.

Meditate for a moment. Allow a few moments of silence to interrupt the reading of this letter, then resume reading. Try to comprehend as much as it is possible for a human mind to comprehend this lavishness of God's love for us. Daily millions of hosts are given in Holy Communion to the faithful throughout the world! Yet each host is Christ, in tremendous love coming to be united to each and all! Christ in the priest can preach to us, heal our souls, and continue to perform greater miracles of grace than he did in Palestine.

Yes, this lavishness of God's love for us should fill our own lives and overflow into the lives of others! The world is filled with God's love. All creatures know it. He came in time. He comes mystically, mysteriously, every year in the season of Advent, the season of preparation for Christmas. It is the season when we should be pregnant with Christ in an intense way, so that always and constantly we give him birth in our hearts. It is the season to be sanctified by him, and to sanctify others by giving him to them, as Our Lady gives him to us.

During Advent we think also of the Parousia when all things will be made new, when finally and forever we shall be united to him in a love that transcends our intellect and imagination, but for which we must prepare *now, every day, every moment of our lives*!

Why is it that our hearts are still so cold? Why is it that our longings for the Parousia, if they exist at all, are so weak? Many are the reasons. It is not our fault that these longings have not been given to us in childhood and early youth. But they are given to us now in Madonna House. Let us open our hearts wide, dearly beloved. Let us accept these longings whole-heartedly. Let us make these longings the food, the strength the goal of our lives!

Let everyday *be the day of the beginning again*, of loving him a little more, or of hungering for him a little more, of turning our faces to him. All we have to do is to look at the person next to us. We must never forget that *we shall be judged on love alone*. There is only one way to love God and to prove it to him, and that is by loving our neighbor.

Our neighbor is the person next to us at any given moment. It may be other members of the community in your house with whom you are working at this moment; the stranger at your gates; the poor you have gone to serve; the priests, religious and lay people who come to visit you. I repeat, turning your face and heart to Christ simply mean turning your face to the one who is next to you *at this moment of your life*.

If we do that, dearly beloved, we shall be saints (with a small "s"). If we do it well, we shall be saints with a capital "S". It really doesn't matter what kind of saints we are as long as we are saints. For the definition of a saint is a "lover of God," which also means, naturally, a love of all human beings.

Listen! Do you hear the cry of a child in the night the Holy Night of his birth? It is God crying, not only for the milk of his mother, but for your love and mine. The cry should be especially piercing to those who are in any way dedicated to him.

It is from him that he expects the milk, the food of love in return. He wants their whole being. With him it is all or nothing at all. Because that is the way that he loved — *totally, completely* — *being born as a child for us, dying on a cross for us.*

This is my prayer for all of us, that we hear the cry of a Child who is also God, hear it in the holy night of every moment of our lives; and that we bring him the food of our love on a platter of the total gift of self, every moment of every day, every day of our lives.

Yes, this is my prayer for you, dearly beloved, I know that when I am saying this prayer I am praying for joy and happiness for you, the Joy "that eye has not seen, and ear has not heard and mind cannot comprehend."

I pray that we should all love him in that way. This is my Christmas present for you. I have nothing else to give you but my love, my understanding my compassion, my prayers, and my service.

Holy, joyous, peaceful Christmas to you, one and all, and a New Year that will set your feet on the road to Bethlehem, Nazareth and Golgotha, so that you too might rise with him.

Lovingly yours in Mary,

Catherine

TEMPTATIONS OF THE CELEBATE

December 19, 1963

Dearly Beloved,

I wanted to discuss with you the difference between a temptation against chastity and a temptation to marriage.

Temptations against chastity are a normal part of the devil's equipment. Chastity is one virtue that he likes to destroy because it leads to purity of heart. Those who practice it to a high degree see God long before they are dead; they possess him long before their house of clay returns to the earth.

The devil also attacks chastity because it is a social virtue. Strange as this may seem to you it brings the very breath of God — of purity, beauty, innocence, childlikeness — to a world surfeited with sin and sexual aberration.

We of Madonna House have experienced the effect that our chastity has on others. True, I myself am not a virgin; I've been married. However, I was successful with prostitutes. Perhaps it was because I have a pure heart, I wouldn't know. But one remarkable thing I do know, and that is that the most successful among us was not the most experienced in life. It was Olga LaPlante, who at the age of 21, was one of the purest and most chaste souls I have ever known. The second was an Irish girl in Harlem who was so good with the same type of women when they came to our clothing room. She too was virginal and pure of heart in the full sense of the word. The so-called sinful women just "ate out of her hand," as it were, and as they did with Olga.

So naturally the devil is going to attack your promise of chastity. God will allow it, so that you might grow in grace and purity while fighting this temptation, as millions of priests and nuns do; as do married people for whom continence is the only way of practicing birth control for long periods. Pagans too have remained chaste because chastity has been a virtue respected from time immemorial. '

The vestal virgins of Rome and Greece, who served at the temples, were highly respected *because* they were chaste. Buddhist and Hindus, monks of all traditions respect chastity and virginity.

It is a virtue that is so "social" that it astounds and amazes people in every civilization and in every age. It is the reflection of God's face. So naturally the devil wants to blot it out. Take it for granted that you will have temptations against chastity. They will come on quiet feet. They will feed on loneliness and aloneness. But you will also have the graces to fight them.

One of our psychologist friends makes this distinction between loneliness and aloneness. *Loneliness* is what every human being has to endure. St. Augustine put it well when he said, "Our hearts are restless until they rest in God's heart." The disappearance of loneliness will come only in the Beatific Vision. Loneliness is hunger for union with a perfect being, i.e. God. If you imagine that married people do not know this loneliness, you are mistaken. Our psychologist friend called on me who has been married twice, to confirm or disprove this. I confirmed it. Much as I love my husband, Eddie, he and I, ultimately, are lonely. We cannot penetrate each other's innermost being.

Aloneness is man-made. Some are alone because they flee from reality or withdraw from life. This is a pathological aloneness, as is also the aloneness of a shy person; but mostly aloneness stems from not knowing that God loves us, or accepting this truth with great difficulty. Also, we don't love ourselves as we should, or our neighbor as we must. Then it is hard for us to even dedicate ourselves to a cause, even to God. We spend part of our time in daydreaming and imagining an ideal partner, a friend, a lover, a husband, a wife, who will "understand" us; but we make no steps toward understanding others. Aloneness in this sense can be alleviated. The temptations against chastity will play on that aloneness through daydreams. Of these we must be aware.

Every time that you overcome these temptations with the grace of God, you become a pure and shining light to the world, and the Apostolate moves forward by leaps and bounds.

Temptations to marriage are a different story. They are temptations against your very vocation — against the very things that you have promised God so solemnly to observe. To leave the Apostolate because *you have decided that you want to get married is to slap God in the face. He has not inspired this decision.*

At the moment you are uninvolved with any member of the opposite sex. You are just coddling yourself with your precious free will, giving in to Satan's subtle temptation. You are reaching out for something good to destroy something infinitely more precious, which is your vocation to the Apostolate. This has been shown to you quite clearly through your being accepted by the directorate of Madonna House who truly represent God.

I confess that I literally shiver with fear and physical trembling before the wrath of God in certain cases.

I'm not judging anybody. I am speaking objectively. To depart from a vocation that has been clarified and reclarified, knowing full well that the seal of that vocation is upon your soul, and then to *embrace another vocation that you imagine you have is a tragic thing.* All I can say is may the Lord have mercy on the soul of those who fall prey to this temptation.

People in the grip of this temptation never seem to stop for a moment in their downward descent and ask their spiritual director, "Father, what shall I do?" They *tell* him. That's *pride.*

As far as the Apostolate is concerned, I am at peace. I know that there will be many defections. If there were defections among the apostles why shouldn't there be amongst us? Religious Orders have them and so does marriage. But I feel cold and my agony returns when I think of what we can do to God.

Let us all be watchful.

Lovingly yours in Mary,

SPIRITUAL DIRECTORS

January 13, 1964

Dearly Beloved,

It seems that we have to clarify the question of spiritual directors once more, so let us review briefly what we already know about spiritual direction.

I am sure that there isn't a member of Madonna House who doesn't realize that the life of perfection to which we are called in this Apostolate demands a total dedication. To live out this dedication under the counsels of poverty, chastity and obedience we must have a spiritual director. The waters of life are turbulent and dangerous, and Satan loves to place pitfalls along the way. Definitely we need a guide.

We are also generally familiar with the procedure of obtaining a spiritual director. First, we must pray very earnestly to God before choosing one. It is a very important relationship that we are entering into with Christ the Priest, and we must turn to him to direct us to the right person. He may do this by giving us a certain spiritual attraction to some priest. Perhaps it is through a sermon, a retreat, or because we heard some spiritual truth expressed by this priest that went straight to our heart. These can be indications that God is directing us to him.

Once we have found the priest, we must enter into a very childlike relationship to him. We must love him as we love God — supernaturally. We must trust him completely. We must obey him implicitly. Otherwise, we wouldn't need a spiritual director. if we try to get around him in the thousand ways we try to get around even God, we will encourage Satan to trap us. One does not do such things to God.

These rules apply to everyone, in and out of the Apostolate. But as lay apostles we should also encourage those with whom we work and serve to have spiritual directors. I repeat: not to have a spiritual director is to be a foolish person, one who is guideless in a great, utterly-unknown wilderness. I expect that you are all convinced of the fact that you should have spiritual directors.

Also, for someone to take a spiritual director who is thoroughly unfamiliar with the Apostolate — and I stress the word ''thoroughly'' — this, too, is acting in a foolish and unintelligent way.

I once had a spiritual director, a Discalced Carmelite, who was thoroughly familiar with Friendship House. But six months after I moved to Combermere, he refused to direct me and rightly so. He said he was utterly unfamiliar with the new accent that our Apostolate had taken, and he could not advise me in this new context. This is a very important point to remember. It doesn't apply to lay people in general, but only to lay apostolates. A priest is familiar with single life in the world. He has been a layman and has known women before he became a priest. He is thoroughly familiar with married life, and usually pretty familiar with the religious life of priests and nuns. But unless a given apostolate is his apostolate, he would not be that familiar with it. If a wife comes to him complaining about her husband and he suspects that she is biased, all that he has to do is to ask her to bring her husband in. Then he can talk to him privately or in front of her, as he wishes, and get both sides of the picture.

But if you choose a priest who doesn't know Madonna House, or knows it superficially, you put him behind the eight-ball, and yourself behind the twenty-ball! Many of them are not at all prepared according to the Madonna House point of view, and will say so if you ask them. They have yet a lot to learn.

You can seek out a priest not of Madonna House, and spin him any kind of yarn that you wish. You can seek from him friendship and compassion and merciful understanding, but your spiritual life will not progress; in fact it will regress. Any priest in his right mind will know this.

True, according to the rules of the Church you are free to choose anyone as your spiritual director. The directorate of Madonna House does not impinge on your freedom. But if you remember the reason for having a spiritual director, it becomes obvious, both in the natural and supernatural order, that since we are blessed by our own priests in the Apostolate who *know* us, and other local priests who are very familiar with our Apostolate, you can and should go to these priests. Intelligence, I repeat, guides your choice. You want to go to God, don't you? You desire rapid, spiritual progress don't you? That means choosing a priest who *knows* our Apostolate.

The majority of you, because you come to Madonna House as a Training Centre, usually choose one of our Madonna House priests. Then you go to the missions. Because you find it difficult to write and to express yourself, because there is a lapse between your letters and your spiritual director's answers, you easily get discouraged.

This should not happen. You are approaching this whole matter of spiritual direction by mail in too natural a fashion. You are depressed. Your emotions get the better of you. Or you have a real problem, so you think (I spoil you a little too, God forgive me! By answering you at length, and usually pretty fast!)

However, your relations by mail with your spiritual director are quite different from your relations to me. I know that you love your spiritual directors, but you do not trust enough, that is, you do not trust God enough. Write without any worries. You are writing about your soul. The priests have the grace to read between the lines. Don't worry about your manner of expression, your grammar, or anything like that. Trust Christ fully. He will see to it that the priest clearly understands the poorest letter.

If you do not receive an immediate letter, remember that *God* sometimes doesn't give any answer for a long, long time, either. Sometimes not until you meet him face to face. Sometimes an answer will come very slowly. This is God's way of clarifying the doubts that you might have. The answer may not make sense to you at this moment, but will make sense if you meditate upon it.

The silence of the spiritual director may mean that he is teaching you patience; that he is teaching you how to grow in trust and obedience; that he is allowing the problem, which he understands very well, to work itself out in you; that he is praying about it. In fact the reasons for delay are myriad, all beautifully hidden from you to make you grow in faith and trust. Do you begin to see what I mean?

So when you go to a spiritual director in Madonna House, you have to *love, trust and obey*. Continue to be his spiritual directee no matter how far away in this world God might send you. That would be the sensible, the supernatural thing to do *if you really want to become saints and live the spirit of Madonna House perfectly*.

Now I want to discuss with you some reasons why you could sever connections with your spiritual director and seek another.

I must admit that there are few reasons for doing this. The first, of course, is if he tries to induce you to sin. This is an almost inconceivable idea, but one that may happen, because the Church has been entrusted to human beings and not to angels. Of course, if such a thing should occur, it is self-evident that you cannot possibly continue to be directed by such a man even though he is a priest.

Another reason: if you begin to realize that though there is no sinful situation at the moment, there might occur a situation which could be considered "an occasion of sin." Now don't jump immediately to the conclusion that this "occasion of sin" means sin against purity, or is necessarily concerned with sex. This, of course can happen if too great an intimacy or natural friendship develops. It normally doesn't, for the priest sees to it, if you don't, that this is kept in bounds. I presume that the members of Madonna House, especially the women, are aware of this, and are always very watchful.

I am not speaking only of these occasions of sin. Others may arise. One happened to me and this example may help you.

I had a very good spiritual director, a secular priest, and everything went along fine for a few months. Then I noticed that, for some reason or another, he began to ask *me* my advice on *his* spiritual life! At first I thought I was mistaken and allowed a few more months to pass. But it became evident that the situation was continuing, and I was becoming his involuntary spiritual director! Our roles were being reversed.

Because this was becoming an occasion of sin for me — pride — (nothing to do with sex, whatsoever), I severed the relationship. It would have been easy for me to convince myself to continue because he was paying me a great compliment. "The man supposedly knows my soul" (so my thoughts might run) "and he thinks I am good enough to advise him. Ho hum! I must be pretty good!" I saw the danger in time. Because I loved, trusted and obeyed the man, I told him why I was severing the connection, and he understood and agreed.

Some moral theology books give another reason for severing connections with a spiritual director: cessation of communications because of conflict. Personally I cannot fathom this possibility. To me this is unclear. I am not a moral theologian, but I look at it with the simplicity of faith.

Let us presume that your spiritual director does not go along with an idea that you think is 100% Gospel, and your communications break down. You're thoroughly persuaded that you should go to the right, and he thinks that you should go to the left. Here is where your trust and obedience should prevail. Without question, you go to the left. If God had wanted you to go to the right he would, in due time, have shown your director that this is so. In the meantime you will earn yourself untold merits, and win many souls for Christ by your obedience.

The story is told of Josefa, the holy Sacred Heart nun who is up for canonization. (She died in 1923, so she is our contemporary). Christ once appeared to her in the chapel, and told her to come back at recreation time. The Sister was very obedient. She revealed her soul (as in this case she should have done) to her superior, for that sort of phenomenon must be known to the superiors as well as to the spiritual directors.

The Mother Superior told her that she was sorry but they would be having a sewing bee on the uniforms of the young children. She could not go to the chapel. Sister Josepha went to the bee without a word. Later she met Christ in a corridor. He smiled and told her, "Had you come to the chapel against the will of your superior, I would not have been there." How much more is he ''not there'' when our wills and ideas clash with him in the priest to whom we have prayerfully entrusted our souls!

If communications have broken down between us and our spiritual directors, it behooves us to examine ourselves and not our spiritual director! Read the lives of the great saints and you will see that they obeyed spiritual directors who seemed to be bereft of any intelligence. Out of that obedience God brought tremendous results for themselves, and for the world around them. So I personally don't ''buy'' this excuse for severing relations with a spiritual director because of a conflict.

However, if things get so impossible that you can neither eat nor sleep then you have one last resort before severing your connection with a spiritual director. That is go to another priest known for his wisdom and sanctity. It should be someone whom you do not know socially, and preferably someone whom you have never met. When you have found this person you should tell him personally or if too far away, write the full details of your situation. Of course, be as objective as you can about your spiritual director, but then accept the decision of this priest as final.

Under no circumstances go to a priest whom you know through the Apostolate, or whom you knew before you came to Madonna House. He is already disposed in your favor. You want God's answer, purified of any human factor. What is at stake is your immortal soul. That should be worth everything to you!

I once had that sort of temptation. Rev. Paul Furfey, my spiritual director, was pretty harsh with me, and had put me in a corner which I did not like. So I sought other advice. And, what is the use of my lying to you: in my loneliness and self-pity I sought out a Dominican priest whom I knew well, whom I knew loved me very much, and who thought I was a pretty saintly Catholic woman. ''He,'' I said to myself, ''surely will understand the situation.'' So to him I went.

When I presented my case to him, he rose from his chair, got a bottle of holy water, blessed me with it, read a short exorcism over me to chase Satan away from my soul, and told me in no uncertain terms not to be such a damn fool and wreck my whole spiritual life by separating myself from Father Furfey! That I should go ahead and do what he told me — period. Then he gave me a cup of coffee. Now that's a sensible man!

At spiritual reading one day I presented the gist of this letter.

Fr. Brière* pretty much confirmed what I said, and added a few words of wisdom. What he said was very simple: you pray for a spiritual director, for someone whom you judge to be competent, and interested in you. Then you love, trust, and obey him, for he is Christ for you.

Fr. Bob Pelton contributed a very profound thought too. He said that competency is self-evident. The priest is trained for spiritual direction, has the grace of the sacrament of the priesthood, and is obviously interested in the salvation and sanctity of souls. But besides this you must enter into the mystery of the Incarnation.

A priest is not chosen for his personality, his intelligence, for his deep knowledge of theology, or for any other traits of person or intellect. He is chosen because he is the incarnation of Christ in this moment of spiritual direction. Fundamentally, you must pray for *faith* because you are *face to face with a mystery of our faith*. This mystery cannot be probed by reason, but must be accepted by faith.

One question came up in the discussion: What's the difference between counselling and spiritual direction? It's a good question because in Madonna House the priests, out of kindness, to both. Because of this confusion, our priests have now adopted a new technique. When they *counsel* you, they preface their counselling by saying, "I speak to you not as a spiritual director, but as a friend and counsellor in the natural order." When that part of the interview is over, and the spiritual part arises, they say, "Now listen, it is your spiritual director talking." Actually, no priest should do too much counselling; it confuses the directee. But because there is no one else to do it, priests do counsel. But now you will know the difference and that is good.

Lovingly yours in Mary,

*A Madonna House priest.

THE NATURE OF MEN

January 25, 1964

Deary Beloved,

A false and dangerous notion exists among the men and women of the Apostolate. It concerns relationships which have a seemingly spiritual motivation. Sometimes the person involved in a relationship with someone of the opposite sex *believes* that the motivation is spiritual (and it may be) especially at the beginning. The only thing that can be said about such a person is that he or she is very innocent or very ignorant — first of oneself, secondly of human nature, and thirdly of the devil and his power.

Because Madonna House puts great stress on "receiving everyone as Christ," or perhaps because this subject has not been discussed as fully as it should have been, the members of Madonna House may not have been alerted to the dangers that arise between men and women.

Let us be very clear when we speak, for instance, of men. We mean not only laymen; we mean also seminarians, Brothers, and priests. It often happens that women get the idea that they can solve the problems of men who come to Madonna House. They believe that they can "help" to straighten out their lives with the varied "bits of knowledge" that they have acquired in Madonna House.

This is dangerous. Actually, I could end this letter right now by simply giving a rule — a fundamental, axiomatic rule — and bluntly state that no single woman of any age can help any man, married or single. But that, I think, would not be sufficient, so let's go into the depths of the matter. Sister Mary Andrew, our psychologist friend, once explained very clearly that this is a psychological impossibility. She described the man's growth in general, and his sexual growth in particular. She explained that at the age of 18 months, a child of any sex recognizes the difference between the sexes. The male child knows that there is a being who is gentle and kind and loving who caters to his needs. At eighteen months he knows that this person is different from the other adult who fills his life, and who represents authority, law, strength and security.

As an aside, Sister mentioned that at her clinic she finds great damage done to babies two to three years old by the very fact that today the baby has difficulty in separating the sexes. Not only does the woman wear pants, but often the woman in the North American civilization is the figure of law, authority, strength and security without the corresponding warmth and tenderness. The child, therefore, is confused. Instead of having a mother and a father, he has two fathers. The man can never be for the child the nursing, female figure that the mother can. Bereft of the mother figure, his personality is already warped and sick at the ages of two or three.

She went on to say that between the ages of three to six (if all is normal up to then); the child will begin to be jealous of his father. He wants his mother for himself; wants to be the center of her interest, and he will compete for the attention of his mother. However, if the father pays great attention to him during this particular stage — plays with him, takes him for hikes etc. — this infantile jealously will soon change to great admiration and imitation of his father, and a normal balance will be restored.

Between the ages of six and nine the male child separates himself from his mother and attaches himself not only to the father, but to the gang. Now he still loves his mother very much, but he doesn't want any signs of affection from her. We all know *that* stage in a boy.

When the child reaches nine and goes on to twelve, he enters the calmest period in his life. He has now established good relations with his father and his mother, and with other boys. This is the time when he will accept girls and will play with them. Sex is dormant, and he considers women as a weaker counterpart of himself.

From the age of 12 onward to 21 or so, he enters the turbulent stage of the male. Because of his anatomy he becomes cognizant of sex. It bothers him very much. His organs grow, and he becomes very aware of them. However, he is unable to bridge the gap between himself and the other sex.

This is especially true between the ages of 12 and 16. It is a painful period in the development and growth of the male. Already, the signs of his maleness are apparent. He fully realizes the difference between the male and the female, and not only anatomically. He is deeply attracted to the opposite sex, and his habits change. We all know one sign: when he begins to care much more about his appearance!

If all goes well, and there is a good background in his home (psychologically speaking), plus a religious upbringing that has fully taught him to distinguish right from wrong, he will quite easily arrive at the stage when he is mature enough to marry.

Next, comes a very important point for us of the Apostolate. Sister showed very clearly how young men approach this marriageable stage. She also showed us how sex works in a man, according to his nature.

1. *Selectivity*. When a man is ready to marry, he consciously or unconsciously "selects". He might have a large group of female acquaintances and friends, but suddenly his eyes, as it were, are open to just one person in their midst. Or, he might enter a room and come upon a sea of female faces, but he will see only one, and the rest are as if they didn't exist.

This is wonderful *for marriage*. Nature has made it this way. But all of us, especially women, must recognize *that this selectivity in the man* is a natural, built-in tendency.

What does this mean for the Apostolate? Very simply, if any male (member of the community, visitor, a seminarian, a priest, a Brother, a married man) selects one person to tell his troubles to, to walk and talk with, or even to just be with in a group, and addresses all of his conversation to that one person, the women of the Apostolate must sit up and take notice. For this is the start of a dangerous situation which the man may not realize and neither does the woman. It is nature's way of leading towards sexual union with the selected one. Danger signals are all around, and they must be recognized as such. The woman must be aware of it immediately, and remove herself at once from this situation.

She must never, under any condition, imagine that she can "help" this particular male. No matter how innocent or spiritual the conversation, the built-in sexual pattern created by Mother Nature in man is already at work in the depth of his unconscious. Few men realize these things at the time.

2. *Protectiveness*. The second built-in preparation by Mother Nature is the male's tremendous desire to protect the one he has selected. His whole maleness is aroused. This, of course, is wonderful *for marriage*, for the husband must protect his wife and children.

How does this relate to a woman of Madonna House? Flattered by being selected, intellectually unaware of the dangers inherent in this selectivity, filled with illusions that she can "help" this person, she begins to bask in the protectiveness of this newly-acquired friend, or, as she sees it in all simplicity, a "person to be helped for Christ".

The nature of woman as described by Sister scientifically and psychologically, is *passive, dependent, in need of strength and protection.* You can see for yourself that a young woman of Madonna House, struggling with loneliness that is inherent in all life, and in all vocations (but at times becomes very acute in the vocation to a life of perfection) unconsciously surrenders to what is natural and normal for her — *the protectiveness of the male.*

What has begun as an unconscious illusion that she can help *him,* now continues in reverse. His protectiveness, his deep interest in her, still without any outward signs of what one calls "men-women relations," calls from her passivity and confidences. *Now* she has *a person* with whom she can talk, and to whom she can impart, still perhaps unconsciously, much more than what she originally planned. Her idea was to listen, console, to talk about God and the things of God — in a word, I repeat again and again, "to somehow help this man solve his problems and find God." But now she is telling him *her* problems, *her* difficulties, *her* needs.

You can see for yourself where this leads. At this stage, in the case of married people, priests, seminarians, and Brothers, the tragedy is already half begun. In the case of single, lay people, one can foresee (without using too much imagination) the forthcoming misery and tragedy.

If any one of these people is psychologically disturbed (and the majority of people who come to Madonna House are) then disaster is at hand. None of us are psychologists or psychiatrists. Can you realize the effects of these unconscious mechanisms (built in by nature) which are already at work and then compounded by psychological problems? Well, anything can happen! A priest can leave the priesthood; a seminarian can leave his seminary; a Brother can desert his vocation; a married man can leave his wife. But over and above these vocational problems, tragic situations such as suicide and scandal can occur. No matter which way you look at it, no good, whatsoever is effected. There can only be harm, tragedy, temptation and confusion — all works of Satan.

3. *Selectivity — Protectiveness*. Two natural steps which lead men and women to marriage now follow. The male will desire to touch, to hold, to look at the object of his selectivity and his protectiveness. This stage has two movements. First looking gently, touching the hand, maybe patting the head and so forth. They are still seemingly innocent gestures, but they are always precursors of sexual desires. It is only a matter of time and opportunity when the bonfire of sex will burst forth and burn sky-high. The first desire to possess will be expressed in a passionate embrace.

Again, I draw the attention of the female staff never to overlook the first two stages, selectivity and protectiveness. They will inevitably lead to the third stage when the damage will be done.

Sister explained that the above steps are normal for people called to the married life. Each of them is good, and if properly handled, will lead to marriage and be consummated there.

She then returned to the childhood and adolescent years of the male. She reviewed the fact that, generally speaking, the boy child and the adolescent love only themselves; especially this is true of the infant from birth to about school age. From school-age on, the boy-child does not yet love the other — his school chums, or the members of his gang etc. He is still in the infant stage; *he loves those who cater to his needs and pleasures*. It is still a form of self-love.

Love of the other begins to develop in adolescence. We see this in many young people who become interested in racial issues, in the poor etc. However, this love is still amorphous and not very well defined.

It is only when the selection of the opposite sex occurs that *true love of another comes forth in all of its vitality*. Now he doesn't matter to himself; *she* does. He truly loves her enough to "lay down his life for her!"

The same process takes place in the female child. She too reaches the moment when she "loves the other", and is ready to "lay down her life for him." After marriage, however, their love for each other matures immensely; the small stream becomes a river flowing into the sea of the children. Now both of them would really lay down their lives for the children.

As men and women mature in matrimony, their love begins to flow even further into the community. You see them becoming interested in other peoples' children. The father becomes a Boy

Scout leader, the mother helps with the Girl Guides. They also become interested in community improvements. Still, their love for these latter will be somewhat limited. Their first concern must be for their family, and only secondarily the community and the nation, and sometimes even international concerns. Now many families even go to mission lands! Beautiful and immense as the vocation of marriage is, it is still only one aspect of the immense Love who is a Person, and from whom all love flows.

The human person is capable of more. We are capable of opening our hearts to love — to the neighbor. Who is this neighbor? It is the world, composed of innumerable individuals who are in need. This universal love begins with *falling with love with Christ*, and for his sake, loving all people in the person of one's neighbor, and the neighbor is whoever comes to the door.

This universal love leads some men and women to forego the founding of their own family, and to engage in strengthening the whole family of humanity to whom Christ is wedded, and to do so for Love's sake, and for humanity's sake. These men and women are ready to lay their lives down for anyone. They have channeled all of their natural and supernatural powers — sex and everything else — into this immense universal river of love.

Instead of founding one family, they have given themselves to the family of humanity. In order to seal their universal, Christ-like love, their wedding with God, they have bound themselves by promises of poverty, chastity, and obedience. In this way they are utterly free. This is the foundation of the life of religious, of secular institutes, and of the thousands of thousands of lay people who have taken private vows.

Having presented this immense and wondrous picture of love, Sister then went on to say very powerfully and truthfully that, contrary to the common notion, that *genital, sexual expression is not essential to the full blossoming* of human life.

This truth cuts sharply across the conscious, subconscious and unconscious ideology of even some Catholics. We believe, secretly (we would not acknowledge it, perhaps) that all unmarried people are probably frustrated people, and that sex and marriage would cure their frustrations. The fact that three out of five marriages on the North American continent fail, doesn't seem to deter us from these false notions.

No, sexual union is not necessary to the rounding out of a human personality. The love of men and women has thousands of ways of fulfilling itself. The greatest, of course, is the way Christ as exemplified in the call of the rich young man. But many other people, for a greater cause, do not marry either. Some Communists forego marriage to be more dedicated. Many scientists, artists, philosophers, ascetics and holy men also forego marriage. Endless is the stream of men and women who have renounced sex and the founding of families for what they saw as a greater good.

Now, we in Madonna House have been called to this *universal love*. We have entered into it with our eyes wide open. We have been given a good preparation for it. At no time did anyone hide from us the pain of the Cross. We responded to God's call voluntarily and sincerely.

But it behooves us to *know our natures*, and to take care not to upset the delicate balance of our own lives and that of our Apostolate. So I would like to summarize what I have been discussing in this letter:

Men of the Apostolate

If you are drawn to selecting one person from among the opposite sex in the Apostolate, recognize what is happening. Stop right there! Discuss the matter with your spiritual director. Be alert! Pray! Fast! Be watchful! Natural danger is stalking you. Satan is seeking to use this chink for his own end.

If you feel protective towards any one of the opposite sex, you have already gone through one stage. Now the danger is real. Now, our natural rhythms are at work. Be frank and very watchful; pray and fast much. Satan has put a wedge into the chink.

Exactly the same applies to people outside of the Apostolate. You will be going to the missions. You will have to work with teenagers, young women, and middle-aged women; follow the same rule exactly. Be watchful for the same signs. (They apply to women as well.)

Never, never think that you can help a woman. Let the priest handle those situations. If a woman or girl seeks your help, hand her over to the nearest woman in your community. Honestly and simply tell her that you are not qualified to assist her.

Women of the Apostolate

More inclined by nature to be "helpful," all of the women of Madonna House must be alerted: *Never, never even try to help a male member of the staff or a man outside of the community, be he a priest, seminarian, Brother, or layman.* It is impossible that you can be of any help to him. It will inevitably lead to tragedy.

Never, under any circumstance, correspond with any member of the male sex on the pretext of "helping him out." Letters are dangerous, because we are more unhibited in letters. Also, they are written proofs of your relations with this person. Suppose that the person whom you are trying to "help" is psychologically unbalanced, or becomes vengeful when the chips are down, and you have to withdraw your friendship and support. Imagine if those letters were brought out publicly as well they might be. How many interpretations can be made of the written word, especially words carelessly written?

I personally know of a woman who was sentenced to life imprisonment because she wanted very much to "help" a married man. She was utterly innocent of any infidelity to her husband or of any sexual relations with the other woman's husband. But she was foolish; she wrote letters. When the wife of the other man was found murdered, the letters were found, and she was condemned (on the evidence of those letters) for the murder which she never committed! Eleven years later the true murderer confessed and she was released.

I leave to your imagination how utterly foolish, how completely dangerous letters may be, especially in the case of priests. You mean well. You try to help. You write. The priest suffers an accident, dies, or becomes ill. The pastor, the police, or some strangers get hold of your letters. Are they letters that any stranger can read? You meant well. But maybe you expressed yourself too freely, and the fat is in the fire!

So to sum up these two points: never imagine, in any way, that you can help a member of the opposite sex, whoever he is, refer him to priests or to other men, or to much older women. Under no condition carry on a correspondence with men, whoever they are. Don't get involved!

Watch for the feeling of "being protected" and of "being selected." Women respond to the selectivity of men. Never make a confidant of any male in the houses of the Apostolate. By this I mean long conversations, even in public. At no time "go for a walk" either on the city streets or in the countryside with any man whatsoever, even if he is old enough to be your grandfather — even if he is a bishop, a cardinal, or the Pope.

While we were discussing all of these things, one of the most saintly, holy, innocent members of Madonna House exclaimed at one point, "Gee, I'm glad to hear that! Last summer a young priest kept asking me to take a walk, and I quite naturally went without thinking anything of it. Nothing exceptional transpired, except that he was telling me about his problems and I didn't know what to do about them anyhow. But now, I ask myself why did he want to walk alone with me when there were plenty of chairs on the lawn where we could have talked. I also ask myself why did he want to discuss his problems with me who know so little of life?" Now, this person saw the light, and I hope you all will.

To sum up, relationship between men and women of the Apostolate must be holy, simple, embracing everybody, never selecting a single person for special confidence. *Do not try to help in any way members of the opposite sex, and never be alone with them.*

Lovingly yours in Mary,

OPENNESS

January 28, 1964

Dearly Beloved,

Again and again in letters and discussions I am requested to explain what openness is. It seems that this little word creates many difficulties.

Yet it is such a simple and clear word. We understand very well what it means when we say, "Mrs. Jones held an *open* house last Saturday on the occasion of the Silver Jubilee of her son, Father Jones." It simply means that the private house of Mrs. Jones was *open* to all who wished to come.

We are quite clear when we say that a contemplative Order held an *open* house on the occasion of the blessing of the premises by a bishop. It means that the hidden (and to us strange) premises of contemplative men and women, for once, are open to the public.

We understand that word when we speak of people who are *open*. You can read on their faces anything they think and feel, whereas others are closed. No one ever knows what they think. We speak, for instance, with warmth in our voices, of places that are "open to all in need." They admit the poor, pilgrims or anyone irrespective of race, color or creed.

In all of these cases the word "open" or "openness" conveys something positive, something pleasant, something warm and friendly, something that somehow we consciously or subconsciously associate with love.

Well, we are right. The heart of Christ was opened with a lance and the Church was born on Calvary. Brilliant or ignorant, all of us Christians understand the symbolic thrust of this lance into the heart of God. To all of us it means that God so loved us that he allowed his Heart to be opened in a painful and brutal manner, so that we might find shelter there. So "openness" must have its roots in love or it isn't openness. We must open ourselves for others to come in and see all the secret chambers of our being. We must open the house of our minds, souls, and hearts to the gaze, investigation and appraisal of others.

But the main topic I would like to discuss with you today is the openness of the members of Madonna House to their spiritual directors, to their superiors and to one another.

We begin with the premise that Christian openness *deals exclusively with oneself and not the other*.

Let us look at this truth in relation to each of the people mentioned above:

Spiritual Director:

Openness with a spiritual director must be utterly complete, without trying to hide a single corner of our inner selves — souls, hearts, minds, or bodies. How can I be close to my spiritual director? There are endless ways that our corrupt, human nature has devised. Let us discuss a few.

We can present a biased, one-sided picture of a situation. There are devious ways in which women, especially, can do this.

We can color everything the way we wish. It will not be the whole truth though it may appear to be.

A person can begin, for instance, by saying that she has a problem with obedience because the head of a department has asked her to do something which she considered stupid. Under the skillful questions of her spiritual director, it develops that the greater problem is not with obedience but with charity! Openness with a spiritual director means stating the facts truthfully and relying on his judgement.

When discussing another personality with a spiritual director, openness would demand that you ask that person to be present if the matter is grave, so that the other can hear the accusation. If you are in the missions that part of your letter to your spiritual director which deals with the specific accusations of anyone in your house should be read by the accused person, so that this person might have a chance to write to your spiritual director his or her side of the question. This would be openness.

Do not attempt to handle by yourself even the smallest temptation, considering it too picayune, too unimportant to bring to his attention. Verbally or in writing, if need be, state very little temptation. If you have a director you must be utterly open. Not the tiniest corner of your soul, mind or heart should be neglected. One grain of sand can stop huge machinery from working in a factory. A temptation that is insignificant today can ruin your vocation tomorrow, because you used your judgement wrongly and were closed to your spiritual director!

If the tragic moment arrives (and it may) when you feel ''out of tune'' with your spiritual director, that is the moment of danger. This is the time to be so utterly open and receptive that you go to him and state this situation in plain, brief sentences. *You must also be widely open to accept his judgement and his conclusions.* If you are open only in the presentation of your problem, and closed to its solution through this holy man, you are only half open and that means closed.

This is a very important part of openness and one of the hardest. Note that it always relates to you and not to the director. You are not asking the director to open his mind, heart and soul to you. That is his business. As a general principle you must always be open to others, but others must not necessarily be open to you.

So to clarify, when you have problems with a spiritual director, *you tell him what your problem with him is, not what you think is wrong with him.* There is a vast difference between the two approaches!

Director General

What is openness to a director general? It is the same openness that has been discussed in all of the previous pages, but it basically concerns the outer forum. The women of the Apostolate may if they so wish, open part of their souls to the director general, especially in that part of their behavior which affects others.

Every act has a moral significance. If one's inner problems begin to affect the common good, then, of course, I have a right to ask the person to discuss these problems with me more deeply. However, your openness should forestall my having to ask. You yourself should be ready to be open as every Christian should be.

You need to be open for your own spiritual and apostolic growth as well as the growth of the common good. Unless there is openness between the members and all of their superiors, direction is impossible and the common good suffers. I needn't point out how many times some tragic problems have exploded in my face and rocked Madonna House, because the members were not as open to me as they should have been. Again and again we have to pick up the pieces because of this lack of openness.

Why do you think that I have given you the obedience of writing to me twice a month? It is to make it easier for you to be open with me. It is because I love you and want you to be open in every way, but especially in wisdom and grace. This is why I desire passionately that you be open with me.

Here again I draw your attention to what openness is. It begins and ends with the words "I" and "me." You are open about yourself; you are not discussing others. You state only the facts about the others, never judging their intentions, ways of thinking or doing things.

If you have difficulty with another, you simply state the bare facts of that difficulty and leave the rest to God and your directors. But about yourself tell the fullness of truth without shame or reticence.

The same principles apply to the Local Directors and the Heads of Departments: at no time do you tell them what is wrong with *them.* That's not openness; that is criticism. If you have a just cause, you come to them and state in so many words, I'm sorry, I was a little upset about your order yesterday. Please tell me what is wrong with *me* that I feel this way.

If you have a matter of conscience relating to your Local Director or Head of a Department, examine *yourself* first. Write or speak to your spiritual director stating the facts about the other, and the facts, emotions, reactions about yourself, wait and be open for an answer.

If it is a matter that concerns both the inner and outer forum, write to your spiritual director (or speak to him if you are here) and to your Director General.

To One Another

Regarding your peers, you may choose different forms of openness. There is the ordinary openness of loving, friendly people banded together by love in an Apostolate tending towards perfection. What kind of openness is this? Well, again it pertains to *you* and only to *you*! You are quite free (and it would be a good idea and in keeping with openness) to tell your brothers and sisters all that is needful for them to know about you. You can tell them about your background, your family, your education, your skills and interests. But you cannot ask openness from them, nor can you probe to find out anything from them which they do not wish to reveal. We pray that everyone may come to the openness that I am describing in this letter, and that is the spirit of Madonna House. But always keep in mind that *openness is always about yourself, and not about the other*.

It is not necessary in the name of "openness" to tell your brothers and sisters the problems of your family, such as that your father is an alcoholic. Here again we come into a delicate field. Remember that openness is about *you*. So you don't have to discuss your parents.

The "confidential discussion" of the problems of someone else is as far removed from true openness as hell is from heaven. This kind of "openness" whose other name is gossip, is a sin against loyalty to Madonna House and Christian love. One doesn't gossip about, doesn't open the sores of confidential problems of the Apostolate. This is like probing Christ's wounds with dirty fingers. And, I repeat, it is as far removed from real openness as hell is from heaven.

There is an openness that you can exercise towards another to help that person. In the case of emotional problems we find that it helps the young ones who come to Madonna House when one of the seniors quite casually says, "Oh, yes, I also had those headaches when I first came. They are of emotional origin and I can tell you how I dealt with them. This type of openness is based on Christian love, compassion and empathy.

Spiritual Directors, Director Generals, Local Directors, Heads of Departments, and Directors of Training are the superiors of Madonna House. You must also understand that every superior is a person set apart by the very nature of their offices. Superiors have to lead and teach constantly both by word and example. Thus they have to teach about openness as well. But their openness is quite different from yours although somewhat similar.

How should they be open? Well, in the same way as you must be open. As Thomas Merton says, "They must be humbly open about their shortcomings and their personal difficulties with you.

I am as open as a Director General could possibly be. If my spiritual director permitted me, I would make a general confession to you, and I mean a confession of *all* my sins. I certainly do not try to hide my shortcomings, my difficulties, nor do I hesitate to apologize when I am wrong. I have opened my soul, heart and mind in my books and articles. Now you are going to get the *History of the Apostolate** which has been one of the most painful things for me to write. That is because I had to be, in obedience, utterly open with you in this History. This is the type of openness that your directorate and your superiors must have with you. And that is the way that you must be when you become a superior.

But God help the superior if he or she has the wrong kind of openness — an openness that comes from their needs, an openness that puts the problems of superiors on the not yet strong enough shoulders of the young. It behooves the superiors to keep much to themselves.

I don't know if I have clarified openness for you. The essence of it is that one talks about oneself and not about the others. So two members discussing what is wrong with another are completely *off base*. To discuss one's own shortcomings is to be "on the beam" — Christ's beam.

Likewise, someone telling a superior what is wrong with him or her is way off base, and not in the spirit of the Apostolate. If

---

*At this time Catherine was beginning to write the History of Friendship House and Madonna House.

there is something really wrong, they have the ways I have described for dealing with the matter.

Lovingly yours in Mary,

[signature]

THE FRAGILE VIRTUE OF CHASTITY

February 21, 1964

Dearly Beloved,

My letter on *Men and Women in the Apostolate* evidently made you think, and clarified for you this area of our Apostolate. Even if this might be repetitious, I want to state once more that that letter was based on scientific facts as presented by Sister Mary Andrew, a Doctor of Psychology. Its main purpose was to make especially the men of the Apostolate (but the women as well) realize that the physical make-up of a man tends to union with a woman long before he is aware. In other words, it means that the natural, bodily rhythms of a man are ahead of his conscious self. This is a fact little known to the average layman and one to remember. These rhythms, begin with *selection*, continue into *protectiveness*, and then reach the conscious stage of wishing to be close to the person whom he likes.

People under a promise of chastity should be aware of this and *not indulge in selectivity, or in the protectiveness of a person of the opposite sex*. The women of the Apostolate, realizing this, must remove themselves from such subconscious selectivity and protection, thereby helping men not to be tempted against the virtue of chastity.

But this does not mean that a man should not ''protect'' every women in the Apostolate. This is part of his being a man. But note the difference: *his protectiveness is directed to all.*

However, our call to chastity means much more than this. Stop for a minute and meditate on the meaning of our chastity prayerfully, especially before the Blessed Sacrament. We will see once more how the immense Wisdom of God never leaves his Church, his Mystical Body, in times of trials and difficulties, but always answers her needs.

Consider our world today. Reams have been written, and are still being written about sexual immorality. Rome at its decline doesn't seem to have been as decadent as our modern, so-called "Christian civilization" is today. Hindus, Muslims, members of pagan religious of Asia, Africa and so-called "backward countries" are simply horrified at the moral decline in Europe, England, and the North American continent. There is more morality and obedience to moral laws in pagan countries than in so-called Christian ones.

The worship of sex and the "body beautiful" is reaching proportions of idolatry. The allied vices of drunkenness, drug addiction, juvenile delinquency, illegitimacy and emotional disturbances have risen to epidemic proportions.

It is a sad state of affairs that we behold. Gently, Christ bends down to his Church in distress, and calls forth some of its members (now already in the thousands) to a new apostolate — a remedy for this idolatry.

He calls into being the various forms of the lay apostolate. He obviously wants to show a chaste, dedicated youth to a world drunk with immorality and self-indulgence. He wants them to live this dedication of chastity right in the marketplaces of the world.

There is an interesting dimension to this call of Christ. Have you noticed that he often calls very attractive men and women? Again his wisdom shines. For if the members of such apostolates were only unattractive men and women, the world would not take notice of them.

No, God is wise. He chooses the best as ambassadors of his beloved virtue of chastity. So, each one of you, my dearly beloved, has been chosen to manifest that virtue in the marketplace. This virtue is so much needed to counteract the idolatry of sex in our day and age. *What a responsibility! What a glorious task!*

I hope that you are beginning to see that this promise of

chastity is vitally important to the Apostolate and to bring souls back to a sense of balance in a world drunk with sex.

You are good; you love God. I feel certain that you desire to serve him in this beautiful and chaste way. However, you are young and inexperienced. You might be innocent as doves, but you are not yet "as wise as serpents." So I write these letters to clarify, to warn and to encourage.

I have already written to you that under no circumstances should young men and women imagine that they can be of any help to a member of the opposite sex of their own age group. But to the women of the Apostolate, I add this warning: they cannot be of help to *any man* no matter what his age or his state in life. This is beyond their competence. They have no graces from God to do so. They must not even try, for it might be an occasion of sin, or even worse, an occasion of scandal.

We hear of influence that our members have on married people, teenagers, the seminarians, and priests. It is a power that comes to them from God and their own cooperation with his grace, and flows from their promise of chastity.

Parents have found us wonderful examples for their children. Seminarians take heart at the mere mention of Madonna House and all seem to say, without saying it directly, "If they can be chaste, so can we."

I need not paint you a picture. Suppose one of our members spent a long time with a member of the opposite sex, sitting alone in a kitchen, drinking coffee, talking about God, and the things of God. You and I know that there is not a shadow of impurity in that meeting. But what do other people see.

Many depend upon some of you for moral support. Perhaps because of you they can fight temptations to adultery and fornication. Then suddenly their lifetime seems to snap because they question *your* chastity. Can you imagine their disappointment? You would be responsible for their doubts.

Chastity is a fragile virtue. It must be guarded. We of the Apostolate must be especially aware of what it means to the world today. What a beacon of light we are supposed to be! Yes, the love and wisdom of God bent with tenderness over the world and called us to show the face of chastity in the marketplace. Chastity is one of the jewels in the crown of virtues which the world needs.

So, dearly beloved in Christ, knowing your innocence, knowing that you do not want to convey these false impressions, knowing that you are pure of heart, I implore you to be watchful, to think seriously and deeply whenever you are dealing with a member of the opposite sex. Try never to be alone with him in a separate room or even in a place full of people. Never allow a shadow of disappointment to enter the hearts of those who watch, and to whom your indiscreet action may be the last straw for one who is tempted.

God love you. I do.

Lovingly yours in Mary,

BOREDOM AND SOCIAL AMENITIES

February 24, 1964

Dearly Beloved,

Today I would like to discuss boredom and good manners.

There are some amongst us who occasionally or for long periods feel a sense of boredom. Do you know what boredom is? It is a kind of death in a human being. It means that people have let their interior resources dry and reach a sort of coma that is akin to death.

It means that their motivation is at an absolutely low ebb. Boredom is a forerunner of emotional problems, or even mental and emotional breakdowns. It may lead to alcoholism or to drug addiction in an effort to escape that sense of uselessness and failure.

A man dreams in his youth that he will achieve great things, and then he gets a job on a production line where for eight hours a day he keeps putting a bolt into a hole. He gets bored. He never sees the completion of his work. He feels that he is not contributing anything to anybody. He is just a cog in a machine. It will become worse in our computerized society. A man will just sit before a panel and push buttons!

Our industrial, technological society creates this monotony. It is understandable that under such conditions anyone would be bored. However, when a *nurse* becomes bored with her work, when a *teacher* becomes bored with hers, when a priest is bored with being a priest, or a lay apostle of Madonna House is bored with being a lay apostle, then his or her motivation has fallen asleep. The breath of Satan is upon that person.

I ask you, how can I be bored writing personal letters to you day in and day out when I love you? How can I be bored teaching the shining truths of God, even to the half-listening ears of the youth? It is not possible! It is impossible to be bored when you are in love with God. Those of us who have become bored have either ceased to love or are in danger of ceasing to be *in love*. This would be a first step to a break-up of the family.

Granted, we live in routine; we get up at a certain tme; we eat at a certain time; we pray at a certain time, we work at a certain time. There are always the same things to do and that becomes monotonous.

We try to escape this monotony through privacy through some kind of break in constantly dealing with the public. These breaks are provided by retreats, days of recollection, holidays, and other ways. But that boredom should enter the mind, heart and soul of a member of Madonna House is hard for me to imagine, unless he or she is beset with temptations; unless Satan is present whispering his weird half-truths.

How is it possible to be bored when we believe the marvelous words of St. Paul *that we can make up what is wanting in the sufferings of Christ!* In his infinite mercy God calls us through grace to become *co-redeemers of the world with him!*

Do you realize this, dearly beloved, that you are co-redeemers with Christ? He has given you this immense power. This seemingly greyish routine of ours isn't grey at all, but resplendent with light, or at least it is in our power to make it so.

How does this work, in our daily lives? If my secretary sitting here typing letters, offers the tiring, routine job of hitting the keys hour after hour under my dictation then she is co-redeeming the world with Christ. The men, by getting up in the morning, performing ordinary routine jobs such as repairing things, driving and cleaning can save souls from the jaws of hell. The women working in the kitchen making the "eternal stew" can bring joy and can bring joy and hope to others.

How in the name of the All Holy can one become bored with this typing, the meat cutting, this potato peeling, this fixing and cleaning; with endless repetitive routine jobs if one knows in faith that everything helps to redeem the world and to render glory to God.

Stop for a moment and think of a member of M.H. being bored. Isn't it incomprehensible in the light of what I have just written? The answer should stare you in the face. This person has allowed his or her love of God and others to sink into a coma. The remedy is prayer, fasting, spiritual reading, retreats, days of recollection and the *examination of our consciences.* Boredom spells danger to the soul. Satan is there!

Now I want to speak of ordinary, social manners. They include posture, ways of sitting, ways of eating, certain niceties such as men opening the doors for women, carrying their parcels and so on. In Madonna House educational or so-called "class backgrounds" of people do not matter at all. Scripture says that God is not a respector of persons. But we do place great value on charity as you all know.

You may not know which fork to use for salad, but charity will make it very simple. Without false shame, you will simply acknowledge that you don't know and you will ask. If you have been used to eating food with your knife, you will soon desist because you will see that no one else does; but you will realize especially that it makes people tense. You can cut yourself and it isn't charitable to make people tense.

Posture is an important part of the Apostolate. A saint teaches by the way he sits, stands and walks. Let that be a lesson for you. Think of how a saint would sit, stand or walk and do likewise. Again charity demands that you assume a posture that doesn't offend others.

Besides these social amenities good manners consists in being concerned about the others.

Neither is it good manners to engage in arguments, and you know what I mean when I say arguments. I don't mean discussions or dialogue in which you can learn from others by exchanging ideas politely, charitably and peacefully. By argumentiveness

I mean that you are holding onto your own ideas no matter what. The discussion becomes heated, unpleasant and uncharitable. We do not argue in this manner because it is uncharitable.

Politeness and good social manners really stem from love. Your concern should be for the other person. So please note this, for this is a very important part of our Apostolate. Being concerned about others should be for you like breathing. Can you imagine Our Lady, like a lump, sitting with her two elbows on the table and taking no part in the conversation? Can you? I can't. Doesn't the Gospel give you a tremendous picture of the graciousness, gentleness, and good manners of Christ, and I'm sure Mary was like him.

In spirit go to Nazareth! And then act in our houses as if you were in the presence of Jesus, Mary and Joseph, and you will automatically be a gentleman and a gentle woman.

Love in Christ, the Gentleman,
and in Our Lady, the Gentle
Woman,

Catherine

ON BEING MISJUDGED

February 27, 1964

Dearly Beloved,

I have had several people write to me about problems of general interest, so I will answer these questions all together. They concern *justifications, misunderstandings and free time.*

Let us begin with *justifications.* Again and again I have stressed the fact that we must not justify ourselves. This attitude is substantiated by Scripture, especially by Christ's silence during his Passion.

I agree with you that it is a bit difficult to know when to justify oneself and when to keep silence when corrected. It is especially difficult if one greatly desires as we all should to strive for perfection.

Let us look at the dictionary. "Justify: to show, to be just, to vindicate, defend; also to make right and just, to adjust or fit, to make exact." The synonyms of this word are "absolve, acquit, approve, authorize, clear, defend. Then it goes on to say "there might be sometimes excuses which cannot be justified. For that which can be justified does not need excuses." Let's look at this last sentence and many things will be immediately clear to us.

That which can be justified does not need to be excused. This is a peaceful, loving approach to life. Let's take an example. Your local director, or anyone for that matter, accuses you of failing to live our vocation. This might be true. So you thank them and say that you will try to do better for you know that every Christian can always do better. Until we die we can always improve.

On the other hand this accusation might *not* be true. You are trying your best at the moment which is all that anyone can do. In that sense you are not a bad member of Madonna House; but you will become a bad one if you start to justify yourself.

The accusation may also be unjust, but in this case you will have great merit if you simply remain silent. Because God is working in his or her soul as well, eventually the person will either apologize to you, or if this isn't done you will grow in sanctity and grace. You will be more like Christ than you have ever been before.

Let's take another example. You have been told to take charge of some event in a house. There will be a party or some affair at which there will be priests and lay people, and you are put in charge of it all. You are also preparing dinner for the family.

You do this with a happy heart believing that you are managing it all very well. Then, when everything is over and the director of the house returns, you report to her in a nice way satisfied that you have managed so many things at once; *you appear to stress the fact that you managed the kitchen well*. The director gets the idea that you were occupied in the kitchen to the neglect of the guests and reprimands you. Here, very simply and trustingly like a child you explain to her how it was, not with the intention of justifying yourself, for there is nothing to justify; it is a misunderstanding. You say that evidently you expressed yourself poorly, for in your heart the kitchen didn't matter; you were just glad that all went well. This is an explanation, not a justification, because here was nothing to justify or excuse; all did go well. Your director didn't understand you. Make yourself clear.

Suppose she still doesn't understand you. Well, here you rejoice! Now you think of the Eighth Beatitude. It becomes almost a false accusation of course, that depends again on her intention. She might be positive in her mind that she understands you rightly, but you couldn't care less because you have made the effort to explain the semantic difficulty and you rest on that. You will win graces and the director eventually will come to the same conclusion in God's time, and all will be well.

If you are accused of something that you didn't do, you have two choices, spiritually speaking: you can simply state the truth which again is not justification in the exact sense of the word, but a statement of the truth or you can remain silent and take the gaff. This latter is considered heroic in the spiritual life, and very commendable.

You see how hard it is to answer your questions, because we are dealing with intangibles. You do not justify yourself; you "make just right and," that is, you straighten out a misconception. However, if it concerns you alone, you might take the high road of heroism and be silent.

To justify yourself wrongly would be something like this. I come into the kitchen and find a messy table. I "blow my top" at the person in charge of the kitchen. If she starts giving me excuses that she had told the girls to do it, that the men came in and messed it up, that is a wrong justification of oneself; because being the person in charge, *she is responsible to see that the mess is cleaned up no matter who did it or what happened.*

To give you an example from real life, I was in Ottawa, founding the Friendship House there when I got a long distance call from the secretary of the Cardinal in Toronto to come to his office immediately. Naturally I went at once. In the meantime I found out that one of the volunteers who had been highly recommended to us by a well-known monsignor had gone berserk. She had gotten drunk, had collected a lot of beer bottles and gone to the Polish rectory and smashed the windows.

I was in Ottawa; I had nothing to do with it. The person in

charge of the Toronto House was officially responsible, but I knew better than to say so to the Cardinal. He wiped the floor with me and rightly so *because I was the highest authority, and bore the brunt of the responsibility.* I took it unflinchingly, and when he was finished I handed him the letter of the Monsignor in order to "make just and right" the situation without defending myself, and he apologized.

Now when anything of this type occurs to you, say the name of Jesus and consider in your heart: will my answer make things "just and right?" Am I alone accused and do I wish to be heroic and silent? Act accordingly.

Since "justify" also means "to defend" you *always defend the other person, if there is an occasion to do so.* Some member of the family accuses another of something that they have not done and you know it. It is your duty to speak up. I know that I haven't done a very good job of explaining this, but it is difficult business. The *key lies* in your intention, but at no time should it worry or upset you. You should always be in perfect peace about it. It is the lack of peace that can damage souls.

About "misunderstandings" the dictionary says, "to understand wrongly, to fail to understand, to disagree." Here we enter the realm of psychology more than that of theology. Consider that misunderstandings mean to "understand wrongly, or fail to understand." Why do we fail to understand? Mostly it is because we hear what we want to hear, and see what we want to see. Our powers of perception are very often limited by our emotional state. Semi-consciously or unconsciously, we select what we want to see and hear.

Most misunderstandings arise because of this. In addition we "project ourselves." I had an example of this one morning at a meeting of the department heads. One of the members had been slowing very much on her job, and I suggested that since we all love her, let us work together to help her to speed up.

There was a moment of silence, but none of the seniors seemed to think well of my suggestion. We had a little discussion. It wasn't too important, but it became immediately apparent that none of them wanted to move in, because all of them, at one time or another, have also slowed down under emotional stress. They were all sitting there projecting themselves as if they were that person, and reacting to my suggestion, not as she would react (that was an unknown quantity) but as they would react if they were she. We clarified the matter speedily. But here was the beginning of many misunderstandings, had it not been clarified.

These emotional reactions are at the bottom of most misunderstanding in the Apostolate. Of course, there is also the desire to be well thought of, to put one's own point across, and to be approved by everyone.

We can also use *wrong words* to express our ideas so that people misunderstand and ideas not not clearly shared. A third reason which we should fight constantly is an emotional dislike of one person or another. As you know by now, there is a big difference between "like" and "love". Here, our emotional prejudices must give way to caritas.

Now to the question of *charity and our free time*. Let us say that you have an hour or two off, or an afternoon or a morning. You are faced with the following possibilities in the order of charity:

You know that your local director needs help in some way or another; you know that one or more members also need help of some sort; you are interested in doing something on your own free time for the gift shop or to beautify the house. Perhaps you feel that you should do some pressing correspondence.

You make a choice and let us say that you are on your way to do some copper work for the gift shop. Another member meets you and knows that you have time off, and asks you to translate a Latin Hymn. You finish that and someone asks you to look up some symbols for him.

So what are the demands of charity in this example? Frankly, there is no one who can tell you this. This is where your free will has to make its own decision. However, if I were asked to give an order of charity, the hospitality to guests takes precedence over everything else. The local director's needs must be met if they are urgent. The needs of the other members who ask me to do this or that should be carefully examined and perhaps I would say that I was very sorry, but that I had an urgent letter to write. Urgent letters to parents and immediate relatives would come next. The gift shop would be the next step. Other letters would come after that.

But I would not be worried at all if I didn't follow this sequence, because the free time that belongs to me by the grace of God and his mercy is at his disposal, and no matter what I do, if I have the intention of loving, I have done the right thing.

I hope that this clarifies the latter for those who have asked me. If not, let me hear from you.

Lovingly yours in the
Lord of Wisdom,

[signature]

LOYALTY AND LETTERS

March 6, 1964

Dearly Beloved,

Today I want to discuss letter writing within the Apostolate.

You come to Madonna House as working guest. You become a Visiting Volunteer, an Applicant, and eventually a member of Madonna House, if this is your vocation. You find that in Madonna House you meet many people. You meet lay people, bishops, priests and seminarians. Madonna House is a crossroads of the world and you meet people from many countries.

Because of the nature of our Apostolate, visitors of all types may happen to talk to one member of Madonna House more than to anyone else. Perhaps they will get to know one of you better than they know the others. That makes them feel ''in,'' especially if they know several of you well. That's understandable, for all those who come to us are usually predisposed to like us. They come for information about the Apostolate. They do not always differentiate your status here. They do not know whether a person is a guest or a member of Madonna House. They group you all together as part of this lovable whole that is Madonna House.

I don't want to offend you at all, but just to state the obvious truth: if they had met you, young and inexperienced as you are, outside of Madonna House, it might be that they would not pay any attention to you. You can't imagine a bishop casually meeting someone, becoming interested in them and remembering them. This would be outside of a bishop's normal dealing with the laity.

If you would chance to visit at the home of people who come here, you wouldn't expect to be invited after a couple of visits like that, to address the Christian Family Movement. No one would think that you were qualified to do that. But as members of the Apostolate of Madonna House, bishops and priests, seminarians and married people would listen with interest and respect to your opinions, *especially on the Apostolate, its foundations and goals.*

You will find also that if you go to a mission house where there are few members of Madonna House, where there is a homey atmosphere, and where it is easy for people to know you individually, all of the above will be enhanced. I'm sure that people will like you for yourself because you are likeable; but do not make the mistake of thinking that this is the only reason why people are kind, interested, and inquiring. You are important to them *because you are members of an Apostolate — a whole with which they totally identify you.*

Should you leave the Apostolate, the reactions will be different. If you try to keep contact with the people whom you met through the Apostolate, you will find out that people will keep their allegiance to the Apostolate. Though they might like and sympathize with you, your relationship with them will eventually peter out. For what attracted you to them in the first place was that you sold what you possessed, took up your cross, and followed Christ in a rugged, lay apostolic way.

Be that as it may, you may have to get it into your lovely heads that you have made these friends not as an individual in your own right, but as a member *of an Apostolate*. What you write to the friends you have made through the Apostolate is a reflection not only on you personally but on the Apostolate as well.

Let us take, for example, the case of a member who has been in one mission house and made many friends. She is then transferred to another house. Let us presume, for sake of an example, that this person is, humanly speaking, not happy about it, but obeys anyhow. During the time of readjustment she goes through all kinds of emotional stages. She lacks the desire to express it to her spiritual director and to her superiors. So she proceeds to write about her emotional states and reactions to those friends of the

Apostolate whom she considers individual friends.

What is the reaction of those friends outside of the Apostolate? You as members may not know the reactions, but we of the directorate do. These people write to us or they simply go to the local director of the former mission house. They bring your letters with them and discuss them. They wonder why you do not seem as dedicated as they thought you were, or they demand explanations and want to know why you are being so badly treated. They explain that now they are getting the real "low-down" on the Apostolate a look behind the scenes.

Be that as it may, this sort of thing does not do the Apostolate or you any good. So please do not use the friends whom you made in the Apostolate to give vent to your emotional problems, difficulties or black moods.

Do not tell them anything that they should not know about the Apostolate. Such letters would be disloyal to the Apostolate, which means to God. Pray over it, and be very careful not to harm God's works, for this is one thing that arouses God's just anger. And who wants to enter the awesome anger of God?

Lovingly yours in Jesus Christ our Lord,

SEEDS OF LOVE AND FORGIVENESS

July 2, 1964

Dearly Beloved,

Recently I received several letters from one of our staff in the East. Her letters made me stop and think. She raises some profound missionary questions. One concerns the whole Moslem missionary apostolate. The other concerns adaptation to the East. Here are my answers:

"Yes, I understand exactly how you feel about Moslem country. True they have a missionary spirit. They are zealous, loyal and true to their religion. They believe in God; they revere Mary. Christ to them is a great prophet. The roots of our faith grow from the same biblical soil. In other words, Judaism, Christianity and Islam have a common father in Abraham, and the Bible is revered by both. In a sense the Old Testament is the mother of the Koran as it is the mother of the New Testament.

"But I would say that Islam is still in the process of development as far as religion is concerned, much as the Jews were for thousands of years. The Jews *expected* the Messiah, but Islam, when the Messiah came, *acknowledged* him only as a prophet. So they are marching over longer roads. The beginning of Christianity for them will have to be the belief that *God has come — has been incarnated among us* — that the real Messiah has come to them even though their belief in Mohammed has blurred his Image. Yet they believe in Allah, the one true God. In centuries to come there will be changes, but note the words I use *in centuries to come*. That means that we who have been so strangely called to the Divine History are little signposts of the truth that God has come. That makes our little seed of belief that Jesus is God even smaller than a mustard seed.

"Yes, there is this to consider and meditate upon, but as far as you are concerned, there is more. In your case that *more* is a very special grace from God! You are called to exemplify in your person, not only hiddenly, but also vividly and obviously, Christ's greatest commandment of all: 'Love thy neighbour as thyself.' However, in a few cases like your good self, the Lord asks you to go higher, and to *love your enemies!* Moslems have been the enemies of your people; they have murdered and martyred your people for generations. Your people, emotionally speaking, have for centuries harbored in their unconscious and conscious life a great fear and an emotional hatred for them.

"You are asked now to till the soil of these Moslems souls and to plant the tiny seeds of love. The furrow that you are beginning will be long, and you will not realize how long until you see God face-to-face. That furrow will extend for generations. Members of Madonna House will, in turn, plant seeds of their lives in that mission which you are pioneering.

"That is what I see without even visiting your house. This is what my intuition tells me about you and the Moslems. Strangely, I rejoice that this is so! That one of my spiritual daughters is so clearly, so simply called by the Lord to love her *enemies*. You will do this simply "by being among them, and witnessing to the fact that Jesus is not only a Great Prophet, but he is Allah himself! They will come to see that Allah is One in Three and Three in One.

"Look at your vocation and your mission in this world — with the eyes of God. It is already resplendent in glory in proportion to your perseverance and your understanding. You have been called to a tremendous task. I envy you with holy envy".

She told me also that she had met a certain nun who had lived in India for a long time and whose Order still had no vocations. She has been confronted by religious and laity and even by the police with this one question: "How long have you been in the country, and how many vocations have you?" She said that invariably she had to answer that she had been in India for twelve years, but that as far as any native vocations were concerned, there were none. Her Order was replenished from the West.

That nun didn't mind any personal humiliation that she experienced nor the reflection that seemed to be cast upon her Order. What worried her was that the whole Roman Catholic Church was not adapting to India. She knew that there would be many vocations if this adaption was made.

One reason for the lack of vocations she said is that her Order is a very modern and a very active one, though they have a contemplative side. It so happens, the Sister went on to say, that *the active life has never* impressed the East. Ghandi, among others, was tremendously impressed by a Trappist monastery which he saw in Africa.

Another problem that the Sister mentioned was the fallacy of sending native vocations to Europe, Canada, or to the United States for training. None who were sent persevered because the cultural gap was too great.

I agree fully with that nun. Yet, I feel that our Apostolate must be active; yet, also we must be contemplatives. How do I reconcile these two in our Eastern missions?

Very simple. All of us in Madonna House must be contemplative in the sense that I try to express in all of my writings.

Perhaps this sense of contemplation has a Russian accent, but nevertheless, it blends with the rest of the East, for we Russians are predominately people of the East particularly in the religious sense.

But over and above our all being contemplatives, we should in future times have a truly contemplative, Eastern-Type, hidden, quiet, inactive community or group. This is how I visualize it. There may be a center there some day when our mandate is clarified. And next to them, in days to come, living poorly, humbly, yet not quite in the destitution of those around them, there will be a group that will pray and do penance. They will earn their living at handicrafts, so dear and beloved by the East, and be hidden as Charles de Foucauld was in the desert, as the Russian saints were in the Poustinia. Yet they will be as hospitable and available as these others were to those who come to talk to them about God and the things of God.

Yes, dimly but clearly, I foresee that some day this will take place for Madonna House is always open flexibly and pliantly to new ideas or to traditional ideas in new settings. We must always remember that charity, hospitality, and availability are our foundations and that there are thousands of ways of crying the Gospel with our lives.

Lovingly yours in Mary,

BIBLIOGRAPHY

Dear Bishop. Milwaukee, Wis: Bruce Publishing Co. 1947.

Apostolic Farming. Madonna House Publications 1980.

Dear Father. Alba House, New York, 1979. New Edition Madonna House Publications — 1988.

Dear Seminarian. Milwaukee, Wis.: Bruce, 1950 — Reprinted Madonna House Publications 1986.

Dear Sister. Milwaukee, Wis.: Bruce, 1953.

Doubts, Loneliness, Rejection. New York: Alba House, 1981.

Fragments of My Life. Notre Dame, Ind.: Ave Maria Press, 1979.

Friendship House. New York: Sheed & Ward, 1946.

Gospel of a Poor Woman. Denville, N.J.: Dimension Books, 1981.

Gospel Without Compromise. Notre Dame, Ind.: Ave Maria Press, 1976.

I Live On An Island. Notre Dame, Ind.: Ave Maria Press, 1979.

Journey Inward. New York: Alba House, 1984.

Lubov. Locust Valley, N.Y.: Living Flame Press, 1985.

Molchani. New York: Crossroads, 1982.

My Heart and I. Petersham, Mass.: St. Bede's Publications, 1987.

My Russian Yesterdays. Milwaukee, Wis.: Bruce Publishing Co., 1951.

Not Without Parables. Notre Dame, Ind.: Ave Maria Press, 1976.

Our Lady's Unknown Mysteries. Denville, N.J.: Dimension Books, 1979.

People of the Towel and the Water. Denville, N.J.: Dimension Books, 1978.

Poustinia. Notre Dame, Ind.: Ave Maria, 1975.

Sobornost. Notre Dame, Ind.: Ave Maria, 1977.

Soul of My Soul. Notre Dame, Ind.: Ave Maria, 1985.

Strannik. Notre Dame, Ind.: Ave Maria, 1978.

Urodivoi. New York: Crossroad, 1983.

Where Love Is, God Is. Milwaukee, Wis.: Bruce Publishing Co., 1953.

Translations to other languages not included.

APPENDIX

THE WRITINGS OF CATHERINE DOHERTY

POUSTINIA

Poustinia is the Russian word for desert. Catherine leads us into a deeper dimension of prayer based on the Christian Spirituality of the East. She speaks of the Journey Inward which every soul must arise and take into the Heart of her Beloved. Over 100,000 copies of this moving book have been printed. Truly a Spiritual Classic.
ISBN 0-87793-083-X

FRAGMENTS OF MY LIFE

In this book Catherine tells the story of her life, not the purely factual, but, rather, the story told through her interior vision of how God has led and molded her through her more than fifty years of apostolic life.   ISBN 0-87793-194-1

SOUL OF MY SOUL

Catherine shares some of her writings over the years on prayer. It is not a book on how to pray, but a book on becoming a prayer.
ISBN 0-87793-298-0

DOUBTS, LONELINESS, AND REJECTION

This is a book which speaks to our human anguish and how to find meaning in the Passion, Death, and Resurrection of Christ.
ISBN 0-8189-0419-4

SECRETS OF THE HEART

Catherine's poetry and conversations with her Beloved—a 3-volume series.

JOURNEY INWARD

This first volume is taken from Catherine's poetry. It reflects her interior journey over many years. This book, with its moving images and haunting revelations, captures the simplicity and the mystery of our union with the Lord of love. Both the intense joy and pain of the inner life are opened to us from Catherine's own experience.   ISBN 0-8189-0468-2

LUBOV: THE HEART OF THE BELOVED

Lubov: the Russian word for love. In this second volume, Catherine presents her life, her deepest interior conversations with God. She never wrote these for publication. They were poured forth, in silence, into the heart of the Beloved. Now Catherine shares them with us.   ISBN 0-914544-60-8

MY HEART AND I

This is the third volume of Secrets of the Heart. Anyone who ever met Catherine knew that she possessed a spiritual personality with many facets. It can be seen that she, like St. Paul, became all things to all men for the sake of the Gospel. What is it that goes on in the soul of a person that brings her to such a state of spiritual greatness? Read and see. ISBN 0-932506-59-3

PRIESTHOOD

DEAR FATHER

This book springs from Catherine's heart as a profound message of love for priests. It reveals the depths and heights of the priesthood. In this revised edition, several new chapters have been added from writings of Catherine which were not, until now, available. The vocation of the priest in the Lay Apostolate is unfolded. The book is inspiring for both priest and lay person.

ISBN 0-921440-00-6

DEAR SEMINARIAN

Catherine's wisdom for those preparing for the priesthood. It is quickly becoming a light on the path of Bishops, Priests, and Seminarians. Truly a message for the priest in the church of today and tomorrow. Because Catherine's understanding of the priesthood springs from a deep faith in Christ in the priest, it will always be a timeless book. ISBN 0-921440-05-7

THE LITTLE MANDATE

THE MOST IMPORTANT SPIRITUAL LEGACY CATHERINE HAS LEFT THE APOSTOLATE. *Journey to the Lonely Christ* and *Love Love Love* are the beginning of a series, which will be explored for years to come.

JOURNEY TO THE LONELY CHRIST

by Fr. Robert Wild

An exploration of the essence of the Spirit of Madonna House as found in Catherine's writings. The first of three volumes.

ISBN 0-8189-0-509-3

LOVE LOVE LOVE

Volume II of the Spirit of Madonna House as found in Catherine's writings. by Fr. Robert Wild

---

Tumbleweed
by Eddie Doherty

Biography of Catherine originally published in 1948. Now available in New Edition 1989. 0-921400-12-X

RESTORATION: our newspaper, published 10 times yearly.

Written by the staff of Madonna House, this paper has been in continuous publication since the arrival of Catherine and Fr. Eddie to Madonna House in 1947.

Subscription $3.00 yearly. Gift subscriptions available on request. Sample copies also available.

OTHER LANGUAGES

A listing of Publications in French and other languages is available on request.

AVAILABLE FROM:

**MADONNA HOUSE GIFT SHOP
COMBERMERE, ONTARIO
CANADA   K0J 1L0**